TEXAS WOMEN

Frontier to Future

Ann Fears Crawford

Crystal Sasse Ragsdale

TEXAS WOMEN

Frontier to Future

by
ANN FEARS CRAWFORD
and
CRYSTAL SASSE RAGSDALE

State House Press
Austin, Texas
1998

Library of Congress Cataloging-in-Publication Data

Crawford, Ann Fears.
Texas women : from frontier to future /
by Ann Fears Crawford and Crystal Sasse Ragsdale.
p. cm.
Includes bibliographical references and index.
ISBN 1-880510-52-9 (hardcover : alk. paper)
ISBN 1-880510-53-7 (pbk. : alk. paper)
ISBN 1-880510-54-5 (lmt. ed. : alk. paper)
1. Women—Texas—Biography.
2. Texas—Biography. I. Ragsdale, Crystal Sasse.
II. Title.

HQ1438.T4C72 1998
305.4′092′2764—dc21   98-10698

Printed in the United States of America

FIRST EDITION

cover design by David Timmons

STATE HOUSE PRESS
P.O. Box 15247
Austin, Texas 78761

In celebration of the life of my beloved aunt
Lucille Fears Kucera
and for her great grandniece
Margaret Mellon
spanning the generations of Texas women.

—Ann Fears Crawford

A Salute to the Wallace Girls
My mother Mable
and her sisters Annie, Ida, Ada, Alma, Thelma
who wrote, sang and painted Texas
1880-1990.

—Crystal Sasse Ragsdale

Table of Contents

Acknowledgments

No writer who delves into the realm of women's history writes in a vacuum. Throughout the years during which the authors of *Texas Women: Frontier to Future* have been exploring the role of women in the Lone Star State, many persons have aided in their project. The authors also owe a debt of gratitude to the research facilities across the state that have, at long last, realized the value of collecting Texas women.

The staffs of the Austin-Travis County Collection of the Austin History Center and the local history collection of the San Antonio Public Library were most helpful with research aid, while the staff of the DRT Library at the Alamo provided research help on the lives of Lila Cockrell, Eleanor Brackenridge and Cyndi Taylor Krier. DRT Library Director Cathy Herpich helped with research into the life of Nettie Lee Benson, as did the Reverend John A. Lewis of Lampasas and Bill Brock of the Austin Presbyterian Seminary.

As always, the researchers at the Center for American History at the University of Texas at Austin gave support to both authors, and the staff of the Texas State Archives helped with exploring documents and newspapers. Vickie Hocker, director, and the staff of the Dittlinger Memorial Library in New Braunfels handled interlibrary book loans and research questions.

Nancy Booth, head of Special Collections, Fondren Library at Rice University, Houston, provided keys to the papers of Frankie Randolph. Will Howard of the Texas Room, Houston Public Library, was most helpful in answering constant queries on the lives of the women of Houston.

The staff of the Texas Room, Dallas Public Library, helped with research on Margo Jones, Kay Bailey Hutchison and Eddie

Bernice Johnson, while Robert Schaadt and the staff of the Sam Houston Regional Library and Research Center, Liberty, aided with the Texas roots of actress Adah Issacs Menken. Kathleen Dillon, Houston Community College, and the Sterling Memorial Library, Texas A&M University, College Station, gathered materials on Mary Martin. Dr. Martha Mitten Allen of Georgetown inspired Ann Fears Crawford's fascination with suffragist Jessie Daniel Ames.

Ethel Soshin of New York helped with research on Jane Cazneau, Amelia Barr and Helen Corbitt. Nancy Graff-Floyd of Waco provided information on Amelia Barr. Martha McCabe helped with research on her native New York. Dominique de Menil kindly answered questions concerning her Paris childhood and her life in Texas, and Phil Heagy of the Menil Collection in Houston was helpful.

Paul Porter shared memories of his aunt, Katherine Anne Porter, and David Bland of the Porter Museum in Kyle helped with a chronology of Porter's life. Reisa Rogovein and Linda Rosenkranz, Crawford's colleagues at Houston Community College, provided critiques and comments on Porter's writings.

In exploring the life of Nettie Lee Benson, Crystal Sasse Ragsdale was aided by director Laura Gutierrez-Witt and archivists Wanda Turnley and Jane Garner of the Nettie Lee Benson Latin American Collection. Annie Benson offered her view of life in the old Benson home in Sinton, while Jeannine Krumnow of Houston contributed personal accounts of Benson's life.

Margaret Hale Magness supplied primary source material on Norway relating to Elise Waerenskjold, and Olive Forbes of the Perry-Casteñeda Library, The University of Texas at Austin, provided help with women's fashions of the 1840s. The staff of the General Land Office, State of Texas, provided help with Spanish and Mexican land titles, and Doug Barnett, Linda Newland and Mary Standifer of the Texas State Historical Association aided with unpublished selections from *The New Handbook of Texas* files.

Sallie Reynolds Matthews' son, Watt Matthews, and Margaret Putnam opened the door to the Texas ranchwoman's life. Archivist Janice Sabec of Trinity University, archivist Bob Tissing of the Lyndon Baines Johnson Library, and Heather Lammers of the McNay Art Museum, San Antonio, were helpful with material relating to Martha Mood. Mary McComb and Glenna Robbins located additional appliqúe hangings of the Texas artist, and Dolores Latorre shared memories of her friendship with Mood. Jack Rhodes, executive director of Miami University, Hamilton, Ohio, and Glenda Terrell Rhodes, head of the Lane Public Library, Oxford, Ohio, helped with material on Mood's New Harmony period.

Hallie Groos Slaughter, a student of Helen Corbitt's at The University of Texas, gave an intimate look into the life of the woman who became the authority on good food in Texas.

Carole Rylander, Sarah Weddington and Ann Richards have contributed memories and opinions on Texas politics. Rose Campos in Senator Judith Zaffirini's office, Mike Green in Congresswoman Eddie Bernice Johnson's office, and the Washington staff of U.S. Senator Kay Bailey Hutchison provided help with photographs and questions.

Billie Carr and Frankie Randolph's granddaughter, Molly Luehrs, shared reminiscences of the woman who helped create the Harris County Democrats, while J. Edwin Smith, Ed Cogburn and that most literate of Texas politicians Bob Eckhardt shared their memories of years of Democratic politics. Celeste Scalise shared experiences politicking with San Antonio Mayor Lila Cockrell, and Ann Porter provided sidelights on the career of Kathy Whitmire as mayor of Houston. Nadine Eckhardt provided insightful commentary on Molly Ivins, and the late Clif Olafson of the *Texas Observer* shared material on both Ivins and Randolph.

Douglas Harlan provided an introduction to Cyndi Taylor Krier. Harlan and Chase Untermeyer shared their insights into the career of Kay Bailey Hutchison, as did Milton Fox, Gethrel Franke and the late Tabor Ward. Political consultant Karl Rove gave generously of his insights into Hutchison's winning campaign. John Knaggs and R.G. Ratcliffe of the *Houston Chronicle* were most instructive concerning Republican politics in Texas.

June Moll shared memories of working with Margo Jones in Dallas, and the consummate theatre technician Jim Pringle provided an intimate look into Jones' theatrical years in Dallas.

Segments of Allie Victoria Tennant's biography were generously supplied by Robin Salmon, Vice President & Curator of Sculpture of Brookgreen Gardens, South Carolina; Ethel Soschin sought information concerning people and places in the art world which Tennant might have known during her New York years; Dr. Sam Ratcliffe, head of the Jerry Bywaters Special Collections at S.M.U., sent materials on her Dallas career; Roger Carroll, manager of the Fine Arts division of the Dallas Public Library, was very helpful, as were David Hunter of the Fine Arts Library of the University of Texas at Austin, Airene Martin and Natalie Davis of the Dallas Museum of Art, and photography curator Tom Shelton of the Institute of Texan Cultures.

Crystal Ragsdale's sister Ray Heller accompanied her on visits to Benson's homeplace; Christopher Williams was guru of the laptop.

Crawford's administrative assistants Nora Acosta and Felicia Vega managed to maintain order within the files on Texas women, while her research associate J. Ramsey Sutter shared in the adventure of Texas political women. Her greatest debt of gratitude goes to her colleague Jack Keever for his insightful comments on Kay Bailey Hutchison and Texas women in politics; he has earned heartfelt thanks for always being the most intrepid of editors and the best of friends.

Preface

Exploring the world of Texas women in the 1990s has become an even more exciting adventure than it was in 1967 when the authors first began to research women in the Lone Star State. Women as achievers have continued to proliferate since 1982, when *Women in Texas: Their Lives, Their Experiences, Their Accomplishments* was first published. Since then, women have made enormous strides in the fields of literature, art, philanthropy and politics. Women have excelled in sports, medicine and librarianship. The world of the theatre has been enriched by artists who have made Texas theatre among the most exciting in the nation.

Texas women are consummate pioneers with a rich frontier tradition that carries through to women in Texas today. In *Texas Women: Frontier to Future*, the authors trace the heritage of pioneering women from the frontier past to modern-day Texas.

Perhaps no other Texas woman's story is a more fascinating variation on a woman's life in Texas than is that of Harriet Ames (Potter), who lived through decades of notoriety while trying to establish the legality of her marriage. Her memoirs are fascinating reading, as are the diaries and memoirs of many other frontier women that portray life in Texas. Writer Elise Waerenskjold immigrated to Central Texas from Norway and chronicled her experiences for generations of European readers. No stay-at-home writer, however, could equal Jane Cazneau, whose life became one of adventure rare even for frontier women and whose *Eagle Pass* dramatizes life in a Texas border settlement.

Amelia Barr's life was far more dramatic than any of her novels. Her love for Texas began in 1850, and later for almost four decades her novels, poems and essays were set in international locales. Continuing the Texas tradition of "lady scribblers," Sallie Reynolds Matthews chronicled ranch life in the Lone Star State in her *Interwoven*.

Texas roots are especially strong in the writings of Katherine Anne Porter, who carried her Texas-inspired characters onto the national scene. Helen Corbitt inspired a legion of Texas cooks; her witty cookbooks still hold a prominent place in the kitchens of good cooks everywhere. No Texas author more exalts the frontier tradition of Texas women writers, while moving forward into the twenty-first century, than Molly Ivins, whose humorous and pungent articles on Texas politics and culture keep readers *au courant* on all things Texan.

The world of books is not the province of authors alone. Women in Texas have proved to be able, and often courageous, librarians, and no one personifies this role more than Nettie Lee Benson, who went far beyond the traditional woman's library role of "genteel hostess" to establish the world-class Latin American collection that bears her name at The University of Texas at Austin.

Frontier theatre has a rich tradition in Texas, and the nineteenth-century actress Adah Isaacs Menken took her talents from frontier Texas to the Great White Way. "The Menken" became the toast of Broadway and Europe with her flamboyant, often naughty, histrionic talents. Margo Jones pioneered "theatre-in-the round," inspired fledgling playwrights, and mentored other Texas theatrical women. Mary Martin continued the theatrical tradition, creating heart-warming memories for a generation of the world's theatregoers.

Following the philanthropic path blazed by Texan Ima Hogg, Eleanor Brackenridge lent her name and money to educational projects for Texas women, while Jessie Daniel Ames extended progressive reforms and women's suffrage from Texas to Washington.

Art holds a special place in the lives of Texas women, and Dominique de Menil with her husband John gave much of their art collection to their Houston museums: the Rothko Chapel, the Menil collection, the Cy Twombly Gallery, and to the Byzantine Fresco Chapel Museum which opened in 1997. Martha Mood's fabric wall hangings decorate churches, chapels and schools throughout the Lone Star State, while sculptor Allie

Tennant's heroic works capture the spirit of Texas in artistic human form.

Texas women have dramatically displayed their inimitable style in the field of politics, in which Kay Bailey Hutchison has become the first Texas woman to hold a seat in the U.S. Senate and where Eddie Bernice Johnson is one of two Texas African-American women displaying their strengths in the U.S. House of Representatives.

The phrase "A woman's place is in the House—and the Senate" is applicable to Texas Republican Cyndi Taylor Krier and Democrat Judith Zaffirini, who have earned reputations for excellence in the upper chamber; Krier now enhances the judiciary. As Texas approaches the twenty-first century, women occupy every level of the political spectrum, continuing the tradition set by the suffragists of the Lone Star State.

From pioneers to politicians, from artists to authors, from suffragists to theatrical personalities, Texas women have won their place in the state's history. The world of Texas women remains endlessly fascinating; the parameters of Texas women's achievements remain boundless.

The adventure has only begun.

—Ann Fears Crawford
Houston, Texas

—Crystal Sasse Ragsdale
Austin, Texas

July 1997

Jane McManus Cazneau and son William Mount Storms.
Courtesy The Center for American History, The University of Texas at Austin.

Jane Maria McManus
Storms Cazneau

1807-1878

*"A born insurrecto
and a terror with her pen"*

Few nineteenth-century career women lived with such impassioned vigor as Jane Maria McManus Storms Cazneau, headstrong and daring, often rushing impulsively toward new conquests without weighing the consequences. She was a highly motivated individual; energetic, she preferred to work independently in situations in which she was challenged. Jane was attracted to people who shared her choices of action and daring; she may have learned to maintain contact with the right people, those with influence and money, from listening to her father discuss his business operations. In her numerous letters Jane was a name dropper; whether she was recording an actual incident or conversation with a well-known person, or had heard of it from someone else, she cleverly made the retelling so entertaining that the real facts were sometimes obscured.

Jane was the only daughter among the four children of William Telemachus and Catharina Coons [or Kuntz] McManus. The family lived in Troy, New York, a prosperous town and the county seat of Rensselaer County, at the headwaters of the Hudson River not far above Albany. William McManus was a well-to-do lawyer who served as district attorney of Rensselaer County before being elected to the United States Congress for one term, from 1825-1827. At age eighteen Jane fell in love with and married William F. [sometimes listed as Allen B.] Storms, a young lawyer in her father's law office. The couple became parents of a son, William Mount Storms, before their separation in 1831 and their later divorce.

Jane's brother Robert, five years her junior, was to become her companion during her early years in Texas, where he settled and remained her lifetime friend and advisor. Whether or not Jane received the advanced academic training for young women offered at Emma Willard's Female Seminary is not known, but her family possessed an "intellectual tone" and Robert was graduated from Rensselaer Polytechnic Institute, the oldest school for science among English-speaking countries. He worked as a surveyor for the Troy and Bennington Railroad and had his own surveying firm before accompanying Jane to Texas when he was twenty.

When Jane McManus Storms set about preparing for her Texas saga in the fall of 1832 she was twenty-five and her future was falling into place. She sought to establish herself as a woman of property, an empresario settling emigrants of her own colony on Texas lands soon acquired by her from Mexico in December 1832. She certainly was knowledgeable; her father had an interest in the 1830 Galveston Bay and Texas Land Company in which capitalists in New York and Boston holding colonization contracts with Mexico were selling land script to would-be settlers, and she was acquainted with Samuel Swarthout, one of the company's promoters.

She also had plenty of historic lore, for Jane McManus' roots lay deep in Texas soil; a member of her paternal McManus family had been killed in the early 1800s while taking part in one of the freebooter Luis-Michel Aury's numerous battles in Galveston or in the Caribbean. Jane's father had interests in the projects of an infamous Spanish slave-trader and may have financed related businesses in cotton mills and molasses bottle plants in the Troy area, as well as in ships involved in commerce headed for Cuba via North Carolina and Texas. By additional coincidence her father knew the notorious Aaron Burr, having perhaps met him while they were both in Washington, D.C., or in New York where the one-time vice-president of the United States had become an active and constant schemer for land conquests in Texas and Mexico.

With Jane about to set out for Texas, William McManus requested a Texas introduction for his daughter from Burr, and in mid-November 1832 Burr gave her a letter to one of his friends, Judge James Workman in New Orleans.

> Allow me the liberty, my dear Sir, to introduce to your acquaintance A LADY! be not alarmed, for it is not intended that she should tax your Hospitalities nor, very slightly your Gallantry; for she is a woman of business and has great enterprises in view. . . . Young Mr. Mcmannus [*sic*] attends his sister. . . . I have recommended to them Col Austin's settlement. . . . She is eminently qualified for this enterprise and she will be able to send out one or two hundred substantial settlers in less time and better selection than any men or half a Dozen men whom I this day know—she has always professed and adhered to the Catholic faith and religion, and is much esteemed and respected by the clergy.

Jane had grown up in the German Lutheran church; just when she became a Catholic is not known, but the switch would be politically advantageous during her years in Central America and in the Caribbean.

On the following day Burr hurried off another letter to Jane in New Orleans advising her to "recollect that opportunities direct to the Country of your destination are rare—Keep a journal of all that you may see or hear or <u>think</u>" and he closed, "God bless and prosper you." One writer commented the letter was not unlike any number Burr wrote to young women with whom he was friendly.

About the same time, Burr invested in an ill-fated project to settle a colony of Germans on the Texas coast. When his new wife, the wealthy, widowed Madame Stephen Jumel whom he had married in 1833, inquired about the costly, failed enterprise, Burr said it was "no affair of her's and requested the messenger to remind the lady that she now had a husband to manage her affairs. . . ." The couple's estrangement soon followed, and in 1834 her "bill of complaint" against him, aside from her monetary grievances, was also to allege that her husband had recently committed matrimonial offenses at divers times with divers females and specifically at Jersey City with one Jane McManus. The discrepancy of dates later vindicated Jane, however, and when Jane learned of the private divorce hearings which involved her, she was quoted as having exclaimed, "Oh, la! Marcy save us." Whether Jane had an Irish brogue or whether "marcy" was the witness' own pronunciation is not recorded.

Wanting to secure as many trump cards as she could while still in New York, Jane secured yet another letter of introduction, this one to Stephen F. Austin from his cousin, Archibald Austin. His letter speaks of Jane's wanting to make such arrangements "as may be practicable in regard to a Location" for her proposed European settlement. Archibald urged his cousin to "pay her such attention as a Lady and a Stranger may require in a new Country." Austin's monumental correspondence brought many such letters at the same time that more official considerations came to his attention. Austin and his cousin Archibald had carried on correspondence in 1830 regarding their preference for German and Swiss immigrants, and the same year Manuel de Mier y Terán, Mexican Commissioner of Colonization, wrote, "it would be very advantageous to locate about a hundred Swiss or German families in Galveston" under the immediate supervision of the Mexican government. From the 1820s the German peasant-craftsmen were regarded by empresarios in Mexican Texas as less troublesome than other settlers because the Germans were dedicated to farming their own land and had no interest in the land speculation which was a disturbing characteristic of a large number of Texas immigrants.

With the prevailing interest in "good" immigrants and perhaps led by Burr's German immigrant plans, Jane decided that *she* would also introduce German immigrants into Mexican Texas. But before she could embark with her colonists her plans were abruptly interrupted and, in an undated letter to Aaron Burr likely in the latter part of 1832 from her 118 Greenwich address in New York, she wrote that she was "almost distracted," for Charles D. Sayre, a New York state resident and Austin colonist, had "withdrawn his freight and passengers and almost left my vessel empty." She continued, "I have taken some Germans as apprentices for their passage—they are well and firmly bound for 2 years at 12 dollars a year for each working man." She reassured Burr that "once in Texas I could pay my way—could you let me have $250 on any security that I can offer?" Knowing he might think of her father's backing her, Jane added, "I cannot go home, you are aware it drained these means to pay for the land."

With or without Burr's help, Jane and Robert landed at the established port of Matagorda in Texas in early December 1832, their handful of German immigrants in tow. Robert soon became a true Texian farmer, settled in Liberty County on the lower Trinity River, and welcomed his parents from New York when they joined him the next year; William McManus returned home in 1834 where he died the following year in Brunswick, outside of Troy. Mrs. McManus remained in Texas, later moving to Galveston where she is said to have died some years after her husband. Robert secured a position as surveyor for the government of Coahuila and Texas but, as the possibility of revolution continued to grow, resigned his connection with the Mexican government in December 1835 and joined the volunteer army which within months freed Texas from Mexico. Sagacious at acquiring land, he returned to farming and spent the remainder of his long life as a prosperous plantation owner. Throughout her various experiences, Jane would depend on Robert as her legal representative in Texas and as a trusted confidant.

Jane, unlike Texas visitor and traveler Mary Austin Holley who was always a victim of sea sickness, apparently landed in Matagorda with no trouble, in sturdy fine health, and with her remarkable, self-assured style. As a single woman who had traveled to Texas on a professional business venture, albeit to be a failed one, she was "welcomed with a hospitality characteristic of life in the new country."

She arrived with the expectation of settling her German immigrants on an eleven-league grant of land which she thought she had received from the Mexican government. According to one report of her immediate situation in Texas, she "found it impossible to procure the means of going any further, and this caused dissatisfaction among the colonists [she had brought] who broke their contract and decided to settle in Matagorda" on their own. Thus Jane unwittingly joined the coterie of would-be empresarios who for over a decade, beginning in the early 1820s, found that their plans to settle "Germans in Texas failed to accomplish their object," and no record remains of her colony. Not until 1845, the waning year of the Texas Republic, would German contractors themselves create the first permanent large settlements of their countrymen in

Texas, first in New Braunfels then in Fredericksburg.

But as a newcomer to Texas in 1832 Jane had much to learn in the harbor village of Matagorda, at the mouth of the Colorado River. The remote settlement of a few hastily built dwellings and warehouses seemed to cluster uncertainly along the flat, grey, desolate coastline running along Matagorda Bay, but it was important as one of the few entry ports of Mexican Texas. After the ship's passengers landed and Jane's German settlers, as if in private conspiracy, immediately set out on their own, Matagorda alcalde Samuel Rhodes Fisher learned that the thwarted colonizer was without means to settle even herself and "insistently urged her to make her home in his family, for he said very truly there was no decent place of accomodation." Fisher, known for being "extremely hospitable" to new arrivals, probably did not consult his wife regarding the female boarder who "remained in the family for many months making herself so useful and agreeable that all became quite fond of her."

Jane wrote to an unnamed Texas correspondent in a letter dated January 5, 1836, that her main interest was in obtaining land in Matagorda adjoining that to which she had already obtained title, but she feared that her earlier letter had "not been entirely lucid" for she had to attend to the children of the house who were "teasing [her] to play with them." What Fisher's Quaker wife Ann thought is not known, but their impressionable young daughter Annie may have reflected her mother's reaction when years later she described Jane as a "woman adventuress" who was "young and handsome."

During the months of being useful and agreeable in Matagorda, Jane encountered the man whom Annie Fisher described as being "romantically in love with her" and whom over a decade later Jane would marry; William Leslie Cazneau had come from Boston to Mexican Texas in 1830 and established a general merchandise business in Matagorda. He would become intricately involved with several swashbuckling personalities in the Republic's unfolding political and military events.

Jane was walking onto a stage where the drama was already in action. The deadly cholera epidemic of 1832 and 1833 swept the Mexican state of Texas and Coahuila so ruthlessly that "every activity except the constant immigration of Anglo-Americans was paralyzed temporarily." Jane entered a man's world, a country of men destined to become heroes—the young romantic Mirabeau B. Lamar and the pragmatic ultimate politician Sam Houston. Not unlike the majority of new Texas immigrants, Jane arrived already intoxicated with the enormity of the amount of Texas' free land. Scooping up easily available land grants like a gambler gathering up playing cards, she did not yet realize that it was one thing to have one's name on a large land grant but quite another to have it legally surveyed and to fulfill the contract for settlement according to the land rules of Stephen F. Austin's colonial Texas.

Almost immediately Jane applied for and received land which pioneer surveyor Elias Wightmen marked out for her in 1833 next to Seth Ingram's on Trespalacios Creek in Matagorda County. Her name is penciled on an old map, although she never legally owned the land. In May she received a grant of eleven leagues, over 3500 acres, in Austin's Upper Colony just above the present-day Waco on the east side of the Brazos, a remote and inaccessible empire within Indian country. By March and April 1835 she could claim nine more leagues along the Matagorda Bay coastline. Unfortunately, "Jane never followed through on claiming (in one way or another) all of her surveyed lands."

In early 1836 when her brother and the hearty Cazneau joined the Texas revolutionaries, Jane sailed back to New York and tried her hand at borrowing money on her lands, experiencing the joy of contributing her "mite to purchase arms for her brave defenders," but finding it a poor time to borrow money on Texas land with the whole country in the turmoil of revolt against Mexico.

She also needed money to support her young son William, who has remained an enigma through the years; a journalist in Eagle Pass recalled that research had shown the boy's being a "terror" even as a child. Jane in her will of 1877 set down that the "peculiar mental condition of my said son [has] obliged me to make these special and independent arrangements in his behalf." Another of her biographers wrote that William Mount Storms in the late 1850s had "become an inventor and of some note and patented several types of gunlock[s] which were not, however, put to any real use." In the mid-1870s Robert McManus, having Jane's power of attorney and not being able to reach her, sold their joint rights to land in McLennan County and the Waco area; William later brought suit to reclaim the property, "but the statute of limitations had by then expired." Regarding her son, Jane had a situation very similar to Mary Austin Holly's; neither took her handicapped son on her various travels.

New York remained Jane's home for some years, and as a seasoned New Yorker she read newspaper announcements of ship arrivals and departures. In May 1836 she saw a ship's passenger list indicating that Mrs. Fisher, her former Matagorda hostess, was arriving in New York with her family. Jane called on the lady, but some sources recorded that Mrs. Fisher was less than warm to her former boarder, perhaps because Mrs. Fisher had learned of Jane's name appearing in the Jumel-Burr divorce litigation.

Upon her return to Matagorda in 1838, Jane again met malicious gossip on the occasion of a "Ball of 26th instant" held in the town in November. Jane McManus was not invited! In a neighborhood of so few inhabitants, the reason for Jane's exclusion must have been well circulated. Although the women of the Matagorda area had undoubtedly made out the invitation list, it was the six male members of the ball's board of managers who were held officially (and individually) responsible for the stunning insult. A flurry of letters was exchanged between the board's chairman, Colonel V. Howard, and Ira R. Lewis in whose home Jane was staying. Lewis noted that the board was guilty of "an act of intentional disrespect—a wanton outrage upon the feelings and character of a lady who has already suffered by misfortune and injustice." Lewis could have been referring to Jane's ill-fated Texas colonization project, but he could also have been referring to her being named in the New York divorce case. After Lewis' series of written complaints to the six "Managers of the Ball of 26 instant" brought no satisfactory explanation nor apology, Lewis saw no other solution than to meet them one by one in a duel. The hapless Cazneau accompanied by his friend Charles DeMorse delivered the challenge message, but cooler heads prevailed and citizens at a public meeting passed a resolution that it considered the matter "not coming within the code of honor."

Whether or not because of the cotillion snub, Jane was back at home in New York in 1839. Once again she could select the current fashions—the full skirt over petticoats and long cotton drawers, a close-fitting bonnet tied under the chin, then over her shoulders a square or rectangular red, green and black paisley shawl that draped gracefully over the bouffant skirt as no coat possibly could.

In the early 1840s when the United States was recovering from a major depression and there was little hope of her making any financial headway from selling any of her Texas lands, Jane put her Texas colonizing aspirations behind her for a time. Needing to earn her own way, she chose a career in journalism beginning with what she knew, Texas and Texas politics; she sold freelance articles and contributed editorials for Moses Yale Beach's *New York Sun*, championing their joint cause of the annexation of Texas to the union.

At the same time she gathered information on the four Texas presidents Burnet, Houston, Lamar and Anson Jones which appeared as "The Presidents of Texas" in the March 1845 issue of the expansionist *United States Magazine and Democratic Review.* Waxing to the idea of adding to the pressure from some factions for Texas' admission to the union, she enlarged the article into a small paperback book *Texas and her Presidents; with a glance at her Climate and Agricultural Capabilities* which was published the same year under the pen name C. Montgomery. Jane must have enjoyed conjuring up various names during her long writing career—Storms, J.M. Storms, Jane McManus, Jane McManus Storms, Cora Montgomery, C. Montgomery and Jane Cazneau.

Along with her published newspaper pieces, she wrote innumerable letters to Mirabeau B. Lamar, whom she had probably greeted when he arrived in New York in 1844 and visited later during his trip to Washington. He enjoyed an honorary seat in the United States Senate which he used to lobby for the annexation of Texas. In early 1845 she wrote him another of her letters high in his praise, "There is one thing I value more than General Lamar's society. It is General Lamar's fame." Evidently Jane kept in close contact with Lamar; later during a cold Sunday afternoon in February when they were hotel-bound in Baltimore, she joined her long-time friend, writer Ann S. Stephens, and Hamilton R. Boone in writing Lamar a remarkably frivolous letter recalling a recent visit with him in Washington. The good-natured Lamar filed it among his papers for posterity.

Jane also encountered the literary critic for Horace Greeley's *New York Tribune*, Margaret Fuller ("Queen Margaret" as she was known in Boston). In a letter to a friend in June 1845 Margaret mentions that "Mrs. Storms is coming on Saturday with a set of Ionian distingúes to dine here." In October of the same year Jane wrote Lamar from New York revealing her feelings on "poor Miss Fuller" who unwittingly supplied "a summer mischief" with Miss Fuller's blaming Jane and her friends for "their Texian principles of destructiveness." With Margaret Fuller's well-known Bostonian sarcasm pitted against Jane McManus' quick New York tongue, the two women could hardly have maintained a friendly understanding on politics or culture. Jane closed the letter with her usual spirit of banter in her letters to Lamar, referring to a gathering which she, Margaret Fuller and Lamar had attended, "I do think General you are guilty of the most unchristian and never-to-be forgiven inhumanity in not making the amiable to her when we were at Greeleys. We think it a stain upon your character as a man of humanity."

A year later when Lamar had returned to Texas, Jane wrote encouraging him to continue collecting material for a history of Texas, adding, "I was much inclined to favor Mrs. Holley's plans [for her history of Texas] but some others thought she was too Austin for impartiality. I suspect I am too anti-Houston." But for the time being Jane had two other projects for her talents—the Mexican War after Texas' annexation to the Union and the surge of interest in the United States' Manifest Destiny. Jane became a flag bearer for the expansionist philosophy in American politics.

In pursuit of her consuming interest in the political thrust of Manifest Destiny then popular in the United States, particularly concerning the acquisition of Mexico, she turned her journalistic talents to becoming a war correspondent, the first American woman to attempt such a position. She wrote from Mexico City well behind the Mexican lines when she accompanied Moses Beach and his daughter Drusilla on a so-called secret peace mission (and personal business trip) for the Polk administration. Beach had banking and canal-building ventures in mind and Jane, as a Spanish-speaking "vivacious brunette with snapping dark eyes, set in a face of dark and haunting beauty with good breeding and winsome manners to match," was well qualified for both her own reporting and Beach's various ventures in Mexico City. The trio, hoping to avoid detection as enemy Americans, took a circuitous route to Havana, arriving in December 1846. Jane wrote eleven letters to the *Sun* and to other United States newspapers on the "legal censorship and restriction" in Cuba. The British consul gave Beach, accompanied by his "wife" and daughter, a temporary appointment "as bearer of dispatches for the consul."

During their five-month stay in Mexico beginning in early January 1847, Jane wrote sixteen letters for the *Sun* in addition to those she sent to other United States newspapers. Mexico City was in a state of military and civil unrest; although Jane reported on the situation, she continued "to push one of her major themes": that the United States by annexing Mexico could save the country for Mexicans of the poorer classes, a desirable result which could not be accomplished by simply buying off the military leaders then in control of the country.

In mid-March Beach and his daughter, under threat of arrest by Santa Anna, departed abruptly for Tampico while Jane headed for Veracruz where she met General Winfield Scott with his invading army and reputedly advised the general on the state of affairs in Mexico City. Although he may have taken her information under advisement, he nevertheless cautioned Beach against sending important information "by a plenipotentiary in petticoats." When she heard of his criticism of her, Jane evened the score by dubbing him "old Fuss and Feathers," a description so astute that it became permanent in Mexican War annals.

On their return trip to the United States, the trio of New Yorkers stopped in Cuba, where Beach seemed to be "up to his neck in Cuban intrigue" and where Jane met Venezuelan General Narciso López who wanted to free Cuba from Spain. Jane's career seemed to be marked with both listening to and advising men in public affairs; Sperry Beach, a later *Sun* owner, commented that Jane seemed to have a perpetual "axe to grind."

In New York and Washington again, Jane pursued her long-time interest in the United States' annexation of Mexico. Senator Thomas Hart Benton described Jane as a "female fresh from Mexico, and with a masculine stomach for war and politics." According to correspondence between Moses Beach, Robert Dale Owen and Nicholas Trist, Jane seems to have offered advice on the Treaty of Guadalupe-Hidalgo in early 1848, but by then she again had other interests. In a movement to free Cuba from Spain and to improve conditions in Mexico, revolutionary expatriates in New York began publishing *La Verdad*, a short-lived Spanish-language newspaper. Jane took on the editorship, supporting the "general interests of republicanism on the American continent."

Jane's influence in New York was still recognized in Texas; in 1849 David G. Burnet sent this plaintive request from Galveston to Lamar in Washington.

> If you should extend your travel to New York, I beg you will make some inquiry about my manuscript review of Kennedy's *Texas* which you recollect was sent to Mrs. Storms—She wrote me that Bennett of the Herald has borrowed it and refused to return it, at the insistence it is presumed of the scoundrel Houston—I should like to get the ms. back if it can be conveniently done, but don't care to have any fuss about it—it's of no value any how.

Burnet also asked Lamar if [Thomas Jefferson] Green was still with him, if General Cazneau had left, and mentioned that he would "not forget the interest they have taken in my affairs." One can only guess at Jane's advisory involvement with these well-known political figures.

She had reported on a war and continued to write to important people, but Jane was getting no younger. One acquaintance commented that "If she had married old Texan Colonel Anthony Butler, who wanted to marry her, he would doubtless have secured the titles [to some of her Texas lands] for her; she had had a better offer than him—a man worth at least $300,000 in New Orleans."

Whether or not the Texas gossip of Jane's marriage offers was true, some time between 1848 and 1849 she married her long-time friend General William L. Cazneau, who was in New York to select a stock of goods for his purported wagon train sales venture to Chihuahua (he perhaps had California in mind). One of Jane's biographers suggests that Jane's decision to marry him may have been influenced by his being ill with a "bad, serious case of smallpox [which] caused her womanly concern." They had known each other since her first arrival in Texas in 1832—and by now there seemed to be no one else. The marriage of convenience brought Jane back to Texas with Cazneau, whose good friend Charles DeMorse described him fondly, although historian José Gabriel Garcia termed him a "tenacious adventurer."

In 1850, on the cusp of another grand adventure, Jane published two pamphlets, *The Queen of the Islands* to urge the annexation of Cuba, and *King of the Rivers* about the Mississippi and the free and slave states. Jane, apparently in need of money, proposed to the *Sun* that for fifty dollars in 1850 and another fifty dollars in 1851 she would send chapters of her proposed book *Eagle Pass; or, Life on the Border,* written under the name of Cora Montgomery. She did not wait for the *Sun* to decide and the book came out in 1852, the same year as *Uncle Tom's Cabin.* Jane described the Rio Grande border setting which was the first of her and Cazneau's two decades of joint ventures that began when the couple decided to develop the old Antonio Rivas land grant along the river. Jane wrote of her Eagle Pass experiences with references to the conflict of policies on either side of the river, and she urged the United States government to protect its "free-born citizens enslaved for debt in Mexico."

She described life on the Texas border during their two years on the Rio Grande beginning in March 1850. The journey south and west began:

> On St Patrick's day our company mustered for the trip across the broad prairies and untrodden hills that unroll between San Antonio and the Bravo. Our two carriages, three mounted servants, led mules, and escort of friends made a gay and joyous cavalcade. The sides of our carriages bristled with firearms like a brace of small travelling arsenals.

The "vast tree-sprinkled plain" they crossed was little different than it is today in the 1990s—it has long been designated the "brush country" and the native grasses have been grazed off. During the windy weeks of March the party might have experienced the fabled *matacabra* [goat killer], the cruel east wind which freezes the new-born kids. The travelers saw the area's only buildings, the meager structures of Fort Duncan set on a sloping prairie "sprinkled with mesquite like a vast and venerable orchard" and the Rio Bravo "about as wide as the Hudson at Troy." As the party neared Fort Duncan their escort "found two soldiers who had been killed" by the Indians.

The Cazneaus lived for a few months near Fort Duncan, "in a neat cottage," while the general had his office in a "spacious double tent" from which he hoped to develop the Rivas tract into a prosperous "mining region which enfolds us on every side." Jane, seeking reasons for others' investments, made up a suggestion list: since the "soil and climate" of the Eagle Pass country was similar to the grape and wine producing regions of Parras in Mexico and of El Paso, she felt that "at no distant day these uninhabited wastes will echo the merry vintage songs of the distant Rhine," and there was the possibility of growing the medicinal castor bean. Ignoring the age-old local practice of grinding corn on a metate, she blithely observed that there was not a single mill that "turns out bolted flour" and that there were "crying wants" for machinery and machinists "throughout the upper valley of the Bravo."

Jane soon gave up on investment possibilities and turned to concern for human rights and to collecting the experiences of various Mexicans living about her for the vignettes which made up her Eagle Pass book—the lives of the men and women and children of Mexican, Indian and Castilian backgrounds whom she came to know.

No sooner had Cazneau arrived than he began arranging to dispose of their somewhat clouded legal interests in the tract. When Jane was in New York in 1846 she had bought the 1,283 acres from the diary-keeping Adolphus Sterne of Nacogdoches, but in 1851 she returned the title papers to Sterne who "wanted it for [his] friend Wm F. Storms." A few years after the Cazneaus left, anti-slavery propagandist Frederick Law Olmstead, who had read *Eagle Pass*, traveled to the desolate country and wrote that he "should have been a little less disappointed" at the sight of the helter-skelter settlement, if he had known that Jane's optimistic view of the place reflected Cazneau's land-selling schemes.

Perhaps as a result of Jane's letters to President Franklin Pierce and his successor James Buchanan, in 1853 the Cazneaus left Eagle Pass, their "green nook embosomed in this rocky wall," for the lush, damp foliages of the Dominican Republic where he would serve as "special agent" for the presidents. In another ballooning project the couple became involved with Cazneau's old friend Thomas J. Green in recruiting men for the filibustering William Walker and his attempts to acquire control of Nicaragua. Jane is credited with describing Walker as the "grey-eyed man of destiny." In 1857 Lamar was appointed United States minister to Nicaragua where he served for twenty months. Jane continued their correspondence with advice on his public image, on the country's future under United States control, and on gardening for Lamar's wife.

Often the Cazneaus, either separately or together, were their own couriers for their numerous projects, sailing to New York and commuting to Washington where they had an estate. Cazneau was also involved in his own more lucrative work in Santo Domingo—slave selling and illegal shipping in the Caribbean with his partner Colonel Fabens, "the discredited consul at Greytown" in Nicaragua.

Just before the Civil War, the United States became interested in securing Samana Bay, an inlet on the northeast coast of the Dominican Republic. Afterwards in 1865, on one of her periodic business trips to Washington and ever on the alert for an extension of United States domain, Jane mentioned to Secretary of State William Seward the "marked neglect of our government of the rights of our citizens abroad" and recalled the one-time interest of presidents Pierce and Buchanan in acquiring Samana Bay. The following winter Seward, pursuing the conversation concerning the bay project, paid a "mysterious visit" to Santo Domingo and "spent an hour or two at the residence of General C." Despite the information the secretary obtained there, the naval value of the "Gibraltar of the Antilles" was found to be faulty because the bay could be attacked from the land side.

Jane was memorable not only for her constant politicizing but for her own distinctive *persona* which newspaperman Henry Watterson described.

> A braver, more intellectual woman never lived. She must have been a beauty in her youth, she was still very comely at fifty; but a born insurrecto and a terror with her pen. God made and quipped her for a filibuster. She possessed infinite knowledge of

Spanish-American affairs, looked like a Spanish woman, and wrote and spoke the Spanish language fluently. Her obsession was the bringing of Central America into the Federal Union.

Jane and Cazneau seemed to have been a good team, for they lived together over twenty-five years in a continuing adventure of what seemed to be one impractical fantasy scheme after another involving unimproved land to be acquired and developed. Wherever she was Jane continued to write her books, *In the Tropics, by a Settler in Santo Domingo* and in 1878 *Our Winter Eden, Pen Pictures of the Tropics.* The couple lived at Keith Hall, their Jamaica estate near Spanish Town. Included in Jane's papers is a copy of a drawing of the home rendered in flat style with no perspective, showing a lattice-decorated, two-story mansion with palm trees which Clara Driscoll's home Laguna Gloria in Austin much resembles. Shortly before Cazneau's death at Keith Hall in January 1876, the couple gave Robert McManus power of attorney over their Texas properties.

Within a year after her husband's death, the widowed Jane was in New York where she made her will on January 27, 1877. She bequeathed all of her and Cazneau's earthly possessions to her long-time friend Ann S. Stephens of New York with the stipulation "in such manner as she in her discretion shall think best, to the support and comfort of my son William Mount Storms, during his life." Jane carefully listed all of her Texas property—those thousands of acres which were never legally hers. In addition to other lands the couple claimed, she noted the Jamaica estate and the Eagle Pass acreage which they had relinquished in 1851.

During the first week of December 1878, Jane and a woman companion, Mrs. A.M. Storm, boarded the ship *Emily B Souder* bound for Jamaica. Only partially booked before the holiday season, the ship "carried only nine passengers, about one-third the number she could accommodate." The *Souder's* course was reckoned toward Turk's Island due south of New York, but by the tenth of December she was probably sailing far to the east and a little south of Cape Hatteras. The ship's actual location will never be accurately known, for hurricane winds overwhelmed it and the dashing Jane McManus Storms Cazneau died as dramatically as she had lived.

When Mirabeau Lamar dedicated the collection of his poems *Verse Memorials* to Mrs. William L. Cazneau and to General Cazneau in 1857, he wrote, "her name, like that of her husband, is identified with the history of Texas. Both have given their lives to the support of her interests." Jane, her lively thoughts written with an untiring pen, is still a vital *persona* recalled in pounds of documents, innumerable letters scattered in archives collections in the United States, references to her life in magazines and books, facts and fantasies scribbled in personal papers still in private hands, and ultimately in her small books, so determined and so positive in mirroring the woman she was.

REFERENCES

Bard, W.E. [Waco]. Papers. Jane McManus Cazneau Vertical File. The Center for American History, University of Texas at Austin.

Barker, Eugene C. (ed.). *Austin Papers.* Annual Report of the American Historical Association for the Year 1919, vol II, Part 1, 2. Washington, D.C.: United States Government Printing Office, 1924.

Bass, Feris A. Jr. and B.R. Brunson. *Fragile Empires, The Texas Correspondence of Samuel Swartwout and James Morgan, 1836-1856.* Austin: Shoal Creek Publishers, Inc., 1978.

Biesele, Rudolph Leopold. *The History of German Settlements in Texas.* Austin: Von Beckman-Jones Co., 1930.

Bender, A.B. "Opening Routes Across West Texas, 1848-1850." [Map] *Southwestern Historical Quarterly* XXXVII (October 1933).

"Book Reviews and Notices." *Southwestern Historical Quarterly* XVIII (July 1914).

Brown, Frank. "Annals of Travis County and of the City of Austin, from the Earliest Times to the Close of 1875." Typescript, vol. IV of XV vols., Austin History Center.

Cazneau, Jane McManus. Letter to Mr. Wood. *New York Sun.* January 1850. New York Historical Society, New York City.

_____. Papers. The Center for American History, University of Texas at Austin.

_____. "Cora Montgomery." Will, January 27, 1877. Vertical File. The Center for American History, University of Texas at Austin.

_____. "Cora Montgomery." Vertical File. The Center for American History, University of Texas at Austin.

Cazneau, William L. Title to Antonio Rivas Grant, November 12, 1851. Correspondence and Case Files. John Herndon James Papers. Daughters of the Republic of Texas Library at the Alamo.

Dolch, O.L. Jr. "The Last Frontier, Mrs. Montgomery's First Trip." *Naylor's Epic Century* [San Antonio] February 1938.

Durgin, Mrs. James H. Letter to Robert Crawford Cotner, January 18, 1966. Nettie Lee Benson Papers. Nettie Lee Benson Latin American Collection, University of Texas at Austin.

_____. Jane S. Mayer. Papers. The Center for American History, University of Texas at Austin, Box BJ213.

Gulick, C.A. and Winnie Allen (eds.). *Papers of Mirabeau Buonaparte Lamar.* Vol IV, part 1, 2. Austin: Texas State Library, 1924.

Guthrie, Keith. *Texas Forgotten Ports.* Austin: Eakin Press, 1988.

Hudspeth, Robert N. (ed.). *Letters of Margaret Fuller.* "To James Nathan, N [*sic*] Y. 12th June, 1845." Vol. IV of VI vols. Ithaca, New York: Cornell University Press, 1987.

James, Edward T. (ed.). *Notable American Women.* Cambridge, Mass.: Radcliffe College, 1971.

Maverick County [Antonio Rivas Grant]. Map. October 1879. W.C. Walsh, General Land Office, Austin. Daughters of the Republic of Texas Library at the Alamo.

Miller, Thomas Lloyd. *Bounty and Donation Land Grants of Texas, 1835-1888.* Austin: University of Texas Press, 1967.

Montgomery, Cora. *Eagle Pass; or, Life on the Border.* New York: George P. Putnam & Co., 1852.

_____. *Eagle Pass; or, Life on the Border.* Robert Crawford Cotner (ed. and intro.). Austin: Pemberton Press, 1966.

_____. *The Queen of Islands* [Cuba] *and The King of Rivers* [the Mississippi]. New York: Charles Wood, 1850.

Nelson, Anna Kasten. "Jane Storms Cazneau: Disciple of Manifest Destiny." *Prologue, Journal of the National Archives,* vol 18 (Spring 1986).

Olmstead, Frederick Law. *A Journey Through Texas or a Saddle-Trip on the Southwestern Frontier.* New York: Dix, Edwards & Co., 1857.

Reilly, Tom. "Jane McManus Storms: Letters from the Mexican War, 1846-1848." *Southwestern Historical Quarterly* LXXXV (July 1981).

Roach, Sister M. Baptista. "The Last Crusade of Mirabeau B. Lamar." *Southwestern Historical Quarterly* XLV (October 1941).

Sellers, Rosella R. "The History of Fort Duncan and Eagle Pass, Texas." M.A. thesis, Sul Ross University, Alpine, Tex., 1960.

Seward, Frederick W. *Reminiscences of a War-Time Statesman and Diplomat, 1830-1915.* New York: G.P. Putnam's Sons, 1916.

Smither, Harriet (ed.). "Diary of Adolphus Sterne." *Southwestern Historical Quarterly* XXXVIII (July 1934).

_____. *Papers of Mirabeau Buonaparte Lamar.* Vol. VI. Austin: Texas Library and Historical Commission, Austin State Library, 1927.

Soschin, Ethel Uman. Numerous letters to Crystal Sasse Ragsdale, 1996, concerning Margaret Fuller, Jane McManus Cazneau, and the S. Beach correspondence in the New York Historical Society.

Von Hagen, Victor W. *The Germanic People in America*. Norman: University of Oklahoma Press, 1976.

Wallace, Edward S. *Destiny and Glory.* New York: Coward-McCann, Inc., 1957.

Wardell, Dorothy. Letter to Jane S. Mayer, August 16, 1955. Jane Durgin/Janes S. Mayer Papers. The Center for American History, University of Texas at Austin, Box BJ213.

Williams, Villamae (ed.). Stephen F. Austin's "Remembrances." *Register of Families*. Archives and Records Division, Spanish Collection. Austin: Texas General Land Office, 1984.

INTERVIEWS

Joan Clay Lowe and Crystal Sasse Ragsdale, Austin, Texas, November 22, 1996.

Harriet Ann Moore Page Ames

(Harriet Potter)
ca 1810 - ca 1896

"Loyalty is a commendable virtue,
but it can be misplaced"

For good or ill, the sense of style possessed by Harriet Moore Page Ames, better if less accurately known to Texas history as Harriet Potter, continued throughout her life. On a spring day in late March 1836 after the fall of the Alamo, she was undoubtedly the best dressed of all the frightened women fleeing to safety in the rambunctious Texas Runaway Scrape that had begun in mid-March as Sam Houston's forces hurried ahead of Santa Anna's pursuing Mexican armies. Although her outfit was not the style current in New Orleans, Harriet wore the best clothes she had. Just before she joined the headlong rush to outrun the Mexicans, she had been on her way to visit a neighbor and wore a black silk dress cut low over the shoulders and a white silk crepe shawl. Her small bonnet of black velvet trimmed with white satin ribbon sported a feather decoration of white and aqua blue that matched the blue stone of the large brooch that held the shawl in place.

Harriet was soon to end one relationship which had threatened her life and those of her children and begin another which years later would become a *cause célèbre* in Texas. By the time Harriet became involved in the great sweep of events in the beginnings of the Texas Republic, she had already suffered through a brief and stormy marriage with Solomon C. Page and was now to experience another relationship with rascally Robert E. Potter. After his death in 1842 Harriet was to have her and "Rob" Potter's lives become the subject of open public discussion during an extended civil court litigation.

In the 1880s, years after the twenty-six-year-old Harriet experienced the Runaway Scrape, she began to write her memoirs. From the vantage of time she looked back over her tempestuous past and wrote, "It seems to me that my life was spared these many years in order that I might write this history and let the truth be known about much that has been falsified and misrepresented." Unfortunately Harriet made little use of dates, and her references must usually be guessed at. Memories from six decades earlier can hardly be clear—some historians do not believe all that Harriet wrote is true—but perhaps the essence of her story is what matters.

In 1953 Harriet's manuscript challenged writer Elithe Hamilton Kirkland to create an historic novel from Harriet's story and from the reams of court reports during the twenty years after Potter's death. Kirkland selected her story's title, *Love is a Wild Assault*, from a poetic line in Kahlil Gibran's *The Earth Gods*. After the book came out in 1959, the real Harriet permanently became the remodeled heroine of Kirkland's romantic fantasy.

Harriet Ann was born in New York City, but by 1827 she was living with her father Dr. Francis Moore and stepmother Sarah in Nashville, Tennessee, where she met her future husband Solomon C. Page. Although her father expressed doubts about Harriet's early marriage, his wife thought it a good and settling influence for the girl. The Moores apparently made no investigation into their future son-in-law's means of livelihood, and from the beginning of the marriage Harriet had little security; Page was a compulsive gambler. His gambling losses were characteristically followed by apologies and promises of reform, but he always returned to his luckless "patience, and shuffle the cards" routine.

The first page of Harriet's typed-copy manuscript is missing, but the second page concerns her marriage to Page. Soon after the birth of their son Joe, "affairs became worse and I ceased to look for help from [my husband]." Then yet another "little toddling thing came to fill my heart with added love," the baby girl "Ginny." When Page took his family to New Orleans, possibly in 1831 or 1832, Harriet chose to rely on her own resources and rented a house on Camp Street next to the corner of Julia Street in "Upper Faubourg." Having decided to earn her living, she shopped on Chartres Street with wholesalers and "bought such things as were necessary to stock my little shop and had them taken to my house." She built the shelves and the counter for her small "notions" store with "dressed planks" she had delivered.

Sometime between October 1832 and October 1833, Harriet fell ill to "yellow fever which could be counted upon for the summer months." The approximate dates for her illness are known because she was attended by Dr. Anson Jones, who was in the city during that year before leaving for Mexican Texas. Jones, by his own account, was glad to leave New Orleans for he had "found the pernicious habit of gambling, to which I always had an inclination, was growing upon me."

Harriet's father, Dr. Moore, had already taken the rest of his family from the United States to settle in Brazoria, and so it was not hard for Page to decide to gather his family and seek out his father-in-law's neighborhood with the hope of settling nearby. Whether or not Harriet shared his feelings for going to Texas, she accompanied her husband and brought along "all my little notions as well as my groceries for a shop to be opened in Brazoria." At a time when Texian women were constantly mending and patching their families' worn clothing, Harriet's supply of "thread, needles, and pins" was worth more than jewels.

Dr. Jones met Harriet's boat at Brazoria with the message that her father was too ill to be there. According to Harriet, Jones observed her large supply of furniture and offered to buy her prized "best bed for $100," since she didn't need it on the Brazos. Harriet, not giving it enough thought, readily agreed to the sale, again falling prey to her usual experience with gamblers.

Soon after their landing her brother John met her with horses to take Harriet and the children to her father's farm, but the problem arose of choosing between going immediately to her ill father and of having to leave the as-yet-unloaded furniture, groceries and stock for her store with her improvident husband Solomon. Harriet recalled that

> I begged him not to touch any of my things during my absence, as I would come the next day with my brother to get them; he promised that everything would be safe and that he would stay on board until my return.

Trusting that all would be well we began our ride over the prairie; leaving the Brazos the level prairie lay before us spangled with the most beautiful flowers, as if the bonny face of Texas smiled out from the long soft grasses as welcome to the strangers; no sound was heard but the beat of the horses' feet, the springy turf, the soft rush of the wind through the long grass or the call of a bird for its mate.

In front of my brother sat my little girl and behind him clung my little boy, both radiant with delight at the strange things they saw, and the novelty on horseback.

It was also strange and beautiful to me. At last to the westward a deep belt of timber curved like a great protecting arm about the waist of the prairie, and just on the outskirts of the timber stood a comfortable log house, boarded inside and out, where my father awaited us. He was quite ill and so glad to have us with him that when morning came he would not let me go back to Brazoria.

He asked me if I had brought any flour. I told him that I had two barrels and that one of them was for him.

The next day Solomon drove up to Dr. Moore's house in a wagon holding only a single barrel of flour rolling about—gamblers had swindled him out of Harriet's possessions. The news upset the whole household, and John returned with Solomon to see about recovering the lost goods. Dr. Jones helped recover the furniture and supplies, but the groceries were all gone. In yet another family scene, Harriet's father offered her a section of land if she would leave Solomon and stay nearby; argument followed when Sarah objected to her husband's giving away land which her children needed. After the lively drama, an indignant Harriet went off with her husband in what would become a harrowing and near-fatal experience for her and the children.

While in Brazoria, Solomon heard that a Mr. Merrick needed help and, despite being told that Mrs. Merrick had starved to death there several years before, they set out with somewhat uncertain directions to find Merrick's house. The first house they came to was a dilapidated shell, and after one night there they began the search again and found another house which seemed to be the one they were looking for. They soon ran out of food and, despite Harriet's dread "lest anything might detain him and the little ones left to starve," Solomon rode away with Harriet's "best-bed" money and a "promise to be back in three days." The last of their supply of black-eyed peas was eaten and Harriet "searched the Prairie with anxious eye" for Solomon. She gathered from nearby bushes the "sweet scarlet bunches of parsley haws" for the children to eat and became angry at the "terrible inaction when [her] little ones fretted with hunger." She described the scene years later.

> On the sixth day the sun was setting and the leaves of the trees that grew along the Bayou were tinged with golden light that shimmered over the surface of the water. Hope was not dead yet, and I stood gazing out over the limitless distance when I saw my husband coming towards us. He had not brought one thing to eat.

With Harriet's money he "had bought some clothes to go to the war in; he said that everybody was volunteering to go to the war and that he did not want to be called a coward." Solomon indeed had volunteered and joined the eager Texians setting off for the relief of the Siege of Bejar from mid-November to early December of 1835. As he rode off Harriet ran along the muddy trail screaming, "I wish that you'll be struck in the heart by the first bullet fired and before you die, you'll live just long enough to think of your wife and children left alone to starve in the wilderness." Harriet's son comforted his weeping mother, saying, "When I grow up to be a big man I'll go out and bring you a big bag of meal myself." If Harriet's memory served, they lived another nine days on the haws before anyone else appeared.

Mr. Merrick, who owned the place, fortuitously rode over to the house because of his persistent dream of a woman in the house who was starving. Seeing their situation he unsaddled, "staked out his pony and went off with his gun." He soon returned with a turkey which he skinned and "cutting the breast off he sharpened a stick and ran through it and stood it up before the fire to cook." The hungry children were delighted. Harriet hoped that he would take her away from her "unhappy little home to a settlement of some kind." Even though she told

Mr. Merrick that her husband would not return, she listened in disbelief as he frankly told her that he did not "see any way" to help her "for everyone had gone to war." He rode away leaving Harriet to do what she could with mounds of spoiling meat. After their brief respite of having food the family returned to eating haws, and little Ginny became listless from hunger as more days of waiting passed.

By rare good luck the Episcopal missionary Reverend John Cloud, who had ridden out from Brazoria in search of Harriet, found his way to the lonely cabin when he saw black smoke rising from a thick growth of the broom corn Harriet had set afire so that her children would be entertained with the popping sounds as it burned. Cloud had begun his search after his promise to a friend of Harriet's who had insisted that he go out and find her. He brought cold biscuits, brandy and candles and "other items too numerous to mention." Three days after she watched him ride away toward civilization, a wagon rolled up and Harriet with the children and all of her possessions were taken to Brazoria where she was reunited with her family. In a quick sequence of events Harriet moved into a house in Brazoria and set up her store, and her brother John brought his young wife to stay with her for he had joined the volunteers hurrying off to join the other Texians seeking Sam Houston's forces.

Harriet was soon swept into the mass of fleeing people who had been frightened by the yelling of "old man Norton." Known as a "very hard drinker," Norton had run out of whiskey and, in a "weak and nervous state and on the verge of delirium," had been seized with fright when he heard the gunshot-like popping of burning river cane. He ran through the settlement yelling that Mexican soldiers firing their guns were coming down upon them. On this day of "Norton's Panic" Harriet, on her way to go visiting, grabbed up Ginny in her arms and clutched Joe's hand to crowd in with the others surging toward the north from Brazoria in the flight of the Runaway Scrape.

They had not gone far when a man in a wagon loaded with meat drove past those on foot and agreed to Harriet's plea to give the boy a ride. She ran along behind until she could lift Joe onto the back of the wagon, then she followed, her silk dress dragging along the muddy prairie. Refugees from along the Brazos made a bedraggled night camp on Bailey's Prairie between the river and Oyster Creek. Harriet and the children may have spent the night sheltered beneath the wagon, but next morning the wagon's owner joined other men going down to Velasco on the coast, leaving Harriet and her children in what she described as a "vast concourse of people."

As the Texians gathered up their few possessions to continue their flight, two men with three attendants rode up on horseback to the edge of the crowd; a dark-eyed man with black, curly hair stood up in his stirrups and introduced himself as "Colonel Robert Potter, Secretary of the Texas Navy" who "had orders to take the Brazoria settlers across the bay to safety on Galveston Island"; ships awaited them at the nearby port of Velasco. In her velvet hat Harriet Page stood out amid the sea of women wearing faded cotton sunbonnets and shawls; no man could miss seeing the beautiful woman alone and in need of help. Potter hurriedly talked to his companion Colonel Warren D.C. Hall and, by their glances towards her, Harriet sensed that she was the subject of their conversation. She knew Colonel Hall from Brazoria, but it was the other man who seemed most interested in her.

The other man was "Rob" Potter from Oxford, North Carolina, who had arrived in 1835 in Nacogdoches where journal-keeper Fairfax Gray described him as "a disorganizer" and said that his coming to Nacogdoches was "greatly deprecated by the intelligent and well disposed, courting favor with all his art. . . . [He] is succeeding to a wonderful degree. He can only float in troubled water." Potter, in early December, dispatched a letter to the General Council of the provisional Texian government stating that he was "desirous of serving the country in the present emergency" and that he wanted to command "an armed ship to cruise on the coast of the enemy." While in Nacogdoches he was elected as one of the representatives to the new Texas Convention and immediately became active in convention affairs, although he ill-advisedly made an enemy of Sam Houston. Subsequently Potter received more than he had requested, for as an ex-United States Navy man he was appointed to the Naval Affairs committee and then chosen to be the first Secretary of the Texas Navy.

As Santa Anna's armies continued their sweep up coastal Texas, Potter's most important mission, as commander of the navy, became the immediate evacuation of Texians across the bay from Velasco to Galveston. So it was in the line of duty that he first saw Harriet Page in her finery. He offered her a lead horse which she rode holding Ginny in her arms; young Joe must have ridden with one of Potter's escorts. Fairfax Gray noted that Potter boarded the armed schooner at Velasco accompanied by "a number of ladies from the Brazos whose husbands were in the army, seeking safety in flight." Among them was Harriet, whose attentions from Potter did not escape the other women. There being no place for the women to stay once the ship had docked in Galveston Harbor, they all remained on board, and it was "while on the ship a great sorrow came" to Harriet. Later she wrote,

> My little girl sickened, poor little thing; she had passed through many of the hardships of life; and while she lay there ill it seemed hard that while safety for us seemed so near, she should be beyond reach of it. The end came, and we buried her on the Island. . . .
>
> We all stayed on the ship until after the battle of San Jacinto and then I wanted to go to my grandmother's in Kentucky. I had parted forever from my husband, for he came on board the ship and begged me to return to him, but no inducement could turn me from my purpose, to go away from him and Texas forever. He had left his innocent, helpless little babies and young wife to perish from starvation. No, never, never, would I trust myself nor them to his mercy again.

Harriet transferred to Potter's new ship, the recently captured *Pocket* on which he decided in early May to sail to New Orleans on naval business. When Harriet's plan to go to Kentucky became known in Galveston, a colonist family asked that thirteen-year-old Martha Moore accompany her. Once in New Orleans Harriet, Joe and Martha waited until Potter could arrange for their passage to Kentucky. One day he rushed them out to board a sidewheeler which Potter said was bound up the Mississippi towards Kentucky, but after several days Harriet noted that the waters were not a broad expanse of river but a smaller, deep, tree-lined stream. When she confronted Potter with the apparent change of course, he replied that he had gotten them on the first boat away from New Orleans, away from a yellow fever epidemic, and that the boat was indeed not on the Mississippi but on the Red River. Harriet demanded to leave the boat as soon as it arrived in Alexandria. There Potter located a family going overland to Illinois and willing to take Harriet, Martha and Joe with them. From there the three could travel on to Kentucky.

Potter continued to "ensnare" Harriet; she wrote that "he was weaving a net around me that it would be impossible to break." They continued by boat upriver to Shreveport and overland to a house, on the Texas side of the Sabine River, which Potter rented or perhaps owned. Here the family going to Illinois decided to stay in Texas, and Potter continued to press Harriet to marry him, insisting that her marriage to Page was not legal since, to be valid in Texas, the ceremony had to be performed by a priest; she and Potter could be married by bond for the present until the union was resolved legally. Many years later Harriet wrote of how she came to be "married" to Robert Potter in September 1836.

> He loved me devotedly, and the more I thought about it the better it seemed out of my difficulties.
>
> So one evening according to the custom of the country, the little assembly gathered to see us wedded; the ceremony was a very simple one in those days in that country, but it was just as binding as [if] judge and clergy were present.

Martha Moore's brother-in-law came for her soon after Harriet and Potter had begun living together as man and wife. Solomon Page did not obtain a divorce from Harriet until May 1840; Potter and Harriet never held any other marriage ceremony, and it was well known among their acquaintances that Potter often referred to Harriet as Mrs. Page rather than Mrs. Potter.

The best-dressed woman in the Runaway Scrape became a farm woman supervising the crops of cotton, corn, and fodder for the horses on Potter's Creek in the Sabine River area in what is now Harrison County. Rob Potter was an active, busy lawyer handling his private practice, dealing in land and eagerly pursuing his new political career. With Sam Houston in office as the Republic's first president, Potter could have no part in the administrative branch of government, so he concentrated on becoming an influential Texas politician as his district's representative to Austin.

While Harriet was living at the Sabine farmstead, a neighbor woman revealed to her the dark, sordid story of Potter's
past. His professional life had begun at age fifteen when he left
his home in Granville, North Carolina, with an appointment as
a midshipman in the United States Navy. After several years of
service he resigned from the navy in 1821, studied law and went
into private practice. He was elected to the North Carolina
House of Commons where he made political enemies, but his
electorate did not seem to mind his peppery disposition and
chose him to represent North Carolina in the United States
Congress where he was "brilliant and imposing" during his
two terms. He married Isabella Taylor, a prominent Granville
County girl in 1828, and the couple had two children, a daughter and a mentally retarded son.

Once again at home during the congressional summer re-
cess, he became jealous of Isabella while she was attending one
of the popular annual "protracted meetings" of Methodists
gathered for week-long camp revivals in which young women
and children often became highly emotional while listening to
the spirited sermons. Isabella seems to have been quite moved
by the messages she heard, and when a Methodist minister came
to pray with her, Potter "accused him of breaking one of the
Commandments, namely that of committing adultery." He
sprang upon the unsuspecting man, and one version of the story
(numerous and various versions swept through the country)
relates:

> He jerked out a keen sharp blade that he no doubt
> had sharpened for the purpose, and pounced on the
> unarmed victim like a lion upon its prey, beating him
> senseless and then proceeding to castrate him.

Potter warned the minister that if "he kept quiet" no one would
know of his disgrace. While still in a murderous state of mind,
Potter then sought out a seventeen-year-old Presbyterian kins-
man of Mrs. Potter's whom he suspected of also being too
friendly with his wife and gave him the "same treatment."

When some of Mrs. Potter's relatives gathered at the Potter
home, Rob demanded that they have his wife admit to being an
adulteress. Although Potter claimed she did confess, both the

relatives and Mrs. Potter insisted that he lied. Harriet, in her own version, wrote that Potter, while in Washington, had "become infatuated with a beautiful heiress and became engaged to her"; with both a scandal and a legal separation, he could then be free of his wife in North Carolina. Potter was arrested and jailed without bond, since it was unsure if the victims would survive.

At his trial five days later he conducted his own defense and "charged that rich rogues, harpies, lawyers, and bank officials were persecuting him and dogging him because of his efforts to relieve the people from oppression." From his jail windows, Potter "poured forth such streams of abuse, such assaults of his rich and powerful persecutors as had never been heard before." The jury sentenced him to two years in prison and a one thousand dollar fine. From the Hillsboro jail he wrote and had printed an eighty-page pamphlet entitled *Mr. Potter's Appeal To the Citizens of Nash, Franklin, Warren, and Granville*. In his "usual sarcastic and biting style" he gave his account of the affair; in time the act of emasculating a man came to be known in North Carolina as "Potterizing."

At the end of his prison sentence in 1834, Potter sought election to the North Carolina House of Commons, where he had earlier served two terms, and was elected once again. In December Potter was notified of his wife's divorce and that she had changed her and the children's name to that of her mother's maiden name. December also brought the end of Potter's legislative career when, according to one story, he engaged in an all-night poker game on Christmas night in which, having lost heavily, he drew his pistol and made off with his opponent's winnings. On the second of January 1835 Potter was expelled from the House. He then made his way to the Texas wilderness where, by July 1835, the thirty-five-year-old Potter had outdistanced his old adversaries but where he would make new ones.

By late 1836, freed from his naval duties with the new Republic of Texas and after living some months on the Sabine with Harriet, he found land more to his liking and built a home on "Potter's Point" on Ferry Lake in what is now Marion County. Various names for the lake—Fairy, Ferry and Soda—crop up in the legal documents concerning the land's ownership after the 1850s. When Potter brought Harriet to their new home she wrote that "it was indeed set in the midst of lovely and romantic surroundings," and she and Potter would live there together except for a period when they returned to Potter's Creek because of Indian troubles. Once Potter had established his farm lands and their home, Mulberry Shore, he won election as senator to the Fifth and Sixth congresses from the Red River and Fannin counties district. He joined in law partnership with Isaac Van Zandt, and in Austin Potter was among the politicians who clustered about President Lamar and against Sam Houston. One of the men in this group, whom Potter no doubt knew, was William Cazneau, whose future wife was to be Jane McManus.

During one of the times while Potter was away from home, Harriet gave birth to a stillborn son and later to their daughter, Lakeann, whom he adored, and to their son John. The Potter household at various times included Harriet's brothers John and Abraham Moore and her son Joe Page. During the legislative terms of 1840 and 1842 he spent much of his time in Austin while Harriet managed the farming. Potter was concerned about the crops and the farm animals, but he was especially concerned about his fine horses and their special care and wrote to Harriet from Austin in mid-January 1841 that he was "uneasy about [his] own private affairs at home" for there were tasks there which he could manage with perfect ease but which might embarrass her. In the same letter he informed her that he had "employed Mr. Ames to aid in preparing the farm for a crop." Thus was Harriet introduced to the man whom she would later marry.

Harriet was actively aware of the trouble among the area settlers which became known as the war of the Regulators and the Moderators. The conflicts and confrontations of ill-will among neighbors intensified in the winter of 1839 with the arrival of Captain William Rose of the Regulators. That Potter as part of the Moderators would clash with the "Lion of the Lake" was inevitable although both groups claimed they sought to stem the lawless depredations of a band of men in what is now Shelby, Harrison and Panola counties. Rose had supported Potter's opponent in the previous senatorial race and had possibly been involved in several murders. In a highly charged personal vendetta Potter had persuaded President Lamar in November 1841 to issue a presidential proclamation offering a $500 reward for Rose's capture, and in late February 1842 Potter left Austin and " returned home determined to deal with Rose dead or alive."

Reaching home at the end of February, Potter rode out on the first of March with several of his own men in search of Rose at his farm. Rose, seeing the approaching posse, lay down and had his workers pile brush over him, thus eluding capture. The next day Rose, armed with a writ for Potter's arrest for trespassing on Rose's premises, gathered his men and surrounded Potter's home during the night. Harriet, hearing the dogs barking, could not arouse Potter from his sleep, but at dawn, March 2, Texas Independence Day, she arose to see about grinding the corn for breakfast. First she sent out a young boy of the household and then her brother. When they did not return she ventured out but ran back into the house when shots were fired at the hired men.

Potter at last awakened, "looked through a small crack in the wall" and, seeing the number of the attacking party, told Harriet that if he made a run for the lake he could elude them, being a "fine swimmer." She tried to dissuade him but he grabbed up his shotgun and darted out of the house. He made his run to the lake safely and, standing his shotgun against a tree, dived into the water. As he surfaced, one of Rose's men shot the swimmer in the head with Potter's own gun, and he disappeared from sight.

At the house Harriet, in a frenzy over Potter's disappearance and concerned about the boys, ran to the kitchen to find that they had not been hurt and that the hired man, although shot in the back, was not seriously injured. Harriet dressed his wounds and then, with one of the boys and a neighbor who had heard the shooting, rushed down to the lake's edge, pushed a little boat out onto the water, and "rowed about the lake all day" searching "with a large spy-glass." Even though others came to help, by the time darkness fell the search had not revealed any trace of Potter. By coincidence, the day after Potter was killed a newspaper article in the *New Orleans Daily Picayune* quoted a Texan as saying that "Potter was decidedly the most popular man in the two houses of Congress," that he "was born for action, low in stature, slightly corpulent, address bold and graceful, voice musical and distinct, hair much inclined to curl, dark amber color and worn very short, dark hazel eyes."

Harriet found Potter's body the next day, washed ashore near where he had dived into the lake, and had him buried on a knoll near the house. Knowing she needed to have the record of the murder legally filed, she rode first to Dangerfield and, finding no help there, continued to Clarksville where Potter had friends and where on March 25 she preferred charges against Rose and his men for the murder of Robert Potter.

On returning home, Harriet was horrified to find that her baby daughter Lakeann had fallen into a pot of boiling lye soap and been scalded to death; she buried the child next to Potter's fresh grave. In the fall Harriet married Charles Ames who had been her good friend during the two tragedies and, assuming Potter had left no will, they continued to work the farm lands and live in the homestead. Rose and the eight men involved in Potter's murder were imprisoned in the Nacogdoches jail for a time and finally succeeded in having the charges against them dismissed in May 1843.

But Potter *had* made his will, in Austin on February 11, 1842, and to Harriet's bewilderment when it was probated in January 1843, Potter, her savior, husband, father of their children, had bequeathed to her, "Mrs Harriet Page," only a part of his head-right land out of the "one league and one labor of land which was the amount due a married man living with his wife." The headright had been issued to Potter on March 14, 1838, based on his claim that he "had arrived in Texas, July, 1, 1835." At that time he had not yet met Harriet, and he had been divorced by his wife in North Carolina. Harriet's brother was given one hundred acres out of Harriet's share. In addition to the land, she was to have her choice of two mares from Potter's stable, his cattle, three negro slaves, and the household and kitchen furniture plus the farming equipment. Potter made no mention of his and Harriet's two young children, Lakeann and John.

The bulk of Potter's property he bequeathed to two women friends in Austin: three sections of land to Mrs. Mary Wade Henderson Chalmers, wife of John G. Chalmers, Secretary of the Treasury during President Lamar's administration; and two sections of land including the homestead on Ferry [Caddo] Lake "in consideration of my esteem for her" to Mrs. Sophie Ann Mayfield, wife of Colonel James S. Mayfield, Lamar's Secretary of State. East Texas historian Deolece Parmalee has surmised that Mrs. Chalmers, a native of North Carolina, could have been kin to Potter; of Mrs. Mayfield, gossip suggested that Potter had openly courted her. John Chalmers presented the will for probate in Red River County (or Bowie County since at the time the county boundaries were not certain) in early January 1843.

Mrs. Mayfield apparently never claimed her inheritance, and Harriet and her husband continued to live at the farm on Caddo Lake. In 1852, however, when both Mrs. Mayfield and her husband died leaving six minor children whose support depended on the Potter inheritance, La Grange entrepreneur Samuel K. Lewis acquired control of the estate and instituted court proceedings to affirm his ownership. What followed was one of the most scandalous, and perhaps one of the longest, civil cases in Texas' history.

Harriet declared she had a legal right as Potter's widow to his lands, but Lewis' lawyers secured innumerable depositions from the couple's acquaintances supporting the "common knowledge" that there had been no legal marriage between them. The theme generally expressed was, "It was a notorious fact that she left this county (Brazoria) in the general runaway melee in 1836, and went to Galveston and from thence went away with Potter." Martha Moore Reed, the thirteen-year-old girl who had remained with Harriet from Galveston until after the so-called bond marriage, insisted that as a child she knew nothing of the legal status between the couple.

Harriet and Charles Ames continued to live in Mulberry Shore, Harriet's home, and to work the adjoining farmlands where, at the end of 1859, Harriet's agricultural worth was estimated to be $10,000. Even after Charles' death in 1866 she continued to fight the suit brought against her land claim. Finally in 1875, Texas Supreme Court Justice O.M. Roberts ruled against Harriet's claim on the "closely related limitation features of the case." Thus ended the much-publicized controversy which in its years of litigation contributed hundreds of pages of testimony concerning the "marriage" of Harriet Page Ames and Robert Potter. In 1875 Harriet was forced out of her home and went to live for a time in Linden, Texas, with her son William P. Ames, one of the children she had by Charles Ames. After another change of residence Harriet wrote,

> I am eighty-three years of age now, and live in my youngest daughter's comfortable home in New Orleans. My daughter's husband, Dr. Marrero, is one

of the best men that ever lived, and belongs to one of
the most prominent families in the South. I am very
proud of my two sons: Dr. E.Y. Ames and William P.
Ames.

Harriet, looking back over her life in Texas, concluded her
long memoirs.

In spite of the hardships and sorrows that I endured in Texas I love that State best, for there, too, my
happiest hours were spent.
I am proud of the work that I did for the country
of my adoption, for no women in it did as much as I
to populate it.
And yet, no amount of money could ever tempt
me to live over again the life that I lived in the Lone
Star State.
My pen fails me when I attempt to paint many of
those past scenes in their true colors. But this outline
may give the reader some idea of what it was to live
in a wild country in those early days, and to lead as
eventful a life as mine.
Sometimes I wish that I were in that better land
with those that have gone before, for I miss the
companionship of my dear husband and my deaf-
ness causes me many lonely hours. . . .
None of my children care for the country, but I
miss the sight of green fields; where one's crops grow
as they rest from their labors; I miss the pleasant
sights and sounds of farm life; the cry of the poultry,
lowing of the cattle, and the swisk of the scythe in the
long grass.

Harriet Ann Moore Page Ames died in her eighties, sometime after she finished her memoirs, not too far from the Red
River country of East Texas where she and her family had been
involved in one of the state's most notorious and lengthy legal
battles.

REFERENCES

Ames, Harriet A. "The History of Harriet A. Ames during the Early Days

of Texas Written by Herself at the Age of Eighty-three." P.I. Nixon
Papers. The Center for American History, University of Texas at
Austin.

Asbury, Samuel E. Letter to P.I. Nixon, August 24, 1944 *re* Harriet Ames
manuscript. P.I. Nixon Papers. The Center for American History,
University of Texas at Austin.

Cheshire, Joseph Blount. *Robert Potter*. Photostat copy from *Nonnula*.
Chapel Hill: University of North Carolina, 1930.

Dienst, Alex. "The Navy of the Republic of Texas." *The Quarterly of the Texas
State Historical Association* XII (January 1909).

Dimick, Howard T. "Four John Greggs of Texas." *Southwestern Historical
Quarterly* LI (April 1948).

Donoghue, Mary Kennedy. "An Abstract of Biographical Data In the Texas
Supreme Court Reports, 1874-1881" [Harriet Ames, Sophie A. May-
field]. M.A. thesis, University of Texas at Austin, August 1938.

Fischer, Ernest G. *Robert Potter, Founder of the Texas Navy*. Gretna, Louisiana:
Pelican Publishing Company, 1976.

Gray, William F. *From Virginia to Texas, 1835, Diary of Col. Wm. F. Gray*.
Houston: Fletcher Young Publishing Co., 1965.

Hope, Alonzo P. *A Legend Of Caddo Lake*. V.H. Hackney, ed. Marshall, Texas:
Marshall National Bank, 1965.

Jones, Anson. *Memoranda and Official Correspondence Relating to the Republic
of Texas, 1859*. Chicago: Rio Grande Press, Inc., 1966.

Kemp, Louis Wiltz. *The Signers of the Texas Declaration of Independence*.
Houston: Anson Jones Press, 1944.

Kirkland, Elithe Hamilton. *Love is a Wild Assault*. Garden City, New York:
Doubleday & Company, Inc., 1959.

Lewis & McGinnis *vs* Ames, 44 Texas 319. Texas State Archives.

"Lewis & McGinnis v. Harriet A. Ames." *Cases Argued and Decided In The
Supreme Court of the State Of Texas, During The Latter Part of the Tyler
Term, 1875, and the First Part of the Galveston Term, 1876*. Reported By
Terrell & Walker, XLIV. Houston: E.H. Cushing, Publisher, 1881.

Norvell, James R. "The Ames Case Revisited." *The Southwestern Historical
Quarterly* LXIII (July 1959).

Shearer, Ernest C. *Robert Potter, Remarkable North Carolinian and Texan*.
Houston: University of Houston Press, 1951.

Weyand, Leonie Rummel and Houston Wade. *An Early History of Fayette
County*. La Grange, Texas: La Grange *Journal*, 1936.

Williams, Mrs. Marjorie L., ed. *Fayette County: Past & Present*. n.p., 1976.

INTERVIEW

Deolece Parmalee and Crystal Sasse Ragsdale, Austin, July 23, 1981.

Photo from The Lady with the Pen: Elise Waerenskjold.
Courtesy Norwegian-American Historical Association, Northfield, Minnesota.

Elise Amelia Tvede Waerenskjold

1815-1895

"Faithful Correspondent From Texas"

What prompted seventy-four-year-old Elise Tvede Waerenskjold to ask, in an 1889 letter to her Norwegian homeland from Kaufman County, Texas, "I wonder if Svend Foyn is going whaling again; he will be eighty in June. Could one buy a picture of him?"

She had probably last seen Svend Foyn decades earlier in the mid-1840s after her romance and short-lived marriage to a man who rose above his seaman's status to become the foremost innovator of European whale hunting and a wealthy and powerful man in Norwegian affairs. It had been years since 1839 when Elise and Svend had dared marry without seeking the customary church banns, and then only three years later agreed to a friendly divorce. What brought them together might well have been their youthful joy of living, their robustness, their driving energies, or even the deep-seated missionary penchant they shared for improving people's lives.

At sea Svend demanded complete obedience of his men; at home as a husband he did not change character. Away on his whaling expeditions for months at a time, he brought home the ways of his rough seafaring life, his addiction to potent brandy, and an utter disregard of Elise's wishes for her own life. Outside of his work and his religion few things interested Svend, while Elise pondered a wide range of ideas, read new books from the continent, and studiously recorded her thoughts. She could not follow the strict, narrow dictums of the traditional wife's role her husband demanded, the tedious housekeeping, the intricacies of mindless sewing, numbing kitchen hours, and sitting through unending sessions of church attendance and sermons. Their backgrounds were entirely different, and agreement on a divorce for these two strong-willed Norwegians allowed them to go their separate ways.

Elise's parents were *kondisjonerte*, the well-educated upper class with long-time cultural and family ties to Denmark. Elise's father, Nicolai (Niels) Seierslov Tvede, was a Lutheran pastor who had continued his studies at the University of Copenhagen where he was influenced by the "flowering period of rationalism or the Enlightenment" of the eighteenth century. Returning to Norway he took up his pastorate among poor farmers and became part of the group of "potato priests," a *potetprester*, who urged on his flock lives of temperance by foregoing the customary drowning "of their misery in quantities of cheap but potent liquor." These pastors encouraged their congregations to plant and eat the Irish or white potato as a cheap and hearty food for their meager diets. With a staple such as the potato, coupled with abstention from the strong Scandinavian *aquavit*, water of life, they could upgrade their destitute existence. Eventually thousands of impoverished Norwegian families created a better life when they migrated to the United States, bringing with them their opposition to strong alcholic drink.

Into this environment of new thinking Elise Amelia Tvede was born on February 19, 1815. Her parents lived in Dypvag parsonage in Kristiansand diocese located on the Skagerrak, a broad arm of the North Sea between Norway and Denmark. Elise grew up in the household of intellectual parents and her training began early. She learned to read Scandinavian, German and French. As a child of privilege Elise learned and lived the social graces expected for her class. She had lessons in painting and as much music and voice training as her talent would allow. She listened and grew to understand the conversations between her parents and visitors who brought ideas from the world outside Norway's remote geography. Throughout her long life, wherever she was, she would guide her inked pen to composing letters, essays, articles and religious tracts.

Two years after her father's death, Elise at nineteen was an educated young woman who did not marry immediately. She instead chose to become a teacher and joined a school in Tonsberg, an ancient port for whaling fleets. Some months later she established her own school at Lillesand, teaching handicrafts to girls and, at the same time, visualizing a wider range of classes. Expansion meant additional demands on public funds, a proposal that did not please an education board unwilling to put such monies into a woman's hands. The school did remain open, however, for six more years.

Accepting defeat, she carefully put away her school plans. Besides, she had met Svend Foyn, who wanted to marry, but soon after their marriage her resolve changed from, "I can make this strange, lonely marriage work," to "No! it simply will not work." Svend, far away on his whaling voyages, had second thoughts too, "This is indeed a strange woman, my wife, who prefers reading books and writing down what she thinks." In the assurance of his bottle and his growing income from whaling, the thought must have come often to his mind, "She spends too much time worrying about poor people who drink too much."

They decided on divorce in 1842. Elise took back her maiden name Tvede, and within a short time her writings placed her among Norwegian social reformers. Recalling her father's vocation of helping the poor in their fight against alcoholism, she became the first woman member of the temperance society in Lillesand and soon was a recognized *foregangskvinne*, woman leader, in the temperance movement which she supported with both her money and time. In 1843 Elise published a pamphlet monumentally titled "Summons to All Noble Men and Women to Unite in Temperance Societies for the Purpose of Eradicating Drunkenness and the Use of Brandy, Together with a Brief Exposition of the Deleterious Effects of Brandy Drinking." She was soon aware of the difficulty of being recognized as both a professional and a woman and began signing her temperance articles with a simple "E.Tvede."

Her writings brought her in contact with old friends, the brothers Reiersen, sons of a country sexton. Both Christian and Johan Reinert Reiersen had gained recognition as outspoken advocates of Norway's battle against alcoholism. As a young student, Johan had often read in her father's library then lingered to discuss his ideas with the Reverend Tvede. With missionary zeal, and in hopes of furthering the cause of abstinence, the Reiersens began publishing the liberal journal *Christianssandsposten*. They urged poor Norwegians to migrate to the American West where limitless acres of land were available. They needed only to apply for their own farm acreage and build their homes.

Johan Reiersen sailed for the United States in 1843 to investigate the possibilities for Norwegian immigration. Going first to the mid-West where Scandinavian settlers were settling, he instead chose Texas. On his return to Norway he and Christian established a new monthly journal *Norge og Amerika*, Norway and America, to foster interest in their own Texas settlement project. In the summer of 1845, putting their theories into action, the brothers with their father and sister and several friends journeyed to Texas. Johan mailed back his travel journals which appeared as "Sketches from Western America." Elise edited the material for publication and fell under the spell of the glowing reports.

During the short, dark days she read of a seemingly tropical land twenty degrees closer to the equator than her home in Kristiansand. In Central Texas grasses grew knee-high where cattle, horses and sheep fed through the winter. No mountain winds swept snowy landscapes; instead there was warm sunlight. Later in Texas she wrote of seeing "butterflies flitting about" on Christmas Day and experienced the dry winds of Texas summer that browned the landscape and cracked deep fissures in the dry soil.

By the mid-1840s Elise added another crusade to that of temperance: Norwegians' moving to Texas. She reasoned, "It is not necessary for immigrants to live in the dust of cold, dismal, sod huts they recently built for themselves in the Dakotas." Elise Tvede decided to settle in Texas herself, lured by its light and warmth but also perhaps motivated by a new romance.

Elise's life presents an enigma; a seemingly independent woman, men nevertheless influenced her life's directions, first her pastor father, then Svend Foyn whom she never forgot, then the Reiersen brothers. She next chose Wilhelm Waerenskjold. Where they met or how soon they discovered their mutual interest in migrating to Texas and in each other is unknown. Wilhelm, from the seaport town of Fredrikstad, had been her husband's bookkeeper. He was of an ennobled Danish-Norwegian family, and with him Elise renewed her social place. Although he was seven years younger than she, Elise must have felt they had much in common. Leaving her editorial work behind, and several months past her thirty-second birthday, she and Wilhelm joined another Reiersen group bound for Texas in 1847.

Elise left behind a changing Norway. Her interests had been in temperance and the immigration movements, and her strong religious background had not led her toward Norway's nineteenth-century golden age of the arts. Despite her intellectual talents, her life would not be with writers, artists and composers in her homeland; her decision to go to Texas ended any such involvement. Another phase of her life would begin far away in rural Texas.

Once she had made up her mind, Elise began packing the immigrant chests with books, her Bible, and selected dishes cradled among eiderdown comforters, coats, and dark wool petticoats. She carried her hats in a bandbox, but she would soon learn from neighboring American farm women to wear the washable, soft, cloth sunbonnets. Tied under the chin, they kept the sun off her face and neck and held her hair in place in all weather.

When the ocean voyage was over, Elise and Wilhelm were uncomfortably warm in their Norwegian clothes in New Orleans' sultry air while they shopped for the medicines not conveniently available in their wilderness home. Eagerly they finished with the port city and Wilhelm, struggling in uncertain English, negotiated with the long-experienced teamsters and wagoneers for hauling their possessions. Here he made his first contacts with America's classless working society, both white and black, people with whom he would have but little understanding during the remainder of his life.

The immigrant train headed away from the Mississippi and toward Texas. Each day in the afternoon the strung-out train of wagons stopped where there was water and the animals could graze while the people organized a living routine. At night Elise pulled out the tortoise-shell combs and hairpins and brushed her long hair before braiding it for the night. She loosened her clothing, took off her black shoes, and in dubious privacy away from the campfire, pulled off her stockings. The travelers slept in the open on pallets placed on the ground, and if she awoke fearfully to the sounds of wolves' howling, the night insects' endless droning in the brush lulled her back to sleep.

From Nacogdoches they headed toward the Reiersens' settlements, Brownsboro in Henderson County and on to their destination, Four Mile Prairie in Van Zandt County. After their arrival, the couple chose nearby Prairieville in Kaufman County to obtain their marriage license. The pale-skinned Scandinavians dressed for the occasion wearing their German Romantic-style clothing, Wilhelm in a soft-brimmed black hat, large bow tie, satin vest, and long suit-coat with loose-cut trousers and Elise in a stylish, full-skirted dress and a small beribboned hat. They were married on September 19, 1847, although it was not until 1849 that Elise's divorce from Foyn was finally granted and the stain of the couple's not being legally man and wife was removed.

They bought a square mile of land among their fellow Norwegians, only to find it overwhelming in its flat vastness from which Wilhelm struggled to wrest a livelihood. Their lumber home was not colorfully painted as were Norwegian houses; instead it was an unpainted Texas farm house with a wide dog-run through the center, stone chimneys at each end and a lean-to kitchen strung along the back. An attic story for extra sleeping quarters was tucked under the eaves with shuttered openings to admit light and air. During the day Elise was a farm wife, but in the evening she returned to the security of reading and writing which she would continue for almost fifty years of her life within a small radius in Texas. Each night, wreathed in the light of a smoky kerosene lamp, she wrote a steady flow of articles and reviews of books published in Europe. Her letters concerning Norwegian Texans became a saga in which she unwittingly created a new heroine—herself.

While Wilhelm was locating the site for their house and its outbuildings, he perhaps enlisted the offices of a legendary *Nisse*, a good troll who traditionally watched over the livestock and the fields of growing grain on Norwegian farms. The newcomers found agreement on their dislike for the American food staple, corn, but misunderstandings arose among the immigrants because some of them spoke country peasant dialects while others spoke the *riksmal* or national language.

Far more puzzling for the newcomers, reared in the formalities of the Lutheran church, were the frontier American religious camp meetings. Held in the fall when harvest work was done, farm families gathered to live outdoors for eight days, beginning and ending on a Sunday. In a community setting among friends and neighbors they gave vent to their religious expressions. As they listened to sermons under a brush arbor, several among them often took to the woods for "so-called secret prayers." Later, laughing and crying in the "highest state of ecstasy, they would throw themselves on their knees or backs, conducting themselves like perfectly insane people." After witnessing these performances, Elise concluded that the congregation seemed to "believe that they [cannot] get into Heaven unless they take it by storm."

Since there was no Lutheran church in the settlement, several of the Norwegians became Baptists, Campbellites or Episcopalians. In time, when one of her Texan daughters-in-law wished to avoid the tedious religious studies required to become a member of the Lutheran church and joined the Methodist congregation, Elise dryly commented, "I wish very much that we could soon get a good Lutheran pastor."

From her beginnings in Norway and then in Texas, Elise remained true to herself. Following her father's example, she approached her undertakings with strength and vigor. Her "actions were at times brusque" and she was known to express her displeasure with an unexpectedly sharp tongue using unseemingly earthy epithets. Where she acquired the expressions she used is uncertain; perhaps they were learned from hearing Svend Foyn's seaman's vocabulary.

Elise's photographs, made in Texas, belie the fact that she was a small woman; both her likenesses and her actions left the impression that she was a large woman of imposing stature. She parted her hair in the center in a forthright manner, and a portrait painter might view her widely spaced eyes as a balance for her large mouth. A photograph made in her later years reveals a softened though still-quizzical expression, expectant, unflappable. Wresting a living from the Texas soil was cause enough for a questioning gaze, as through the years Wilhelm and Elise's bucolic Eden experienced droughts and floods and insect plagues. Market prices were low when crops were plentiful and rose to unaccustomed highs when yields were scant.

As with most Norwegians, Elise's views on temperance did not exclude all alcoholic beverages. For the traditional Third Day of Christmas 1852 she wrote that she "had not been able to get a simple thing like ale," the heady Christmas draft much used in cooking as well as for festive drink. When recently arrived immigrants brought yeast, members of the community "brewed ale for Christmas," and how they savored that first Texas batch. Elise estimated she had not "tasted a glass of wine in four years." Wines and fruit juices were important "when one is athirst from fever," for it seems "cold water was looked upon as harmful." She probably had already felt the need of "fever quieting" drinks as the couple came to know the various illnesses of babies and children. Their first child, whom they named Otto Christian Wilhelm, was born on May 5, 1851.

They welcomed the birth of their second son on December 12, 1853, and called him Niels Seierslov Tvede in honor of Elise's father. As soon as little Otto could hold securely onto her blouse while sitting behind her on the riding mule, Elise took Niels in her lap and went visiting among the neighbors. Continuing the account of her life, she wrote that she "again expected a little boy," and that "the little baby arrived happy and well" on October 4, 1858. He was christened Thorvald August for a friend's son. Since Elise had her last baby when she was almost past childbearing age and no longer young, she fretted that she might die and "have to leave [her] beloved children." She concerned herself with their schooling and religious training in which Wilhelm took but little interest. Soon after Thorvald's birth she wrote a "Confession of Faith" on her religious beliefs.

Judging from Elise's comments in her letters, her husband's ways of doing things were not always to her liking. Described by friends as "hearty, ambitious, talented," Wilhelm was at times "volatile, unpredictable." He farmed, raised cattle and sheep, organized a local Temperance Society, served as justice of the peace among his fellow Norwegians, and invested in a sawmill and in a flour mill located in neighboring Brownsboro. Before the Civil War he and other Norwegians were speaking out on their allegiance to the Union and in their opposition to slavery. Although there were about six hundred slaves in Van Zandt County before the war, Elise later confessed she did not "really know the laws on slavery" nor the punishments for harboring fugitive slaves. Wilhelm was arrested in 1864 as a Union sympathizer but was soon released. The end of the war did not ease the hard feelings between the Texans and the Norwegians.

To the troubled atmosphere was added the death of the

Waerenskjold's youngest son in early 1866. Elise and Wilhelm buried him in Texas soil, but their frontier debt was not yet fully paid for within months Wilhelm was murdered. The couple had long struggled to understand the fierce nature of their Texas neighbors who were "quick to avenge themselves" in personal disputes. "Every man was his own sheriff," with a "false sense of honor," Elise would write describing the often explosive climate of human relationships in which they lived.

A complete explanation for the disagreement between the aristocratic Wilhelm Waerenskjold and the sometime farmer and "scoundrel of a Methodist preacher" N.T. Dickenson was never found, and the conviction of the murderer had to wait almost ten years. Dickenson's description was that of a "quiet, peaceable man" who did not drink. Yet this "peaceable man" carefully planned the murder, crafted a hunting knife, and worked on his pistol. He boasted that the next time he saw Waerenskjold, he would "hurt him and hurt him bad." The two men met on the porch of the general store and post office in Prairieville. Wilhelm, caught off guard, was brutally stabbed and died almost instantly. Dickenson fled. Later he was caught and, in a long-delayed trial, found guilty of second-degree murder and sent to the penitentiary for ten years of hard labor. The experience was brutal for Elise.

Widowhood brought increased demands on her energies as Elise assumed tasks Wilhelm had directed during their married life. Through the hard times of Reconstruction, she warded off bankers pressing for payment of overdue agricultural loans. Turning to her first husband, she wrote Svend Foyn requesting help and, with the money he sent, saved her lands. Elise was able to rejoice in the mid-1870s when their first, small, frame church at Four Mile Prairie was replaced with a larger one. Although the Texan board and batten structure did not resemble the high gabled, dark-stained lumber *stavkirke* of Norway, it rose in simplicity as a statement of faith.

Elise's sons, born in the decade of the 1850s, came to manhood following the Civil War. She wrote compassionately of their farm ventures and of their lives. After the war she again wrote letters to friends, and her articles appeared regularly in Norwegian newspapers where she had a wide readership. Clad in her black "widow's weeds," she visited friends near home and in Hamilton and Bosque counties. She walked whenever it was possible and was "welcomed just like a bishop" on her arrival in a settlement. Bringing news with her, she was a walking newspaper to the isolated households.

In late 1894 Elise wrote final letters from her Prairieville home of forty-six years. Because she was nearing eighty, it was decided that she should move to her son Otto's home in Hamilton. Before leaving she undertook several trips, even traveling to Dallas, to bid goodbye to old friends.

In Hamilton she wrote her last letters in January 1895 and, as if summoning his spirit from an unforgotten past, noted that Svend Foyn had died late the previous year. Before the first month of the new year ended, Elise died on January 22, 1895.

The writings of Elise Tvede Waerenskjold chronicled her adventurous life that began in early nineteenth-century Norway and continued in Texas until the century neared its close. Her saga was a physical adventure in which she had changed worlds and cultures. It had been more than a new life in a new land; she had journeyed on a pilgrimage. The transplanted *foregangskvinne* had been counsellor, welcomed friend, and tireless observer of her compatriots so far from their remote homeland in Norway.

REFERENCES

Andreae, Christopher. "Two Centuries of Romantic Art." *The Christian Science Monitor* 86 (August 17, 1994).

Clausen, C.A., ed. *The Lady with the Pen, Elise Waerenskjold in Texas*. Northfield, Minnesota: Norwegian-American Historical Association, 1961.

Magness, Margaret (Hale). "Tucsonans Find Numerous Yule Customs To Adopt." *Arizona Daily Star* (December 21, 1958).

_____. "Economical Drinkers Brew Their Own." *Arizona Daily Star* (February 15, 1959).

The Norwegian Texans. The Institute of Texan Cultures. San Antonio: University of Texas at San Antonio, 1970.

O'Leary, Alice. *Trolls and Witches of Norway*. Olympia, Washington: O'Learys of Olympia, 1964.

Reiersen, Johan Reinert. "Behind the Scenes of Emigration: A Series of Letters from the 1840's." Carl O. Paulson, et al (trans.), Theodore C. Blegen (ed.). *Norwegian-American Studies and Records* XIV. Northfield, Minnesota: Norwegian-American Historical Association, 1944.

_____. *Pathfinder for Norwegian Emigrants.* Frank Nelson (trans.). North-field, Minnesota: Norwegian-American Historical Association, 1981.

_____. "Norwegians in the West in 1844: A Contemporary Account." Theodore C. Blegen (trans. and ed.). *Norwegian-American Studies and Records* 1. Northfield, Minnesota: Norwegian-American Historical Association, 1926.

Unsted, Lyder L. "Norwegian Migration to Texas: A Historic Resume with Four American Letters." *Southwestern Historical Quarterly* XLIII (October 1939).

Waerenskjold, Elise. "A Texas Manifesto: A Letter from Mrs. Elise Waer-enskjold." Clarence A. Clausen (trans. and ed.). *Norwegian-American Studies and Records* XX. Norwegian-American Historical Association, 1959.

INTERVIEWS

Margaret Hale Magness and Crystal Sasse Ragsdale, Austin, 1994-95.

Courtesy Harry Ransom Research Center, The University of Texas at Austin.

Adah Isaacs Menken

1839-1868

"Cleopatra in Crinoline"

When the curtain rang down on Captain John B. Smith's production of *Mazeppa* at the Green Street Theatre in Albany, New York, on the evening of June 7, 1861, theatrical history had been made, and the name of the leading lady was on everyone's lips. It was not the play, based on Byron's romantic poem, that had held the audience's rapt attention; it was Adah Isaacs Menken, in a "breeches part" as Count Ivan Mazeppa, that had shocked and stunned the viewers. "The Menken" had made a wild dash across the stage on the back of a fiery steed clad only in flesh-colored tights and a short tunic.

"The Naked Lady," as Menken was soon known, had enjoyed a wealth of pre-production publicity along with Belle Beauty, the "wild horse" that "pawed the dust" and carried "the Menken" from the stage to thunderous applause. Captain Smith had drummed up publicity for his production by parading thirteen horses through Albany's streets, proclaiming them as "The Menken Stud", while Menken's press agent, Edwin James, had entertained reporters with his fledgling star's mysterious background.

Was she in reality Dolores de Ricardo Los Fiertes, daughter of a Spanish Jew and an aristocratic French Creole woman? Or was she perhaps Marie Rachel Adelaide de Vere Spencer, daughter of an English duke who had escaped over the convent walls? Or perhaps merely a second-rate vaudeville actress married to heavyweight pugilist John C. Heenan? Whoever she was, she was a sensation in Albany; one theatrical reviewer commented, "the Menken is without a rival in her special line—but it is not a clothes line!" The "naked hussy on horseback" sold out the play's run in Albany and played to the largest theatre audiences ever recorded in the city.

"What's in a name?" Menken sighed to rapt reporters before repeating her success as Mazeppa on the New York stage. Even though the critic from the *Baltimore Sun* had panned Menken's performance, noting that "We recall Miss Menken on our stages in one or another roles that were mercifully brief. She is a dreadful actress," the Broadway Theatre was sold out for her New York opening night on June 13.

The cream of New York society, along with nine Union generals, one rear admiral, seventeen colonels, and Edwin Booth and Ada Clare, the reigning figures of the New York stage, were all there for a glimpse of "la Menken" in what one critic called "one of the worst plays ever written." Press agent James had fanned the flames of promotion for his star, arranging public appearances with her on the arm of the poet Walt Whitman. With her rich Creole coloring, her shockingly short hair, and dressed in a velvet Byronic costume, Menken was nothing short of a sensation.

The "celebrated artiste" completed her publicity antics by smoking a cigarette in public after consuming a dinner at Pfaff's restaurant of raw clams, chicken soup, a hearty steak, and fruit pie. The owner of Pfaff's obligingly prepared a turkey sandwich for her to eat during the play's intermission to keep up her strength for her plunging, scantily clad horseback ride.

Prior to the play's opening, whispers had spread through New York that the Louisiana-born Menken was less than enthusiastic for the Union cause. In response Menken composed a poem, *Pro Patria—America 1861*, which the management obligingly circulated among the audience before the curtain went up and a fife-and-drum band marched onstage to play "Yankee Doodle." Despite lukewarm press reviews, Menken's theatrical reputation was made, and she continued her shocking ride as Mazeppa through theatres in Europe and the American West.

But who was she? What were her origins? Menken could be as fanciful about her parentage and her birthplace as she was adamant about her status as a star. Knowing good publicity when he saw it, Edwin James continued to play up her "illustrious beginnings" in the press. Knowledgeable Texas theatregoers, however, ardent in their theatregoing since the days of the Texas Republic when the city of Houston had claimed a theatre before it had an established church, had been speculating about "the Menken" since she first appeared on the Texas boards.

Menken's beginnings mystified historians for years, but it would seem that she was born in 1839 as Philomene Croi Theodore, the daughter of Auguste Theodore, a wheelwright and free man of color living in New Orleans, and his wife Magdaleine Jean Louis Janneaux. The couple had another child named Benigne, and in later life Adah claimed to have only one sister. Although she boasted of an early dancing career with her sister on the New Orleans stage, no recorded evidence exists for their performances. By the time of her birth as Philomene and her appearance in Liberty, Texas, Philomene had transformed herself into Ada Theodore and her sister had become Annie Josephs, perhaps a married name. As Ada Theodore, the woman who was to become "la Menken" advertised in the *Liberty Gazette* on October 8, 1855, that she would be giving a series of four readings from Shakespeare during the upcoming months.

During November and December the *Gazette* published three of the aspiring poetess's poems signed "Ada Bertha T— e." One of the poems written in Washington, Texas, and titled *The Bright and the Beautiful*, was dedicated to her sister Josephine, who must have been Annie Josephs. However it was another poem written in Austin City and dated November 23, 1855, entitled *New Advertisement* and dedicated to R.M.T., that announced to frontier Texans that the poetess was looking for a Texan to marry. In the poem an ardent Ada Bertha Theodore described herself for prospective bridegrooms.

> I'm young and free, the pride of girls,
> With hazel eyes and 'nut brown curls';
> They say I am not void of beauty—
> I love my friends, respect my duty—
> I've had full many a BEAU IDEAL,
> Yet never—never—found one real—. . . .

Ada Bertha toured Texas, visiting the communities of Livingston, Liberty, Austin, Washington-on-the-Brazos, and

Galveston, delivering her Shakespearean readings and branching out as a writer and poetess while continuing to send poems and articles to the *Liberty Gazette*.

Despite her ardent search for a husband, Ada's articles reflect a decided feminist slant, deploring the fact that young women were "trained that the ultimate end of every accomplishment is to please the opposite sex. To win for herself a wealthy husband is the lesson. . . ." As a young woman, obviously talented and outspoken, alone and touring frontier Texas, Ada experienced rejection, criticism, and notoriety. In her ardent way, she picked up her pen to deplore the actions and comments by young men "who imagine it adds to their dignity to play off mean jests, to bandy unclean doubts of woman's honor; and this even passes as a wretched substitute for wit. . . ." In her "Fugitive Pencilings" to the *Gazette*, she further expanded on her feelings, crying out that "A man discovered America, but a woman equipped the voyage. So everywhere; man executes the performance, but woman trains the man. . . ."

Despite the feminist slant of her writings, a husband was soon in the offing for the poetess. Whether or not R.M.T. responded to the poetess's "advertisement," Alexander Menken, a musician and orchestra conductor touring Texas, obviously succumbed to the "hazel eyes and nut brown curls" of Ada Bertha, for he was soon courting the poetess. Ada B. Theodore and Alexander I. Menken were married on April 3, 1856, in Livingston, Texas, by D.D. Moor, the justice of the peace for Polk County. The couple had met when she was dancing at Neitsch's Theatre in Galveston while he played in the orchestra. The honeymooners lived at the Minter Hotel in Livingston, where Alexander Menken was attempting to set up classes in dancing the Highland fling, polka, and mazurka.

Evidence exists of an earlier marriage between Adda Theodore and composer W.H. Kineass in Galveston on February 6, 1855. If this is, in fact, Ada, then she was already married when she eloped with Menken. With the extravagant Ada anything was possible, and she was later to remarry yet again before the papers of her divorce were delivered.

In later life "the Menken" would make much of her Texas days, claiming to have been captured by Indians and escaping with the help of the Indian maiden Laulerack and being miraculously rescued by Texas Rangers. According to the tale, the rescued actress was taken under the protection of General William Selby Harney, commander of the Eighth Military Department posted near Austin in 1852. Here, according to "the Menken," she translated Spanish documents and helped the general in the command of his soldiers.

The fanciful tale, told by the actress to William Wallis in Paris and printed in a pamphlet after her death, resembles nothing more than one of the wilder Western dime novels, but Menken carried the story into her poetry, eulogizing "Laulerack, the dark-eyed one" in one of her romantic, idealized poems.

If ever "the Menken" had a press agent for an apocryphal life in early Texas, it was Texas bon vivant and international playboy Thomas Peck Ochiltree, former Texas Ranger and a major in Hood's Texas Brigade. Stories told by Ochiltree circulated throughout Texas and even in Europe well down to the twentieth century and form much of the mythic folklore of the actress's life.

According to Ochiltree, he and Adelaide McCord were schoolmates in the "old Spanish pueblo" of Nacogdoches where her father or stepfather was an "old clothes" man. Later, Ochiltree claimed, he saw the actress riding in her carriage and bet a friend that he could gain a ride with her. Menken greeted him cordially and Ochiltree won his bet. So pervasive were Ochiltree's tales that Menken is known in some Texas histories as Adelaide McCord.

In truth, "la Menken's" Texas days were short lived; the Panic of 1857, which created a depression across the United States, also affected the theatrical world. In New Orleans, however, The Charles Company was looking for an actress for a benefit performance. Taking the professional name of Adah Isaacs Menken, the aspiring actress and her husband were off to New Orleans and a triumph for Adah in *Fazio or the Italian Wife's Revenge* at the Gaiety Theatre in August 1857. Although the production was only a benefit performance, the *New Orleans Daily Picayune* commented on the "accomplished and talented Menken," and the couple were soon producing their own plays, all starring Adah. By the time she had played Lady Macbeth in Nashville for William H. Crisp, Adah was determined on a career on the boards with her husband as her own impresario.

Adah resolved to carry her professional career on to Cincinnati, the "Queen City of the West," where Alexander's family were both prominent and prosperous merchants. She used her Creole looks and dark curls and cited her illustrious forbears, the mythic "Los Fiertes," to convince Alexander that she too was Jewish. Alexander was not so sure that his family in Cincinnati would welcome an actress, but Adah, intent and ambitious, gained a booking at Wood's Theatre and flooded the Cincinnati *Israelite* with her poetry and articles.

The *Israelite* welcomed their "favorite and ingenious poetess" to Cincinnati, and audiences cheered "la Menken" in *The Soldier's Daughter*, *The Jewess*, and *The Hunchback*. Not only was Adah a Cincinnati theatrical success, she was a social success as well, attending tea parties and dinners, sprinkling her conversation with Latin axioms and French phrases, and delivering readings from Shakespeare. Then it was on to Dayton, where she scored another triumph singing "Comin' thro the Rye" and performing a Spanish dance during the intermission of *Sixteen-String Jack* in which she played her first "breeches part."

When Adah was awarded an honorary commission in the Dayton Light Guards, gaining her headlines and comment in newspapers across the nation, Alexander displayed his jealous side and walked out in a huff while his conservative family registered shock. Adah went to great effort to mend her shaky marriage, but it received still another blow when John Carmel Heenan, "The Benecia Boy" and the self-titled heavyweight champion of America, made an appearance at the theatre where Adah was performing and called on the actress.

Alexander wanted to settle down in Cincinnati, but Adah was consumed with passion for the New York stage and, no doubt, "The Benecia Boy," and the couple received a rabbinical diploma of divorce. Adah relocated to New York to fulfill her destiny on the stage and in Heenan's arms. The news that the prizefighter and the actress had secretly married on September 3, 1859, soon hit the newspapers, and Adah was soon pregnant. When Alexander Menken wrote to newspapers that he and Adah were still legally married, the new Mrs. Heenan was labeled a bigamist. Heenan sailed for England for the world heavyweight fight, and Adah took up her pen to defend herself in the press.

Abandoned by Heenan, Adah suffered further over the death of the child she had borne, closely followed by her mother's death. Even though additionally burdened with a suit for nonpayment of a bill filed by her hotel, poems and prose flowed from her pen deploring the role of nineteenth-century women in America. She even wrote a flattering critique of Walt Whitman's *Leaves of Grass*. The literary editor of the *New York Sunday Mercury*, Robert Henry Newell, published her poems and soon was seen about town with the actress.

Adah could also be seen in the company of another flamboyant actress, Ada Clare, and the two "Ada's" scandalized New York by wearing their hair short, dressing in shocking clothing, and smoking cigarettes in public. Aided both by a new agent and by her publicist Ed James, Adah was ready for another theatrical success. A triumphant tour followed with Adah playing *The Soldier's Daughter* and soon adding to her repertoire the part of the lovesick sailor William in *Black Eyed Susan*. One critic gushed of her audiences, "The beautiful Adah carried them by storm."

Nothing, however, rivaled her triumph as Mazeppa, a role she was to carry to Europe and, to the bane of many actors and actresses, the American West. Robert Newell thought the project absurd but admired the lady poet, feeling that she should relocate herself from the theatrical world into the literary. His first step toward his goal was marrying her on September 24, 1862; his second was to announce that her place was not on the stage but in the home, turning her hand to poetry, to housekeeping, and to her husband.

Typically "la Menken," she removed herself from home and husband and onto the stage of Baltimore's Front Street Theatre in the heart of Dixie in the midst of the Civil War, once again clad in flesh-colored tights and romancing the role of Mazeppa. After a thunderous benefit performance and the receipt of a diamond bracelet, Menken determined that someday she would be "the greatest artiste in the World."

Menken's Southern sympathies created yet another scandal when the actress demanded that her dressing room be redone in Confederate grey, despite the fact that Baltimore was in Union hands. Menken was arrested and accused of spying for the Confederacy, but she was dismissed with a warning. Her advocacy of the Southern cause gave rise to yet another Menken myth: that in defiance of a Union general in love with her, she allowed a Confederate flag to flutter from her hotel window.

Cold weather and illness incapacitated her, while Newell was begging for a reconciliation. Perhaps she considered a husband a necessity for the splash she now planned to create at McGuire's Opera House in raffish San Francisco. In the wake of Southern losses at Gettysburg and Vicksburg, the West must have seemed promising indeed. After a trying journey across the Isthmus with Newell in tow, Menken, "a vision in yellow," embraced San Francisco while Western audiences embraced Mazeppa.

With her fiery steed and Junius Brutus Booth, Jr. as her leading man, "la Menken" became a San Francisco sensation, enlarging her repertoire to play six parts in one of America's first musicals, *Three Fast Women*, a title well suited to the actress's flamboyant style. Menken even accepted a bet that she would not visit the infamous Barbary Coast with its brothels and gaming tables. Not one to turn down still another "breeches part," Menken, dressed as a Gold Coast dandy and smoking a cigar, not only went, but returned with two thousand dollars in winnings from the tables.

Menken threw herself into literary pursuits and embraced the West Coast *literati*. She could often be seen in the company of poet Joaquin Miller, writer Bret Harte, and the aspiring actress Lotta Crabtree, but one journalist, Mark Twain, claimed that Menken was "a circus rider who belonged under canvas." Twain's comment, however, was made before he saw Menken in her famous role on the boards in Virginia City, Nevada, in March 1864. The miners loved her and her flashing ride on the "Wild Heart of Tartary," and Twain sang her praises.

Riding her horse, gambling, traveling from saloon to saloon, laughing and applauding when the saloonkeepers hung her picture over the bar beside her former husband "The Benecia Boy," Menken relished the life of the Comstock region. She even pondered settling down in the West and writing a novel, but Europe beckoned and Menken accepted a parting gift of a silver brick from the miners and stock in the Menken Shaft and Tunnel Company in the heart of the mining area named "The Menken." One local poet summed up the miners' fond farewell.

Menken, adieu! No more shall lusty "boys"
Applaud Mazeppa, till hoarse throats grow hoarser;. . .

Taking her leave of the miners and her husband for the final time, Menken returned first to Baltimore for a reprise of Mazeppa. War-weary Baltimorians, however, failed to applaud and, with box-office receipts flagging, Menken devised a scheme of posing as a Southern spy to be taken into custody, questioned, and sent under armed guard to Washington. After her release, and determined to seek her theatrical destiny in London with Ed James promoting the tour, Menken opened at London's Astley's Theatre under the direction of Edward Tyr-rell Smith, who promoted the production of Mazeppa by playing up the "naked aspect" of the play. Her opening night was a smashing success, and she received the greatest curtain call of her career.

The *London Times*'s critic commented that "The lady's costume is certainly not one that Queen Elizabeth would have recommended to her maids of honour. . . ," and *Punch* printed a verse ending with the refrain, "'Bring forth the horse!' Yes Mr. Smith, But don't bring forth the Menken!" Another bit of doggerel which circulated through London was:

> Lady Godiva's far outdone,
> And Peeping Tom's an arrant duffer;
> Menken outstrips them both in one
> At Astley's—now the Opera Buffer. . . .

London audiences loved the production, and Menken relished in her publicity in the vulgar press, dancing to the *Mazeppa Waltz* and the *Mazeppa Galop*, taking in the comic pantomime *The Cream of Tartar*, and collecting comic songs that dubbed her play "death by crinoline." At the end of the six-months' season, she had collected possibly more than five thousand pounds.

Her tour of the provinces brought even more money, fame, and satisfaction to "la Menken," as did her latest lover, "Captain" James Paul Barkley, her "Prince." Although the "Benecia Boy," was in London, hoping once again to gain her affections, Menken paid him off and shipped him back to the United States. When Barkley fell ill in New York, Menken also sailed for the United States and returned to the boards as an international star in the well-worn *Mazeppa*.

Finding herself pregnant by Barkley, Menken cancelled a tour of the play and married Barkley before discovering that he was professional gambler. She fled to Paris, while indulging in laudanum to salve her sorrow, and a "suicide attempt" was duly reported in the press. Georges Sand, Menken's constant companion in Paris, served as godmother to Menken's baby, whom she christened Louis Dudevant Victor Emmanuel Barkley.

In Paris Menken was absorbed with her latest epic, *The Pirates of Savannah*, especially commissioned for her and featuring duels, swordfights, ballets, and an even more thrilling horseback ride. Overcoming "la Menken's" lack of French, and with true French panache, the dramatists created their heroine as a mute. On opening night, September 29, 1866, French critic Theophile Gautier commented that Menken "mimes with rare intelligence a mute protectoress of persecuted innocence." A fall from the fiery steed resulted in bruises, broken fingers, a sprained wrist, and a torn ear, but it also rushed a famous royal lover to her bedside. King Charles of Wittenburg danced attendance, and rumors had it that Emperor Napoleon III sent his own physician to oversee her cure.

Paris took "la belle Menken" to their hearts, and soon her likeness appeared on shaving mugs and scarf pins while Parisians adopted hairstyles, coats, and trousers *a la Menken*. Even the illustrious Alexandre Dumas, Père, praised the actress, and the two spent many hours discussing poetry, novels, the theatre, and romance. Rumors of a May-December love affair soon circulated through Parisian intellectual circles, and the two were photographed with Menken on the author's lap, her hand holding a book. Dumas signed photographs to "My dearest love," and Menken responded to "My dearest friend." Dumas's family filed an injunction to stop the sale of the photographs, but they had already been widely circulated.

Indeed, "la Menken" was one of the first actresses to realize the value of photographs for publicity purposes, posing for *cartes de visite* with local photographers wherever she was appearing on the stage. Thousands of photographs circulated throughout her lifetime; at her death she was the most photographed woman in the world. The nude photographs done in Paris, showing the actress totally nude except for a sheer loin cloth, became true collectors' items.

After her Paris triumph, Menken was ready for yet another European adventure and accepted an engagement in Vienna at the Theatre am dier Wien. Instead of her usual standing-room audience, "La Menken" failed to please Vienna and was vilified in the press. The Austrian adventure, however, led to one more mythic tale of the mischievous Menken.

According to Noel Gerson, who eulogized Menken as the "Queen of the Plaza," after the actress arrived in Vienna she received a caller, Baron Friedrich von Eberstadt, who had earlier seduced her when she lived in New Orleans. She bartered for the dubious honor of living with him; the price of her amorous affections was the honor of being presented at court. The baron supposedly arranged for the actress, heavily veiled, to be presented before the austere Franz Joseph. When presented, Menken whipped off the veil to reveal herself in the flesh-colored tights of Mazeppa fame and was banished from the staunchly puritanical empire.

Sobered by the ridicule and poor press she had received in Vienna, Menken fled to Paris only to receive the news of the death of her son. Now was the time to make a change in her artistic life, to expand her adventures into the world of the intelligentsia. A love affair by correspondence, with the San Francisco poet Charles Warren Stoddard, provided her the inspiration to collect and publish her poems, and she initiated her intellectual adventure in London. Earlier she had offered to send her poems to Charles Dickens for his critical comment, and now she began to collect her "soul poems" for an epic anthology that she fantasized would bring her fame and fortune. Working frantically although ill, Menken rushed to ready her works for the publisher. Thirty-one of her poems were to form *Infelicia*, for which Menken would be forced to pay the publication costs.

Taking time from her work, she encountered the Pre-Raphelites, a group of Bohemian poets, writers, and artists dedicated to breaking the barriers of Victorian English manners. Capturing her fancy was Algernon Charles Swinburne, a homosexual opium eater obsessed with flagellation and, according to the Pre-Raphelite Brotherhood, a poetic genius. Needing a noted figure to polish her verses, Menken determined to save the esthete from his exotic and erotic debauchery by setting him to work as an editor.

She appeared unannounced at the door of his Dorset Street chambers one night, and subsequent nocturnal visits gave rise to wild speculation about their "affair." One friend of Swinburne's told the poet's biographer Edmund Grosse that Menken, when she asked the poet for help with her poetry, was told by Swinburne, "My darling, a woman with such beautiful legs should not bother about poetry."

For their "affair," Menken reprised her old "Los Fiertes" *persona* and called herself "Dolores," the title of one of Swinburne's poems. The poet wrote a short poem in French in the actress's album. Said to be inspired by Menken, the poem *Doloriada* ends

> Love flatters us with signs
> And kisses on mouth and eyes,
> For one day and a night,
> Before his flight.

A photograph of the couple circulated through London and caused one more Victorian scandal, although today one cannot imagine why. A somewhat blowsy and tired-looking Menken sits with the poet's hand in hers; the actress's other hand rests on his shoulder. The so-called "affair" nevertheless shocked the prudish Victorians, and the photograph shows the intimacy of the couple.

In London Menken appeared once more at Astley's Theatre in *Mazeppa*, but one evening during the wild ride on horseback, the horse veered too close to the scenery and Menken was injured. A doctor from the audience dressed the wound, and Menken left for Paris to plan yet another production and to complete *Infelicia*. Perhaps it was for the best that she was to die of cancer caused by the wound rather than to be exposed to the criticisms concerning the publication of *Infelicia*. One visitor to her Paris rooms reported her propped up in bed, smiling but admitting, "I have received my death-wound. . . . I am lost to art and to life."

She died on August 10, 1868, and was buried in the Cemeterie Père la Chaise in Paris. Her ever-loyal press agent Ed James and a group of theatrical friends had her body moved to the cemetery at Mountparnesse, where her tomb carried the inscription "Thou Knowest."

Menken once wrote of the poems that made up the volume *Infelicia* that "They are strange and beautiful to me. . . ," but when her poems were published a week after her death, the critics were not kind. The critic for the *Pall Mall Gazette* wrote that "Tears, so to speak, bedew every page. . . ," and others wondered that a woman who on stage made such "indecent displays" could even presume to turn her hand to poetry.

Dante Gabriel Rossetti admired her work, and his brother William included her poems in an anthology of American poetry, noting that they reflected "a life deeply sensible of loss. . . ." One of her biographers, Allan F. Lesser, comments that Menken's poetry is reminiscent of that of her old friend Walt Whitman, but he concludes that her poetry's faults are due to lack of editing on Menken's part. A more modern biographer, Wolf Mankowitz, correctly finds Menken's poetry reflecting the plight of nineteenth-century feminists, calling for women to be in control of their lives and their bodies.

> All her lives and writings project the same revolutionary sentiments: that a woman belongs to herself; that she has her own genius; that she has her own Eros; that her body is hers and hers alone. . . .

Today her poems seem well within the mainstream of feminist writing, revealing much about the actress and the woman. The actress, a theatrical sensation treading the boards in her flesh-colored tights and astounding audiences as Mazeppa, cried out in her poetry that her heritage

> is to live within
> The Marts of Pleasure and of Gain, yet be
> No willing worshiper at either shrine;
> To think, and speak, and act, not for my pleasure,
> But others. The veriest slave of time
> And circumstances. Fortune's toy. . . .

"La Menken" deplored the fact that her heritage was "to watch The glorious light of intellect Burn dimly, and expire; and mark the soul. . . ." The woman who embraced numerous husbands and lovers through her lifetime, concluded that "Life is a lie; and Love a cheat," and marveled at her life and career as a "Cleopatra in Crinoline," as one critic called her, wondering "Is this what dreams are woven of?"

REFERENCES

Berg, Annemarie. "They Came To See: The Actress Who Struck It Rich With Comstock Lode Miners." *True West* (December 1982): 10-13.

Brooks, Elizabeth. "Adelaide McCord" in *Prominent Women of Texas*, 156-61. Akron, Ohio: The Werner Company, 1896.

Cofran, John. "The Identity of Adah Isaacs Menken: A Theatrical Mystery Solved." *Theatre Survey* 31 (May 1990).

Davis, Kate Wilson. *Adah Isaacs Menken: her life and poetry in America*. M.A. thesis, Southern Methodist University, Dallas, Texas, 1944.

Falk, Bernard. *The Naked Lady*. London: Hutchinson & Company, Ltd., 1934.

Fleischer, Nathaniel S. *Reckless Lady*. New York: Press of C.J. O'Brien, 1941.

Gerson, Noel Bertram. *Queen of the Plaza*. New York: Funk & Wagnalls, 1964.

Hutchins, John K. "That's Why the Lady Was a Terror." *Saturday Review* 73 (October 24, 1964): 43-47.

James, Edwin. *Biography of Adah Isacs Menken*. New York: E. James, circa 1881.

Lesser, Allen. *Enchanting Rebel: the Secret of Idah Isaacs Menken*. New York: The Beechhurst Press, 1947.

Mankowitz, Wolf. *Mazeppa: The Lives, Loves and Legends of Adah Isaacs Menken*. New York: Stein and Day, 1982.

Menken, Adah Isaacs. Biographical File. The Center for American History, University of Texas at Austin.

_____. Biographical File. Sam Houston Regional Library and Research Center, Liberty, Texas.

Morrison, Ian. *The Sensation*. New York: New American Library, 1963.

Oursler, Fulton. *The World's Delight*. New York: Harper & Brothers, 1929.

Phelps, H.P. *Players of a Century. A Record of the Albany Stage, Including Notices of Prominent Actors who have appeared in America*. Albany: n.p., 1880.

Reynolds, David S. *Walt Whitman's America*. New York: Alfred A. Knopf, 1995.

Winegarten, Ruth and Cathy Schechter. *Deep in the Heart: The Lives & Legends of Texas Jews, a Photographic History*. Austin: Eakin Press, 1990.

Courtesy Archives & Information Services Division, Texas State Library.

Amelia Edith
Huddleston Barr

1831-1919

"Dreams are large possessions"

Amelia Huddleston Barr was over eighty when she began to write her autobiography *All the Days of My Life* recalling the innumerable "visions" she had experienced during her lifetime. Sleep often brought vividly dramatic dreams, harbingers of her future, by whose messages she at times shaped her decisions. At other times she could only wait for whatever the visions had foretold. "I entered this incarnation on March the twenty-ninth, A.D. 1831. I brought my soul with me," she wrote, "an eager soul impatient for the loves and joys, the struggles and triumphs of the earthly tabernacle."

Her name Amelia came to her from her widowed Huddleston grandmother. The little girl first knew "the lonely sea-stretches of Silverdale in her birthplace in the little town of Ulverston" located on the lonely coast of Morecambe Bay in Lancashire County. The neighborhood in northwestern England, nearer to rugged Scotland than to London, was "saturated with the spirit and influence of George Fox." She recalled years later that "when the full consciousness of childhood came, I was living among the mountains of the English Lake District, in the ancient town of Penrith."

Life in those "secluded parts of England" was very similar to that of Queen Elizabeth's time, a harsh, brutish, poverty-stricken era with no sanitary conditions in towns and no education for the mass of the people. Sponge-like, Amelia's mind recorded the customs, conversations and people in the places where she lived and visited, and she drew from them for her eighty novels and stories written and published during the decades after she was forty years old.

Impressionable Amelia grew up in a religiously charged atmosphere with her parents, Methodist minister Reverend William Henry Huddleston and his wife, Mary Singleton, who was of Quaker upbringing. Amelia was the second daughter with an older and two younger sisters and three younger brothers who did not live to reach manhood. The birth of her first brother rearranged the family hierarchy; Amelia lost her place of importance as one by one the three baby sons replaced their sisters in their parents' interest and preference. Amelia later wrote, "I had already learned that little girls were of much less importance than little boys." But after the loss of the boys, the parents again took notice of their daughters and Amelia thrived on the renewed close association.

Although newspapers were considered "the peculiar luxury of men," Amelia was free to read any books in her father's library. When the seven-year-old opened a copy of John Wesley's *News From the Invisible World*, she marveled at this religious man's "god-sent" experiences with "ghostly visitations and wonderful visions." Years later she emphasized the wide reading of her childhood—from the Asian splendors of the *Arabian Nights* she claimed that she "owed more to Queen Scheherazade than to any mortal." She was shipwrecked with Crusoe, crossed the Sahara with Denham and Clapperton, wandered hungry and forlorn with Mungo Park on the Niger, and went round the world with Anson and Cook. She suffered with "every one of Fox's martyrs," and Defoe's book of the Plague of London made her "walk softly" and "cast a hush over life for days and weeks." She emphasized that she "not only read through books," she also "felt through them."

The Reverend Huddleston was educated as an Anglican minister, but "being a born evangelist" he became imbued with the crusading spirit of the new Methodism and its concern for the poor. He chose to leave the Church of England, and his family was constantly shifted from one locale to another in accordance with the Methodist church practice of periodically reassigning ministers. The first move was to Penrith in Cumberland, then to Shipley and Ripon in Yorkshire. When her father accepted churches on the Isle of Man, the ten-year-old Amelia found the new environment reinforced her "cradle memory of the great sea." Influenced by her father's books, Amelia wrote a tragedy *Seneca* which she presented to him. Her younger sister Alethia Mona was born in the large-roomed, sunny house in Castletown where they lived for two years before the family returned to England, to Kendal in Cumberland County where her youngest sister Mary was born.

Being of independent means, her parents were able to give their daughters good educations; while the family had been living in Shipley, a not-yet-five Amelia had attended a *dame school* where she had "only reading, needlework and knitting." Her tiny fingers were able to manage a needle and thread and master the basic sewing techniques—to "hem and to seam, and to fell [to finish a seam by sewing the edge down flat], and to stroke and to backstitch, and when I left I could read any of the penny chap books I could buy." Other schools followed as Reverend Huddleston was transferred from one town to another; at Miss Pearson's fashionable school Amelia pursued her lifelong appreciation of literature and music.

The family's comfortable way of life ended suddenly when her father's business partner ran off to Australia with funds entrusted to him. To help support the family, Amelia's mother planned to establish a school which she and her oldest daughter Jane would manage. Amelia was to be one of the teachers. In preparation for the project, Amelia at sixteen left home to assist in a private school in Downham Market, Norfolk County. She became an instructor in music, drawing and English, at twenty-five pounds a year with her board and lodging.

At the end of the school year Amelia returned home bringing twenty pounds from her teaching salary, her first-ever earned money which she offered to share with her father. After he refused she sought out her mother, who accepted the gift in tears. During the past months Mrs. Huddleston had received an inheritance of rents from a row of cottages, and the extra income had done much to put the Huddleston household into a more comfortable state, but Amelia's father had taken control of the additional funds. Amelia never forgot the financial helplessness which her mother endured, and which most of the women of the world faced. In her 1912 autobiography, concerning the position of women she did not wonder "at any means they now take to emancipate themselves." In an interview shortly before her death Amelia commented that she had written "mainly for the kindly race of women. I am their sister and in no way exempt from their sorrowful lot."

Amelia's parents never doubted that she would finish her schooling and enter teaching as a career. A Methodist minister aided her in securing a scholarship to a school in Glasgow financed by the Methodist Weslyan Board of Education. In early January 1849 Amelia set off for Scotland and began her studies in the new, co-educational, American-style normal school for training teachers. She "left home and traveled to a distant school" where she soon found her familiar English-oriented world challenged by, among many things, a new vocabulary spoken with Scots accents. She became acquainted with a society foreign to that which she had known in England. After one Saturday evening's party when Amelia marveled at the bravura of the gaiety and singing, a woman there told her that "After dark and over the toddy the men were brave Scots but by day they were getting their shillings for shillings' worth." She joined a group of friends on a summer cruise to the Orkney and Shetland islands, and decades later she would draw on her memory of those people and the scenery to write her most popular novel, *Jan Vedder's Wife*, as well as others.

Her training completed, Amelia remained in Glasgow fulfilling her pledge to repay her school debt by teaching in the Methodist Board-sponsored school, mostly for poor children. But for the fulfillment of one of her prophetic messages, Amelia would have paid off her obligation; in a dream she went shopping for wool yarn and, on entering a yarn warehouse, passed "many men at desks writing, but no one spoke." Pushing open a door into another room she saw a young man writing; he turned to her "saying in a pleasant, authoritative way, 'Come in, Milly. I have been waiting for you'."

A few days later the dream became reality when Amelia went to a woolen warehouse to buy tickets to view, from a window there, a parade in which Queen Victoria and her family would ride. The astonished Amelia was met by a smiling young man, Robert Barr, who greeted her and promised to deliver the tickets. She knew this was the man whose fate "good or bad" she must share, and an inexpressible sadness possessed her. Overwhelmed, on returning home she lay down and fell into a deep sleep; when she awoke she was reconciled to her fate.

Barr became an attentive and persistent suitor and the

eighteen-year-old Amelia soon fell in love with the Scotsman, son of a Presbyterian minister and a successful businessman. Seven years Amelia's senior, he often came down to Kendal from Glasgow to court her. After her father had given his permission for their engagement and marriage, Reverend Huddleston announced that Amelia was still in debt to the Methodist Board for seventy pounds. In a show of gallantry, the love-smitten Barr wrote out a two-hundred-pound check for her release.

Amelia fondly remembered her wedding dress, a "small polka jacket" of white lace and trimmed with satin atop her bouffant-skirted, white satin dress "of ordinary length" just four or five inches above the ankle. Her small "bonnet" was trimmed with white lace and orange flowers and she wore satin slippers. Over her going-away dress of pale blue she drew an expensive white silk Indian shawl before donning a "bonnet trimmed with blue flowers."

A photograph made the year before her marriage reveals a large young woman whose daily childhood fare had included large amounts of starches—bread and butter, bread and milk, Yorkshire pudding, rice or tapioca pudding and, often for tea, a thick-sliced sweet loaf perhaps with currents and caraway seeds and sugar sprinkled on top. Years later when she became a well-known writer, her newspaper and magazine pictures reveal a portly, round-faced Victorian matron.

Amelia had married an affluent young Glasgow businessman; their first home, tastefully furnished, included some of Amelia's family pieces. In the evenings they went to plays and operas; on other nights they read to each other or Amelia played the piano and sang Scots songs which Robert liked. During that first year in Glasgow, Amelia met Henry Ward Beecher, a minister and prominent speaker from the United States who was an outspoken opponent of slavery and interested in the growing movement for women's rights. He encouraged her to "hunt him up" if she ever came to New York, but it would be seventeen years before she sought him out.

Soon after their marriage Amelia tried to win Robert's confidence and "share his hopes and plans only to be made to understand" that she was going beyond her sphere. Early in their marriage Robert acquired a new business partner; after Robert brought him home for dinner Amelia told her husband that the man was "a rascal from his beard to his boots" who

"could not tread his shoes straight," quoting a Yorkshire prov-
erb for a rogue. Robert ignored her suspicions. Shortly afterward Amelia became "very busy with a diminutive wardrobe."
Although she was to have nine children, she never mentioned
being pregnant, only the assembling of clothes for the new baby.
The couple's first child, Mary, was soon followed by Eliza or
"Lillie" as she was called.

Shortly after their first wedding anniversary the pleasant
tenor of their lives ended when Robert's business venture with
his new partner failed and he lost nearly everything he owned.
As news of Robert's bankruptcy became known, their friends
shunned them and businessmen who spoke to Robert blamed
him for his financial failure. To escape the unpleasantness the
couple decided to leave Glasgow. Although wanting to remain
under English rule, they nevertheless dismissed going to Australia and instead chose Calcutta. Soon after their decision,
Amelia dreamed of the city as great blocks of burning coal and
awoke with a scream. Believing the dream a bad omen, they
next considered Canada but instead decided on going first to
New York and from there on west.

They gave up the house and began selling off many of their
possessions. Robert's mother offered to buy some of the furniture and rent it back to the couple. Perhaps in reaction to Mrs.
Barr's hard-bitten offer, Amelia went for a walk and impulsively bought two Scots-agate bracelets. Neither was of expensive workmanship nor of any great value, but she kept them
and years later used them in an important exchange. Robert left
for Liverpool to buy the sailing tickets and to arrange for
shipping their possessions. Amelia, as she was to do numerous
times afterward, packed for herself and the children, paid off
the servants and caught the train to meet Robert. "Events that
are predestined require but little arrangement. They manage
themselves," she confided in her diary, a statement she could
never again make so blithely.

After the ocean journey to New York Robert hurried his
family west, reached Chicago in early 1853, located a partially
furnished "too large house" and hired servants. He opened an
office on Lake Street and advertised himself as an accountant. In
January after the birth of their third daughter Edith on Christmas Day, Amelia opened a "Ladies School." There were four
boarders and twelve day pupils, and she wrote to New York for

a "resident teacher who could speak French and teach music."

Although the venture began well enough, the couple was soon catapulted into a series of unfortunate episodes. Baby Edith died during the summer and, as hard luck followed them, the hapless Amelia sought and found recourse in her enduring faith in the goodness of a caring God. Robert Barr seemed destined to associate himself with unscrupulous men who, sensing his trustingness, betrayed him. The newly arrived Scotsman began trying to adjust to Chicago, a city rapidly growing with enormous numbers of foreign immigrants. With mistaken judgment he became involved with the Know-Nothings, an organization opposed to foreign immigration including the importation of slaves. In what appeared to be a malicious set-up, Robert was induced to speak at one of the group's meetings. A near-riot ensued in the audience, and the following morning Robert's name appeared in a Chicago paper as being a part of the night's fracas.

The next days and nights were fraught with fear for the couple, and they decided that Robert should leave Chicago immediately. Amelia's explanation for Robert's involvement remains veiled; in her memoirs she reveals little except that for ten days and nights "Robert was in the power of his enemy." By Thanksgiving he was at home again, saying he had won a "great victory" and that he would remain in Chicago, but a party member urged Robert to leave town because his "life was not worth a cent" and there would be an attempt "to arrest him for debt."

Robert fled, catching a train to Cairo, Illinois, and thence down the Mississippi to Memphis. Since it was Thanksgiving, Amelia's students had gone home, and she wrote their parents asking payment for their schooling. The servants were paid and dismissed, and she followed Robert to Memphis where he had found a job as bookkeeper and a small, furnished house. As soon as they had enough money, they sent for baby Edith's body and buried it in the new garden cemetery at Memphis. But with the return of warm weather came its accompanying specter, cholera. People who could, fled, and the Barrs, gathering their possessions, boarded an ominously quiet river boat carrying slaves from the Memphis market down to New Orleans. The stop in that city was short, for cholera was widespread, and the travelers boarded another boat bound for Texas, although

Amelia suggested returning east or to Scotland. Their boat was not allowed to land at Galveston because of the yellow fever quarantine, so from Houston they took a stage to Austin.

Amelia fondly remembered the first few years in the capital as living in "Arcadia." Robert's accountant training brought him a job with the Ways and Means Committee of the 1856 Session of the Texas Legislature, and later he secured a position in the state comptroller's office. Amelia opened "Mrs. Barr's Ladies School" with sixteen pupils, and Robert taught drawing, painting and map coloring. The curriculum extended beyond the "3 Rs" to "all branches of ancient and modern literature." For music and singing they charged one dollar per lesson. Years afterward, some of her students wrote to her and even met her in New York.

Overlooking the Presbyterian congregation, the Barrs instead attended St. David's "pink adobe" Episcopal church where Amelia sang in the choir and played the organ. The couple was well received in the community, and Robert must have captured the interest of the townspeople with his appearance at the capitol where he worked, always impeccably dressed in high silk hat, gloves, white flannel shirt, dark tweed trousers and broad leather belt. Suspenders, a waistcoat and Wellington boots completed the carefully chosen wardrobe of a model mid-nineteenth century Victorian gentleman. Amelia did not record how soon he changed to more comfortable dress which reflected both the climate and the frontier. Austin women chose simple at-home dresses of cotton and linen, but those they wore in public had full skirts pushed out by voluminous starched petticoats over bell-shaped hoops. Amelia noted in her diary that she had spent "all day making over my hoop."

Through a wonderful generosity Amelia had the use of a private library from which she borrowed the classics to read daily to her children and to Robert in the evening. She was a serious scholar and established a truce with the children, reserving for herself half-an-hour each day when, with a cup of tea and usually with a baby in her lap, she would read to herself. The children knew that if they interrupted her there would be no reading to them that night.

The family lived in various houses while they were in Austin, and each time they moved Amelia and Robert worked at making the new place livable. Despite the numerous moves,

Amelia still had boxes and barrels packed with "plenty of fine bedding and table damask, china and plate, bits of bric-a-brac, and a good deal of Berlin wool work and fancy needlework." In poignant memory years later, Amelia recalled one of the houses, "I am sitting in the little wood house, with its white-washed ceilings and unpainted stairway and one sits at my side, who left me forty-five years ago." She would always remember her forty-year-old husband, his Scots brogue, his pleasant expression, and the beard extending around and under his chin from the ends of his sideburns.

At one particularly uncertain time Robert decided he wanted to have a dairy farm in the country. Amelia was relieved when he got out of the notion, for she well knew who would have to ready the milk and make the butter her husband dreamed of selling in town. Amelia was nevertheless maternal and domestic, a "fine house keeper," a good cook who daily baked bread and cakes, who constantly sewed, and who knitted stockings for her husband and children. During the couple's first years in Austin two sons, Calvin and Alexander Gregg, were born. They lost a baby daughter, Ethel, but a later baby daughter, Alice, survived.

The pristine new capitol building sat on a low hill at one end of an alternately dusty or muddy Congress Avenue that extended down to the wide river, which rose during flood times in unhindered majesty sending its muddy waters rippling into the town. Dry-weather days were filled with the unending sounds of clopping horses and mules and the grinding of the metal-rimmed wheels of buggies, carriages, wagons and lorries. Picket fences encircled the governor's mansion as well as the capitol grounds; Austin was a town of picket fences, of chimneys and flues, and milk cows in little sheds behind the houses. Soon after they moved to Austin, Amelia traded her two agate bracelets for a milk cow.

One night in late 1859 a troubled Amelia fell asleep and visioned herself in a dark, lonely place in a downpour. She saw a "great white arch" across the heavens, which suddenly broke in two. Half of the arch fell to the ground; beside it a *"Presence"* appeared and cried out for the *"birds of prey."* Turning to the north, west, south and east, it screamed, "Come! and I will give you flesh to eat!" She awoke Robert to tell him of the spirit message to which he responded, "It is war, then, Milly, and may

God help us."

In Austin the Barrs had soon become aware of Sam Houston's mystique. In December 1859, on the eve of the Civil War, Houston gave his inaugural speech as governor. Standing before the simple Alamo commemorative obelisk, he asked his listeners to think not as Southerners or Northerners but as Americans. As the powerful Secessionist faction clamored its pro-slavery stance, Houston lost control of state politics. On the fourteenth of March in 1861 Amelia sat in front of the gallery just above the speaker's desk where a copy of the Ordinance of Secession was spread. She watched state officials swear allegiance to the Confederate States and saw Governor Houston refuse. Amelia considered Houston the "grandest and most picturesque figure in American history," and in the first pages of her popular novel *Remember the Alamo* described his "true imperial look which all born rulers of men possess."

Amelia wrote that Austin was a "scandalously Yankeefied Union loving town," although the Secessionists had sponsored a "splendid procession" with several young women's riding horseback carrying flags of the Southern States. Despite his anti-slavery beliefs, Robert continued his job with the state during the war because he was an "expert accountant;" pro-Confederate Amelia "wrote some stirring articles for the Austin paper." As war times "began their hard pinch," the Barr children gathered leaves from wild yupon bushes and dried them as a poor substitute for Amelia's tea. Often Robert was not paid, and the Barrs keenly felt their restricted financial situation. For additional income Amelia worked for the state, compiling tax rolls, ruling paper for the lists and making envelopes. On the twenty-eighth of March 1865 she noted in her diary with some desperation, "We have no money, and very little clothing in the house—neither have I anything ready, either for myself or the child I am expecting."

With Lee's surrender Austin became an unruly place, but by the end of July three thousand Union soldiers had entered the capital. Early in August Amelia wrote that her "dear little Archibald was born at half past six" that morning, and several weeks later the family moved to the "Morris place" just back of the capitol and almost in the center of the camp of the Union's Sixth Cavalry. It was a fortuitous location, for the whole family soon found the officers to be courteous, friendly and helpful neighbors.

The Austin Amelia and Robert had known changed, and Robert was unable to find a position with any local businesses. He was planning on going job-hunting in San Antonio when the baby, Archie, became quite ill. The doctor from the army camp advised Robert not to leave home; the baby died the next night. Robert later accepted a position with a cotton firm in Galveston and left his family. Amelia stayed in Austin three months longer, until October past the yellow fever season, then she packed their household goods, left the furniture with an auctioneer, and gave away the cow she had exchanged for her bracelets. The family had lost a son and a daughter in Austin; now with three girls and two boys Amelia was not sorry to leave her "Arcadia."

Without the two oldest daughters, Mary and Lillie, the management of the family through the years would have suffered greatly. Lillie, a hearty outdoors person, intelligent, questioning and at times willful against authority, early assumed the lifelong care of her mentally retarded younger sister Alice. In Galveston Mary grew "tall, pretty, and very graceful and soon began putting on young lady airs." When Robert was at home, he devotedly visited with his two young sons. Their children were, above all, the enduring constancies in the vagaries of the couple's lives.

In Galveston Robert rented a small house with a good cistern for the rain water. Amelia wrote Jennie Cohen in Austin in late October 1866 that she liked Galveston very much and that she "could not help crying when she saw the sea again," for being near the water was part of her heritage. In April 1867, when yellow fever first appeared in Galveston, the couple left the inhabited area and rented a remote, freshly renovated place near the water, a short distance from the U.S. Army camp. None of the family liked the house; Amelia immediately felt an "indefinable repugnance" for it seemed a bewitched house with its dark and shadowy rooms. One evening Amelia and Robert returned from a walk to find the children alone and frightened; their German maid had fled. When she returned the next morning, she explained that she had been terrorized by "dreadful men going up and down the stairs." A visiting neighbor, expressing surprise that the Barrs would move into the house, explained the evil spirits—the deserted, isolated house, then painted blood red, had earlier been the refuge of pirate Jean Lafitte's men.

As yellow fever spread, Robert asked Amelia to take the children away from Galveston. She refused, then within a few days a quarantine ended any hope of escape. Years later both Lillie and her mother wrote of the following weeks; Amelia in her autobiography titles one chapter describing the family's illnesses "The Terror By Night and Day," followed by "The Never Coming Back Called Death."

At the beginning of those tragic days Amelia recalled a prophetic dream.

> It is as clear in my inward vision this hour as when I awoke from it. I was by the side of a river, a river black and motionless. Great trees overshadowed it, and all its banks were hidden in a lush growth of rushes and long grasses. It was a horror of marshy earth and dead water. And among the long rushes and dead water, a human figure lay, a man unnaturally thin and tall, with a yellowish, deathlike face, surrounded by long straight black hair. He lay prone as if asleep, but slowly raised himself, and looked at me. Then with a languid air, but a voice of fate, he said, "One shall be taken, and the other left."

A few nights later, unable to sleep, she sat at an open window screened by wooden blinds. Hearing a faint stir in the hedge she "stopped rocking and sat motionless listening." She then heard three tremendous blows on the blinds, as if a hand had struck them. Hurrying to her family, she found all safely asleep. The next morning Robert investigated and saw the imprint of a huge hand on the unbroken blinds; soon after the "hedge turned black and was covered by a loathsome sweat or moisture."

In early September the children became ill. When Amelia also contracted yellow fever, Robert and volunteer Scots friends helped care for them. During her illness the two boys, nine-year-old Calvin and Alexander, five, died. Robert returned from their burials ill with yellow fever, died two days later, and was buried near his sons on the seventeenth of September 1867. Amelia and the three girls recovered. After September the fever declined and the following month a hurricane swept the island bringing a feeling of renewal. Amelia's last child, a son Andrew, was born the first week of December but showed signs of yellow fever and died within a week. The baby was buried next to Robert and the boys.

After Robert's death Amelia and the girls were almost destitute, with only a little money from his family and various Galveston friends. In early January 1868 she opened a boarding house on Tremont Street which did not prosper (Amelia never could manage her finances even in the best of times), so on the first of November she gave up the project and decided to go to New York with Mary, seventeen, and Alice, seven. Fifteen-year-old Lillie sailed to Scotland to stay with Robert's mother.

In New York Amelia, armed with a letter of introduction from a Galveston acquaintance, subsequently met William Libbey who encouraged her to open a small school in Ridgewood, New Jersey. Libbey also suggested that Amelia write an article on the Confederacy in Texas, which she sold to D.Appleton and Company for thirty dollars. She recalled saying, "Why I can write three or four of those things every week!" Lillie, whose vivaciousness did not please her Scots grandmother, returned home, and she and Mary found jobs that allowed them to be at home at various time to look after Alice.

Nineteen months was long enough for the family to live in the remote New Jersey countryside, and Amelia moved her family to New York City where they lived in rooms in a "large, brick house" on Amity Street within a short walk of the Astor and Mercantile libraries and the Historical Library on Second Avenue. Recalling Mr. Beecher's offer of help if she were ever in New York, Amelia wrote him mentioning their meeting years earlier. When she greeted him, he commented that if she could write as well as her pathetic letter asking for help, she surely could contribute to the *Christian Union*, a paper in which he had an interest.

With that job she began a routine of research and writing often ten hours a day for the next fifteen years in her special alcove in the South Hall of the "vast, inspiring, vaulted rooms" of the Astor Library. She was "nearly thirty-nine years old when [she] became a student at the Astor." Even with her continued writing and help from her daughters, they did not have enough money; at times Amelia had to choose between buying an apple for her lunch at the library and having the money to ride "the cars" home at the end of her day's work. Finally, in anguish she sold the diamonds from the circlet ring she wore with her wedding band.

Amelia next joined the staff of a Christian periodical, *The Working Church*, writing religious news, columns, poems and essays. Her output became so great that editors in various publications used two separate pen names for her. When her finances improved she chose a flat on Lexington Avenue, rather far from the Astor Library. She furnished the rooms pleasantly, rented a piano, and for a time the flat became a gathering place in the evening for literary men and women, although she generally passed those hours drinking her beloved hot tea and, in the days before typewriters, recopying the day's work which "doubled the labor," for the press copy had to be written "very clearly" with pen and ink.

Amelia was a compulsive writer and the quantity of her writings was prodigious—weekly short stories for the *Ledger* as well as various ones for the *Christian Union*, the *Illustrated Christian Weekly, Harper's Weekly, Harper's Bazaar, Frank Leslie's Illustrated Weekly* and the *Advance*. She sold pieces to the *Leisure Hour* and the *Sunday Magazine* in London. Hundreds of verses came easily from her mind, although she admitted that she "never considered herself a poetess in any true sense of the word." Her poems nevertheless "got the money, and the money meant all kinds of happiness" for herself and her daughters. Working eight or nine hours a day, Amelia began writing novels, often two a year, although at first they were never money-makers.

Amelia's personal life was bound, in what she wished to be a permanent pattern, with both Mary and Lillie's working but still having strong ties to her and to Alice. Despite her novels about independent women, Amelia could not accept her daughters' considering marriage. In the early 1880s when thirty-three-year-old Mary married Kirk Monroe, an editor for *Harper's Young People*, Amelia felt unappreciated. She also worried about the unworthiness of Lillie's suitor, whom her daughter subsequently married and divorced. Despite their marriages, both daughters continued to be helpful to their mother.

Amelia's life was restless and peripatetic, perhaps sparked by the daily commute to various libraries. She made numerous trips to England to sell her writings and to Scotland where she visited her mother-in-law in Glasgow and went to see where she and Robert had lived. During one visit she met a former beau whom she found uninteresting. She made one trip to the West when, urged by her daughters, they moved to Denver for a year. Her one permanent haven, Cherry Croft, was a large home and grounds at Cornwall on the "top of Storm King Mountain" on the west side of the Hudson where she could "look out over 60 miles of the Hudson and the hills and valleys surrounding" her. Here she maintained a home for almost thirty years. During the months of moderate weather she entertained guests, gardened, and harvested the cherries and apples from her orchard. She and Alice spent the winter months in the stylish New York Hotel just above Washington Square, and at times they sought a few weeks of milder weather in Atlantic City.

Amelia never forgot Texas, where she was made an honorary member of the Daughters of the Republic of Texas in 1902. Of Austin she wrote one friend saying, "My life in Austin was a very happy one and I love the place with all my heart." In a letter in which she enclosed her photograph taken on her seventy-eighth birthday, she commented that it fit her "very well yet. Literary work is living work. The infusion of mind & spirit into flesh & blood every day keeps the flesh young." Well-dressed, she sat for innumerable photographs used by her publishers, often commenting in her letters on their quality and availability. Amelia always tied her experiences to the spiritual world, and in 1899 she allotted time to read in depth on various religious beliefs—Christian Science, theosophy and spiritualism.

During her years of writing Amelia would engage in conflicts with her literary editors and endless misunderstandings with her publishers. She often lost royalties on her books published in England and on pirated translations made in France. Her first novel *Eunice Leslie* appeared in serial form in the *Working Church* in the early 1870s, but it was not until 1883 that the moderate acclaim of the novel *Cluny McPhearson* convinced her to devote much of her time to writing novels. With the publication of the successful *Jan Vedder's Wife* in 1885 and *The Bow of Orange Ribbon* in 1886, she became an accepted American novelist, turning out romantic historical fiction often at the rate of two a year. Her popularity was well enough established that in 1888 her main publisher, Dodd, Mead and Company, paid her a thousand dollars for *Remember the Alamo,* which was published in England as *Woven of Love and Glory.* The firm printed forty-two of her novels from 1885 to 1911, and she had nineteen other novels issued by other publishers during this same time. Unable to create a moving drama script, she gave up trying to turn her stories into plays, and she was never able to recreate the Evangeline Arcadian story into a novel.

Through the years Amelia maintained a daily diary and, using it as her guide, in early September 1911 began her autobiography *All the Days of My Life,* completed in 1912. "On Christmas, 1913 A.D." she gave a presentation copy to the New York Public Library, the successor to her beloved Astor Library. In June 1918 she finished her last novel *The Paper Cap,* a story of factory industrialization in England. At the time of her death she had yet another novel in the planning stage.

Throughout her life she suffered continual ill health and serious illnesses, although the long bout with her over-worked right hand and fingers was immediately ended when she began using a typewriter in 1887. She died just short of her eighty-eighth birthday on March 10, 1919, after a fatal stroke in her last home in Richmond Hill, Long Island. She was buried in the plot of a good friend, her editor Louis Klopech, in the Tarrytown (now Sleepy Hollow) Cemetery. Her daughters Mary Munroe, Lillie Munro and Alice Barr survived their mother.

REFERENCES

"A Belated Centenary." *New York Times Book Review* (March 16, 1919).

"A Cromwellian Romance, Amelia Barr, *The Lion's Whelp.*" *Literary Digest* (February 15, 1902) [review, portrait].

"A Woman Novelist's Phenomenal Success." *Literary Digest* (January 29, 1898) [portrait].

Adams, Oscar Fay. "The Novels of Mrs. Barr." *Andover Review* XI (March 1889).

Adams, Paul. "Amelia Barr in Texas, 1856-1868." *Southwestern Historical Quarterly* XLIX (1946).

"Amelia Barr." *Review of Reviews* (May 1919) [portraits].

Barr, Amelia E. *All the Days of My Life: An Autobiography.* New York: D.Appleton and Company, 1913.

_____. *Joan. New York Times Book Review* (February 18, 1917).

_____. Letters to Jennie Cohen, John G. Palm, Mrs. S.S. Posey. Amelia E. Barr File, Center for American History, University of Texas at Austin.

_____. *Remember the Alamo*. New York: Dodd, Mead and Company, 1888.

_____. "When I Was A Girl." *Ladies Home Journal* (December 1891) [portrait].

"Famous Novelist, Amelia E. Barr, Dies." *New York Times* (March 12, 1919): D-14.

Gideon, Samuel. "Amelia Barr: Why Is She Famous?" *Austin American-Statesman* (April 24, 1932) [illustration of Barr home].

_____. "Mrs. Barr On Way To Home Here." *Austin American-Statesman* (April 24, 1932) [illustration of Barr home].

_____. "Beauty of Austin In Early Days." *Austin American-Statesman* (May 1, 1932) [portrait].

_____. "Civil War Days Here Recounted." *Austin American-Statesman* (May 1, 1932) [portrait].

Graham, Philip. "Texas Memoirs of Amelia E. Barr." *Southwestern Historical Quarterly* LXIX (July 1965).

Greene, A.C. "The Durable Society: Austin in the Reconstruction." *Southwestern Historical Quarterly* LXXII (April 1969).

Hawthorne, Hildegarde. "Amelia E. Barr—Some Reminiscences." *The Bookman* (May 1920).

Howard, Mary Eby. "The Novels of Amelia Barr." M.A. thesis, University of Texas at Austin, June 1943.

Linder, Lionel, ed. *The Appeal of Memphis, A Retrospective of 15 Decades, 1841-1991. The Commercial Appeal*, Memphis, Tennessee (April 21, 1991).

Mabie, Hamilton W. "Amelia E. Barr." *The Book Buyer* VIII. New York (September 1891).

"Mrs. Barr's Ladies School." Letters received 1822-1858. Lucadia Christiana Niles Pease Collection. Austin-Travis County Collection, Austin Public Library.

Notable American Women, 1607-1915, A Biographical Dictionary I. Cambridge, Mass.: Harvard University Press, 1971.

Repplier, Agnes. "Amelia Barr, *Was it Right to Forgive?*" *Saturday Evening Post (November 4, 1899)* [review].

INTERVIEWS

Ethel Uman Soschin and Crystal Sasse Ragsdale, New York, 1996, 1997.

Martha McCabe and Crystal Sasse Ragsdale, Austin, 1996, 1997.

Courtesy Austin History Center, Austin Public Library.

Mary Eleanor Brackenridge

1837-1924

"Working for High Purposes"

On March 7, 1916, the San Antonio Federation of Women's Clubs honored Mary Eleanor Brackenridge on her eightieth birthday with a luncheon at the Gunter Hotel. Women, speaking on behalf of the city's clubs, lauded the founder of many of the clubs and spoke of her "broad vision of womanhood . . . her interest in all lines of woman's work . . . and her dignified advocacy of 'Votes for Women'".

Brackenridge had served as the founder and first president of the Woman's Club of San Antonio in 1898, the first club in San Antonio to endorse the movement for suffrage for women. Speaking at her inauguration as president of the club, she had noted that

> Women's clubs are no longer amusing; they are the solemn rising of the good women of the land who organize to stand together as a unit to work for high purposes. . . .

The woman honored by her city had devoted her life to "high purposes." Over and above the philanthropy and dedication to education which had marked the history of her family, her own efforts toward the education of women and children, despite color or race, became the driving force of her life's work and are remarkable for their time.

Born in Boonville, Indiana, on March 7, 1837, Mary Eleanor Brackenridge was the eldest daughter of John Adams Bracken-

ridge and his wife Isabella Helena McCullough. The Brackenridges had eight children, but two daughters, both named
Elizabeth Ann and called "Lillie," died in childhood. The second of her three elder brothers, George Washington, was to
become a formative influence in her life.

An eminent lawyer, John Adams Brackenridge represented
his district in the state legislature and, although a Whig, supported Henry Clay for president. He possessed an extensive
law library, and Mary Eleanor often recounted the story that
Abraham Lincoln walked miles to study law with her father.
Other stories centered around a family that could point with
pride to a Scots grandfather, John Adams Brackenridge, who
had served as the first Presbyterian minister of Washington City
and been a strong advocate of education. His wife, Eleanor
White Brackenridge, set an example of family philanthropy by
organizing the first orphan asylum in Washington, D.C.

In 1853 ill health led their son, John Brackenridge, to move
his family to a ranch near Texana, Texas, where he established
a mercantile store. During the Civil War he refused to accept
Confederate money and instead insisted on payment in bales
of cotton. By the end of the war he had collected thousands of
bales, which became the basis of his family fortune.

Both Mary Eleanor and her brother George remained in
Indiana to complete their educations. After graduating from
Anderson Female Seminary in New Albany, Indiana, Eleanor
joined her family in Texas while George completed his education at Harvard University.

As a young girl, Mary Eleanor had written in her diary, "I
want to make the world better and therefore happier for all, not
just for Eleanor," and she joined her father as one of the nine
founders of the Presbyterian church in Texana. She began making the world "better and happier" for many young women of
the community by teaching them to read and write. She also
collected books, magazines and newspapers, carrying them
around the county and often discussing current events and
books with her neighbors. Observing the poor health and lack
of adequate medicines among the country people during a time
when doctors often traveled long distances by horse and buggy,
she took a nurse and medicines to those in need until the doctor
could arrive.

The Brackenridge family was torn apart by the Civil War.

Three of Eleanor's brothers marched off to fight for the Confederacy while her brother George, like his father a supporter of the Union, served as assistant secretary of the U.S. treasury stationed in New Orleans after Union forces captured the city. When his father died, George took over the mercantile business and sold the bales of cotton for a tremendous profit.

In 1871 Eleanor and her mother moved to San Antonio to join George, who had relocated his business there. Isabella purchased a stone home called "Head of the River" located in what is now Brackenridge Park, and later George built a Victorian mansion called "Fern Ridge," now the property of the Sisters of Charity of the Incarnate Word and part of San Antonio's Incarnate Word College. George expanded his business interests in the cotton firm of Brackenridge, Bates, and Company by organizing both the San Antonio National Bank and the San Antonio Loan and Trust. Eleanor's appointment to directorships of both financial institutions was a rarity in nineteenth-century Texas. In fact, as a businesswoman herself, she was later to help organize the Business Woman's Club and did much to break down hostile social attitudes toward business women.

Her mother began the organizational work for the San Antonio Children's Home, and the charter granted by the state of Texas on July 27, 1886, lists both Eleanor and her mother as trustees of the corporation. Eleanor's interest in what became the Protestant Orphan's Home did not end with its founding; throughout her lifetime she encouraged gifts to the home and invited the children to visit with her at her home. Although she used her own money to benefit education programs for young women and children, she also enlisted the aid of her brother in her educational projects.

Neither George nor Eleanor ever married, but they made their home together in San Antonio until the end of their lives. Family legend tells that, while still a young woman, Eleanor fell in love with a young man whom her mother felt was not of sufficient character to marry her. While working on an island, he made a fortune he hoped to use to convince Isabella he was worthy of Eleanor's hand, but he developed tuberculosis and Isabella Brackenridge would not allow her daughter to marry a desperately ill man. Eleanor's young beau lived only a year after the end of their ill-fated romance, and he left his fortune to Eleanor. Once again Isabella intervened, stating that Eleanor could not accept any part of the money, and the fortune passed to the young man's brother and sister. Eleanor retained the memory of her tragic romance and visited her young lover's grave until the end of her life.

Eleanor and her brother supported the construction of the Madison Square Presbyterian Church in San Antonio. Although her brother became a trustee of the church and donated the organ and steeple to the building, he never affiliated with the church nor with any institution of organized religion. Eleanor, on the other hand, sponsored Bible-reading activities and invited the Sunshine Girls to meet at her home for Bible discussions.

It was in the burgeoning women's club movement, however, that Eleanor Brackenridge found the forum for both her educational and reform impulses. Although the women's club movement was a middle-class enclave imbued with a high moral tone, it gave to women a sense of networking that began with literary pursuits and expanded to include calls for women's suffrage. Working through the women's clubs she helped to found in the Alamo City, Brackenridge became one of the "movers and shakers" of the progressive reform period, promoting the need for educational opportunities for women and children in Texas and then moving forward to embrace the cause of votes for women.

Following the Civil War, women's clubs proliferated throughout the United States. By the 1890s nearly 100,000 American women were actively involved, and by 1910 there were 800,000 women serving as members within a variety of clubs. Well before the organization of the first women's club in San Antonio, Brackenridge had been inviting groups of women to meet in her home to discuss history and literature. "Any lady with a taste for literature" could become a charter member of Our Reading Club of San Antonio, organized on May 17, 1892, for the express purpose of encouraging the study of literature.

As a student of history and a member of the Texas State Historical Association, Brackenridge helped organize the San Antonio History Club on September 15, 1896, and expressed the aims of the club at its first meeting.

> This is to be a woman's improvement club. . . . We are
> hoping to do some Spring, Summer, and Fall brain

cleaning; we are going to make up our minds in the latest style. . . .

She went on to help organize the Eleanor Brackenridge Literary Club on September 28, 1901, in Edna, in Jackson County where her family had first lived in Texas. The purpose of the club, still active today, was the promotion of the Jackson County Library.

Her attendance in 1898 at meetings of both the Texas Federation of Literary Clubs and the General Federation of Women's Clubs in Denver provided the stimulus for Brackenridge to form the first department club in Texas; The Woman's Club of San Antonio, organized on October 1, 1898, with a nucleus of women from the literary and historical groups, began an ambitious program of progressive reforms, spurred by Brackenridge's inaugural address as the group's president.

> . . . it seems to me that the time is not ripe to work in any department except that of informing ourselves of the best methods of taking hold of work. . . . The Department Club has dealt with the tramp most successfully; it has also helped the respectable poor through its Pingree Gardens, where the waste land around the city became a garden. . . . They say, however, that the women and the children did most of the digging and cultivating, while the men crept into a hole somewhere. . . .

Under her leadership, the Woman's Club worked to clean up the city streets, maintained a sewing school, helped organize the city's charities, established traveling libraries for the counties, and provided the motivating force for obtaining a Carnegie grant for the establishment of the San Antonio Public Library. In addition, Brackenridge paid the salary of the city's first policewoman, and the board successfully campaigned for policewomen on the city's payroll. She was also the motivating force behind the club's awarding of scholarships to young women, encouraging the club to seek federated scholarship loans for worthy students, and she paid for three young women to keep notes at the club. Believing that women were subjected to prejudice and injustice under the law, she organized the club's Committee of Appeal to provide relief for women and children.

A tireless supporter of the rights of women, Brackenridge promoted the concept of women's serving as members of the schoolboard and promoted legislation favorable to women. She served on the Outlook Committee to study bills before the state legislature that should be endorsed by the Woman's Club. When the Philanthropic Department of the club sponsored a law class, Brackenridge taught the class, focusing both on parliamentary law and Texas laws that pertained to women and children.

With her encouragement, the Woman's Club backed the Free Kindergarten Movement, and Brackenridge gave scholarships to teachers to train at the San Antonio Kindergarten Training School, while also supporting a kindergarten for African-American children with her own money. Realizing that future homemakers were necessary in society, she encouraged the Woman's Club to conduct classes in cooking and sewing. Home economics moved from these classes into the public school system, and Brackenridge continued to contribute sewing machines and stoves for student training.

She also enlisted the help of her brother in promoting manual training and home economics courses. As a schoolboard member, he not only encouraged the teaching of manual training classes in the schools, he donated the training buildings for the schools and equipped manual training and home economics centers for African-American students. The two donated the first Home Economics building in San Antonio, and Eleanor provided more scholarships for young women who wished to pursue homemaking in college.

The two Brackenridges shared a belief that there should exist within the city a sheltering environment for children. George donated land adjacent to their first home in San Antonio for the creation of Brackenridge Park, a greenscape of immense beauty, and then contributed land for Mahncke Park, stipulating that both sites must be used for park purposes and that no alcoholic beverages would be allowed.

Prohibition of alcoholic beverages was one of the main goals of progressive reformers, and Eleanor was an active and vocal member of the WCTU, promoting Mothers' Clubs to work against the manufacture and sale of alcoholic beverages. In honor of her work for temperance, the WCTU donated an oak tree, tables and seats in Brackenridge Park. George, even though he stocked his own wine cellars with vintage wines, joined her in the temperance fight. As publisher of the *San Antonio Express* he saw that articles advocating temperance appeared regularly in the pages of the newspaper.

The needs of children were well within the impulse of progressive reforms, and Eleanor Brackenridge contacted Judge Ben Lindsey of Denver, "the children's judge" who had pioneered in the humane treatment of youthful offenders. When her brother donated land for the Southwestern Juvenile Training School for boys in San Antonio, she encouraged members of the Woman's Club to solicit funds and then served on the Board of Control and established a library for the school. She also encouraged Alexander Joske to donate funding for the Bexar County School for Girls.

While encouraging the Woman's Club to work for legislation that promoted the welfare of women and children, Brackenridge also embraced the educational mission of the General Federation of Women's Clubs. Serving as the only founding member from Texas, she became the first vice-president of the Texas federation organized in Waco in 1897. The San Antonio club affiliated with the state organization in 1901, and Brackenridge was instrumental in the founding of the City Federation of Women's Clubs of San Antonio in 1904.

George, sharing his sister's mission to promote education, served on the board of regents of The University of Texas, donated a scholarship in their mother's name to aid young women in attending the university's medical school, and provided funding for both the university's school of home economics and for a dormitory for women at the medical school campus in Galveston. He also donated the land for the Eleanor Brackenridge School, an elementary school for which Eleanor served as president of the school's Parent-Teacher Association, an outgrowth of the Mothers' Clubs she had promoted for the temperance movement. She then organized the San Antonio Council of Mothers, later the Texas Congress of Parents and Teachers of San Antonio, again speaking out for the need for legislation protecting women and children.

Eleanor Brackenridge served on the first board of directors of the San Antonio Young Women's Christian Association, and she paid the salary for an employee of the group's travelers aid department. The association remained one of her primary philanthropic recipients throughout her lifetime, and when she died she left generous bequests to both the white YWCA and the branch dedicated to African-American women.

The fight for suffrage was a natural outgrowth of progressive reforms emphasizing efficiency in government. There was an implied understanding that women would "clean up government," and Brackenridge, holding her advanced views on the abilities of women to work for change, stood in the forefront of the Texas movement. Although suffrage had been an active issue among Texas women since 1893 when the Texas Equal Suffrage Association was formed, the cause had been inactive since 1905.

In 1908 when Dr. Anna Howard Shaw, president of the National American Woman Suffrage Association, lectured in Austin, she inspired local women to found a suffrage club. It was Brackenridge, however, who provided the organizing impetus to the movement when the San Antonio Woman's Club made suffrage a prime goal in 1908. She was also active in promoting the issue before the state's Federation of Women's Clubs.

In February 1912 Brackenridge organized the Texas Equal Franchise Society of seventy-five women and began suffrage schools to help women study the issues inherent in gaining the vote. The time was right, soon local clubs were organizing in other cities, and Texas women began working in earnest for the right to vote in primary elections. Dr. Shaw again spoke in San Antonio in May 1912, encouraging the women of San Antonio to intensify their efforts on the suffrage issue.

Brackenridge undertook a long-term commitment to educate women concerning their legal rights. Two of her pamphlets, *The Laws Pertaining to Women and Children* and *The Legal Status of Women in Texas*, gave further impetus to the suffrage movement. On March 26, 1918, Governor William Pettus Hobby signed a bill that give Texas women the right to vote in all state primary elections and in all nominating conventions, and in June Mary Eleanor Brackenridge became the first woman in Bexar County to register to vote. Like other suffrage workers, however, she realized the battle was only half won and intensified her efforts to work for nationwide suffrage. Suffrage leaders launched a drive for votes for the passage of the Nine-teenth Amendment on Brackenridge's birthday, May 7, 1919, and she rejoiced on August 26, 1920, when the amendment passed extending women's suffrage nationwide.

Like many progressive reformers, Brackenridge believed inherently that women would purify politics, but only if they remained vigilant both on issues and at the ballot box. At a luncheon honoring her on March 8, 1921, she implored San Antonio women not to weaken their powers

> by indulging in partisanship politics. You are not going to purify politics in that manner. Give your strength to principle; do not elect men or women to office because they are agreeable to you; investigate their principles; vote for the man or woman whom you have found kept the faith. It is you who are largely responsible for the men and women in places of power. . . .

In 1902 Brackenridge's fight for suffrage, the rights of women and children, and her philanthropic efforts led Gover-nor Joseph D. Sayers to appoint her one of three women to serve on the board of regents of the Texas Industrial Institute and College for the Education of White Girls of the State of Texas in The Arts and Sciences, later the College of Industrial Arts and now Texas Woman's University.

Long an advocate of the rights of women to higher educa-tion, she had worked with other women across the state for ten years before legislation was passed establishing the college. In the forefront of the movement was the Texas Federation of Women's Clubs, who supported not only the initial legislation but also continued to press for financial support for the school. Brackenridge asked for and received the clubwomen's support for a move to insure that women graduates of the college gained teachers' certificates entitling them to teach in the Texas public schools. Justly proud of the college and her role in its founding, Brackenridge commented in a speech in 1922 that

> this college is unique, because students are there prepared to meet the demands of life equally equipped for society, the classroom, the home or the

professions.

To obtain this object, two faculties were necessary; a faculty of educated teachers of practical training, paralleled by a collegiate faculty, from the best
known universities and colleges. This college is
unique! There is no other first-class college of this
kind in the Southern States.

Reflecting its name change to the College of Industrial Arts,
the college focused on homemaking for young women, offering
courses and degrees in home economics, dietetics, nursery
education, nursing, institutional management, music, interior
designing, costume designing, art education, and occupational
therapy in addition to commercial courses, kindergarten-
primary education, home demonstration for county agents,
and vocational home economics. The college pioneered in the
establishment of a kindergarten, and offered residence cottages
for training in home management. Brackenridge also sponsored a curriculum in rural arts, encouraging students to study
botany and horticulture. She sponsored a "Special Farm Scholarship" to pay the expenses for four years for a student interested in poultry and dairying.

Just as her brother lavishly donated funds to The University
of Texas, Eleanor came to the rescue of the College of Industrial
Arts, when a summer school session was endangered, by per-
sonally financing the 1907 summer term with a bequest of one
thousand dollars, provided the state legislature appropriated
the funds for summer sessions in 1908 and 1909. She also
donated scholarships through her various clubs and established the Mary E. Brackenridge Loan Fund to allow young
women to advance their education. The club women founded
the Mary Eleanor Brackenridge Club in 1907 to advance the
causes of women and children. The first dormitory erected at
the college was named Brackenridge Hall to honor her, and she
remained a benefactor of the college throughout her lifetime,
leaving additional funds to the school on her death.

The first women's club to celebrate the birthday of Mary
Eleanor Brackenridge was at the College of Industrial Arts in
1908, but she herself set the tone for the establishment of her
birthday as "Friendship Day" when, at the celebration of her
eightieth birthday, she told well-wishers, "If one day is dedi-

cated to friendship, the world will be a gainer thereby." In 1939, fifteen years after her death, Governor W. Lee O'Daniel officially designated May 7 as "Friendship Day" in Texas. On March 7, 1941, a portrait of Brackenridge was unveiled at the Friendship Day celebration by the San Antonio Woman's Club. Although Brackenridge never married nor had children, the Council of Mothers honored her as the "Mother of all Mothers" for her work with children and designated her birthday as a day to be celebrated by San Antonio schoolchildren. A speaker at one birthday celebration asked, "What has she not done for Texas?"

Brackenridge remained active in her club work well after her eightieth birthday and died at her home, Fern Ridge, on February 14, 1924. Both she and her brother were buried beside their parents in the family cemetery near Edna in Jackson County. She had lived to see prosper the causes she had sponsored and the college for which she had worked so tirelessly become Texas State College for Women, now Texas Women's University at Denton and a primary educational institution for the women of Texas.

Alarmed at the discovery that the Brackenridge Club at Texas State College for Women had ceased to function, Annie Andrews Schwartze, a recipient of a Brackenridge scholarship, organized M. Eleanor Brackenridge clubs in Washington, D.C., and in foreign countries. The clubs stand as monuments to the woman who was in the forefront of the fight by Texas women for the right to vote, and who through her philanthropy and leadership promoted the enlightened education of Texas women.

Throughout the years women have continued to celebrate the Texas woman who stood as "the beautiful spirit of friendship," the model of the enlightened clubwoman, and a woman who, through both her philanthropy and enterprise, stands as a leader of progressive reform in Texas, a true progressive leader who spent a lifetime "working for high purposes."

REFERENCES

Blair, Karen. *The Clubwoman as Feminist: True Womanhood Redefined, 1868-1914.* New York: Holmes and Meier, 1980.

Brackenridge, Mary Eleanor. Files at The Center for American History,

University of Texas at Austin; Women's Collection, Blagg-Huey Library, Texas Women's University; Daughters of the Republic of Texas Library, San Antonio; History Collection, San Antonio Public Library.

"Brackenridge Name Lauded." *San Antonio Express and News* (March 6, 1960): A-11.

Christian, Stella L. *The History of the Texas Federation of Women's Clubs.* Houston: n.p., 1919.

Clifton, Catherine. *The Other Civil War: American Women in the Nineteenth Century.* New York: Hill and Wang, 1984.

Crawford, Ann Fears and Crystal Sasse Ragsdale. "Texas's 'Petticoat Lobbyist': Jane Yelvington McCallum." *Women in Texas: Their Lives, Their Accomplishments; Their Achievements.* Austin: State House Press, 1992.

"Death Claims Aged Texas Worker for Woman's Cause." *San Antonio Evening News* (February 15, 1924): 1.

Easley, Tex. "Brackenridge Name Significant for Her." *San Antonio News* (February 25, 1960): D-1.

Fenwick, Marin B., ed. *Who's Who in American Women of San Antonio and the Southwest.* San Antonio: n.p., 1917.

Flexner, Eleanor. *Century of Struggle: The Woman's Rights Movement in the United States.* New York: Atheneum, 1974.

"Friendship Day." *San Antonio Express* (March 7, 1948).

Leach, William. *True Love and Perfect Union: The Feminist Reform of Sex and Society.* New York: Basic Books, 1980.

Malsch, Brownson. "The Brackenridges—Ahead of Their Times." Unidentified clipping in clipping files. San Antonio: Daughters of the Republic of Texas Library, San Antonio.

Menger, Johnowene Brackenridge Crutcher. *M. Eleanor Brackenridge, 1837-1924, A Third Generation Advocate of Education.* M.A. thesis, San Antonio: Trinity University, August 1964.

Moreland, Sinclair. *Texas Woman's Hall of Fame.* Austin: Biographical Press, 1917.

"Progressive Women Have Organization Whose Influence Is Felt Throughout Busy Life of San Antonio." *San Antonio Express (October 11, 1914)*: 23.

Rosenberg, Rosalind. *Beyond Separate Spheres: Intellectual Roots of Modern Feminism.* New Haven: Yale University Press, 1982.

Schwartze, Annie Andrews. *Life of M. Eleanor Brackenridge—History of Friendship Day—M. Eleanor Brackenridge Clubs.* Washington, D.C.: n.p., 1940.

Seaholm, Megan. *Earnest Women: The White Woman's Club Movement in Progressive Era Texas, 1880-1920.* Unpublished doctoral dissertation. Houston: Rice University, 1988.

Taylor, Elizabeth. "The Woman Suffrage Movement in Texas." *The Journal of Southern History* XVII No.2. Richmond, Va.

Sibley, Marilyn McAdams. *George W. Brackenridge, Maverick Philanthropist.* Austin: University of Texas Press, 1973.

Sochen, June. *Movers and Shakers: American Women Thinkers and Activists, 1900-1970.* New York: Quadrangle/The New York Times Book Co., 1973.

Williams, Mason. "Recollections of George W. Brackenridge." *The Alcalde* VIII (February 1921).

1880 wedding portrait of John Alexander Matthews and Sallie Ann Reynolds Matthews.
Courtesy Old Jail Art Center and Archives, Albany, Texas.

Sallie Ann Reynolds Matthews

1861-1938

"We were living in the Golden Age but I do wonder where the time goes"

To understand Sallie Ann Reynolds Matthews, step back into the nineteenth-century history of a Texas now long passed. Her paternal Reynolds and Barber families were of Welsh descent, and her maternal Scots Campbell family was "rocked in the iron cradle of Presbyterianism." Her parents and their two young sons left Alabama in 1847, transferring the life of plantation farming to Shelby County in East Texas. Just prior to the Civil War when the family of children had increased to six, they moved again and headed west into a land which, as her mother was told, was "a fine country for men and dogs, but hell for women and horses." She nevertheless made a home for her family while the men were "at war with the Indians or out battling for a living."

The "fine country" to which they moved was near the edge of the Great American Desert, a land of little rain, good range grasses and, until the mid-1870s, the age-old habitat of the immense, migrating buffalo herds that traversed the ancient hunting grounds of several Texas Indian tribes. Sallie lived on ranches most of her life in this area one hundred and fifty miles west of Fort Worth in Throckmorton and Shackelford counties.

The youngest of the family of two daughters and five sons, Sallie was born in Stephens County on May 23, 1861, when the ground was carpeted with primrose, gaillardia and yucca blossoms. All of her life Sallie would look with wonder and love at this annual festival of blossoms which too-briefly carpet the

West Texas pastures with color. She was to spend little time at her birthplace on the Cantrell Ranch near the present town of Breckenridge, where the Reynolds met the "westering" Matthews family, into which she would marry. The Matthews had arrived in Texas in 1858 and shared mutual friends in Alabama with the Reynolds family.

When she was in her mid-seventies, Sallie was to rely on family lore, journals, letters and diaries to craft her memoirs with irrepressible good humor and understanding. She named her autobiography *Interwoven*, using the connotation of weaving to symbolize the interconnectedness and stability of the Reynolds and Matthews families—four of Sallie's brothers married daughters from Matthews families. By the 1880s the area around the Clear Fork of the Brazos had become a lure for a generation of family relatives who had matured after the Civil War and who sought to escape the hopelessness of a devastated economy east of the Mississippi River. Nephews, nieces and cousins headed west seeking their Reynolds and Matthews kinsmen already established on their large Texas ranches, and innumerable interfamily marriages resulted.

Early in her book, Sallie began describing the simple pattern of these intermarriages with her oldest brother George T. Reynolds' marriage to Bettie Matthews, sister of the man who would become Sallie's husband. The closeness between the two families is evident in Sallie's comment that, after her marriage to John Alexander Matthews, she had to begin calling him "John" instead of "Bud;" it was unseemly for a wife to refer to her husband with such informality even though she had known him all her life.

Sallie's father, Barber Watkins Reynolds, had followed the beckoning lure of the western frontier. His continuing search for different locations to make a living involved moving his family to fourteen different locales before settling at last on the Clear Fork of the Brazos River. At their temporary home on the Dawson Ranch in Miller Valley, also near the present town of Breckenridge, Sallie quoted her mother's description of their house as built of logs and "much better" than the one they had just left. Although his wife may have regretted continually moving again almost as soon as she had gotten her family settled in, she "stayed by the stuff" which, in the vernacular of pioneer women, meant she maintained a home and "took care of things" wherever her husband chose for them to live. Her life, as with the lives of other frontier wives and mothers, can be symbolized by the bonnet, the apron and the diaper.

Growing up as the baby of the family, Sallie Ann spent much time with her mother as the older Reynolds children moved away to establish their own lives. On a "sad, dark day" in late 1861, her seventeen-year-old brother George rode off to join the Confederacy, and in 1862 Sallie's sister Susan married Samuel P. Newcomb, a young surveyor from Connecticut. Years later Sallie wrote from hearsay that "guests came from far and near" to the nuptials.

> Preparations had been going on for days beforehand. Improvised tables were placed in the yard and dishes borrowed from the nearest neighbors. Piles of cakes, chess pies, egg custards and tea cakes had been baked, turkeys and chickens roasted and beef barbecued. We did not have raisins, currants and other fruits, with the flavoring extracts that we have now, there being only spices for flavor. If one did not have plenty of eggs and butter the neighbors would contribute, and they always helped with the preparations. There was not only dancing but also a candy pull with a big kettle of molasses candy to add to the festivities.

Soon after the wedding, Father Reynolds relocated his family briefly at the Hanna Ranch, remote from even their closest neighbors yet not far enough away to escape the reality of the Civil War. When the United States withdrew troops from their border forts, the settlers no longer had any defense against the Indians. Even though the state of Texas soon organized the Frontier Regiment, the raids continued and in 1865 the Reynolds, with one hundred and twenty-five other persons from their neighborhood, gathered fifteen miles below old Camp Cooper on the Clear Fork and "forted up" in their own Fort Davis in Stephens County. While living in the primitive conditions of the "picket stockade fort," young Sallie went to Sunday School and began her formal schooling. By the time she was five she was learning to read, piecing out the words in her mother's Bible and in Foxe's grisly, illustrated *Book of Martyrs.*

A year after the end of the war Mr. Reynolds, in a move reminiscent of an ancient clan migration—men, women, his little girl Sallie and her sister's baby—led his household to what they called the Stone Ranch on a small creek that flowed into the Clear Fork, the branch of "sweet" water which ran into the salty Brazos River. The house stood some five miles above Camp Cooper and about twenty miles upstream from Fort Davis. Buffalo "by hundreds and by thousands" migrated over the open country twice a year, and every day and night the settlers were haunted by the threat of attacks on their homes by horsestealing Indian marauders.

The dangerous situation changed when the United States government, in a show of strength against the Indians in the vast area, located Fort Griffin on the Clear Fork in 1867. Just below the fort a town sprang up, and the sudden influx of hundreds of people into the "flat" marked the beginning of a fourteen-year period that changed the tenor of life among the long-time resident ranchers and farmers. The Reynolds' ranch headquarters was close enough to the town for Sallie to attend school and for her mother to make friends with the wives of the officers of the fort. Realizing the advantages for his family, Mr. Reynolds built a home nearer Fort Griffin and they lived there for a short time.

But it was not long before Barber Reynolds moved his family again, in 1869 with only his two youngest sons and Sallie, to begin farming near Weatherford. In this populated country-side there were schools and camp meetings to attend. Best of all, members of the family came for extended visits, including the Matthews with their only son Bud who, at eighteen, was eight years older than Sallie.

Three years later Mr. Reynolds sold the farm for a good profit and, with his even smaller family of Sallie and the Reynolds' youngest son "Phin," left Texas in the luxury of a pullman car. Sallie was "just under thirteen" when they traveled to Point of Rocks near Rocky Ford, Colorado, to spend the winter with the oldest son George and his wife "Sister" Bettie Matthews. In their home Sallie took music lessons on a "cottage organ" and read in their extensive library. Noticing her talent and her interest in music, her father gave her a little Estay organ of her own which remained "a source of pleasure" for years.

Sallie attended school whenever the family lived near

enough to one, and during the winter of 1873-74 Mr. Reynolds hired a governess for Sallie and her brother. While they were in Colorado, Sallie's brother Bennie and twenty-year-old Bud Matthews delivered two herds of cattle from Colorado to Nevada, then traveled west to visit San Francisco. Mr. Reynolds "filed on a tract of land," put in a crop and lost it to grasshoppers. Perhaps it was this farming fiasco and the rigorous Colorado winters which turned his thoughts to the familiar sites along the Clear Fork; he brought his family back to Texas and chose a place not far from Stone Ranch and Fort Griffin. From there Sallie, without fear of Indians, often rode on her sidesaddle eighteen miles to the Matthews Ranch below the fort to visit two of Bud's sisters who were near her age.

After the eradication of the buffalo, ranching took on a more aggressive character. Longhorns had grazed for a time over the open range, but it was not long before ranchers introduced cattle breeds such as Durham and Hereford which flourished on the grassy prairies within fenced pastures. As familiar as a rancher's own name were his cattle and horse brands—Sallie's father used the Spanish gourd, her husband registered the upright A with a horizontal A beside it, and the Reynolds Cattle Company chose the Long X laid sidewise. The image of both country and cattle was captured by artists such as Frank Reaugh, who depicted the alert, hearty longhorns and the Texas trail drives, portraying them in the "illimitable distance" of Sallie's world. Years later, artist E.M. "Buck" Schiwetz, using her descriptions, drew the "outdoor museum" of houses Sallie knew along the Clear Fork.

Although the frontier arcadia on the Clear Fork had the protection of Fort Griffin, during its "unruly heyday" the Flat below the fort was "teaming with wild and reckless characters of both sexes, adventurers, gamblers, desperados, horse thieves and cattle rustlers." Sallie mentions these unruly denizens of the Flat, but she skirts mention of the character who most affected the lives of the Matthews and Reynolds families—John Larn, the charming stranger from Alabama who rode into the Clear Fork country about 1870 and two years later married Mary Jane Matthews who, after being widowed, was to be Sallie's future sister-in-law. Larn built two houses for his young wife and baby son but then, not satisfied with being rancher and sheriff, crossed over to the wrong side of the law. Larn and

his accomplices were suspected of committing several unex-
plained murders, and they "stole so damn many of his neighbors' cattle that they just couldn't stand it longer." By mid-1878
the community was in a "terrible stage" as Larn's "squads
terrorized the Grangers [farmers] and ranch people in their
homes at night."

The "forces of decency" organized into the Shackelford
County Vigilance Committee to settle the violence once and for
all. Their posse easily captured the unsuspecting young criminal at his remote ranch and hurried him to jail in Albany, where
he was shot by his masked captors. Although the Larn episode
lasted only eight years, it remained a dark strand in the harmo-
nious pattern of the Matthews and Reynolds family experiences.

In 1876 a June flood on the Clear Fork washed out Mr.
Reynold's corn "in tassel" as the waters rose into the "lower
yard" of their home. A month later the country was at least dry
enough for Sallie and her family to attend a wedding near
Albany and, the following day, join friends in town for the
Fourth of July centennial celebration of Independence Day.
There were patriotic speeches, and a half-century later Sallie
remembered the fanciful tournament presented by young
ranchers who ran (not galloped) their horses to spear rings off
of posts like knights in the Middle Ages. Afterwards the young
people danced all night and the girls slept on "shakedowns" in
a space above a local store.

Before July was over Bud, Sallie's knight, her "school-
fellow and friend of childhood days," proposed to the fifteen-
year-old girl. He wanted to marry immediately then go on a
wedding trip to the Centennial Exposition in Philadelphia but,
reared in a family of sisters, Bud should have known that no
girl wants to be rushed through her exciting wedding-day
preparations, and the date was set for Christmas Day. Sallie
later wrote that "another link in the chain which bound the two
families was forged by this wedding."

As always, frontier family celebrations became collective
affairs—Sister Susan would make the bride's two dresses, using
Paris-inspired *Harper's Bazaar* patterns as guides; her brother
George and his wife, who *did* go to the Centennial Celebration,
sent back the white, half silk and half alpaca wool fabric for the
wedding dress. Mr. Reynolds, on a business trip to Weatherford,

sought out a woman cousin who selected other fabrics and a hat, "only one" Sallie emphasized. Years later she described both dresses.

> The wedding dress was made with a train, not very long, just medium, and had a wide pleated flounce around the bottom. There was a long tunic or over skirt all tied up from the underside making it puff out in the back with a bouffant effect, and a tight little basque with lace on the bottom of it. The so-called second-day dress was of greyish tan, trimmed in blue buttons and blue collar and cuffs. It was made with a long Polonaise which had three rows of little blue bottoms all the way from top to bottom in front and three rows on top of the sleeves from cuff to shoulder seam. The buttons were the common little rice shirt buttons and I covered every one of them with blue material.

The wedding dress is preserved in the Costume Collection of the Ranching Heritage Museum at Texas Tech University. Sallie wore her "second-day" dress at the customary "infare" given by Bud's parents, who had invited a large gathering to enjoy the "usual feasting and dancing."

After spending the winter with Sallie's parents, when the icy winds had moderated in the early spring of 1877, Sallie and John started out in their buggy toward their first ranch home on the California Ranch near the old California Trail, followed by a wagon's bringing their wedding gifts, supplies and two little pigs. Sallie set up housekeeping on the first ranch to be established in Haskell County where, she recalled, "I was to be on the outside border again; it seems to have been my lot in life to be on the edge of things." But, she added, "I was quite content and feel that 'the lines have fallen unto me in pleasant places.'" Although Sallie and John's ranch was isolated, they were not alone for they had the companionship of various family members who lived with them from time to time and of the cowboys who rode in from their remote line camps for musical evenings and to replenish their provisions.

In November Sallie, traveling carefully in the buggy, returned to her parents' home where the first of her nine babies was born, Annie Caroline who was to die before her fourth birthday. Soon afterward the couple decided to move "where there were more people and where we could get a little more in touch with the world." They bought a little ranch on a public road between Albany and Throckmorton on Tecumseh Creek about eight miles from Fort Griffin, where they had almost too much company. After perhaps a decade, as family ranch ownerships changed, the couple lived on the Camp Cooper Ranch in southwest Throckmorton County for a short time, then in 1882 they began housekeeping at the Hoover House on the Clear Fork. Today these houses on Reynolds Bend of the Clear Fork, whether in ruins or restored, chronicle decades of family lives and histories.

Within three years another business arrangement, this one of great family importance, was agreed upon when John withdrew from the Reynolds and Matthews ranching partnership to strike out on his own. The subsequent realignment of ranch lands was of lasting influence, for the couple came into the ownership of lands in "Lambshead Valley, which were located on the Clear Fork just above the point where Lambshead Creek runs into it." The Matthews ranch headquarters became the now-fabled Lambshead Ranch.

There were other changes on the Clear Fork. With the relocation of the Tonkawa tribe to the Indian Territory, Fort Griffin was abandoned after fourteen years and, by the early 1880s, several businesses moved to Albany on the new terminus of the Texas Central Railroad. Two of the Reynolds brothers, along with other members of the family, supplied both the capital and the officers for the first Albany bank. Sallie recalled that there began "a real exodus" of families leaving their ranches to move to town, and the couple soon joined them. Sallie came into friendly contact with other women of the town, but there was more than socializing for she took out membership in the Chautauqua Literary and Scientific Circle with its correspondence courses in scientific, musical and literary subjects. Soon the whole family became involved in the activities of the Presbyterian Church, and in 1886 Sallie joined the Ladies' Missionary Society in which she was to remain a member for over fifty years.

But nature intervened to keep Sallie from becoming involved in too many cultural interests; the drought of the mid-

1880s withered the pasture grasses and bushes of West Texas. As springs and ponds dried up, thousands of cattle perished for lack of water, and the following winter an ice storm blanketed the entire state killing most of the weak cattle which had survived the dry months. In the devastating aftermath of livestock losses, cattle prices remained low and John had to mortgage the entire ranch. He and Sallie decided it would be cheaper for John to take over the active management of the ranch and for the family to live at Lambshead; she long remembered that they "left Albany, October 16, 1887, on a cold, misty day" driving in a "comfortable carriage" the thirty miles to the ranch. Luckily that fall there was an especially fine crop of pecans along the Clear Fork, and Matthews and a number of neighbors harvested the crop to supplement their livestock income. They were to continue to harvest pecans for years.

The hard times which brought families back to the Clear Fork presented a challenge for the children's education, and the community built a small school and hired a teacher. With their accustomed generosity Sallie and John not only provided a place in their home for the teacher to live and boarded several children who lived too far to ride over every day, they also rigged up a "little one-horse buckboard" which the teacher drove to carry several of the younger children to school each day. Soon after the pupils were assigned to their grade "readers," a Sunday School for young and old was organized and held in the schoolhouse. At times a Methodist minister from Throckmorton came to the Bend and gave a sermon. In addition to her household help, Sallie had the guidance of her mother and her mother-in-law, the two family widows.

Cattle prices remained low and John and Sallie, hoping to sell some of their livestock, went to Kansas and made arrangements to deliver them, but ultimately the cattle were marketed at below cost. Although they had sold their home in Albany four years earlier, Sallie and John returned there in 1892. Once again back in town, John became involved with various business interests, and as times became better they joined several of the family members to attend the World's Columbian Exposition at Chicago in 1893. Both families made considerable contributions to their Albany community in 1898 when the Matthews family, honoring their father Joseph Beck Matthews, built the Matthews Memorial Presbyterian Church; the Reynolds family,

honoring their father Barber Watkins Reynolds, financed the
construction of the Reynolds Presbyterian Academy.

Considering their own lack of schooling, Sallie wrote that
she and John were "struggling and bending every effort for the
benefit of our children's education and culture." Her mother
wryly commented, "Sallie, if your children are not a whole lot
better and a whole lot smarter than you are, there is lots of time
and money wasted on them." At first the two families, wanting
to keep the "first cousins, double first cousins and near double
first cousins" at home, sent their children to the Reynolds
Academy and largely provided the funds to run it, but within
a short time the young people were being sent off "in groups"
to attend boarding schools which offered a better quality of
education.

In their continuing search for schooling, Sallie and John
brought their family to live for a time in Austin where the
children attended various schools. Then, in 1908 while the
children were all looking forward to the Christmas holiday and
the celebration of their parents' thirty-second wedding anniversary, Sallie and John's fourteen-year-old second son John Alexander became ill and died suddenly several days before Christmas. Instead of a joyous holiday celebration, Sallie and John
took their surviving five daughters and two sons on the long
Texas Central train trip through the bleak mid-winter landscape
for young John's burial in Albany.

The demands for acquiring knowledge which Sallie required of her children she equally embraced for herself. She set
about learning the botanical name and history of every Texas
wildflower and the name of every Texas bird. Her youngest son
Watt wrote that, beginning with Sallie's childhood Bible reading, she became in time a "profound scholar," and with her love
of study possessed "accurate information on practically every
subject." He recalled that, as children on the long buggy trips
from the ranch to Albany (three hours with a trotting team and
five hours with a walking team), he and his sisters and brother
learned to recite Psalms and were "quizzed on the 205 questions" of the Presbyterian Shorter Catechism. Her children
recalled pleasant, clear nights when she led them out into the
darkness to search the skies for the constellations. At various
times the children had music lessons and learned to play instruments they liked. Sallie took more piano lessons and instruc-

tions in painting; her still life with trout hangs in one of the
restored ranch homes in the Bend. Before the 1920s when oil
was discovered on their ranch lands, Sallie borrowed money to
send several of her daughters on a European tour. Watt, graduated from Princeton in 1921, returned to spend his life as the
manager of the Lambshead Ranch.

Although Sallie had a small sewing machine among her
wedding gifts, she always preferred reading, particularly botany books, playing her organ, and memorizing Bible passages
to sitting and sewing. Dressmakers sewed for her and her
daughters and blocked the needlepoint pieces she had completed. But Sallie liked stylish clothes, and for her eldest daughter's marriage in 1899 she ordered the bride's wedding gown,
a creation in "elegant simplicity of white, silk taffeta trimmed
with chiffon, seed pearl-beaded fringe, and swags of pearls
down the front skirt panel."

Sallie and John reestablished their permanent home in Albany, and in 1930 when they built a large, brick house, Sallie
oversaw the plantings and landscaping for, as historian J.
Marvin Hunter described her, "she loved nature beyond all
comparison." Six years later, finding the summer a better time
for celebrating their Christmas Day sixtieth wedding anniversary, the couple arranged for a week's gathering at Lambshead
Ranch for their children and grandchildren. Sallie seemed reluctant to leave her life, for she lay ill for over a year before she
died in her home in Albany on September 14, 1938. John, her
only sweetheart, died on April 25, 1941.

Together Sallie Reynolds Matthews and John Alexander
Matthews experienced the threat of Indians, the magnificence
of migrating buffalo herds, vast numbers of longhorns and trail
driving, the rise and disappearance of life on the Flat at Fort
Griffin, and the settling of West Texas ranch lands. Sallie's
autobiography *Interwoven*, published in 1936, endures as a rec-
ollection of frontier life in the West. Without the sturdy framework Sallie recorded of life from the 1840s to 1900, the "trials
and tribulations" in her "rambling chronicle of two families"
which she wrote for her children and grandchildren, the citizens of Albany, Texas, would most likely not have begun the
annual, long-running, popular folk opera "Fandangle," nor
perhaps would the myriad of books have been written about
the characters, good and bad, who at one time or another lived

in the Clear Fork area. Her memoirs pay homage to an epoch never to be repeated, and to a Texas love story which lasted a lifetime.

REFERENCES

"A Mother's Day Tribute from Great Westerners Hall of Fame." *Fort Worth Star-Telegram* (May 10, 1981).

Biggers, Don H., Joan Farmer, ed. *Shackelford County Sketches.* Albany & Fort Griffin: The Clear Fork Press, 1974.

Blanton, Thomas Lindsay. *Pictorial Supplement To Interwoven.* Albany, Texas: John H. McGaughey's *Albany News*, 1953.

Degas, Edgar. "At the Louvre." New York: The Metropolitan Museum of Art, c. 1879. [This pastel drawing of two well-dressed women shows styles worn in France that were made available in the United States by patterns in *Harper's Bazaar* and which American women, including Sallie Reynolds Matthews, copied.]

Frank Reaugh, Painter to the Longhorns. Donald L. Weismann, Introduction. College Station: Texas A & M University Press, 1985.

Evans, Glen L. "Geology of Lambshead Ranch." Addendum in Frances Mayhugh Holden, *Lambshead Before Interwoven* (see below).

Eyrich, Claire. "Albany; Will Pioneer Fandangle Epoch II." *Fort Worth Star-Telegram* (May 31, 1970).

"Fort Griffin Fandangle." "Written and Directed by Robert Nail. Music Arranged and Played by Alice Reynolds." The Center for American Studies, University of Texas at Austin, 1955.

Galland, China. "The Soul Of A West Texas Town." John E. Hall, photographs. *Westward* magazine, *Dallas Times Herald* (October 20, 1983).

Grant, Ben O. "Explorers and Early Settlers of Shackelford County." *West Texas Historical Association Year Book* II (1935).

Holden, Frances Mayhugh. *Lambshead Before Interwoven. A Texas Range Chronicle, 1848-1878.* John Guerin, illustrations. College Station: Texas A&M University Press, 1982.

Holden, H.C. "West Texas Drouths." *Southwestern Historical Quarterly* XXXII (October 1928).

Hunter, J. Marvin, comp. and ed. *The Trail Drivers of Texas.* Nashville: Cokesbury Press, 1925.

"J.A. Matthews, Jr." *Austin Daily Statesman* (December 23, 1908): 3.

Jenkins, John. *Basic Texas Books, An Annotated Bibliography of Selected Works for a Research Library.* Austin: Texas State Historical Association, 1988.

Knight, Betsy. "Lambshead Ranch, Texas." *The Magazine of Antiques* CXIV (August 1978).

McConnell, Joseph Carroll. *The West Texas Frontier* (2 vols.). Jacksboro, Texas: 1933.

Matthews, Sallie Reynolds. *Interwoven, A Pioneer Chronicle*. E.M. Schiwetz, drawings. Austin & London: University of Texas Press, 1958.

———. Vertical File. The Center for American History, University of Texas at Austin.

Mills, Betty J. *Calico Chronicle*. Lubbock: Texas Tech Press, 1985.

"Mrs. Sallie Reynolds Matthews Passes On." *Albany News* (September 15, 1938) in *Frontier Times* (November 16, 1938).

Old Jail Art Center. Library Archives. Art Museum, Albany, Texas.

Pocket Map of Texas. Omaha, Nebraska: Bromley-Lewis Land Company, 1909.

Poe, Sophie A. *Buckboard Days*. Caldwell, Idaho: The Caxton Printers, Ltd., 1936.

Ragsdale, Crystal Sasse. "Notes on a visit to Lambshead Ranch, Reynolds Bend and the Putnam Ranch" (June 1978).

Reaugh, Frank. Papers 1878-1986. Inventory. The Center for American History, University of Texas at Austin, 1986.

Robinson, Charles M. III. *The Frontier World of Fort Griffin: The Life and Death of a Western Town*. Spokane, Washington: The Arthur Clark Company, 1992.

Rye, Edgar. *The Quirt and the Spur. Vanishing Shadows of the Texas Frontier*. Chicago: W.B. Conkey Company, 1909.

"Shackelford and Stephens Counties." *The Texas Almanac for 1871-1872*. Galveston: Richardson & Co. Publishers, January 1, 1871.

Throckmorton County Scrapbook and Obituaries. The Center for American History, University of Texas at Austin.

"Throckmorton Pioneer, Judge Reynolds, Recalls West's Wildest Days." *Breckenridge Sun* (March 1, 1934).

Wharton, Clarence. "Joseph B. Matthews" and "George Thomas Reynolds" in *Texas Under Many Flags*, V. Chicago and New York: The American Historical Society, Inc., 1930.

Wilson, Laura. *Watt Matthews of Lambshead*. Austin: The Texas State Historical Association, 1989.

INTERVIEW

Mrs. Margaret (Carroll) Putnam and Crystal Sasse Ragsdale, Albany, Texas, March 23, 1996.

Courtesy A. Frank Smith, Jr. Library Center, Southwestern University.

Jessie Daniel Ames

1883-1972

"The Last Suffragette"

In 1965, seven years before her death, the pioneer suffrage worker and social reformer Jessie Daniel Ames recalled the Texas fight for suffrage. "We were idealists," she told *Austin American* reporter Anita Brewer. "We thought that when we got the vote the whole pattern of politics would be greatly improved and would be dominated by women. . . ."

Although Ames's dream, and that of many other women across the United States, was never completely realized, Ames lived until 1972, long enough to see the beginnings of the woman's movement that would lead many women in her home state of Texas and across the nation to seek and win elective office. Women have yet to dominate politics as Ames and other suffragists had hoped, but the woman that Brewer called "the last of the great suffragettes" was part of the ferment of the suffrage movement that gained for Texas women the right to vote in the Democratic primary in 1918, two years before women across the United States could vote.

Working for suffrage was only one of the causes that absorbed the life of Jessie Daniel Ames. She became one of the organizers of the League of Women Voters, an offspring of the equal suffrage organization, served on the Texas Committee on Prisons and Prison Labor, and founded the Texas branch of the American Association of University Women. Chairing a woman's committee of the Texas Interracial Commission, she became a director of the national Commission on Interracial Cooperation and founded the Association of Southern Women for the Prevention of Lynching.

Jessie Daniel absorbed a sense of community service from her mother, Laura Maria Leonard, who often spent her days helping nurse victims of diphtheria, smallpox, and typhoid, the summer scourge of the South. Married in Camden, Indiana, to railroad station agent James Malcolm Daniel, Laura attended Battle Ground Methodist Institute and taught in a country school before her marriage.

Reluctantly Laura followed her husband to frontier Texas, where Daniel was determined to make his fortune working for the railroad. In the railroad town of Palestine, Texas, on November 2, 1883, the Daniel's third child Jessie was born. Soon the couple moved to Overton, where Jessie remembered the town's main street as "One long, treeless road of white sand running parallel with the railroad track. . . ." There Laura Daniel spent her days nursing fever victims, and when her best friend died Laura dressed her for burial in her own clothes and covered her with flowers. Hot summers also led to violence against the town's blacks, and lynching was commonplace during young Jessie's girlhood. Years later she was to reflect that "Mob rule is the typhoid fever of the emotional life of the South. . . ."

Although the Daniel children joined the Methodist church and Laura taught a Sunday school class, the Daniels were viewed as "Yankees" and outsiders to the townspeople. A harsh and often domineering parent, James Daniel favored his oldest daughter Lulu, taking her on a trip to the Chicago's World Fair when she graduated from high school. To keep Lulu from falling in love and marrying, James decided she should go to college and moved the family to Georgetown where Lulu attended classes at Southwestern University. The entire family took an active part in the Methodist church and the cultural and educational life of the community.

His two eldest children, however, proved a disappointment to James Daniel, who told Jessie on her own first day at Southwestern, "I want you to understand right now that . . . the first time you fail in your classes . . . you come out of school and go to the kitchen. . . ." She attended classes in Southwestern's "Ladies Annex," but her father refused to allow her to attend any social functions. His ideas on women's place in the world was largely determined by his disapproval of the work of his half-sister, Annie Sturges Daniel, a medical school graduate and early suffragist who had been active in tenement and prison reform.

When James Daniel was transferred to Laredo in the Rio Grande Valley, Jessie became enthralled with the Mexican ambience and people of South Texas. Waiting "for the big event" to enter her life, she was courted by army surgeon Roger Post Ames, thirteen years older than she. Then tragedy struck the Daniel family when the youngest child James was struck with a baseball and killed. His father became permanently despondent, and Laura Daniel took over the running of the family.

Jessie and Roger Ames were married, but Jessie was too young and immature to accept the role of partner in a sexual relationship and was resented and snubbed by Roger's Mississippi family who depended on him for their support. Assigned to New Orleans to help quell a yellow fever epidemic, Roger sent Jessie home to Texas.

Although Jessie gave birth to three children, Frederick, Mary, and Lulu Daniel, the marriage never prospered. She alternated between living with her husband in exotic places and with her sister in Georgetown, and later said of her relationship with her husband, "I could not live away from him. I could not live with him. I always returned in hope and joy. I was always sent away in despair." When Roger died of fever in Guatemala in 1914, Jessie was fearful of his family and did not even attend his funeral.

Alone, widowed, and with three children to support, Ames joined her mother in running the Georgetown Telephone Company, a business that James Daniel had acquired before his death. Working as bookkeeper and manager of the women operators in a large common room, Ames rapidly developed into an able organizer and administrator. Soon she was using these talents as one of the mainstays of the fight for women's suffrage.

Spearheaded by Southwestern professor John C. Granbery and his wife Mary Ann, the fight for woman's suffrage was both a controversial and timely topic in Georgetown. When the Texas Equal Suffrage Association began organizing for a precinct drive, Ames held a meeting at her home for thirty-five men and women, and the Georgetown Equal Suffrage League was formed with Jessie Daniel Ames as president. Working with Granbery, an impassioned speaker and head of the men's suffrage league, Ames helped organize the first public meeting on women's suffrage in Georgetown.

On February 22, 1917, Minnie Fisher Cunningham, president of the Texas Equal Suffrage Association, spoke at the Williamson County Courthouse to a group of both men and women suffragists. Working with the dynamic Cunningham proved an inspiring experience for Ames; Cunningham encouraged her to write articles for the *Williamson County Sun* and to speak out for the women's vote. Speaking at the 1917 association convention, Ames called on women to devote their efforts fulltime to winning the vote. To allay the charges of antisuffragists that women working for the vote were spinsters and old maids, Cunningham circulated a photograph of Ames in her parlor reading to her three children.

When the *Williamson County Sun* endorsed votes for women, Ames was ecstatic and soon moved beyond the local scene, taking on the duties of treasurer of the Texas Equal Suffrage Association. Long hampered by opposition from U.S. Senator Joseph Weldon Bailey and Texas Governor James E. Ferguson, Texas suffragists joined in the fight to impeach Ferguson. Suffragist Jane Y. McCallum wrote that if women had the right to vote, they would impeach Ferguson themselves.

Ferguson's veto of the appropriations bill for The University of Texas gave his enemies, including the suffragists, the ammunition they needed to seek Ferguson's impeachment. While the ex-students' association set up offices in Austin's Driskill Hotel, the suffragists took to the streets. Stationing themselves along Congress Avenue, the main thoroughfare to the state capitol, the suffragists displayed banners carrying the words "Women of Texas Protest." For sixteen hours, speakers decried the governor's stand against suffrage and called for his impeachment.

The Texas House of Representatives brought charges against Ferguson, and the Senate voted to impeach the governor. Bowing to the inevitable, Ferguson resigned before the Senate could bring in its verdict. Working through members of the legislature who supported suffrage, women immediately began bombarding the new governor, William Pettus Hobby, to call a special session of the legislature to take up the issue of women's suffrage. Hobby bowed to the pressure for a special session but instead made prohibition the primary order of legislative business.

Spurred by their partial success, the suffragists mounted an avid campaign—letters, petitions, and lobbying efforts daily at the state capitol—keeping the issue constantly before the governor and state legislators. Finally on March 26, 1918, two years before women had the right to vote nationwide, a bill granting Texas women the right to vote in the Democratic primary was signed into law by Governor Hobby.

Armed with the vote, the suffragists registered women and conducted classes to apprise them of issues, and Jessie Daniel Ames was in the forefront in her district, holding mock elections besides arranging restrooms for farm women coming in from the countryside. And come they did, as Ames cited, "by wagon, by hack, by foot," and on July 3, 1918, when the totals were counted 3,800 Williamson County women voted for the first time, carrying their reform ticket to victory. "Hurrah for the women!" Ames exulted, noting that for the first time women were comparing "ideas on politics and candidates not clothes or recipes."

Now it was time to join in the fight for the passage of the Nineteenth Amendment. Cunningham went to Washington, and Ames joined Jane McCallum in working to see that the amendment was ratified by the Texas legislature. They found that legislators were working against the amendment, pairing it with a prohibition measure and one that would disfranchise aliens. Although Carrie Chapman Catt urged them to work to defeat the measure, Ames and McCallum continued to support it. On August 26, 1920, American women gained the right to vote—a major triumph for the suffragists and one that had been long in the making.

On October 10, 1919, the Texas Equal Suffrage Association merged into the Texas League of Women Voters with Ames as its first president. Working to organize citizenship schools, Ames began an ambitious program aimed at increasing voting and pushing for progressive reforms, including full participation on all committees of the Democratic party. Along with many Anglo women of her era, Ames worked for the payment of poll taxes by women, thus assuring that the participation of women in politics would be restricted to Anglo, middle-class women better able to afford the tax. The League of Women Voters also worked for compulsory use of the English language in the state's public schools.

Many times Ames was divided in her feelings, working on committees for the Democratic party to advance certain issues, while also holding to the nonpartisan philosophy of the League of Women Voters. She served with Cunningham on the Democratic party resolutions committee opposing Senator Joseph Weldon Bailey, a committee that the senator dubbed as "six sissies and two sisters." During a period when Ames was ill, Cunningham set up an alternate League office in Dallas, and Ames felt Cunningham had usurped her authority and gone too far in moving the League into Democratic politics.

Splitting with her mentor over political tactics, Ames nevertheless joined willingly with her to help defeat Senator Bailey. With Cunningham and two other women, she attended the Democratic National Convention and saw Bailey defeated. Although Ames often had to loan money to the League, she continued to build the group's support. A boost came in 1923 when a number of women's organizations, determined to lobby progressive reforms through the legislature, came together in the Joint Legislative Council. The League of Women Voters was in the forefront of what was known as "The Petticoat Lobby," helping to prepare position papers on public schools, prohibition, prison reform and other progressive issues.

The Council put its support behind state matching funds to augment the Sheppard-Towner Maternity and Infancy Protection Act that brought support and services to pregnant women and infants. Opponents in the Texas legislature were avid in their determination to defeat the measure, labeling the measure communistic and designed to promote both birth control and free love. When the bill passed, it was regarded as the foremost victory for the "Petticoat Lobby."

Jessie Daniel Ames then turned her interests to prison reform and served as a member of the Texas Committee on Prisons and Prison Labor, an experience that shocked her when she realized the corruption inherent within the system. More shocking to her was the treatment of the inmates, both men and women, on the state's penal farms. Seeing the intolerable conditions experienced in prison by young African-American women, she worked to help set up a training school for delinquent African-American girls.

She had less success when she turned her efforts to Texas

labor. Child labor acts protected children from industrial work but allowed them to work long hours on farms. Wage and hour standards for women working in Texas industry were largely ignored, and discrimination was standard. Hispanic women often worked alongside Anglo women but earned less, and African-American women were barred from working in most industrial plants. Joining with Dallas lawyer Sarah T. Hughes, Ames tried to obtain property rights for married women but saw the bill go down to defeat.

Fighting for suffrage and working with the "Petticoat Lobby" and the League of Women Voters, Ames expanded her sentiments towards social justice and realized the plight of Texas women could best be advanced through better educational opportunities. In 1926 she helped bring the American Association of University Women to Texas and served as its first president. The goal of the group was to offer equal opportunities for professional training and advancement for women in education.

Ames's interest in social justice increased her awareness of the plight of African Americans in the South, and she worked to acquire funding for a high school for African-American students in Georgetown. As director of woman's work for the Texas Interracial Commission, Ames gained a reputation for her efficiency and expanded her own view of the plight of African Americans in the United States, especially of the plight of African-American women.

Working for social justice for African Americans was no easy task, and by 1929 Ames had enlisted the help of Methodist missionary societies. As a salaried field worker for the interracial commission, she called for an end to violence and carried her message throughout the South. She joined with African-American women workers in protesting the work of the Dallas Community Protective League in attempting to isolate African Americans from Anglo residential areas.

Then Jessie Daniel Ames found the cause that was to occupy her energy and resources until the end of her life—the battle against the continued lynching of young African Americans throughout the South. Stereotyping of African Americans and fears of sexual assaults on Anglo women by African-American males exacerbated racial intolerance throughout the South; mob violence and lynching were the results. Ames experienced the racial intolerance even in her own community, where she often found herself branded as a "nigger lover."

In 1929 she moved to Atlanta to take a job as director of women's work for the Commission on Interracial Cooperation, and in 1930 she founded the Association of Southern Women for the Prevention of Lynching. Although African-American men gained admission to the interracial commission in 1924, integrating women into the work of the commission proved difficult. Through missionary societies, Methodist women moved toward social justice reform, and the integration of African-American women into the YWCA provided a base for future leadership roles.

When the Depression began, lynching of African-American men increased along with other incidents of racial violence, and Ames was the force that centered the woman's social justice movement on the lynching problem. As Jacquelyn Dowd Hall points out, Ames exchanged "her identity as a Texas progressive for a place in the ranks of an indigenous southern racial liberalism."

Her first target had been the activities of the Texas Ku Klux Klan, and she supported Jim Ferguson's wife Miriam for governor over the Klan candidate Felix D. Robertson in the 1924 election. Later noting that Ferguson was supported by the "liquor interests," she recalled, "I figured the Ku Klux Klan was worse than drink." She also grew apart from other suffrage leaders, including Cunningham and McCallum, differing over methods of working toward social justice. At about this time her daughter Lulu contracted infantile paralysis, and Ames took on the difficult task of caring for a crippled child at home.

The move to Atlanta broadened Ames's perspective, leading to the founding of the Association of Southern Women for the Prevention of Lynching. Perceiving lynching as primarily a "women's issue," she honed all her political skills and organizational techniques to work for its prevention. An outgrowth of white supremacy throughout the South and aimed primarily at African-American males, lynching also served as a means of social control designed to spread fear and to serve as a means of intimidation.

Focusing on the fears of sexual assault on white women by African-American men, Ames gathered facts and figures that belied the supposition of assault by African Americans. Prejudice and superstition were prevalent throughout the South, and women association workers, trying to protect African-American males, often found themselves threatened by white men. Standing in the face of superstition, prejudice, and a prevalent caste system, Ames and her women mounted an effective campaign using statistics, facts and effective press relations to meet their goals. "The men," Ames later recounted, "were out making studies and so the women had to get busy and do what they could to stop lynchings!"

While African-American women had long worked against lynching, Ames brought the fight to the white, urban middle-class at a time when the South was expanding its industrial and commercial base. As Ames pointed out, the prevalence of lynching proved poor advertising for an economically expanding South. Mobilizing women's church and civic groups to secure funding, Ames set up state councils, concentrating efforts in states such as Mississippi, Georgia, Florida and Texas where lynchings were most prevalent.

Often meeting opposition from church groups that refused to support the aims of the association, Ames turned to club women, and by the 1940s there were 109 groups supporting the association's campaign. In addition, church women sent educational materials aimed at preventing racial violence into the rural, agrarian South.

The Methodist Woman's Missionary Council proved the strongest supporter of the association's programs, with members signing anti-lynching pledges. Women from other denominations added their active voices, and the YWCA served as a means of distributing anti-lynching literature. Imbued with the spirit of social gospel and energized by victories in the prohibition and suffrage movements, Southern women worked avidly against lynching, making Jessie Daniel Ames's crusade their own.

Although African-American women participated in the association and worked behind the scenes to further the anti-lynching campaign, they were never officially part of the organization. Like many Southern women of her time, Ames felt that social justice for African Americans would be best accomplished by the white community, working within religious and social justice movements.

Of the association's 44,000 members, the majority were white women from small towns involved in the missionary societies of their local Protestant churches, primarily Southern Methodists. Many had attended colleges or female academies; many had worked outside the home; most were married and had children. Like Ames they were Southern women accepting the conventions of their times. However, like Ames their contact with the outside world heightened their sense of social justice and propelled them toward social reform.

Jessie Daniel Ames skillfully guided her Southern women toward a broader sense of the social injustices inherent within lynching in the South. The members of the association rejected the rape-centered philosophical backbone of the lynching movement and asserted their rights to protect themselves. They also stood by the fact that lynching throughout the South gave the United States a poor image, and by the 1930s they were using the label "communistic," linking lynching with other subversive activities. They also made a strong appeal for the need for law and order throughout the South.

In 1931 the Scottsboro case brought their cause to the fore-front of the country's newspapers. Traveling on a boxcar through rural Alabama, nine African-American young men took part in a fight and were accused of raping two white women. Although one of the two women later admitted that no sexual assault had taken place, the young men were rushed to conviction at Scottsboro. Eight of the nine were sentenced to die in the electric chair. The International Labor Defense led a court battle, but Ames and her group stood by their single-issue campaign against lynching.

Nevertheless the case aided Ames's efforts to broaden the thinking of association members, citing the fact that African Americans were severely punished while white crime leaders were allowed to go free. Although deploring mob violence, association members stood by the criminal justice system. The Scottsboro case heightened fears of rape and intensified Ames's probing of interracial affairs where white women were in-volved with African-American men. Her findings revealed that many times white women entered into affairs willingly. Never-theless, attacks on the virtuous stance of white women re-mained unpopular throughout the South.

Anti-lynching association members met with African-

American women to discuss exploitation and the double standard of moral conduct, meeting behind closed doors with no men present. Encouraging her membership to respect African-American women and to protect young women, Ames advanced an understanding of the shared plight of American women regardless of skin color.

Ames and her members also focused on lynching as a problem of class, spurred on by friction between African Americans and lower-class Anglos' vying for jobs and status within Southern rural communities. Ames carried the study even further by exploring the role of the southern tenant farmer and praising the work of such New Deal agencies as the Farm Security and the Works Progress Administrations. Carrying her message that the only preventives for lynching and other social ills throughout the South were education, fairer conditions, and understanding among people, Jessie Daniel Ames and her members joined with the NAACP in addressing social issues relative to African Americans in the South. Ames, however, reached an audience that NAACP literature never could, even going one step further by placing the responsibility for lynching in the 1930s directly with ruling Anglo elites.

Throughout the 1930s and early 1940s, Ames hammered away at her message, mastering public relations techniques and bringing her anti-lynching message and the cause of social justice to women across the South. Never afraid to upset the complacency of middle-class church and club women, Ames used her compelling speaking techniques to move women toward a greater understanding of social justice. Hoping always to make anti-lynching a "women's issue," Ames in 1937 could celebrate the fact that eighty-one state, regional, and national organizations had endorsed anti-lynching.

By 1944 at age sixty-one, Jessie Daniel Ames had resigned from the Commission on Interracial Cooperation and the anti-lynching society. She retired to Tyron, North Carolina, but lived through the ferment of the civil rights movement in the 1960s, a cause that brought to fruition social justice for African Americans.

In her later years she came home to Texas, living in Austin with her daughter Lulu Daniel Ames. She died there on February 21, 1972, a Texas woman who had taken up the mantle of social justice for over forty years, working toward raising the consciousness of women through the temperance, suffrage, and civil rights movements. While many regard her as a woman before her times, she might more accurately be described as a woman who helped create her times.

REFERENCES

Ames, Jessie Daniel. File, Austin-Travis County Collection, Austin History Center, Austin Public Library, Austin, Texas.

_____. File, The Center for American History, University of Texas at Austin.

_____. File, Lorenzo de Zavala Archives, Texas State Library, Austin, Texas.

Bateman, Audray. "Texas suffragists fought hard for vote." *Austin American Statesman* (August 26, 1982): A-4.

Bowles, Willie D. *The History of the Woman Suffrage Movement in Texas*. M.A. thesis, August 1939, University of Texas at Austin.

Brewer , Anita. "Suffragette Recalls Her 1918 Vote fight." *Austin American* (May 24, 1965): 24.

Brown, Norman D. *Hood, Bonnet, and Little Brown Jug*. College Station: Texas A&M University Press, 1984.

Crawford, Ann Fears and Crystal Sasse Ragsdale. "'Mrs. Democrat: Minnie Fisher Cunningham'." *Women in Texas: Their Lives; Their Accomplishments; Their Achievements*. Austin: State House Press, 1992.

_____. "Texas's 'Petticoat Lobbyist': Jane Yelvington McCallum." *Women in Texas: Their Lives; Their Accomplishments; Their Achievements*. Austin: State House Press, 1992.

Cunningham, Minnie Fisher. Papers. Houston Metropolitan Research Center, Houston Public Library, Houston, Texas.

_____. File. Austin-Travis County Collection, Austin History Center, Austin Public Library, Austin, Texas.

Flexner, Eleanor. *Century of Struggle: The Woman's Rights Movement in the United States*. New York: Atheneum, 1974.

Foster, G. Allen. *Votes for Women*. New York: Criterion Books, 1966.

Fountain-Schroeder, Joanna and Jon D. Swartz. *Jessie Daniel Ames: An Exhibition at Southwestern University*. Georgetown, Texas: Cody Memorial Library, 1986.

Hall, Jacquelyn Dowd Hall. *Revolt Against Chivalry: Jessie Daniel Ames and the Women's Campaign Against Lynching*. New York: Columbia University Press, 1979.

Humphrey, Janet G. *A Texas Suffragist: Diaries and Writing of Jane Y. McCallum*. Austin: Ellen C. Temple, 1988.

Paulson, Ross Evans. *Women's Suffrage and Prohibition: A Comparative Study of Equality and Social Control.* Glenview, Illinois: Scott, Foresman and Company, 1973.

Courtesy Texas Observer.

Katherine Anne Porter

1890-1980

"The Native Land of My Heart"

In 1962 the Texas Institute of Letters presented its native daughter and world-renowned writer Katherine Anne Porter with its prize for the best book of fiction written by a Texan. The winning book, *Ship of Fools*, was Porter's only novel, had been twenty years in the writing, and was to be made into a major motion picture with a galaxy of Hollywood and foreign stars playing the host of characters.

The award from the institute must have been deliciously ironic to Porter, because in 1939 the Texas group had overlooked the native Texan from Indian Creek to give its first and most prestigious award to J. Frank Dobie for his *Apache Gold and Yaqui Silver*, citing the "indigenous nature" of Dobie's work and claiming he had stayed in Texas to work.

Many felt that the institute revealed its parochialism in passing over Porter's collection of three short novels, *Pale Horse, Pale Rider*, which had gained critical acclaim throughout the nation after its publication in 1938. It was also painfully ironic that the institute granted its award in 1962 to *Ship of Fools* which, despite its bestseller status, most critics regard as inferior to Porter's short stories and novellas. Porter's acclaimed biographer Joan Givner, who does much to set the record straight on the writer's life, claims that Dobie's "aggressively masculine style" probably would have won over any woman writer in Texas in the 1930s.

Recognition for Porter's short stories, however, came in 1965 when *The Collected Short Stories of Katherine Anne Porter* won both the Pulitzer prize and the National Book Award. In her acceptance speech, Porter looked back over her often arduous and colorful career, noting that "it was a long war and an exhausting one. . . .But just the same, I wouldn't have missed the life that I've had, just as it was, for anything. . . ."

The life that the Texas writer led began on May 15, 1890, in a small two-room house nestled among mesquite, fruit, and pecan trees in Indian Creek, Texas, a hard-scrabble Central Texas community that acquired its name from the creek that trickled into the Colorado River. Callie Russell Porter, who was to gain fame as Katherine Anne Porter, was the fourth child of Harrison Porter and his wife Mary Alice, both of pioneer Texas families. Callie's older siblings were Annie Gay and Harry Ray, whose name was later changed to Harrison Paul, but a second brother Johnnie died of influenza in the same year that Callie was born.

Just two months after Callie's second birthday, tragedy struck the Porter family once again when her mother died after giving birth to a third daughter, Mary Alice, called "Baby" by her brother and sisters. The loss was one that struck Harrison Porter hard; finding the task of raising his young family an impossible one, he turned to his mother, Catherine Anne Skaggs Porter, widowed wife of Asbury Porter, who had already raised nine children of her own in frontier Texas.

The indomitable "Aunt Cat," a formidable force in young Callie's life and the source of many of the strong women characters of her fiction, took the young family back to her farm home in Hays County, close to the thriving community of Kyle. Although in later life Katherine Anne Porter painted a picture of her life as one of genteel graciousness, the reality of country life in turn-of-the-century Texas was quite different.

"Childhood is a terrible thing to remember," Porter once wrote, but remember she did, drawing again and again on a childhood haunted by unhappiness and mired in poverty. "Aunt Cat" was sixty-five years old when she took on her son's family to rear. Times were often hard and her house, built for a solitary widow, often crowded. Callie was acutely aware that her clothes, while clean and well-mended, were often the shabby, hand-me-downs of solicitous neighbors. The young girl, always sensitive to her surroundings, was obsessed throughout her life with having proper, and often glamorous, clothing. "If I get a little money, I must always have clothes," she later wrote.

Family members and people from her childhood appear again and again throughout her writing. In juxtaposition to the strong and forceful women based on her grandmother are the male characters based on her father, whose gloomy depression began in his youth and continued throughout his lifetime. "I have sometimes felt myself under a curse with such a father," Porter wrote her sister Gay in 1942. A curse it must have seemed to a young girl growing up without a mother, seeking stability and affection from a father who often transferred his attention to whichever daughter he deemed the prettiest. As numerous critics point out, one of the recurring themes of Porter's writing is the triumph of strong women over weak men, and both "Aunt Cat" and her father strongly influenced both Porter's life and her writing.

Like many frontier women, Catherine Anne Skaggs was a born storyteller, and it was from her that young Callie learned the arts of constructing a story, of using words to capture scenes and people, of depicting the starkness of the Texas land, and of the use of distinctive idioms of Texas speech. It was her grandmother who led young Callie to explore the endless world of the imagination. And it was Aunt Cat whom Porter used again and again as the model of frontier women in her stories.

Having no mother nor role model of a Southern wife and mother to emulate, however, might well have released Callie to find her own way, to break with the stereotypical Texan and Southern view of women as domestic drudges. Although her sister Gay, who had known their mother before she died, became consumed with home and family, Callie was free to create her own role, to rise above stereotypes to become a writer, and to break with her Texas past to live a life of adventure, a woman who embraced lovers more than husbands.

In 1901, when Callie was eleven years old, her grandmother died. In her short story "The Grave," Porter captured the feelings of the country people toward the Porters: "It was said the motherless family was running down, with the Grandmother no longer there to hold it together." Harrison, shunning his mother's fundamentalist religious views, sank into depression and did little to provide for his children either emotionally or financially. When Gay was graduated from the Kyle school,

Harrison moved his family into San Antonio, renting a house near Woodlawn Lake. Eventually poverty forced them to move again into a rented apartment.

In San Antonio Callie made a decision concerning her career, telling her childhood friend Erma Schlemmer that she would become an actress on the stage. Gay and Callie attended the Thomas School, taking both music and dancing lessons. During her term at the school, Callie received instruction in formal good manners, avidly participated in dances and parties with the male students from Peacock Academy, and described herself as "mad for love." Adventurous and daring, Callie was also developing the spectacular good looks that marked her more mature years. At the school Callie received dramatic instruction from an aging actress who, impressed with her student's talent, suggested she take part in summer-stock productions at Electric Park.

During the years that Porter lived in the Alamo City, she was fascinated by its Mexican ambience, and she further explored the southwestern flavor of Victoria, Texas, when the Porters moved there in 1905. Harrison Porter rented rooms for the family on Juan Linn Street and set up a studio on Santa Rosa Street for Gay and Callie to teach "music, physical culture, and dramatic reading." It was here that Callie adopted the name Katherine Russell, but liked to be called "K.R."

Among the many visitors to the rooming house where the Porters lived were the members of the ranch family of Henry Clay Koontz, of Swiss descent. Soon Katherine was part of their warm, Catholic family circle at their Inez ranch and met their son, John Henry, who worked in Louisiana for the Southern Pacific Railroad. It was "love at first sight," and when Katherine turned sixteen the couple was married in a double civil ceremony alongside Gay and T.H. Holloway.

The Koontzes, believing that John and Katherine were both too immature to form a successful marriage, disapproved of the demonstrative Katherine. Her thrifty, businesslike husband also looked askance at his wife's spending his hard-earned money on clothes and presents for her family. Although her marriage was a troubled one, Katherine relished exploring the folk art of the Cajuns in Louisiana, but soon the couple was on the move to Houston where John worked as a clerk. When Gay gave birth to a daughter, Mary Alice, Porter reveled in the role of an aunt, often pretending the baby was hers. In Houston, Katherine converted to the Catholic faith, having been exposed to Catholic dogma by a number of Catholic priests who lived at the Koontz ranch in Inez.

Another move by the couple, to Corpus Christi, placed them in close proximity to both families, and soon strong animosity toward each other's families put additional strain on the often troubled marriage. However, with her husband on the road for long periods of time, Katherine discovered modern literature, wrote poetry, and began working on short stories. Soon the confines of her marriage became too much for her, and in an adventurous stroke of independence she left her husband in what she later described as "my wild dash into that wilder world."

Many of the circumstances of Porter's first marriage remain mysterious. In her dramatic way she claimed her husband was a "monster," and her eventual divorce petition was to claim abusiveness. Still, the marriage lasted nine years, and Porter later claimed he was simply not the man for her. When she became famous as a writer, Porter often ignored her first marriage, and when questioned about it said, "I have no hidden marriages, they just sort of slip my mind." John Koontz never mentioned that he had been married to Porter, and he subsequently married happily and had children. As for Katherine, she was off to Chicago seeking a career in the silent movies.

Although she gained work as an extra with the Essanay Company, the work exhausted her. Feeling a decided failure after six months, she returned to Texas and visited her sisters, helping with their children. She found work performing on the Lyceum Circuit touring small country towns in Louisiana, then she abandoned her acting and sought office work in Dallas while filing for divorce from John Koontz.

Ill and exhausted, Porter was diagnosed as having tuberculosis and had to seek treatment in a charity hospital where she was fed only dry bread and soup, deprived of the milk and fruit she needed to recover. Her brother Paul came to her rescue, and in 1916 she entered the Carlsbad Sanatorium near San Angelo in dry West Texas. Forbidden any exhaustive work and finding no books to amuse her, Porter spent time whiling away the hours talking to a new friend, another victim of tuberculosis named Kitty Barry Crawford, a Texas newspaperwoman and founding owner with her husband of the *Fort Worth Critic.*

Through her chats with Crawford, Porter shared the adventures of one of the newspaperwoman's friends, foreign correspondent Jane Anderson, and became enchanted with life as a journalist. In turn she romanticized her own humble beginnings, spinning tale after tale to Crawford of her youth and marriage. When Crawford returned home to Fort Worth, Porter accompanied her and moved in with Crawford's family. She began writing a society column and covering theatrical performances using the byline Katherine Anne Porter, adopting her grandmother's name for her professional one and legally changing her name in 1915. Porter had found her profession, and Callie became a part of her past.

A summer visit to Denver with Kitty Barry Crawford, still recuperating from tuberculosis, resulted in Porter's being hired by the *Rocky Mountain News*, soon becoming one of Denver's most popular reporters. Then, in 1918 as World War I was ending, an epidemic of influenza swept the city and Porter became critically ill. Gay rushed to nurse her sister, and the *Rocky Mountain News* set her obituary in type. A group of interns gave her an experimental injection of strychnine, and she was on the road to recovery.

"I had what the Christians call 'the beatific vision' and the Greeks called the 'happy day,' the happy vision just before death," Porter wrote later. After her recovery she became enlivened with the desire to become a great writer and a great artist. Her brush with death was to become the basis for her 1939 work *Pale Horse, Pale Rider*, in which Porter developed the fictional persona of Miranda Gay, a character who reappears in the stories that form the basis of "The Old Order" and "Old Mortality."

Although she had gained an excellent reputation in Denver for both her newspaper stories and her theatrical performances, and had also picked up socialite Parke French as a fiancé, Porter felt her destiny lay elsewhere. Before she could make plans to leave Denver, however, her niece Mary Alice died of spinal meningitis and Porter was plunged into grief once more. She lacked the courage even to visit Mary Alice's grave, but carried with her throughout life the "deathless love, and faithful memory," only writing about Mary Alice once in the short story "A Christmas Story" published in 1958.

Katherine Anne wrote her sister that she was leaving for New York to write and felt that one day she would write as well as anyone in America. The Greenwich Village to which she arrived was teeming with the excitement of an artistic explosion not only in literature, but in art and theatre. Released from the strains of conventional society and surrounded by artists and writers, Porter found work as a movie publicist, a position which gave her time to write on her own. When her fiancé pursued her, she tossed his ring down to him from her apartment window.

Her first opportunity for foreign travel came when the *Magazine for Mexico* offered her a job. While in Mexico, she finished ghost writing the book *My Chinese Marriage* and plunged into observing people and the events of Mexico in the chaos of the revolution. She wrote a number of analytical essays on the revolution for American magazines, but it was not until 1922 when she returned to New York that she published "María Concepción," pitting the strong woman triumphant over the weaker man and embodying themes of adultery, betrayal, and violence set in a typical Mexican village. Published in *Century* magazine, "María Concepción" was the first of her stories to bring Porter critical acclaim.

Another trip to Mexico, to prepare a catalog of Mexican folk art for a proposed exhibition, resulted in further short stories with typical Mexican settings and an essay "Why I Write About Mexico" published in *Century* magazine and detailing her fascination with the exotic land south of the border. "The Martyr" appeared in 1923, the story of a weak-willed Mexican painter weeping over the loss of his model, loosely based on the real love affair of Diego Rivera and his first wife, followed in 1924 by "Virgin Violetta," the story of the seduction of a young Mexican girl.

An ill-fated love affair with Chilean Francisco Aguilera, a doctoral student at Yale and twelve years her junior, sent Porter scurrying to an artist colony in Connecticut to write and cure her aching heart, but soon she was back in New York writing book reviews and working on her short stories. She began a love affair with a handsome and charming World War I pilot, Ernest Stock, and the two were married. Soon, however, Porter was aching to free herself from the confining strains of the marriage, and the two separated in 1926.

More important to her literary development were friendships with important women writers. For many writers of this period, biography was in the words of Robert Penn Warren "a step toward fiction," and Porter embarked on a projected biography of early American divine Cotton Mather. Although she worked on the project throughout her lifetime, she never completed the book.

Like many writers and intellectuals of the period, Porter became incensed over the Sacco and Vanzetti case, marched with protesters, and was repeatedly arrested. She returned to New York to yet another unsuccessful love affair. Her short story "He," written in 1927, makes use of the poverty and hostile environment of her Texas background, and 1928's "Rope" utilizes both a rural environment and the weak, ineffectual male that sprang from both her relationship with her father and the men who were her husbands and lovers.

Porter's short story "Magic," based on a tale that Porter had heard from her maid, was published in 1928. The tale is told by a serving woman idly brushing her mistress's hair, and with its Gothic elements and embellishments, the plot bears a strong resemblance to the tall tale so much a part of the Southwestern genre. The often anthologized "The Jilting of Granny Weatherall" followed in 1929 with its memorable portrait of a life wasted on yearning for a faithless lover.

While working as a copy editor for a publishing house in 1928, Porter embarked on yet another disastrous love affair, this time with the author Matthew Josephson, who took an interest in Porter's work. The couple parted when Josephson's wife gave him an ultimatum—she and their son or Porter. Suffering from recurring bouts of influenza and the aftermath of tuberculosis, Porter left for Bermuda to join a group of friends. Living in a lush, tropical paradise at the plantation "Hilgrove," Porter absorbed an ambience evocative of the old South and relished a time of peace and solitude to write.

Bringing into focus her experiences in revolutionary Mexico, Porter produced "Flowering Judas," filled with Christian imagery and pitting the forces of good and evil against one another. The story of the revolutionary Laura and the braggart Braggioni reveals Porter as a master of her craft.

Ill-health once again drove Porter to seek the warmer climate of Mexico. She was determined to complete a novel, but her social life among such literary figures as Malcolm Crowley, Dorothy Day and Hart Crane often kept her from her work, along with the attentions of Eugene Dove Pressly, an aspiring writer who for six years was to be her lover and eventually her husband. A sojourn on the set of Sergei Eisenstein's movie *Qué Viva México* led to the short story "Hacienda," a compelling portrait of Mexico and its class structure, and also Porter's final "adios" to the country.

Years later when *Ship of Fools* proved a bestseller, Porter commented that her trip to Germany aboard the *S.S. Werra* had been a "God-sent opportunity," but she had really wanted to use her Guggenheim fellowship to write in France. Pressly wanted to go to Spain, and the two compromised on Germany since the *Werra* was cheap and leaving from Tampico. Ever the acute observer, Porter absorbed the people on board and noted the construction of the ship, from captain's bridge to steerage, which was to form the structural basis for *Ship of Fools*.

While Pressly left to seek work in Spain, Porter settled in Berlin, recording notes that might prove fruitful for stories and enjoying the social life of the Third Reich. On one occasion she described Hermann Goering's escorting her home from a party, embracing her at the door "like a big bear." Although she was afraid she was suffering once again from tuberculosis, she found Berlin a place of inspiration and completed her novella *The Leaning Tower* while continuing to gather notes for the manuscript which was to become *Ship of Fools*, writing characters from her native Texas into both works.

On the night before she was to leave Berlin to join Pressly in Spain, Porter drank and caroused with fellow writer Robert McAlmon and his friend William Harlan Hale. Hale saw her off, and the two began an affectionate correspondence. Stopping in Paris, Porter fell in love with the "City of Lights," "on sight and without reservation," reveling in the companionship of the American expatriates who gathered at Sylvia Beach's bookshop and writing more letters to Hale, who later visited her in Paris.

She became so absorbed in the Parisian lifestyle that when she arrived in Madrid, only to be met by Pressly brandishing a wedding ring and a rented apartment, she fled back to Paris with Pressly in pursuit. When Pressly was transferred to the American embassy in Basle, he wrote letter after letter imploring her to join him. Caught up in the literary set that included Caroline Gordon, Ford Madox Ford and Glenway Wescott, Porter transformed herself from a young, unworldly woman into a fashionable woman of the world with elegant clothes and stunning white hair—a transformation that the poet and critic Allen Tate noted as her playing the role of a "Great Personage."

Despite the allure of Paris, she joined Pressly in Basle, and when he was transferred once again to Geneva he joined her on weekends. The Calvinistic strictures of Basle turned her thoughts back to her native Texas, and she began noting experiences from her past that would form the basis for "Noon Wine." For the next four years she worked intermittently on the project while also working on the manuscript of "Pale Horse, Pale Rider."

Ecstatic when Pressly was transferred to Paris, she rushed back to her beloved city and the two were married on March 18, 1933. Her love affair with Paris continued, if not that with Pressly. She later wrote that during this period "her point of view fell into focus," and she was intensely productive. She translated a *French Song Book,* revised her story "The Hacienda," and completed "The Circus" and "The Grave." An anthology of her short stories, *Flowering Judas and Other Stories*, was published in 1935.

Although Porter felt stifled in her marriage, the Presslys formed a literary portrait in Ford Madox Ford's novel *Vive le Roy* in which he portrays Katherine Anne as an artist interestingly named Cassandra Mather. Satisfied with her work but unhappy in her marriage, Porter journeyed to Boston to look for new inspiration for her biography of Cotton Mather.

While the biography languished, Porter found the real roots of her inspiration in what she called "the native land of my heart." Traveling to Texas for the first time in fifteen years, she visited her family and explored her early years. Her nephew Paul Porter remembers his first memory of his aunt and the impression that she made on family members and friends.

> She wore a sleeveless white pique evening gown made from a design by Schiaparelli. No jewelry, but her earlobes were rouged! Astonished, her sisters and the other ladies made indulgent little jokes about it among themselves. Of course they had rouge on

their cheeks, Aunt Baby quite a lot of it, but they thought rouged earlobes were outlandish, unseemly, just the kind of thing you would expect of someone who went off to live in Paris and exposed herself to the well-known wicked habits of the French. If Aunt Katherine was aware of what they were saying, she ignored it; and she rouged her earlobes for the rest of her life. . . .

Ever attuned to her surroundings, she visited her mother's grave, absorbed the Central Texas environment, and even took notes on family members. Harrison Porter reinforced her image of him as pitiable, weak, and ineffectual, while her sister "Baby's" fondling and kissing her pet bulldog was to inspire the Huttons' indulged bulldog Bébé in *Ship of Fools*.

Always eager to return to Pressly when the two were apart, she returned to Paris eager to show him glamorous nightgowns she had bought in New York. Equally eager to complete the stories that were now completed within her mind, Porter's marriage began to disintegrate and the couple often fought in public. Separated from Pressly and seeking a quiet place to work and possibly to live, she went to secluded Doylestown in Bucks County, Pennsylvania. There she began work on "Promised Land," the story that twenty-five years later would evolve into *Ship of Fools*.

Her marriage over, although Pressly was to form the character of David in *Ship of Fools*, she took another trip to Texas, traveling once more to her mother's grave and absorbing Texas characters and landscape. Her nephew Paul Porter recalls that she once told him that

> she loved her family, but loved them best from 2,400 miles away. I think she felt the same way about Texas. She couldn't live here, but it was a central part of her being, among those influences which shaped her. . . .

An invitation from Allen Tate and Caroline Gordon to join them at a writer's conference in Michigan ended with her spending time at the couple's plantation home in Tennessee. Here she met young Albert Russel Erskine, a master's student at Louisiana State University and business manager for the *Southern Review.*

Erskine propelled his ardent enthusiasm for Porter's work into an ardent affair with the writer herself. Porter's enthusiasm for him embraced the entire South, and she was soon settled in an apartment in New Orleans's historic French Quarter, working on the manuscript of "Promised Land." With Erskine proposing marriage, Porter escaped to Houston and the warmth of her sister Gay's family and taught a class in creative writing. Erskine persisted, and Porter divorced Eugene Pressly, returned to New Orleans, and married the younger man on April 16, 1938. Erskine was appalled to discover on their wedding day that Porter was nearly fifty, and people seeing them together often mistook them for mother and son. Humiliated, Porter quickly ended the marriage.

Pale Horse, Pale Rider: Three Short Novels appeared in 1938 to critical acclaim, along with "Old Mortality," and Porter began giving a series of readings from her works. With the news that the Texas Institute of Letters had rejected the work, giving its prize to Dobie, Porter sought refuge from her disappointment and her broken marriage at Yaddo, an artists' colony in New York where she relished the time to write.

Seeking a stable home, she bought a house in Silver Springs, Maryland, and made extensive repairs to the home she called Spring Hill. Porter had dedicated her three-novel collection to Harrison Porter, and the death of her father in 1942 after a long illness interrupted her work and turned her thoughts back to family and her Texas roots.

In 1944 her publishers released *The Leaning Tower and Other Stories* while Porter was involved in yet another love affair doomed to failure. Realizing that she was producing little fiction and desperate for money, she took a job as a Hollywood scriptwriter and soon was part of the movie colony but missed her literary associations in the East.

When the novelist Wallace Stegner arranged for her to teach at Stanford University in 1948, Porter relished the change and admitted any student who wanted to enter her classes. Deluged with reading papers and responding to student work, her academic association was not a success. At the end of the year she fled to New York and began a mentoring relationship with the aspiring writer William Humphrey, a fellow Texan, reading and commenting on his stories. When his successful novel *Home from the Hill* was published, he acknowledged that Porter had helped focus his writing in his own Texas roots.

Another Texan, William Goyen, acknowledged his debt to Porter's work when his novel *House of Breath* was published in 1950. Porter had helped him win a place at Yaddo, and they became lovers. Soon, however, with great anguish she determined that the affair with the much younger man was indeed hopeless and asked for her letters back. She journeyed to Paris, as part of the American delegation to the Conference for Cultural Freedom, and returned for the publication festivities surrounding her collection of essays *The Days Before*.

Looking for a place to satisfy her urge for working with young writers, Porter taught at the University of Michigan and at Washington and Lee, and a Fulbright lectureship took her to the University of Liége, all the while working on the novel that her publishers anxiously awaited. Her "safe harbor" seemed on the horizon when she lectured at The University of Texas in 1958 and was led to believe that Harry Ransom, head of the university's Humanities Research Center, would arrange a building or room to house her manuscripts and papers. She planned to settle nearby and reestablish her roots in Texas, but a master's thesis on her work by the wife of a faculty member enraged her, and Ransom, although intent on collecting manuscripts of modern American and British authors, never carried through with any plans for a repository for her papers.

Still busy with lectures, inundated with honorary degrees and armed with a Ford Foundation grant, she was intent on finishing her novel with its complex cast of characters. She moved to Washington where another young admirer, Rhea Johnson, helped bring order to her papers, recovering in the process a number of unpublished stories that found their way into print.

Ship of Fools, a novel some twenty-five years in the making, was finally published in 1962 and became a great popular success. Plans were made to make it into a movie, and Porter was busy with her own plans—how to spend the money the novel made. Her first purchase was an emerald ring much like the Condessa's in *Ship of Fools*, and she took her niece Ann for an extended stay in Italy. She returned to Washington to spend Christmas among old friends, surrounded by the glow of success that her novel had brought. Then came the Pulitzer and National Book awards for the *Collected Stories.*

The largess from *Ship of Fools* had provided her with a large home in Spring Valley, and the nearby University of Maryland provided a "Katherine Anne Porter Room" decorated with her furniture and housing her manuscripts and papers. Barrett Prettyman, a lawyer with literary aspirations of his own, served as literary executor and the object of Porter's amorous desires, still strong although she was in her seventies. Even though the relationship with Prettyman remained platonic, she pled with the love of her heart to "love me as long as you can, and as you may. . . ."

A fall made living in her home a physical impossibility, and her nephew Paul Porter moved her to a townhouse in College Park, Maryland, near her library. In 1970 when *The Collected Essays and Occasional Writings* was published, she was in the hospital. Porter remained active, however, and armed with a new assistant and a yet smaller apartment she went to work on a book about the Sacco and Vanzetti case. When Howard Payne University in Brownwood, Texas, near her birthplace, offered a course on her works with a conference honoring her, she went and again journeyed to Indian Creek to place a bouquet of pink roses on her mother's grave.

Her last years in her apartment in Silver Springs were "taken up with dying." After a series of strokes, surrounded by nurses and family members and embracing the solace of her adopted Catholic church, she died on September 18, 1980. The young girl from Indian Creek, who had dreamed of becoming a famous actress or writer, had found her "place in the story of American literature." Her nephew Paul believes that the thought of her being a part of the world of Texas literature never really crossed her mind, "she aimed to be a world artist, and she was, and it was something she probably wouldn't have been if she had stayed in Texas. . . ."

Porter chose to be buried beside the mother she had never known in Indian Creek, in the farming landscape of Central Texas from which she had drawn so many of the characters of her stories, and in the area she had called "the native land of my heart."

REFERENCES

Allen, Charles A. "Katherine Anne Porter: Psychology As Art." *Southwest Review* 41 (1956): 223-30.

Barrett, Deborah J. "Katherine Anne Porter" in *The Biographical Dictionary of Contemporary Catholic American Writing.* Westport, Connecticut: Greenwood Press, 1986.

Bayley, Isabel, ed. *Letters of Katherine Ann Porter.* New York: Atlantic Monthly Press, 1990.

Bode, Winston. "Miss Porter on Writers and Writing." *Texas Observer* (October 31, 1958): 6-7.

DeMouy, Jane Krause. *Katherine Anne Porter's Women: The Eye of Her Fiction.* Austin: University of Texas Press, 1983.

Emmons, Winfred S. *Katherine Anne Porter: The Regional Stories.* Austin: Steck-Vaughn Company, 1967.

Gaston, Edwin W. Jr. "The Mythic South of Katherine Anne Porter." *Southwestern American Literature* 3 (1973): 81-85,

Givner, Joan. *Katherine Anne Porter: A Life.* New York: Simon & Schuster, 1982.

_____. "Katherine Anne Porter: The Old Order and the New" in *The Texas Literary Tradition,* edited by Don Graham, James W. Lee, and William T. Pilkington. Austin: University of Texas Press, 1983: 58-68.

_____, Jane DeMouy, and Ruth M. Alvarez. "Katherine Anne Porter" in *American Women Writers: A Critical Reference Guide from Colonial Times to the Present,* edited by Lina Mainiero. New York: Frederick Ungar, 1979.

Gordon, Mary. "The Angel of Malignity: The Cold Beauty of Katherine Anne Porter." *The New York Times Book Review* (April 16, 1995): 17-18.

Hendrick, Willene and George Hendrick. *Katherine Anne Porter,* rev. ed. Twayne's United States Authors Series. Boston: G.K. Hall & Co., 1988.

Machann, Clinton and William Bedford Clark, eds. *Katherine Anne Porter and Texas: An Uneasy Relationship.* College Station: Texas A&M Press, 1990.

McMurtry, Larry. "Southwestern Lit?" in *In a Narrow Grave: Essays on Texas.* New York: Simon & Schuster, Inc., 1989.

Nance, William L. "Katherine Anne Porter and Mexico." *Southwest Review* 55 (Spring 1970): 143-53.

Porter, Katherine Ann. "Notes on the Texas I Remember." Unidentified article sent to Ann Fears Crawford by Paul Porter.

_____. *The Old Order: Stories from the South.* New York: Harcourt Brace Jovanovich, 1972.

Porter, Paul. Letter to Ann Fears Crawford, June 9, 1995.

_____. "Remembering Katherine Anne Porter." Speech given at Texas A&M University. Typescript provided to Ann Fears Crawford by Paul Porter.

_____. Speech given at conference on Katherine Ann Porter, Georgia State University. Typescript provided to Ann Fears Crawford by Paul Porter.

_____. Speech at University of Maryland Conference, 1991. Typescript provided to Ann Fears Crawford by Paul Porter.

Tanner, James T.F. *The Texas Legacy of Katherine Anne Porter.* Texas Writers Series, 3. Denton: University of North Texas Press, 1990.

Unrue, Darlene Harbour. *Truth and Vision in Katherine Anne Porter's Fiction.* Athens: University of Georgia Press, 1985.

Vliet, R.G. "On a Literature of the Southwest: An Address." *Texas Observer* (April 28, 1978): 18.

Warren, Robert Penn. "Irony with a Center: Katherine Ann Porter" in *Katherine Anne Porter, Modern Critical Views* edited with an introduction by Harold Bloom. New York: Chelsea House, 1986.

Courtesy Molly Luhrs.

Frankie Carter Randolph
1894-1972

"The Conscience of the Party"

In the summer of 1952, Houston lawyer and political activist Ed Ball was manning the telephones at the Harris County "Adlai Stevenson for President" headquarters when a stocky woman with a shock of short, graying hair walked in and handed him a check for a thousand dollars, a sizable political contribution in those days. "I'm Frankie Randolph," she said. "What can I do to help?"

The name "Frankie Randolph" might have meant very little to Ed Ball or other liberal Democrats in 1952, but within two short years Frankie Randolph had become a force to be dealt with in Texas politics. Liberals blessed her fundraising ability and her organizational genius while conservatives, or "pseudo Democrats" as former Congressman Bob Eckhardt likes to call them, shuddered at the mere mention of the name "Frankie." Whatever their politics, none of the politicians in the Lone Star State from the 1950s to the late 1960s held lukewarm opinions about the legendary Mrs. Randolph.

Born in Barnum in Polk County on January 25, 1894, Frankie Carter grew up in Camden, a lumber town established in 1898 by her father, W.T. Carter, who built a steel-and-concrete lumber mill in the town in 1909 and then constructed a forty-room house for his family of two sons and four daughters. Her mother, Maude Holley Carter, instilled in her a sense of fairness and social justice, planting in young Frankie's mind the idea that there was another way of life other than the one of wealth and social privilege their family enjoyed.

The seeds of social justice flourished in the minds of both Frankie, who embraced politics with a vengeance, and her sister Agnese, who was one of the founders of Planned Parenthood in Houston. Her father, an admirer of Woodrow Wilson, often discussed politics at home, and the Carter children were exposed to the issues of their state and world.

Rebellious even as a young girl, Frankie never could settle down to school and was kicked out of a number of them, made F's in her classes, ran barefoot through the piney woods, and generally defied her father. After her mother's death, her father hired a tutoress, Willie Hutchinson, who became an inspiring teacher and a surrogate mother to Frankie. She instilled in her a love of history, helped discipline the young woman's mind, and taught her the organizing skills that were to help make her a force in the world of Texas politics. Her flamboyant acts and wild deeds continued, however; ever the hoyden, she was once stopped by police for riding her horse through Houston's Herman Park brandishing a pistol. She relished the outdoor life, riding horses and becoming an avid sportswoman.

W.T. Carter moved his family to Houston in 1914, joining his eldest son in the exclusive residential section of Courtlandt Place close to downtown. W.T., Jr. had built his home at No. 12, and his father chose Birdsall Briscoe to design a house at No. 14.

The move to Houston plunged Frankie into social activities. In 1914, celebrating the near-completion of the Houston Ship Channel bringing a deep-water port to the Bayou City, the Deep Water Jubilee of the NO-TSU-OH carnival saw King Retaw I, Eugene Arthur Hudson, crown Frankie Carter as his queen. She never let mere social activities interfere with life's adventures, however, and in the days when women, much less teenaged girls, simply did not drive, Frankie blackmailed her brother into teaching her to drive in the ruts of the lumber trucks in Camden. When she was proficient enough behind the wheel, she could be seen careening down Houston's Main Street in her roadster. Her aunt fainted dead away when she heard of Frankie's daredevil adventures. On another occasion, young Frankie was asked to leave the Baptist church because she was caught dancing.

With World War I and the trenches of France calling the country's young men, Houston's young set said tearful "goodbyes" at ice-cream socials and yachting parties. Frankie Carter could often be seen on the arm of young Mike Hogg, soon to don a uniform and leave for France. Marguerite Johnston points out in her fond remembrance of Houston during this era that on one boating excursion, a young naval lieutenant, Robert Decan Randolph, fell overboard. Frankie dived in after him, and Mike Hogg knew his days as Frankie's suitor were numbered and simply gave up.

"Deak" Randolph, a classmate of her brother Aubrey at The University of Virginia, met Frankie while she was a student at the Baldwin School for Girls in Bryn Mawr, Pennsylvania. One of the pioneer flyers for the fledgling Naval Air Corps, he trained in Canada and then went overseas. The couple were married on June 14, 1918, and their granddaughter, Molly Luhrs, says her grandmother had to be coaxed into having a large, formal wedding. In all the wedding photographs, Molly states, she looks "madder than hell." After his service in the naval air corps, "Deak" Randolph returned to Houston to begin his career as a banker, rising to the executive vice presidency of the Texas National Bank in Houston.

As a young matron, Frankie Randolph helped found the Houston Junior League in 1924 and served as the group's president in 1926. She spearheaded the group's efforts to launch a downtown tearoom where they served lunch to their husbands, brothers, and friends to help raise funds for community projects.

She also made up a foursome to play golf, a new sporting diversion for women. They first played at a nine-hole golf course across from Jeff Davis Hospital and then moved on to the Houston Golf Club, which eventually became the Houston Country Club. An enthusiastic golfer, she would stroll onto the links clad in a striped, ankle-length skirt, a white shirt and tie, jacket, high-topped boots, and a snap-brimmed Panama hat. She later helped to found the Houston Ladies Golf Association.

Frankie and her husband, who shared her love of horses and played polo at a club on Westheimer, hired renowned Houston architect John Staub to design stables for their horses on Post Oak Road. With their two daughters, Aubrey and Jean, they spent a good deal of time at the stables riding and jumping their own horses until World War II.

Frankie might well have remained a typical southern society matron had not she and a partner, Georgina Williams, established the Patio Shop, a dressmaking and millinery business in the Junior League Building. When Williams's black

chauffeur contacted syphilis but could not obtain treatment at
Houston's Jeff Davis Hospital, the two women were outraged
and forced the hospital to treat him. They began going to city
council meetings, became involved in city charter revision, and
took an active role in city politics.

"Frankie" Randolph was also instrumental in the founding
of the Wednesday Club that brought together people of a variety
of interests to discuss issues of the day, and she began working
with the Houston League of Women Voters. A loyal Democrat,
she helped campaign for Franklin Roosevelt in 1940 when he ran
for a third term and defeated Wendall Willkie, then she went on
to support Lyndon Johnson in his hard-fought campaign against
Coke Stevenson to win a seat in the U.S. Senate. Her hardest-
fought fight, however, was in the 1950s when, along with Houstonian Will Clayton, his wife, and a strong labor coalition, she
worked in support of a referendum that would bring more
public housing to Houston. Strongly opposed by private housing interests, the proposal went down to defeat, but the fight
provided Randolph with experience in the political arena and
helped to develop her organizational skills.

Although liberal Democrats in Texas supported Lyndon
Johnson in his Senate race against arch-conservative Stevenson,
their alliance with him was an uneasy one. As Johnson began
to take a more conservative stance, moving closer to Houston
construction magnates George and Hermann Brown and de-
pending on them for his campaign support, the liberal group in
Texas often found themselves at loggerheads with their senator.

By the 1950s the issue of race and states rights was paramount in Texans' minds during both statewide and national
elections. In 1952, when Texas Governor Allan Shivers switched
his alliance from the Democratic party in order to support
Republican candidate Dwight Eisenhower for president, the
liberals maintained their loyalty to the Democratic party and
began gearing up for a fight. An important issue for Texans was
the right to revenues from Texas's oil-rich tidelands; Eisenhower agreed the revenues belonged to the states while Democratic candidate Adlai Stevenson felt the federal government
was entitled to the revenues. When Shivers filed for the governor's office on both the Democratic and Republican ballots, the
liberals had a fight on their hands.

Women had been active in Democratic party ranks since the

progressive era's fight for suffrage, and Randolph found herself carrying the Democratic banner along with such party stalwarts as Lillian Collier and Minnie Fisher Cunningham, who had unsuccessfully challenged Coke Stevenson in the 1944 gubernatorial election. Randolph established the Woman's Division of the Harris County Democratic Party, an organization that later melded with the Harris County Democrats. Attorney J. Edwin Smith served as the first chairman of the organization, labor leader Chris Dixie the second, and labor attorney Bob Eckhardt the third. Eckhardt, a former Congressman from Houston, remembers that by 1952 "Mrs. Randolph was running the show, she raised the money, and she did the work. She was the force of liberalism in Houston."

One liberal activist that Randolph recruited to help organize at the precinct level was Bud Mosier. Often they would attend two meetings in one night, but Randolph would be back at the office hard at work the next morning by nine. In a taped interview, Mosier recalled their work during 1953 and how effective Randolph was at encouraging other liberals to devote themselves to the cause.

> She was the most remarkable person I ever met in my life, and after I found out she really meant business, that she wasn't just 'whistling Dixie,' I just got totally committed.

Democratic loyalists were determined to hold the state for the Democratic party, despite the fact that all candidates, with the exception of Democrat John White, then running for commissioner of agriculture, had crossfiled on both tickets. When Eisenhower won the presidency, taking Texas into the Republican column for the first time since 1928, and with Allan Shivers' maintaining strong control of the Texas governor's office, liberal-loyalist Democrats were forced to take a backseat in Texas politics.

Two organizations evolved to work toward regaining Democratic control of Texas. Speaker Sam Rayburn set up the Democratic Advisory Council to protect the interests of the party in Texas, and by 1956 labor-liberals had formed the Democrats of Texas. In addition, the liberal wing of the Texas Democratic party developed an effective journalistic voice with which to attack the Establishment. In 1954 a group of liberals, including

Randolph, acquired the *State Observer* and melded it with the *East Texas Democrat* to form the *Texas Observer* Publishing Company to produce the *Texas Observer*, an independent voice in Texas journalism. Randolph loaned the corporation $5,000 and another $5,000 was sold in stock. Before the name was even settled on, liberals wrote out blank checks for stock in the publication.

Randolph was instrumental in choosing Ronnie Dugger as editor of the fledgling *Observer*. Billie Carr recalls Randolph's selection of Dugger and her determination that the editor be young, intellectual, and have integrity. "She was the best at picking people there was, and she knew that Ronnie was 'it'." In an interview concerning the *Observer's* initial years, Dugger commented,

> Mrs. Randolph from the very beginning was totally devoted to the idea of independent journalism; of an independent journal, and of the editor running it. . . .

Randolph, merely serving as one of the trustees and as treasurer, gave Dugger a free hand, promising him absolute control of all editorial policy and over all material going into the publication. She lived up to her promise, often disagreeing with Dugger and with his fellow editor, Willie Morris, but not interfering with their running of the *Observer*. Still she was a formidable force, and Dugger recalls that

> Mrs. Randolph trusted me; and when we differed, and I was arguing to her that she was wrong, I can't tell you how carefully I would proceed. . . .

While some liberal leaders, including Bob Eckhardt and Chris Dixie, attempted to work with Senator Lyndon Johnson, Randolph continued her opposition to Johnson's increasingly conservative views. At the Democratic convention held in Dallas in May 1956, Johnson struck back and urged the Harris County Democrats, who were leading an attempt to purge the State Democratic Executive Committee of Governor Allan Shivers's supporters, to back down. They refused. Randolph and Bryon Skelton, both members of the Democratic Advisory

Committee, were both nominated as members of the State
Democratic Executive Committee, but Johnson wanted only
one nominee from the DAC—his own—and instructed his
lieutenants to see that his choice, Beryl Ann Bentsen, wife of
former Congressman Lloyd Bentsen of McAllen, was elected.
Johnson sent word to Randolph that he would see that other
party positions were hers. In typical fashion, she sent back a
resounding "No!."

Knowing she could not possibly muster enough votes,
Beryl Ann Bentsen withdrew, and Randolph's name was placed
in nomination by Houston attorney Jesse Andrews and sec-
onded by Dickinson banker Walter Hall. In his nomination
speech, Andrews cited Randolph's influence, commenting:

> You ask anyone in Harris County—a banker,
> worker, Republican, or Democrat, who is the most
> successful. You get one answer, Frankie Randolph.

When Randolph was nominated as a member of the Democratic national committee, along with Bryon Skelton in a victory
lauded by the labor-liberals who had lost their purge attempt,
Randolph thanked her supporters, claiming victory for Texas
Democrats in the upcoming elections, "I could never thank you
people enough, for this is the greatest honor any woman could
have. . . ." J. Edwin Smith, leader of the Houston delegation
commented, "We won the battle we considered by far the most
important."

During this period, the Harris County Democrats were
steadily organizing their precincts and recruiting leaders to run
for local and state offices. Molding a solid bloc of labor-liberal
voters dedicated to sending a slate of liberals to the state legislature took both organization and compromise, but by 1956 the
Harris County voters had sent five liberals to the legislature.
Among them was Bob Eckhardt, a labor lawyer who credits
three women with helping to get him elected—Minnie Fisher
Cunningham, Marion Storm, and Frankie Randolph.

Randolph often differed with the views of other liberals and
never minded taking one of her own political cohorts to task.
She once sent a telegram to State Representative Dean Johnston,
a dedicated liberal she had helped elect: "Don't Do Anything
Until Tomorrow. You Have Made Enough Mistakes Today."

Her strong views also caused rifts in some of her political partnerships. J. Edwin Smith recalled that his split with his longtime friend Lyndon Johnson, to support Randolph for national committeewoman in 1956, put him "between the Devil and the deep blue sea." He and Randolph later differed over the candidacy of Judge Ben Wilson to the district court—Smith supported Wilson while Randolph backed another candidate—and when Smith ran for associate justice of the Texas Supreme Court, the Harris County Democrats supported him, with the exception of Randolph and her close faction. When Smith lost by a narrow margin, he felt he might have won if Randolph had lent her support.

Realizing the need for a stronger statewide organization, liberals set up the Democrats of Texas dedicated to electing loyal Democrats to local, state, and national offices. Randolph served as chair of the group, telling the media that the group was dedicated to "returning the state to the Democratic Party" and standing in opposition to the Dixiecrats. The DOT coordinated efforts of the Texas AFL-CIO, the NAACP, liberal Hispanic voters, and the Texas Farmers' Union.

In January 1957 Washington reporter Liz Carpenter reported that "high-ranking Texas Democrats" were demanding that Randolph be ousted as national committeewoman because of her association with DOT. Some Democratic officials made charges that Randolph and Houston attorney Roger Dailey had failed to report a $3,000 contribution for a Democratic victory dinner. National Committee Chairman Paul Butler reported that a record of the contribution was found at national headquarters and quickly squashed rumors that he had any intention of removing Randolph.

Infighting for party control continued throughout 1958 and 1959, with Governor Price Daniel's declaring war on DOT and charging that it was a "splinter minority group" dedicated to "sowing the seeds of disunity" among Texas Democrats. The organization supported Ralph Yarborough, who with liberal backing had won a special election for a full term to the U.S. Senate in April 1957, and State Senator Henry B. Gonzalez for governor against Daniel.

The infighting among Texas Democrats continued, and when Randolph called for a "code of ethics" to establish procedures in elections, the move was swiftly opposed by Democratic committeewoman Marietta Brooks of Austin, a longtime supporter of Lyndon Johnson. *Austin American* reporter Sam Wood hailed the battle between the two women as one between the "Tugboat Annie" of Texas politics and the "Dimpled Darling" of the SDEC. Brooks called for Randolph to apologize to the SDEC for calling its members disloyal, while Randolph responded by calling for "personal integrity" on the part of SDEC members.

Randolph also continued to battle with Governor Daniel throughout the gubernatorial campaign. Standing on a platform of states rights and free enterprise, Daniel claimed the DOT would deliver Texas industry to union control. Randolph charged back: "Is he running against me or [Henry] Gonzalez and [W.Lee] O'Daniel?" She also took on her fellow national committee member Byron Skelton when he decried the existence of the DOT.

With the Democratic party headed for convention in September 1958, rumors spread that Randolph would be ousted as national committeewoman for failing to cooperate with the national party. She continued to oppose Lyndon Johnson as he planned a "favorite-son" candidacy for president of the United States in 1960, and she continued to call for loyalty oaths, despite Johnson's opposition to them.

The Johnson forces prevailed, however, and the DOT's went down to defeat. Even though Randolph marched her forces out of the convention hall in Austin and into a rump convention at Barton Springs, Johnson gained his favorite-son nomination. As one liberal expressed the group's disillusionment, "We weren't defeated—we were massacred." Randolph suffered further defeat when she was replaced as national committeewoman by Johnson loyalist Hilda Weinert of Seguin.

The 1960s, however, opened long-promised doors for progressive forces in Texas and across the nation. Long advocating civil rights for African Americans, progressives looked to John F. Kennedy, the Democratic presidential candidate, to forward legislation that would advance the rights of the country's African Americans. Long before Kennedy's election, Frankie Randolph had been actively working for the rights of African Americans to participate equally in society. Former Houston city councilman Gould Buck remembered that "it always pained her to see black delegates to county conventions shunted off to the rear of the balcony," and when she organized her first political banquet, she demanded that Houston's Shamrock Hotel admit African Americans.

Throughout the 1950s and early 1960s, politicians knew that Frankie Randolph would be holding court at her special table in a back corner at Rudi's, one of Houston's private clubs that served mixed drinks to its members before liquor-by-the-drink was legal in Texas. Molly Luhrs recalls one late afternoon when the only other people in the club were two men sitting at a table near them. Overhearing a remark offensive to her, Randolph rose and hit one of the men soundly over the head with her overstuffed purse. The maitre d' came running, and the victim was furious, vowing to sue Randolph for assault. Letters and recriminations flew back and forth but nothing ever came of the case.

On another occasion Randolph decided to have lunch at the club when she was in the company of Cora Guerin, an African American and wife of Texas Southern University professor Nick Guerin. When the two entered, the long-suffering maitre d' told her, "I'm sorry Mrs. Randolph. We don't serve blacks." Randolph shot back, "Well, you do now." The two women marched right in, had lunch, and no other comments were made.

Throwing their support solidly behind the Kennedy-Johnson ticket, on a rainy August 29, 1960, the Harris County Democrats sponsored a Kennedy Ladies Tea with Lady Bird Johnson, Eunice Shriver, and Ethel Kennedy attending. Prominent among the Texas Democratic women present were Jean Daniel, wife of Texas governor Price Daniel, and Frankie Randolph.

On September 12, the group rallied for Kennedy at the Houston City Coliseum, where Frankie Randolph received an ovation second only to the candidate's. After the rally, Kennedy left to attend the meeting of the Greater Houston Ministerial Alliance at the Rice Hotel, where the Catholic presidential candidate successfully defended his stance concerning church and state.

During the years of Kennedy's presidency, Randolph devoted time to encouraging the entrance of African Americans into the mainstream of the voting public. She encouraged black college students to join a Democratic coalition to assist in a poll tax drive and took part in a statewide poll tax effort. In addition she served on the Houston Council on Human Relations, and she chaired the Commission for Better Local Government on which a fledgling politician named Barbara Jordan served. The group recruited and encouraged qualified individuals to run for public office and supported their candidacies.

By 1965 Randolph was winding up her active political career and wrote to Latane Lambert, the secretary of the Texas Organization of Liberal Democrats, that she was retiring from all active political work and resigning as a member of the organization. She also declined an invitation to attend a coffee for Congressman Jim Wright, writing to Warner L. Brock that she was giving up meetings under doctor's orders and telling Brock that she was not sure she would support Wright, but was "looking at his record."

Still her interest in state and national politics remained strong, and she wrote a letter to liberal Democrats as the 1968 elections approached warning them that 1968 was a critical year for Democrats and encouraging them to vote.

> The Republican nominee and the third party candidate are both dangerous threats to progressive government and to lasting brotherhood among men. . . .

The last years of her life were difficult ones. According to her granddaughter, Molly Luhrs, she suffered both a mental and physical breakdown. The strains of politics, coupled with a difficult marriage, took their toll. She was bedridden for a year and a half before her death and contemplated divorcing her husband. Fearing that her reflections on divorce might be the result of hardening of the arteries, coupled with angina, her family intervened to keep the marriage together.

While her grandmother was ill, Luhrs ran for precinct judge with the help of Billie Carr. Although they campaigned door to door, Luhrs lost, but she continues to work behind the scenes in Texas politics, aiding Billie Carr and the Harris County Democrats. "It was wonderful to have her [Randolph] as a mentor and role model," Luhrs recalls. "She really educated me, and made me feel I would be able to do things. I adored her with my heart and soul."

To the end of her active life, Randolph fought for progressive government and candidates she thought would carry the liberal banner, and she rightly earned the accolade that her colleague Billie Carr bestowed on her, "the conscience of the

Democratic party." When Frankie Randolph died on September 5, 1972, her family received numerous expressions of sympathy, telegrams, and letters from political colleagues and friends.

The telegram from Ralph Yarborough would no doubt have pleased her most, "Mrs. Randolph's support and encouragement more than that of any other one person was a major factor in my going to the U.S. Senate." Her longtime associate, Ronnie Dugger, said of her, "She is surely loved by more people in the community of good in Texas than any other woman."

REFERENCES

Adams, Ann. *Firestarter Files: The Public and Private Letters of Franklin Jones, Sr., 1981-1984*. Oak Harbor, Washington: Packet Press, 1985.

Baskin, Robert E. "No Harmony Seen By Mrs. Randolph." *Dallas Morning News* (December 6, 1958).

Bailey, Ernest. "Houston Demos Lose on Ouster, But Win on Mrs. Randolph." *Houston Press* (May 23, 1956).

Brooks, Raymond and Sam Wood. "Capital A." *Austin American* (July 15, 1958).

Carpenter, Elizabeth. "Democratic Bigwigs Hastily Deny Plan for Ouster of Mrs. Randolph." *Houston Post* (January 8, 1957): 4:8.

Corporation Record Book, East Texas Democrat and Texas Observer [original in possession of Molly Luhrs, Houston, Texas].

Duckworth, Allen. "Move to Oust DOT Head Foreseen for Convention." *Dallas Morning News* (August 24, 1958).

Dugger, Ronnie. "On Mrs. Randolph." *Texas Observer* (May 23, 1956).

_____. *The Politician: the life and times of Lyndon Johnson*. New York: W.W. Norton, 1982.

Duncan, Dawson. "Frankie Randolph, Liberal." *Dallas Morning News* (February 2, 1958).

Johnston, Marguerite. *Houston: The Unknown City, 1836-1946*. College Station: Texas A&M University Press, 1991.

Jones, Franklin, Sr. "The birth of the Observer." *Texas Observer* (March 11, 1977): 28.

Kinch, Sam and Stuart Long. *Allan Shivers: The Pied Piper of Texas Politics*. Austin: Shoal Creek Publisher, Inc., 1973.

Lacey, Margaret. "Houston Country Club Golfers Share Memories." *Houston Post* (January 14, 1957) 2:1.

Landrum Lynn. "Ethics in Conventions." *Dallas Morning News* (January 1, 1958).

"Liberals Reorganize as Democrats of Texas." *Houston Post* (May 19, 1957): 1:11.

Mathis, Jim. "Mrs. Randolph Shows No Temper, No Axes—But Many Principles." *Houston Post* (May 24, 1956).

"Move On To Oust Mrs. Randolph." *Houston Post* (September 13, 1956): 1:12.

"Mrs. Randolph Elected to National Committee." *Houston Post* (May 23, 1956): 1:1.

"Mrs. Randolph May Face Party Committee Ouster." *Houston Post* (January 6, 1957).

"New Protest Filed On Anti-Randolph Reports." *Houston Post* (January 18, 1957): 4:12.

Phelan, Charlotte. "As a Democrat, Mrs. Randolph Is Controversial and Dedicated Person." *Houston Post* (May 29, 1960).

_____. "Frankie Randolph: A Junior League founder, who became a scrapper in the tough world of Texas politics." *Houston Post* (September 15, 1972): A-2.

_____. "Frankie Randolph Leads Defeated DOTs Back Home." *Houston Post* (June 19, 1960).

Randolph, Frankie. File, The Center for American History, University of Texas at Austin.

_____. File, Texas Room, Houston Public Library.

_____. Papers. Woodson Research Center, Fondren Library, Rice University, Houston, Texas.

"Randolph Pioneered in U.S. Naval Air Corps." *Houston Post* (October 18, 1955): 6:6.

Smith, J. Edwin, Letter to Ann Fears Crawford, Houston, 28 September 1995.

Spinks, Brian. "Titled Texan: Liberalism Just Simple Progress to Mrs. Randolph." *Houston Post* (June 10, 1956).

Staples, Ann. "The Liberals in Harris County and the 1960 Presidential Elections." Unpublished research paper in Frankie Carter Randolph Collection, Woodson Research Center, Fondren Library, Rice University, Houston, Texas.

Wood, Sam and Raymond Brooks. "Capitol A—Ladies Night." *Austin American* (January 23, 1958).

INTERVIEWS

Billie Carr and Ann Fears Crawford, Houston, 18 May 1995.

Former Congressman Bob Eckhardt and Ann Fears Crawford, Austin, 26 May 1995.

Molly Luhrs and Ann Fears Crawford, Houston, 15 July 1995.

J. Edwin Smith and Ann Fears Crawford, Houston, 9 September 1995.

1935 photo of Tennant with full-scale model of Tejas Warrior.
Courtesy The Jerry Bywaters Collection on Art of the Southwest, The Jake and Nancy Hamon Arts Library, Southern Methodist University, Dallas, Texas. (Photo credit: DeWitt Ward, New York City.)

Allie Victoria Tennant

1898-1971

"A Weakling Should Not Take Up Sculpture"

Always bold and independent, Allie Tennant probably drove her own car on her trip in the late 1930s from her Dallas studio to Electra, Texas, in Wichita County just below the Red River, for an in-depth investigation of the site before beginning her metal sculpture "Cattle, Oil, and Wheat." During the Depression Allie had joined the large number of artists of all ages who created the "art of America" for the W.P.A. (Works Progress Administration), during "a period that infused art with life and gave artists a place in the world. It took art out of the field of dealers and New York cliques and spread it over the country."

In a typewritten memoir whose spelling and punctuation lead one to wonder if her parents were so intent on art training for their precocious child that they ignored her basic "3 Rs," Allie nevertheless expressed the eagerness for things American which she shared with contemporary artists as she gathered ideas for the mural of aluminum panels she would construct for Electra's post office, reconstructing with words her search for the essence of the world which she chose to duplicate.

> After visiting Electra and surrounding country and talking with residents, I decided on "Cattle, Oil, and Wheat," for the subject matter of the pannels.
>
> Before the discovery of Oil, that section of Texas was devoted principally to the raising of Cattle and Wheat.
>
> When Oil was discovered, derricks and storage

tanks, sprang up like mushrooms, almost over night, so now it is almost impossible to look in any direction without seeing a tank or a derrick.

The raising of cattle and wheat has apparently not been much effected by the Oil industry, for thousands of Hereford cattle roam the plains and wheat fields stretch as far as the eye can see. One of the largest ranches in Texas adjoins the town-ship.

I had the feeling when I looked over the rolling prairies, that, Oil, was not crowding out the cattle and wheat, but was simply taking its plase along with them and that there would be cattle on the plains long after the Oil was exhausted.

For that reason and for the sake of composition, I included derricks and tanks in all three pannels, stressing Oil in the center one and Cattle and Wheat on either side, placing the horizon line the same distance from the top of all three pannels to help unify the design.

The cattle on most of the ranches is the Hereford, a short, stocky beef cattle. In order to become familiar with the breed I visited ranches and stock shows, and talked with the cattle men. I also got splendid help and information from the Editor of the Agricultural department of the Dallas Morning News.

Cattle is a large subject to depict in a 1 ft, 10 in by 4 ft, 3 in pannel, so in order to give the impression of a large heard, and to give them the proper scale I designed it so that some cattle would be coming into the composition and others going out of the composition, and repeating the horizontal lines of the back of many, reseeding into the background, and scaling down the cowboy on the horse, to give distance, and just letting him enter the composition to help give the feeling of movement in the herd.

The Wheat pannel is treated in much the same manner, bringing the man into the fore ground for scale and, letting the wagon recede, and be partly out of the composition.

The center pannel which is 3 ft 4 in by 4 ft, shows three oil field workers studying a map, preparatory, perhaps to laying pipe line.

The three figures are brought forward into the first plane and scaled to almost life size. In order to permit this large a scale, only about one half of the figure is shown. The tanks and derricks are designed to balance the composition on either side, and to create the illusion of distance.

The figures of the men were modeled from memory, and are typical, but not portraits, a model was employed for an hour or so to check the anatomy.

By 1940 Allie Victoria Tennant was forty-two years old and had become the professional sculptor she had seemed destined to be. Born in St. Louis, Missouri, the fourth of five children, she was the only daughter of Englishman Thomas R. Tennant and his Georgia-born wife Allie Virginia Brown. Tennant was an accountant who had emigrated to New Orleans in 1872; he was also a watercolorist and soon after his arrival organized a group of fellow artists. The family eventually resettled in Missouri, but by 1910 they had established a home in Dallas on Holmes Street. In the mid-1920s after Tennant's death, the family moved to their home at 5315 Live Oak Street. Allie told the story on herself that she often made mud pies; even as a little girl she "liked the feel of the earth." When she was eight years old she created a red-clay sculpture bust which the family recognized as being of George Washington. She "proudly put it in a window to dry"; that night it rained and the next morning it was "just a little mound of mud on the window-sill."

Allie's parents were interested in training her artistic talent and enrolled their young daughter in the innovative Aunspaugh Art School with the indefatigable painter-teacher Vivian Louise Aunspaugh. It was the first school in the Southwest to offer classes in fine and commercial art, and also the first to use live models, nude and draped. Allie attended the Saturday drawing classes, and a corner in the studio was set aside for her to model in clay. Later Allie had a place at home to work, in which she "inveigled the neighborhood children to pose" for her. Allie also studied with a Professor Meyer, a Munich artist living in Dallas. The young artist was fortunate to "grow up" with a well-rounded art education and to have Aunspaugh nearby years later to continue to critique her work. Allie admitted that if a clay model remained for long in the studio, she could not resist taking it apart and recreating it.

Allie's brothers lived at home for several years even after establishing themselves in the business life of Dallas, and her unmarried brother Roger remained there after the others moved away. After her student and formative years in New York, Allie needed a working place in Texas and, in the late 1920s, chose to establish it in her family home on Live Oak Street. Dallas architect Walter Sharpe designed her studio with a vaulted ceiling, large north window, and shelves and niches for her work lining the walls. Amid these familiar surroundings Allie worked on her sculpture for the remainder of her life.

In her early years of art training as she studied painting and drawing, Allie learned that "there is no conceptual difference between painting and sculpture." She became acquainted with the problems of a sculptor which, she wrote, "are comparatively few and have hardly changed in the long course of the history of western man," as with the sculptor's tools, which have changed little since the ancient Greeks: the point or punch, which is used with a mallet or hammer to knock off relatively large chips of stone, the various chisels: flat, bull-nosed and the claw or toothed chisel, the drill, the files and rasps used in smoothing a figure's surface, and abrasives for polishing off rasp marks.

Then there was the stone itself; Allie learned the varying qualities of granite, onyx and the marbles—Vermont, Tennessee, Italian—in addition to the inherent nature of woods. In her adult classes, Allie had the fortunate advantage of studying and drawing from nude models, unlike the earlier artist Eleanor Onderdonk of San Antonio who, in her New York studies, had to limit herself to miniature portraits of faces and shoulders because women art students were not permitted to attend drawing classes using nude models.

Allie began intensively training when she enrolled in 1927 at the Art Students League in New York. Through 1928 she studied anatomy and had lecture courses with George Brandt Bridgeman, who wrote a number of books on constructive anatomy, life drawing, and on hands, features and faces. She attended the Viennese artist Eugene Steinhof's lecture classes in 1933. Her sculpture training was done under Edward McCartan, whose work shows a close kinship with eighteenth-century

France gained from his Paris studies, and who was influenced by Rodin and Houdon. In the United States McCartan created a number of statues, for public places, and other works of architectural sculpture; Allie's style reflected both McCartan's "quality of line" and his lyricism. The well-known sculptor Lorado Taft praised her student work as promising, and in 1927 her "Head of a Soldier" won second prize at the Texas Artists' League exhibition at Nashville, Tennessee.

The "Roaring Twenties" were exciting years to be an art student with her own sculpture studio in New York. American art was celebrating the brief period of Regionalism with its appreciation of the culture and spirit of the lives lived by ordinary citizens in familiar, everyday American settings. Thomas Hart Benton, John Stuart Curry, Grant Wood, Charles Sheeler and other artists painted and interpreted the various facets of the American spirit for appreciative audiences.

At the same time, American architecture followed the new international decorative style of Art Moderne, later known as Art Deco, whose unmistakable characteristics dominated public and private structures throughout the United States. In New York, William Van Alen's Chrysler Building was a new skyscraper with provocative tower designs, the same type of designs seen in jewelry and furniture. Even the cabinets of the first radios showed the often exotic Art Deco imaging. In New York Allie undoubtedly was familiar with the works of the well known sculptor Paul Manship, whose influence she expressed in her 1936 sculpture "Tejas Warrior" which became her best known work.

Allie also became acquainted with a new approach (but an old technique) of creating sculpture known as "direct carving." Earlier in the twentieth century a number of sculptors in Europe had returned to the technique of working directly in stone and wood, the "true road to sculpture"; in the United States sculptors William Zorach and Robert Laurent became the "leading advocates of direct carving" in the 1920s. This approach broke away from the age-old process of modeling the image in clay and baking it into terra cotta, then stepping aside and turning the model over to a technician who made a plaster cast and transferred it into stone or bronze in which much of the original subtleties of light and shadow were lost. With direct carving the artist is continually involved, working on all sides of the statue as the figure is developed by a process revealing the image as a whole.

In her visits home Allie found that in Texas women were the sculptors; men were the painters. Allie's contemporaries were four other Texas women sculptors, Evaline C. Sellors, Ione Ruth Franklin, Mabel Fairfax Karl and Dorothy Austin, who all lived either in or near Dallas and who shared the same interest in direct carving, partly because of the expense of shipping their works long distances to be cast in metal foundries. American sculptors were producing figures and monuments in three accepted styles, Egyptian, Classical or Equestrian, which the general public seldom found controversial.

In Dallas, which Artist Tom Stell described as a "pivotal kind of town" and a "hot-bed of enthusiasm and euphoria about the art going on," the famed "Dallas Nine" group of men painters were attracting national attention. Allie lived and worked in an atmosphere of art exhibitions and artists' gatherings; local newspapers printed news of the local art scene in their art sections. When New York artist Nicholas R. Brewer brought an exhibition of his painting to Dallas, he painted Allie's portrait.

In those heady early years, Allie worked with an amazing swiftness of creativity producing, in what came to reflect her particular talent, portrait busts as well as small figures. During the summer of 1929 Allie remodeled a head she had done of Virginia Louise Marvin, who took the plaster model to Pisa and had it sculpted in marble. Two portrait busts which Allie exhibited at the 1929 Dallas State Fair were of Dr. Edward C. Cary, dean emeritus of Baylor University School of Medicine, a commissioned cast bronze of a "greenish tinge" mounted on a marble base, and of Frank Klepper, a Dallas artist, in "sunburned bronze mounted on a Belgian marble base."

Other commissions were portrait studies of Dallas citizens Captain W.H. Gates, a head of William Brotherton, Jr., and a small bronze of Stuart Wright in his track suit "crouching as if ready to begin a race." The portrait shoulder bust which she modeled of Mrs. George K. Meyer, a sensitive and touching glimpse of a well-known, intelligent and generous Dallas art patron, won a purchase prize and became part of the Dallas Museum of Art collections. A portrait bust in bronze which Allie created in 1950 of her fellow artist E.G. Eisenlohr shows his soul-searching face, his sensitive right hand on his crossed arms at the figure's base. Eisenlohr, who painted Texas landscapes for forty years, had been among the local painters and art conscious citizens who in 1903 had formed the Dallas Art Association, one of the earliest art-interested groups. Allie, working in another style for an Amarillo home, created an over-the-mantle bas-relief of a moving herd of buffalo, "heads slightly lowered," marching across the plains with the lines of a mesa in the background.

Regarding her approach to portrait sculpture, Allie said that "Aside from satisfactorily assembling the features so that a likeness is achieved, [the figure] should interpret the character of the subject, and should convey, to those viewing it, the immediate presence of the sitter—a feeling of his soul." "Imaginary Head," a woman's head thirteen inches high, reveals Allie's keen interest in early Greek and Roman sculpture and her use of direct carving. During one of the times she was at home from her New York studio in the mid-1930s, she chose that archaic style when she chiseled the head from one of the red sandstones she had obtained when the old Dallas Courthouse tower was demolished.

Allie's interest in water pieces and fountain figures extended back to her student days, reflecting the influence of her sculpture instructor Edward McCartan who had created a number of fountains with figures. Before she settled permanently in Dallas, Allie spent a year in Europe touring Italy where, in addition to visiting the treasure-filled museums, she could study the centuries-old garden architecture of Roman villas with their flowerless gardens planted in intricate patterns of grey and green shrubs surrounding artfully designed fountains of "water art" often with classical figures. In Paris Allie spent endless hours at the Louvre viewing classical sculpture, visiting studios and galleries, and strolling through the parks decorated with outdoor sculptures and fountains.

Although the form and line of European fountains and figures are evident in her fountains, Allie's inspirations came from the world around her in Texas, such as the "small boy with plump legs crossed" which she seated on the edge of a sunken pool behind a garden gate in her own yard. "Water Lily Baby" emerged from her study drawings of a young Waco boy holding up a water lily bud. Enraptured by the movement of waves and water during a holiday in Galveston, she created several pieces of figures in the surf. One she called "The Surf-Rider," a young man's balancing himself on a wave crest for which she had a young athlete pose in her studio. Years afterward, when she no longer had the physical strength to create monumental figures, she returned again and again to designing small fountain figures.

As her extensive list shows, Allie was insatiable when it came to entering her sculptures in exhibitions all over the eastern and southern United States, and many of her pieces were acquired for the permanent collections of a number of Texas museums as well as for private holdings. "The Darling April," a thirty-one-inch figure of a seated girl with pigeons carved in pink Tennessee marble, received the sculpture prize for a garden figure from the Southern States Art League exhibition in 1932.

The 1933 decision to celebrate Texas' one hundred years of independence and to have the celebration centered at a Centennial Fair in Dallas in 1936 set Allie, still in New York, to work designing a sculpture for her entry. History was the "theme predominating throughout the Exposition," and the buildings of the Centennial were to represent the classic, modern and traditional styles as well as Aztec or Mayan styles. Allie designed her figure "Tejas Warrior" to relate to the dimensions of the architectural plans for new construction at the Fair site; she may have known Dallas architect George Dahl, the official Centennial planning director in charge of the Fair's overall design, who was the final authority for all work.

During the time working on her fair pieces, Allie had opportunities to study other artists' figures with archery bows at the Metropolitan Museum of Art—Augustus Saint-Gaudens' "Diana" and McCartan's bronze "Diana". Allie chose to portray a mythical ritual by using the human figure poised in the tension of shooting an arrow. She submitted her "Tejas Warrior" figure and, after the fifty-three-inch high model was approved, completed the eleven-foot figure in gold leaf on bronze. It shows an influence of Paul Manship's "smoothly abstract figures" which she had known in New York and was a significant "turning away from the Beaux-Arts and Renaissance models" of Rodin "as seen in the work of Borglum."

Allie completed the original figure in her New York studio

and had the bronze statue cast at the Roman Bronze Works foundry in New York. A 1935 photograph of Allie shows a handsome woman with classic features wearing a long-sleeved artist's smock, a dark beret covering her hair, sitting on a tall, slanting wooden platform-ladder below the back of the warrior's head with its mohawk haircut. The muscular figure wears a native American Indian breechclout; his right arm is pulled back, bent to hold the arrow while his left arm, following a diagonal line as the figure aims upward, pushes the bow into an encircling curve. The two arms suggest the invisible arrow.

The statue was shipped to Texas and placed in the most impressive building of the Fair, the Texas Hall of State located at the end of a long reflecting pool at the point where fairgoers began their view of the Centennial's impressive collection of Texas history items. The figure stood in the imposing entrance on a "horizontal bar above the bronze and aluminum doors, against a blue and gold mosaic background." The dynamic image of this powerful Indian would remain in fairgoers' memories long after the centennial celebration had passed. Thirty years later Allie recalled the spirited inspiration and completion of the "Tejas Warrior" and wrote that she had "decided to use an Indian as the subject, because the State of Texas got its name from the Tejas Indians who were friendly to the early settlers. The Indian word, Tejas means friend." Allie's other work on the Centennial site was a panel with images of sea horses and fish for the Dallas Aquarium.

A month before the Fair closed in November, Allie secured permission from the Texas State Board of Control to sell the working model of "Tejas Warrior" to sculptress Anna Hyatt Huntington and her husband Archer Huntington, who wanted the figure for their Brookgreen Gardens, a nine-thousand-acre nature preserve at Murrells Inlet in South Carolina, the first public garden in America created specifically to exhibit sculpture out of doors. The warrior was originally placed in the lower right wing of the garden's butterfly design, set against a warm-toned brick wall with silvery-gray foliage plantings. During a redesign of the garden fifty years later, the statue was moved to a new site so that it now is "framed by an arch and set in a raised flower bed." At Brookgreen, Allie's warrior joins her instructor Edward McCartan's gilded "Dionysus," which he had originally designed in 1923, his two other "Dianas," and Paul Manship's gilt-bronze "Diana."

Although the Texas Centennial celebration in Dallas in 1936 was the most spectacular, with its crowds of an estimated six million people, it was not the only celebration to commemorate the hundred years of Texas independence; an additional allotment of funds had also been set aside for various historic memorials. For another two years original works of art inspired by Texas history were installed throughout the state, and Allie was one of the few Texans and few women sculptors, along with Waldine Tauch and Bonnie MacLeary of San Antonio, to receive commissions and grants of federal funds amounting to $7,500 for each statue they created.

Following the popular style of "heroic classicism" in vogue among sculptors of the period, Allie created two dramatic statues in dark bronze of heroes of the Texas Revolution. The "James Butler Bonham," his fateful ride from Fannin in Goliad to the Alamo completed, is shown in determined stride, spurs attached to his knee-high boots, message packet hanging around his neck and a calling horn dangling from his left shoulder. As if in a final gesture of determination, Bonham crumples his flat-crowned hat in his right hand at his side. The compelling eight-foot bronze figure, located on the southwest corner of the courthouse grounds on the square at Bonham, Texas, rests on a monolithic octagonal foundation of pink Marble Falls granite.

Her second statue, hone-finished, interprets a different Texas hero; José Antonio Navarro is portrayed in more formal dress, Mexican-style riding pants and boots with a cape falling from his shoulders to drape onto the pink-granite block where the statue is seated, hands resting on a cane, staring out from the courthouse lawn in Corsicana, the county seat of Navarro County.

Allie's artistic and appealing craftsmanship is dramatically revealed in the works she cut directly into stone. The twelve-inch "Negro Head," a compact image in black Belgian marble, its surfaces polished to a glistening finish, was acquired in 1936 by the permanent collection of the Dallas Museum of Art through the Keist Memorial Fund Purchase Prize from the Dallas Art Association. Janet Kutner, art critic of the *Dallas Morning News*, wrote of the work, "Tennant immortalizes the power and beauty of the black race in her sleek black marble," and Dallas artist Harry Carnohan termed the prize-winning sculpture "a sincere and forceful piece of work that would hold its own in any exhibition in this country." Two other compelling pieces are "Negress" in black bronze, probably created in 1936, and an undated sculpture of a wide-eyed cat sitting delicately on a base, a figure which art historian Kendall Curlee declared "carried simplification to a greater extreme for expressive purposes."

In early 1942 a number of Texas artists who lived in the Dallas area met at Allie's studio to organize a Texas sculptors' group for which Allie was elected president, Dorothy Austin vice-president, and Octavio Medellin the secretary and treasurer. Plans were made for an out-of-doors show to be held at the Dallas Museum of Fine Arts with work in "stone, wood, terra cotta, synthetic stone and other available materials." Allie and her contemporaries, however, were meeting at a turning point in American sculpture, which would soon come to include work and media never before considered by artists. After World War II, a new generation of sculptors began creating pieces no longer tied to traditional images of the human form; "Cubism with its fragmented and broken planes, overlapping shapes, and skewed perspectives" had begun to influence twentieth-century sculpture, as did the new style of Constructivism which was gaining popularity with its "building and layering over, or collaging on top of geometric abstracted shapes."

From her Dallas studio Allie continued to find opportunities for her varied art interests and talents; besides her own creative work she taught sculpture at the Dallas Art Institute and the Dallas Evening School and lectured to various associations and clubs on such subjects as "Sculpture," "Methods and Materials," "Garden Sculpture" and "National Monuments," often demonstrating with clay and metal armatures the various techniques for working in sculpture.

Her interest in garden sculpture and fountains continued and she was a frequent speaker at area garden clubs. She remained a member of the Dallas Art Association, the Dallas Woman's Club and the National Sculpture Society. When local artist Jerry Bywaters began his long tenure as director of the Dallas Museum of Fine Arts in 1941, he started gathering information on Texas artists, among them Allie Tennant, and in time the comprehensive Jerry Bywaters Research Collection on American Art became part of the Southern Methodist University's definitive archives on Texas Artists.

Texas sculptor Allie Victoria Tennant, who had devoted her life to creating statues, died at her studio home in Dallas on December 21, 1971. Her sculptured forms and figures and images remain lasting memorials in many private collections and in the permanent collections of institutions such as the Dallas Museum of Art, the Brookgreen Sculpture Gardens in South Carolina, McMurray College in Abilene, the Southland Paper Mills in Lufkin, and at Highland Park and Hockaday schools in Dallas.

REFERENCES

Auerbach, Arnold. *A Brief History of Sculpture*. New York: Studio Publications Inc., 1952.

Brookgreen Journal. 1996 Annual Report. Brookgreen Gardens, Murrells Inlet, South Carolina.

Cranfill, Mabel. "Allie Tennant." *The Dallasite* (November 16, 1929).

Dryfhout, John H. *The Works of Augustus Saint-Gaudens*. Hanover and London: University Press of New England, 1982.

Hendricks, Patricia D. and Becky Duval Reese. *A Century of Sculpture in Texas 1898-1989*. Austin: Archer M. Huntington Art Gallery, University of Texas at Austin, 1989.

Jones, William Moses. *Texas History Carved In Stone*. Houston: Monument Publishing Co., 1958.

Kutner, Janet. "A Century of Sculpture in Texas" in "The Arts," *Dallas Morning News* (June 10, 1989).

Lance, Mary. *Lynn Ford, Texas Artist and Craftsman*. San Antonio: Trinity University Press, 1978.

Manship, John. *Paul Manship*. New York: Abbeville Press, 1989.

O'Brien, Esse Forrester. *Art and Artists of Texas*. Dallas: Tardy Publishing Co., 1935.

Proske, Beatrice Gilman. *Brookgreen Gardens Sculpture*. Brookgreen Gardens, Murrels Inlet, South Carolina, 1968 edition.

Ragsdale, Kenneth B. *The Year America Discovered Texas, Centennial '36*. College Station: Texas A&M University Press, 1989.

Smith, Goldie Capers. *The Creative Arts in Texas*. Dallas: Cokesbury Press, 1926.

Stewart, Rick. *Lone Star Regionalism*. Austin: Texas Monthly Press, 1985.

Tennant, Allie. "Electra Texas Post Office Decoration." Art Files, Dallas Public Library.

Texas Painting and Sculpture: 20th Century. Exhibition catalogue. Dallas: Dallas Museum of Fine Arts, 1971.

Windels, Susan Bean. "The Art of the Texas Centennial Central Exposition of 1936: A Kaleidoscopic Reflection of the Art and Society of the Early Nineteen Thirties." M.A. thesis, Dallas, Southern Methodist University, 1979.

Zorah, William. *Art Is My Life.* Cleveland, Ohio: The World Publishing Company, 1967.

INTERVIEWS

Roger Carroll and Crystal Sasse Ragsdale, Dallas Public Library, July 1997.

Dr. Sam Ratcliffe and Crystal Sasse Ragsdale, Southern Methodist University, Dallas, August 1997.

Robin R. Salmon and Crystal Sasse Ragsdale, Brookgreen Gardens, July-August 1997.

Courtesy General Libraries, The University of Texas at Austin.

Nettie Lee Benson

1905-1993

"An Anglo Tejana"

"Adiós, amigita. Vaya con Dios." The good wishes rose from the cluster of Nettie Lee Benson's Monterrey friends and students waving goodbye to the young lady who was leaving after teaching for two years at the Methodist-run high school *Instituto Inglés-Español.* The tall, friendly blond woman had no idea that this sojourn had been just the beginning of almost five decades of travel to Mexico and Latin America. Once she "drank the waters of Mexico," the countries south of the Rio Grande would be her lodestar. Her abiding interests and studies in the history and languages of Latin America were to guide her life.

Wherever she went, the role of "Miss Benson" as a teacher never changed, although her focus would expand to include an avocation she did not dream of early in her teaching days. During her long life, she was to pursue a multifaceted career which, in a way, she created for herself. In addition to teaching Latin American history and librarianship at The University of Texas at Austin, in the early 1940s she became director of the Latin American library holdings. She was "fascinated by Mexico and Latin America and by books" observed Laura Gutiérrez-Witt, her successor as director of the Nettie Lee Benson Latin American Collection at The University of Texas at Austin, and this fascination provided the basis for her ability to add to the Collection's treasures of rare books, maps, illustrations and manuscripts which she often bought on generous long-term credit from Latin American booksellers. Nettie Lee Benson's thrifty shopping after poking around in dusty book stores so enriched the Collection that it has become one of the most important Latin American libraries in the world.

Nettie Lee Benson was born on January 15, 1905, to Jasper William and Vora Anne Reddell Benson in Arcadia, a little town in Galveston County. She was the fourth child and second daughter born in Arcadia, but the couple later had four more sons and a stillborn daughter. The 1900 Galveston storm had wiped out the Bensons' farm, and J.W. and Vora eventually decided in 1908 to move to the newly opened San Patricio County to recreate their own "Arcadia." Loading their small herd of Jersey cows on the train, they set out for Sinton, the new county seat in the central part of the county where developers had opened blocks of ranch pastures to be sold as small farms. The land, cleared of mesquite thickets and prickly pear clumps, felt the plow blade for the first time. The heavy, black clay soil was good for raising vegetables, but it created hazards for horse and buggy travel during the frequent rains. Nettie Lee's father, in his job as San Patricio County's first county agricultural agent, sensibly chose to ride a motorcycle when he visited the farms in his district.

The Bensons bought land on the south side of West Sinton Street for their barn and two-story house. J.W. designed the structures on much the same plan as the old home in Arcadia, ordering all the boards cut to his specifications so that the pre-fabricated house and barn could be assembled in Sinton. He first built the barn where the family lived while work was continuing on the main house. When it was finished they moved in—all but Nettie Lee. Not convinced that the new house was a better place to live than the barn, she remained behind until she had made up her mind that being with her family was more important than staying alone. Then, taking her books and her clothes, she claimed her own room and joined her brothers and sister in the new house.

One day when Nettie Lee was six, her oldest brother Jasper, Jr., decided that their children's wagon would be easier to pull if a nail could be driven in the tongue. When the hammer struck the nail, it flew up and struck the little girl's left eye. The cure, the doctor said, was to "bandage the eye and Nettie Lee must stay in a darkened room." Instead of waving to her brothers as they walked off to school, the little prisoner listened to their calls of "See you later, Ol' Patch" and "Good-bye, One-Eyed

Spec," for next to the black eye-patch her face was covered with freckles.

Vora Benson resumed the role of teacher she had given up when she married. Down from the shelves came the books for each day's reading—the Bible, Lamb's *Shakespeare's Tales for Children,* and English poetry. The little girl's dim room became the launching place for her imagination, while the daily routine of absorbing well-written passages led her to intense study and encouraged her to love books and reading.

It is hardly surprising that Nettie Lee's parents contributed so much to their children's well-rounded lives and good educations. Vora had been graduated from Buffalo Gap Presbyterian College and had earned her teaching certificate. J.W. had been reared by an aunt and uncle in Cotton Plant, Arkansas, and began his book learning as a boy in Presbyterian prep schools in Virginia before attending Hampden-Sydney College. He dropped out after two years when an illness affected his hearing and vision and also left him with limited use of his right side. Seeking a change of scene on the Galveston coast, he pitted his physical disabilities against a primitive life of hunting and fishing which challenged him to excel, a quality that shaped his life and was to greatly influence his children.

The Bensons enjoyed their Sinton home for several years before they made another move; the growing family needed more space for the children to play as well as for J.W.'s increasing nursery and dairy businesses. The new site, just off the Mathis road west of Sinton, was far enough from town to escape the often-flooding Chilipin Creek and lay within a brushy wilderness that abounded with wildlife—migrating ducks and geese in the fall and spring, fish in the ponds, and whitetail deer all year around. There were pastures for the cattle and horses. On his Sinton acreage J.W. Benson planted and grafted citrus trees and even developed a cross between a grapefruit and an orange. In keeping with the tropical style set by land developers of the time, he set out date palm trees around the main school building in Sinton and on his own place as well. Some of his venerable, ragged old palms still grow near the Benson homestead and in the community cemetery across the road. As a little girl Nettie Lee once said that she liked the birds and butterflies which lived among the citrus trees growing about the house and never wanted to go away from them, ever. Years later she recalled that she "loved grafting trees" because it gave her "an opportunity to be outside."

Her father constructed a green house and dug nearby a large, high-banked irrigation tank, filling it with a pump that tapped into a shallow well. He taught his sons to channel water along the rows of trees and to the family vegetable plots. He was especially proud of his fine, late-winter strawberries and enjoyed hearing the bright chatter of Nettie Lee's visiting schoolmates as Vora Benson served shortcake with the large red berries ladled over with thick, yellow cream.

On the new country acreage the two-story house was of Southern style with porches on the east, south and west sides. By 1916 the framework for the house was up, but a tropical hurricane's rains warped the timbers and the structure was pulled down, nails hammered out and straightened, and work begun again with new lumber. The ample white house looked like a Mississippi riverboat set down amid the green trees. Nettie Lee never really left this home During the early years of her various jobs, and even later when she established her own home in Austin in the 1940s, the Sinton homestead remained the enduring touchstone to which she returned again and again during her long life. At one time she even paid for its considerable repair after it had fallen into neglect.

As the children grew older their father coached them in tennis, basketball, baseball, volleyball, football on the level ground near the house, and in swimming in the irrigation tank. Their team spirit and competitiveness led a sister-in-law to recall decades later that the Bensons were the "most hard-headed bunch I ever saw." They formed an orchestra; J.W. Benson played the banjo and guitar, Vora and her eldest child Jennie played the piano, the brothers played cornet, clarinet and the piccolo while Nettie Lee chose the flute. At other times they gathered around the piano singing as Vora played.

Nettie Lee matched her brothers' energies with her own. "I was a terrible tomboy; I loved it," she remembered years later. The children worked in pairs, and Nettie Lee most often teamed up with her older brother Ben. The time of enforced solitude which she had experienced, however, was to influence all of Nettie Lee's life. Even the dim image of Vora Benson, her hair in heavy braids wound round her head, would remain with her so that she too, as a grown woman, would plait her own hair in braids and wind it round her head in a style remembered by her Latin American friends. Not until the last years of her life, and only then because of arthritis, did she have her hair cut. The new bobbed hairstyle framing her face with flattering soft lines created a new and gentler likeness to remember her by.

Even though her injured eye had healed, Nettie Lee did not enter school until she was nine, but she immediately began skipping grades. "I read all the time," she recalled, "and I studied all the time, and so I went through very rapidly." Her parents and her teachers quickly recognized that Nettie Lee should be in the grade suited to her intelligence, and besides, she said, "I just loved school, you see, and that was all. I jumped along, I had to get with people my age."

"I slowed down when I got to high school, but I enjoyed every minute of it. I played tennis and was in the band—played the flute and the clarinet." She took all the Spanish courses the school offered. As she grew older there were exciting weekends when Nettie Lee, with her young friends, visited each others' church groups—Christian Endeavor at the Presbyterian Church, the Baptist Young People's Union, and Epworth League at the Methodist church. She confided later that denominations were not important to her, since "we were all heading for the same place, anyway." Yet she contributed to a Presbyterian children's home all of her life, following her parents' longtime dedication to the Presbyterian church.

Much of Nettie Lee's energy was spent in the Sinton High School's physical education program. The girls played volleyball against rival schools in nearby Odem, Taft and Sodville amid rumblings from some Sinton parents concerning the team's bloomer uniforms with black cotton stockings up to their knees. They "teased" the hair growing near their faces into puffs, then pinned the puffs over their ears and called them "cootie" garages; a term learned from World War I American soldiers' description of the body lice encountered in European battle trenches.

Nettie Lee was valedictorian of her 1922 graduation class and with her scholarship might have chosen The University of Texas. Her parents, however, thought her too young for the large school and she instead attended the two-year Texas Presbyterian College for girls in Milford where her older sister Jennie was already enrolled. Both girls studied music, and since the school had not offered scholarships, Nettie Lee waited tables as payment for her meals.

By 1924 Nettie Lee's parents agreed to her studying at The University of Texas. She signed up for Spanish courses and attended Dr. Charles Wilson Hackett's Latin American history classes. By the time she completed her three college degrees, she had taken all the history classes offered by the university. She established her membership in the University Presbyterian Church, then sought campus organizations which appealed to her. The university band forbade women from membership, but the Women's Racquet Club gave her a chance for the sports she enjoyed. Much of her spare time was spent with the University Volunteers in working with various young people's activities in Austin. At a Volunteers' gathering in the spring of 1925, she listened as a friend read a letter from the Methodist Board of Missions announcing an opening for a position in Monterrey, Mexico, teaching high school English, history and math at the *Instituto Inglés-Español*, a girls' boarding school.

Nettie Lee "stood right up in meeting" and spoke out, "Give me the letter." She got the job, but even at the train depot her parents continued to insist that she was too young and that life was too dangerous in Mexico so soon after the revolution. She laughingly recalled, "I was practically getting on the train and they kept calling, 'You can't go! You can't go! You can't go!' But I got there." Back in Sinton, whenever Vora and J.W. read unsettling news from the northern Mexican border they wired her to come home. At the school her teaching went well, although there were times when gunfire sounded from the streets and lights went out in her boarding house, but she could honestly say that nothing ever threatened her in Monterrey. After two years Nettie Lee returned to Sinton, her first experience in Mexico completed. If she ever fell in love, it was with the Mexicans and Mexico in an enduring mutual love affair that continued through her life.

Vora Benson's health was frail and for a year, from 1927 to 1928, Nettie Lee remained at home to help care for her young brothers. That year she also taught the second grade in the Sinton schools. During a family gathering Nettie Lee assured her four-year-old nephew William Wheeler Sharp that she would help him attend The University of Texas after his graduation from high school.

Nettie Lee herself enrolled at the university in the fall of 1928 to continue her work toward a degree in history. She earned money to pay for her college courses by working as a part time YWCA employee at the International House on Nueces Street, arranging social activities for Spanish-speaking young people who also wanted to learn English. After receiving her B.A. degree in 1929 Nettie Lee accepted another YWCA job in Dallas, yet within a short time she answered a notice advertising for a school teacher and accepted a position which took her to the Panhandle. What had qualified her for the fifth-grade teaching job in Hartley, Texas, was not her aptitude in Spanish, mathematics, English or sports, but rather her ability to play the flute; the school superintendent was a musician who wanted a local orchestra to help pass the time in the remote Texas town. One year of winter snows' blowing under the school's door and dust's seeping through windows and walls was enough, and Nettie Lee returned to South Texas in 1931.

Now in her late twenties, she accepted a teaching position in the Ingleside high school and remained for eleven years. Nettie Lee kept such detailed accounts of the high school football games that on Mondays the coaches and students would come to her for game replays. She taught English and Spanish courses, worked at establishing a school library, stayed after school to coach tennis, traveled with her debaters and speakers to annual county meets, and accompanied each graduating class on a senior trip to Monterrey. During her years at Ingleside she influenced the addition of the eleventh grade to the high school and the integration of Hispanic students into the student body. Never "keeping house" during the Ingleside years helped her find enough time for all of her activities. "She always boarded with some family in the community," recalled her sister-in-law Annie Benson.

During the Ingleside years Nettie Lee spent her summers attending classes at The University of Texas and, in 1936 when she was thirty, completed her Master of Arts degree with her thesis, "The Preconstitutional Regime of Venustiano Carranza, 1913-1917." Her nephew William Sharp finished high school, and in 1941 Nettie Lee, remembering her promise to help him go to college, took a year's leave of absence from her Ingleside teaching, not realizing that she would never again be a high school teacher nor that she had set out on a career best suited to her talents and education. At the university she "simply signed up for any graduate courses relating to Latin America," particularly in the newly created Institute of Latin American Studies under the direction of Dr. Hackett.

At mid-semester in 1942 a vacancy opened in the position of director of the Latin American Collection when her longtime colleague Dr. Carlos E. Castañeda left the library. Since her knowledge of Latin American materials was already well known among her professors, they urged her to apply for the job. "Actually, it was dumped on me," she recalled candidly, insisting that she did not feel qualified for the monumental responsibility. Her objections were overruled and she accepted the job. Her faculty friends suggested that she now complete her doctoral dissertation, and in 1944 she set out for a brief trip to northern Mexico in search of historic materials between 1820 and 1824, the period of Mexican history she found challenging.

Early on Nettie Lee had become interested in the years of early Mexican independence and the national policies which followed, so she chose as her topic "The Provincial Deputation in Mexico: Precursor of the Mexican Federal State." While she was devoting some fifty hours a week to the Collection, she began researching materials for her work. Although she wanted to write a biography of José Miguel Ramos Arizpe, the father of the Mexican Constitution of 1824, her dissertation developed into an in-depth examination of early nineteenth-century Mexican politics. The dissertation, completed in June 1949, became a landmark study in modern Mexican history; her mother and a sister-in-law were delighted to "have somebody with a Ph.D in the family." The work was translated into Spanish and published by *El Fondo de Cultura Económica* in Mexico City in 1955, and in 1992 an expanded edition was published by The University of Texas Press as *The Provincial Deputation in Mexico: Harbinger of Provincial Autonomy, Independence, and Federalism.*

From 1942 until her retirement in August 1975, Nettie Lee Benson remained in charge of the Collection. In 1954 there had been approximately 67,000 volumes in the library; on her retirement the number had increased to 305,503. By 1960, in addition to her directorship of the Latin American Collection, she was holding teaching positions in the History Department and in the Library Science School. She had already gained stature in her Latin American writings, translations and articles, and in

1960 she was asked to represent the prestigious Latin American Cooperative Acquisitions Project (LACAP) in acquiring publications for several Latin American collections in United States universities and for the New York Public Library. After an interview in August in New York, she was doubtful that she could make the necessary arrangements. "I didn't see how I could do a thing like that, be gone for six months and doing that kind of thing," she recalled years later.

The library director at the university, more trusting of her talents, thought it would be good for her to "get acquainted with the book business" in Latin America and "to meet people." He could not, however, give her any money to buy books for the university. Nettie Lee considered it a poor decision not to purchase books needed by the Collection while she was visiting all of those bookstores, so she sought out Harry Ransom, then president of The University of Texas, and obtained a note "saying that he approved of using $25,000 for publications purchases." The amount was an overwhelming largesse because the Latin American Collection's annual purchase budget had been only $100 a year since 1943.

The directors of LACAP could not have made a better choice than the librarian from Texas. Once she arrived in a country she did not confine herself to the nation's capital city but took trains out to university towns where she located rare and important publications, often in limited editions. Academic works of Latin American authors were usually published by the government and the books given to the authors to be distributed or given away as they chose. As a result, important scholarly books were often available only in the university centers. Numerous times she located the authors of important publications she wanted for the Collection, only to have them insist on a personal interview in order to explain what the book was about; the sale of their books was less important than having the opportunity to discuss their work. In 1969 Nettie Lee Benson's expertise in Latin American librarianship was again recognized when she was named a member of the International Council of the Museum of Modern Art to select art books for twenty-three universities, museums and libraries in ten Latin American countries.

For years Nettie Lee Benson typed her own letters in English or in Spanish. Although the university "did not provide additional help for writing letters," it "never cut down on postage or stationery," she recalled. Nettie Lee's incoming mail did not languish unanswered on her desk; she responded promptly, almost eagerly, in letters long enough to cover the subject at hand. To friends she discussed points of history, to booksellers the importance of books which the Collection needed. Her responses to serious scholars and students were thorough and knowledgeable; letters of recommendation revealed a genuine and personal regard for her students. At a time when even rare books were circulated from the Latin American library, the high rate of loss of valuable books must have given her the idea that all the rare books in the Collection should be microfilmed for public use.

As a faculty member she attended countless meetings, made endless reports, and sought advice from her fellow professionals. Neither shy nor timid, she constantly badgered for the money to pay for staff, space and materials. In 1960 one donor was so surprised to discover how little clerical help the Collection had that he urged the State Legislative Board to increase the financial aid for special research work at the university libraries, but the request was denied. When a friend of the Collection thought to have a thousand copies of Benson's dissertation reprinted and distributed, she responded with characteristic logic that she did not "honestly think any more money should be spent" on it "since it [was] already in the hands of most people who would be interested in it."

As head of the Latin American Collection, Nettie Lee Benson met visiting dignitaries and well-know writers: Anita Brenner, author of *The Wind that Swept Mexico*, came to the library looking for a collaborator for her proposed popular "History of Mexico"; Emily Edwards, artist and historian from San Antonio, arrived to pursue materials she needed; Prince Felipe of Spain's royal family was perhaps the most celebrated visitor to be met by a now-elderly Miss Benson in the rare books room of the Collection. In recognition of both her work for the Collection and for her publications, in 1979 President José López Portillo of Mexico presented her with his government's highest award recognizing services rendered to Mexico or to humanity by non-Mexicans, *La Orden Mexicana Del Aguila Azteca*, The Order of the Mexican Eagle.

Nettie Lee Benson remained intensely loyal to the library's

friends. In her 1962 terse overview *The Making of The Latin American Collection* she wrote, "the building of a superior collection of books, periodicals, manuscripts, and other research materials is dependent for its success on every person who contributes to it in any way." First among those she credited were the Texas taxpayers without whom, she concluded, "nothing could have been done." Next were the private builders of outstanding collections which the university had purchased, for they had "unknowingly contributed to the richness of the Latin American Collection." But "just as valuable," she wrote, "has been the contribution of knowledge by professors, students, users, and interested visitors." She deemed that the original organizers of the acquisitions of Latin American materials in the 1920s had played important roles in the Collection's development.

Materials relating to Latin American history flowed in to the Collection for years, eventually exceeding the capacity of the library shelves crammed into a space on the third floor of the general library in the Tower of the Main Building. In a 1965 letter she noted, "What a paradox for this to occur in Texas" where space was supposedly of easy access. In a letter written in 1971, almost three decades after she had begun working on the Collection, she was able to apologize to a correspondent, "Please pardon my delay in answering your letter of December 29, 1970, but we have been occupied in moving our library into new quarters and getting everything organized again." The Collection's new home occupied three floors of the south section of the Sid Richardson Building overlooking the east campus.

During Nettie Lee's life in Austin she would share her home and her life with her nieces and nephews as they enrolled in the university and came to live with Aunt Nettie Lee under her rule, "Don't wake me up after eleven o'clock to let you in." She welcomed researchers, writers and friends of long standing to her home; one woman guest helped nail screen wire to a window frame which needed repairing. Company was always involved in the cooking and serving of meals, and her guests often experienced some of the lively energies of Benson family life. On Thanksgiving or New Year's Day, they joined her to watch The University of Texas' football games. A student remembers Miss Benson's body English and her "directions" to the UT football coaches during a memorable TV game broadcast. She was an energetic card player, and joining her in the vigorous game of "Spite and Malice" was unforgettable.

One student recalled Miss Benson's office which, she insisted, was necessarily dark to protect the rare books she was working on. The student privately wondered if the darkened room was not more the result of the months she had spent in dim light after her childhood eye injury. Many of the recollections of her are good-naturedly humorous; one often mentioned was her pronunciation of the name of the Mexican leader Santa Anna, whom she always referred to as "Santianna" in the old Texas vernacular. The personal remembrances of "Miss Benson" by her associates remain a bond among her numerous friends and ex-students.

In her honor when she retired in 1975, her beloved library became known as the Nettie Lee Benson Latin American Collection Library. At first she used her newly acquired free time and research skills in tracing her family genealogy, but she was soon back at the Collection among her proteges and the thousands of books she considered as longtime friends. Even during the months she was in a nursing home, she continued to write, translate, and send page-proofs of her latest writing efforts to her publishers. To a friend she railed against the layout of a book, insisting that the press did not understand the "importance of visual images."

Nettie Lee Benson died on June 23, 1993; funeral services were held in the Presbyterian church her parents had helped establish in Sinton. She was buried in the cemetery just across the road from the arcadian world she never forgot. The young minister concluded the rites of passage with, "*Vaya con Dios, Miss Nettie Lee.*"

REFERENCES

Benson, Annie Odell Haynes. Letter to Crystal Sasse Ragsdale, June 6, 1994.

Billings, Harold. "Nettie Lee Benson Dies." *Library Bulletin* XXII. University of Texas at Austin, July 2, 1993.

Brown, Lyle C. "Nettie Lee Benson Oral History Memoir." Baylor University Program for Oral History. Waco, Texas: Baylor University, June 23, 1972.

Danciger, Jack. Correspondence. Nettie Lee Benson Papers. Nettie Lee

Benson Latin American Collection Library, University of Texas at Austin.

Krumnow, Jeannine. Letter to Crystal Sasse Ragsdale, September 23, 1994.

Long, Amy Jo. "Nettie Lee Benson and the Latin American Collection." *Texas Times*, University of Texas at Austin (January 1969).

Neff, Nancy. "Paredes Awarded Aztec Eagle by Mexico." *On Campus*, University of Texas at Austin (December 3, 1990).

Nettie Lee Benson Papers. Nettie Lee Benson Latin American Collection Library, University of Texas at Austin.

"Nettie Lee Benson: A Legend in Her Time." *ILAS Newsletter* 23 (Winter 1990).

Purcell, Mabelle, Stuart Purcell *et. al. This is Texas*. Austin: Futura Press, 1977.

Ross, Stanley R. "An Interview with Nettie Lee Benson." *The Hispanic Historical Review* 63(3) (August, 1983).

Vásquez, Josefina Z. "In Memoriam Nettie Lee Benson, 1905-1993." *Historia Mexicana* XLII (Abril-Junio, 1993).

INTERVIEWS

Annie Odell Haynes Benson and Crystal Sasse Ragsdale, Sinton, November 5, 1993; June 6, 1994; September 23, 1994.

Alta Bel Owen and Crystal Sasse Ragsdale, Sinton, November 5, 1993.

SELECTED LIST OF PUBLICATIONS BY NETTIE LEE BENSON

"A Governor's Report on Texas in 1809" (trans. and ed.). *Southwestern Historical Quarterly* LXXI (April 1968).

"Bishop Martin De Porras and Texas." *Southwestern Historical Quarterly* LI (July 1947).

"La Elección de José Miguel Ramos Arizpe a las Cortes de Cadiz en 1810." *Historia Mexicana* 33 (Abril-Junio, 1984).

"Letters." *Southwestern Historical Quarterly* L (October 1946).

Report That Dr. Miguel Ramos De Arizpe . . . Presents the Condition of...The Four Eastern Interior Provinces of the Kingdom of Mexico (trans., annotations and introduction). Austin: University of Texas Press, 1950.

"The Making Of The Latin American Collection," *The Library Chronicle of The University of Texas* VII. The University of Texas at Austin, 1962.

"The Benson Trace" IV. Benson family publication, July 1983-December 1985.

"The Contested Mexican Election of 1812." *The Hispanic American Historical Review* XXVI (August 1946).

Courtesy Dallas Public Library.

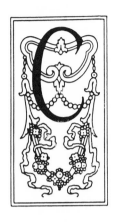

Helen L. Corbitt

1906-1978

*"The dining room
is one of the last
out posts of civilizations"*

"Oh, Miss Corbitt."

"Yes, Mr. Marcus?"

*"I just wanted to tell you that the Sauce Provençale on today's veal
is as good as I have eaten in France."*

"Thank you, I'm glad it pleased you."

*"However, I do need to mention the matter of expense. You well
know that our Zodiac Room, even before you took over, has not been a
financial success. There is a need to cut back somewhat on the cost of
the dishes we serve here at Neiman-Marcus. You do understand?"*

*"Yes indeed, I do, but you didn't mention money when you
employed me, Mr. Marcus. You simply said you wanted the best food
in the country, and I've given you that."*

Helen Corbitt, her face flushed to match her red-gold hair,
waited for an answer from her boss. His "wild Irish genius" of
a chef, as he later called her, had for the moment sauced his
goose. Both of them, however, soon came around, and Helen
agreed to produce Dallas' best food and to retrench somewhat
on the expense of ingredients in dishes the Zodiac Room served
for their luncheons, suppers and party foods.

When Neiman-Marcus enlarged the store in 1950, it had
added its own restaurant with a catering service to "attract
more people to the downtown area and as a service to those
customers from out of town" for a day of shopping. For several
years Helen Corbitt had rejected Stanley Marcus' offer to become food director of the floundering dining room, then one

day she called him to say that she was "tired of the hotel food business and was willing to talk" to him. She became the Merlin of the Zodiac Room in the Neiman-Marcus Camelot, filling a role that lasted for over a decade.

This wizard of good foods was born on January 26, 1906, in the Benson Mines District of St. Lawrence County in northernmost New York State not far south of the St. Lawrence River; her brother Michael was two years younger. Helen was tremendously proud of being Irish. Her father Henry J. Corbitt was born in New York City the son of Irish immigrants. Helen's mother Eva Marshall listed her parents as Canadian-Irish and Canadian-English; from her English heritage Helen traced her lineage to the *Mayflower* settlers.

During Helen's growing-up years she shared the Corbitt family's more-than-usual interest in the preparation and enjoyment of good food. One of her childhood memories was that her mother always dipped a teaspoon into almond extract before measuring vanilla or lemon extract; childhood dining memories included her Canadian-English grandmother's hard sauce which accompanied the traditional plum pudding at the joyous conclusion to a Christmas dinner. When Helen was a little girl she prepared a dish of macaroni and cheese with egg and milk, "almost a custard," and at seven she baked a June Cake, "a sort of pound cake." Years later as she cooked over gas and electricity she recalled the stove in the family kitchen, "You know, I don't think pot roast ever tasted as good as when it was cooked in a coal stove."

Her education included a boarding school in Watertown, New York, followed by a bachelor of science degree from Skidmore College in Saratoga Springs, New York. At about the time she was graduated, with plans for further education in medical school, her father, a prominent lawyer, lost even the family home in the stock market crash of 1929. The financially difficult years which followed, and the loss of a way of life she and her family had enjoyed, left an enduring mark on Helen's approach to money and expense.

So lasting in her memory were those lean years that in her third cookbook, *Helen Corbitt Cooks for Company* which came out in 1974, she divided the menus into "three categories: expensive, less expensive, and inexpensive." She reminded her readers that caviar started at thirty-nine dollars a pound and to plan accordingly, for it was out of the price range of most cooks. One woman who received the cookbook as a wedding present in the middle 1970s recalls that, among her young married friends whose husbands were just beginning their business careers, using the inexpensive recipes started them on a lifetime of selective food buying and careful menu training which they never forgot.

With the Depression still weighing heavily on the national economy, Helen's medical plans were out of the question. Instead, she entered the job market and found an opening in the field of food preparation at the Presbyterian Hospital in Newark, New Jersey, as dietitian and large-quantity menu planning supervisor. By tasting and comparison she early came to the basic tenet of good quantity cooking, "even though you must cook for large numbers, cooking should be done in small quantities." She practiced "ratios" so that she didn't "have to remember recipes."

Soon after she assumed her new position, she shared in a northern New Jersey custom reserved for strangers, a "throw a buffalo" party. She was told the menu was buffalo meat and, being Helen Corbitt, she remembered the cooking procedures. Members of the buffalo conspiracy and the newcomer gathered outdoors at a picnic area where a large hardwood fire had burned down to red-hot embers which the cook divided into a number of small, glowing piles. At the right moment "large, thick, healthy steaks at least two or three inches thick" were pitched on the coals and turned frequently until they were "charred enough," then after brushing off the ashes with a stiff scrubbing brush they were "dunked into a pail of melted butter," cut into chunks and eaten with the fingers. "You will never believe steak could taste so heavenly," she wrote later.

Helen remained for six years as therapeutic dietitian at the New Jersey hospital, then she secured a position with better pay as a dietitian in the Cornell Medical Center in New York City. She made the most of the gourmet opportunities of the city, discovering the herb-flavored foods of northern Italy, and wrote about foods in her letters home, describing with appealing detail the wonders of the exciting new cuisines she was encountering. But she still needed more money and turned from her weekday routine of large-quantity cooking to baking rich, dark chocolate cakes for the wives of some of the hospital directors.

On Saturday morning her alarm clock rang at three o'clock to allow enough time for baking the cakes in the little stove in her small apartment. Orders increased as her reputation spread as a fine cake baker.

In 1940 with times still hard, Helen at thirty-four was not one to stagnate on a job which had become either too confining or was not paying enough. She sent out applications for a change of employment and took the position that paid the most, at The University of Texas in the Home Economics Department teaching large-quantity cooking, nutrition and restaurant management. Texas was far from her family, but she packed her bags and cast her New York life and work behind her. She boarded the train for her first trip south below the Mason-Dixon line and finally arrived at the depot in Austin, near Congress Avenue within easy view of the capitol, unwittingly planting her feet solidly on Texas soil where she would spend the rest of her life. Very soon neither Helen Corbitt nor Texas cooking would ever again be the same.

Helen learned about Texas foods during the brief time she managed the University Tea Room where she taught Home Economics majors to create appetizing food in quantity and how to manage an eating establishment. The large, one-story building, now gone, was of cut, white Texas limestone nestled among the trees northwest of the Texas Memorial Museum on San Jacinto on a triangle of land bounded on the east by a channel of water which flowed through the Frank Dobies' side yard and into Waller Creek on the west. Soon Austinites were crowding into the dining rooms on Sundays to eat the "best food in town" planned and prepared by Helen Corbitt's university students.

During her first few weeks at the university Helen was asked to create a menu for a large group using just Texas products. When it came to serving black-eyed peas she consulted her cookbooks and, finding nothing that intrigued her palate, came up with the most unconventional recipe the venerable Southern staple had ever been subject to—she decided to pickle them! In a now time-honored recipe called "Texas Caviar" she drenched them in garlic, onion, vinegar and oil and served the dish cold. Neiman-Marcus later canned and sold the pickled peas to thousands of Texans who celebrated New Year's Day by eating them for good luck in the coming year. She was also warned by her fellow home-economics faculty members not to put sugar in the cornbread, Yankee-style, which she had had no intention of doing.

Since Helen had no car and her garage apartment near the old Seton hospital was not in walking distance of the campus, one of her senior nutrition students, Hallie Groce Slaughter, picked her up each morning and came to know her professor. "She demanded a lot of you but she always demanded more of herself. Every time you looked around she was working harder than you were." The secret of Helen Corbitt's phenomenal success? Hallie Slaughter thoughtfully commented that it was her "having really superior taste buds—like some people have perfect pitch or an infallible color sense."

Helen's reputation for creating good food traveled to Houston, where directors of the Country Club offered her a job overseeing their dining room. She accepted after the university did not match the thirty-dollar-a-month raise the Houston club offered. Helen thought the new job would tide her over until she could go back to New York; she relished telling the story, that for the first six months she didn't unpack her suitcases, "then I unpacked the suitcases, but I didn't unpack my trunk. After a year I unpacked the trunk and decided to stay." She fondly remembered the University Tea Room workshop time, and especially "the most happy days of my food career, the Houston Country Club" where she continued to work during the World War II years.

For a December gathering of women golfers she created her own recipe for eggnog, and during those years of food rationing she held back enough butter and sugar for coconut pie which she served the men golfers on Saturdays. Helen began using pecans for the first time in her cooking and often had plates of Travis House Cookies at teas, coffees, "even cocktail parties." She advised cookie makers to "stir, never beat cookie dough." While still at the country club Helen began writing "Kitchen Klatter," a weekly column on food which appeared in the *Houston Post*, the *Arkansas Democrat* and the *Dallas Times-Herald* for twelve years. For the next thirty years she traveled about the country giving lectures on cooking and entertaining; in time she began using color slides for her "Fashions in Food" talks. A one-week itinerary might include White Sulphur Springs, Atlanta, Mobile and New Orleans, talking to restaurateurs and

club managers on the innumerable problems of serving food to
the public, including how to serve good food prepared in
quantities.

Helen Corbitt possessed classic features with a noticeable
fold of skin over the outer edges of her eyes which gave her a
slightly whimsical gaze. With a dark wig and heavy earrings
she would have resembled a face from an early Middle East
Christian Era mosaic. Finding her irregular teeth a constant
source of displeasure each time she looked in the mirror, she
had all of them removed before coming to Texas; afterward her
ready smile revealed well-matched teeth. Columnist Dick Hitt's
memory of Helen was that of a "sedate and delicately attuned
lady."

She fielded the question of her not marrying but admitted
to having been engaged three times. "I may have been ahead of
my time," she admitted, "I've always been dedicated to my
work, and I couldn't see myself being limited to any one man.
I don't have any regrets." Despite not wanting to share her
career with marriage, she nevertheless did not rule out men
from her life; she adored her father and brother and dedicated
her first cookbook "to the men in my life." The large diamond
she always wore on her right hand might have been an engagement ring from a fiancé who insisted on her keeping it as a
remembrance of his admiration.

Helen eventually left the country club and tried working
for Joske's Houston department store as manager of their restaurant, the Garden Room, and as director of their catering
department. The job was of short duration, however, for she
"was fired," a "combination of not making enough money and
not seeing eye-to-eye with some of the executives." She maintained that it was the best thing that ever happened to her, for
it propelled her away from the booming oil town of Houston
and back to Austin and the Driskill Hotel to the world of politics
among the good ol' boys and the "pols" who spent a great deal
of their time at the hotel, an easy walk down Congress Avenue
from their offices at the capitol.

Helen began the new year of 1952 as director of the dining
room in the famed hotel, often catering parties, large and small,
"for every one who wanted one." She had a range of menus,
competent help and a savoir faire which stood her in good stead
with the statewide clientele which often made Austin a second

home.

At the Driskill she planned dishes to please the appetites of people who enjoyed both familiar foods and new recipes. She recalled that she would often be introduced by her fans as the "Hashed Brown Potatoes with Sour Cream Girl." Some years later while in England researching foods for Neiman-Marcus, she planned a dinner for the United States Ambassador and his all-male guest list. With "real prime beef" she served her memorable Texas hashed brown potatoes with sour cream, and "every Englishman there wanted the recipe." Another prize recipe, one she brought to the Driskill from the Houston Country Club, became a permanent Driskill dessert choice, Orange Chiffon Pie with Prune Whip Top. An enduring favorite for which townspeople returned time and again was her superbly flavored Canadian Cheese Soup. The pie was certainly of Southern influence, the soup undoubtedly a New York state concoction. Lyndon Johnson's favorite dessert was tapioca, over which Helen crumbled a few candied violets to spruce up the dish's lackluster color.

A standard favorite of the holidays was Mildred's Eggnog Pie which her chief baker created. Mildred was the mother of nine children and weighed over three-hundred pounds. Helen enjoyed a good story on herself and often told of having asked Mildred what her husband, a minister, thought of his wife's having to work on Sunday. "Aw, Miss C.," she responded, "You can't live with God and work at the Driskill," to which Helen added, "'and with you,' I'm sure she meant."

After almost four years at the Driskill, in 1955 Helen packed her cookbooks, her collection of china plates and her suitcases and traveled to Dallas to her new domain as manager of the Zodiac Room at Neiman-Marcus. In one last grand gastronomical fling before she left Austin, she was asked to plan her own farewell-supper gala at the Headliners Club. The menu for the buffet was so elaborate (and she worked so hard on it) that she included it later in her famous *Helen Corbitt's Cookbook*.

In Dallas after years of attempts, Stanley Marcus had finally prevailed on Helen to take over the restaurant and make it the success he had envisioned when the store was enlarged five years earlier. Appreciating her fine-tuned expertise with flavors as well as her acknowledged ability to run a tight kitchen, Marcus once introduced her as the "Balenciaga of Food." In her new domain she continued "to produce new taste sensations and to satisfy the eye as well as the palate by her dramatic food presentation." She so excelled in her varying menus and imaginative catering that the Zodiac Room became a gigantic success, not only in Dallas and Texas but internationally as her name became synonymous with innovative serving coupled with an enchanting new approach to the enjoyment of good food.

A Zodiac Room meal often began with small surprises, to whet the diner's appetite, such as a small cup of chicken consommé and the traditional single popover. When he came to know her better, Marcus understood her "uncontrollability, her genuine Irish temperament, and her sheer genius in the field of food." In one of his Monday *Dallas Morning News* columns in March 1958, the "Neiman-Marcus Point of View" featured Helen Corbitt and the Zodiac Room, mentioning schedules for brunch, lunch and tea, menu suggestions, and the daily style shows. Helen returned Marcus' admiration with a deep and life-long regard for the man who sincerely appreciated her consummate talent with food.

As large Texas towns became cities after World War II, Dallas, enriched by oil, agricultural, merchandising and investment money, became the undisputed financial capital of the state. It was already the railroad center and soon became the airline hub when Braniff Airlines established headquarters there and everyone had to fly to Dallas to catch planes to anywhere else.

None of this extravagance of riches was lost on Neiman-Marcus director Stanley Marcus who, while on a trip to Europe, came up with the innovative idea of "Fortnights" to replace an earlier Neiman-Marcus Award for Distinguished Service in the Field of Fashion. The memorable annual fortnights were two-week festivals of merchandising combined with an array of fine consumer goods oriented to the American buyer and produced in the country or countries the fortnight featured. The event, staged during the mid-October business lag, involved the Dallas cultural and business communities, which joined with Neiman-Marcus to create a well-orchestrated entertainment often beginning with an opening gala ball benefiting various cultural charities such as the Dallas Symphony, the Ballet, or the Civic Opera, and introducing the special foreign guests of honor and other celebrities to Dallas.

For Helen, months of Zodiac Room planning were required for the special foods and decors featured during the fortnight. Marcus chose to feature France, the capital of style, in the first fortnight in 1957; despite the continued and difficult period of her recovery after World War II, Paris continued to live up to her reputation as the style center of Western fashion. A master chef with four assistants from a French passenger-ship line were imported with a liaison chef from New York. Their first day in the Zodiac kitchen began in a memorable though turbulent manner. Helen recalled that from early that morning the Frenchmen spent a great deal of time "drinking wine, brandy and beer," and they began giving it to the kitchen help in Helen's domain. The next morning, with no apology to the visitors, Helen called her people together and warned them, "If I catch any of you drinking today you're fired."

Although the visitors spoke little English, they "seemed to understand and work habits cleared noticeably," she recalled. During this gala fortnight, Neiman-Marcus' patrons entering the store on Ervay Street found the building's familiar, first-level facade transformed to resemble Paris boutiques on the Faubourg-St.Honoré. The Zodiac Room became Maxim's restaurant in Paris, and in the kitchens Helen and her staff catered to the chef's "awesome creation" of one entree each day for lunch, one dinner for the wine connoisseurs' *Confrerie des Chevaliers du Tastevin*, and another dinner for customers.

Soon after this first fortnight, Marcus sent Helen to Europe as a "thank you," and she chose to travel on the French ship *Liberté* on which the fortnight's French chef had his kitchen. She remembered the voyage as the "most fascinating gastronomical binge one could imagine," and she admitted to weighing one hundred and eight-five pounds afterwards.

Helen and Neiman-Marcus learned much from the French chef experience, and in the fortnights to come Helen herself created the food specialities in her kitchen, adopting the menus to her "customers' taste," for they "didn't seem to give a hoot about foreign chefs." Several years later at the opening of the South American Fortnight, she planned the menu for the introductory gathering at the Marcus' Black Mark Ranch by serving an *asada* of barbecued beef, lamb and chicken roasted on "metal cross-like holders" with Texas sourdough biscuits, an inspired accompaniment for the meats. At the store, an open bar with various South American coffees was open each day for Neiman-Marcus' customers.

In preparation for the 1960 Italian Fortnight, Helen spent two unforgettable weeks on a cook's tour through northern Italy, sampling the endless variety of antipastos, the ubiquitous pastas, and the fettucini she finally chose as her favorite, which she called "Mama food" because it soothed her and others "gastronomically and spiritually." The Italian Fortnight banquet for 1,200 people was held in the large Dallas Sheraton Hotel where she worked in conjunction with a Swiss chef. Helen demanded that different wines be served in different wine glasses, which taxed Dallas' restaurant supply houses but did not daunt her plans. During the fortnights, she relished the challenges of creating good food served in beguiling settings both for the store's customers as well as for famous foreign guests. France and England were twice honored with fortnights.

During her visit to Switzerland in preparation for the Swiss Fortnight, Helen discovered that, despite their legendary hotel and restaurant schools, the Swiss focused largely on international cuisines, so she set out to find what the Swiss ate at home. She "came back with a great respect for veal, cheese and wholesome delicacies of cheeses in quiches and fondues and their classic preparations." At Neiman-Marcus the response to the dinner opening—a beer hall setting like one she had seen in Lausanne with tables pulled together and food served family style—was overwhelming, and reservations were planned for two seatings. She later wrote about the affair and that she organized an impromptu "third sitting which meant more elevator men, more air-conditioning, more security." The next day, meeting with her bosses, she had to listen to all of the reasons why the third serving was ill-advised and not to be repeated. She later admitted that Neiman-Marcus did not belong to her and that such costly decisions should be left to the top management. Nevertheless, after that three sittings were planned for the special weekend gala fortnight openings. At times, if interest seemed to suggest it, a Monday night opening was added as well.

The visit to Denmark in preparation for the Danish Fortnight introduced her to Scandinavian fruit pastries and to the high-calorie, open-faced sandwiches with the bread covered with so much butter one could hardly taste the "variety of things the Danes put on them." Planning for an Austrian Fortnight meant visiting Salzburg and learning how to prepare the vast array of national dishes. She relished the gusto of *skeller* foods and drink, but her visit to Vienna's famed Sacher Hotel pastry kitchen was dampened by having her guide, the head of food services, addressed by his staff as *"doktor."* By the time she returned to Dallas she had gained ten pounds from so much food *mit Schlag.* Back in her own kitchen far from the *doktor's* intimidating presence, she recreated her own version of the famed *Sacher Torte.*

Before the Far East Fortnight she flew to both the East and West coasts, visiting restaurant chefs in their kitchens in San Francisco and New York to learn about the "foreign" ingredients and sauces and the basics of preparing Chinese, Japanese and Indian foods. She later wrote that by "researching, tasting and talking to many chefs," she and her associates "turned out some acceptable and interesting Oriental menus." On the Indian night she wore a stunning blue sari which complimented her blue eyes.

For the finale of the Far East Fortnight, decorators transformed the Zodiac Room into a set from *The King and I* with three buffets—Indian, Chinese and Japanese. The idea was that guests would choose one of the buffets; instead they chose all three! The unexpected demand of the delighted guests' appetites challenged the kitchen staff and Helen's creative cookery. For the evening she had decided on being an authentic Chinese; her robe, hair and makeup fooled even Stanley Marcus in the receiving line. She didn't mind the cumbersome obi, but the shoes were impossible. It was five a.m. before she had seen to the last of the party, and she decided that instead of going back to her apartment she would check into a downtown hotel where, without luggage and still in costume, it was some time before the manager identified her and gave her a room.

From the recipes she found in her working cookbooks, Helen created her own distinctive dishes. The Cheddar Cheese Soup at the Driskill, she mused, had been a part of her life for so long that "it may have come with the stork." Perhaps the most famous recipe attributed to her is her Poppy-Seed Dressing, which she never claimed to have originated. She had first tasted it in New York, "so many years ago I hate to recall, but I did popularize it when I realized that on the best grapefruit in the whole wide world, the Texas pink, it was the most delectable dressing imaginable." Poppy-seed dressing has come to be widely used for all fresh fruit, although some omit the onion juice as a flavor out-of-place with the sweeter fruits. Her Lime Honey Dressing, also for fruit, was inspired by having to use-up several quarts of sour cream. Cream, sour or sweet, and butter were essential ingredients in all of her cooking.

Helen Corbitt was a noted dinner-party giver who made entertaining in the kitchen acceptable, close to food, stove and icebox with all of the dishes, glasses and cutlery within easy reach. For years she held monthly cooking gatherings, in her apartment, for fourteen men whom she found to be "adventurous" in their food interests. On a different night each month she entertained a number of women who were close friends. None of her guests objected to an evening of non-smoking, and non-drinking except for the dinner wines.

One of her special annual activities was the well-known three-day cooking school conducted in the Zodiac Room, sponsored for seventeen years by the Junior Group of the Dallas Symphony Orchestra League. These popular annual events, last held in the ballroom of Southern Methodist University in 1977, added more than one hundred thousand dollars to the support of the symphony. She also scheduled innumerable other fundraisers sponsored by Dallas groups and held in Zodiac Room facilities.

Helen's fourteen-year direction of the Zodiac Room ended in 1969 after Stanley Marcus invited Helen to become the food consultant of the Greenhouse, a luxurious health and beauty spa in Arlington. Changing to a less demanding atmosphere, she created the menus and recipes for all meals—breakfast trays, poolside lunches, and dinners in the dining room using linens, china, crystal and flowers with caring attention to the guests' personal diets.

Helen L. Corbitt (she kept secret what the "L" stood for) was, as one columnist wrote, "the high priestess of haute cuisine," yet she was as American as apple pie. She liked to gather people into friendly informality while eating, such as the old-fashioned church supper with country-fair food which she organized for one of the fortnights' evening opening galas. Her five cookbooks reflect an exuberant approach to good eating and good company, and her radiant *joie de vivre* helped sell thousands of them at book signings and at cooking schools—by 1974 Neiman-Marcus had sold 80,000 copies of her first and most famous, *Helen Corbitt's Cookbook.*

Helen had hundreds of friends, and she refuted the charge from her employees that she had a bad temper, responding "I don't think I have a temper. I think I have a tremendous amount of patience. I have a sense of humor, and sometimes when I'm joking people take me seriously." Word circulated from her kitchen that whenever she was irritated she threatened to go to "Ireland and never come back!" At the party honoring her retirement from directorship of the Zodiac Room, one of her longtime helpers presented her on behalf of her staff with a ticket to Ireland. Blinking and feigning hurt she said, "So you want to get rid of me completely?" "No ma'am," he responded, "If you'll notice, that ticket is round trip."

Helen Corbitt received numerous honors; in 1972 she was among the fifty most outstanding graduates honored at the 50th anniversary celebration of Skidmore College, and she served on the school's board of directors. In Texas she was listed among the ten most influential women in the state. For her special achievements in food preparation and restaurant management, in 1961 she was the first woman to win the Golden Plate Award for Food Service Operator presented by the Institutional Food Service Manufacturers' Association. Among her honors was the Escoffier Gold Plaque of the *Confrerie de la Chaine des Rotisseurs* awarded in 1968. She was a long-time, honorary member of the Dallas Symphony League, an honorary member of the *Tastevan du Chevaliers* gourmet society, and she served on the Texas Agricultural Board and on a study commission on dietetics. She was elected to serve a three-year term on the Board of Governors of the Culinary Institute of America, an outstanding school of its kind in the United States. She is listed in *Who's Who of American Women* and in *Foremost Women in Communications.*

Despite her outward gaiety and charm, Helen was hard-working, methodical, painstaking and thorough. She bequeathed the Dallas Public Library more than six-hundred recipe books, now shelved for general circulation, along with her cooking school lectures. Her most-used cookbooks are dog-eared and often spattered with grease or butter; among her favorites are *Fanny Farmer's Boston Cooking School Cookbook,* a longtime basic reference, and her *New England Yankee Cookbook,* "one of the most thumbed volumes in her collection." No chef is without Escoffier's bible of French cooking; Helen's was a paperback printed in 1920. Books on quantity cooking were necessities for her special expertise; beautiful recipe volumes were for cocktail-table conversations. Much of her personal collections is at the University of Dallas at Irving.

Helen Corbitt died in Dallas on Monday, January 16, 1978. Her obituary requested memorials, in lieu of flowers, to the University of Dallas Fund for the Helen Corbitt Lectures on Excellence. She was buried in Dallas, in the state where she had planned to stay only temporarily but where she remained to devote a lifetime influencing Texans not only to read about food but to revel in preparing and eating good food served in pleasant settings.

"She was a no-nonsense woman," wrote Helen's longtime friend Dick Hitt of the *Times-Herald,* "capable of humor, often of the rapier variety, but she used it as she would a pungent spice for hinting at the substance of a point. She was a curious combination of elegance and gusto, impatience and painstaking perfectionism, femininity and jaunty zest," and he continued, "she was subtle and imperious, ebullient and unerringly correct. Lots of things that you wouldn't think would go together in a person, went together in Helen Corbitt. She was a *bouillabaisse* of a person, part administrator, part hostess, part duchess, part Mother Superior."

REFERENCES

Criswell, Ann. "70s Party Style Is Kitchen Buffet, Says Helen Corbitt." *Houston Chronicle* (September 27, 1970).

"Food authority Helen Corbitt dies." *Dallas Morning News* (January 17, 1978).

Hitt, Dick. "Helen Corbitt: The grande dame of gourmets." *Dallas Times-Herald* (January 18, 1978).

Krisch, Nora Louise. "Kitchen trick is a treat." *Houston Post* (November 13, 1970).

"League in Symphony With Cooking School." *Dallas Times-Herald* (February 28, 1971).

Marcus, Stanley. *Minding the Store, A Memoir.* Boston: Little, Brown and Company, 1974.

_____."Neiman-Marcus point of view, things you don't know about the zodiac." Regular Monday column, *Dallas Morning News* (March 28, 1958).

Mark, Carolyn Bengtson. "Helen didn't want compliments for meal." *Austin-American* (January 19, 1978).

Raffetto, Francis. "Culinary Queen. Helen Corbitt's Food Still Reigns Supreme." *Texas Star* (March 26, 1972).

Stone, Marvin H. Letter to Crystal Sasse Ragsdale, August 19, 1996.

Sweeney, Julia. "Helen Corbitt: Name has pickin' privileges." *Dallas Times-Herald* (March 7, 1976).

_____."Helen Corbitt adds her touch to class." *Dallas Times-Herald* (March 14, 1977).

Thirteenth Census of the United States: 1910 Population. Township of Clifton, Benson Mines District, Hyland Avenue, New York. Department of Commerce and Labor, Bureau of the Census. Roll 1074, Sheet 2B, April 1910.

INTERVIEW

Hallie Groce Slaughter and Crystal Sasse Ragsdale, August 23, 1996.

ANNOTATED COOKBOOKS:

A Taste of Texas. Jane Trahey (ed.), compiled for Neiman-Marcus by Marihelen McDuff. New York: Random House, 1949. This cookbook, sponsored by Neiman-Marcus, foreshadowed Stanley Marcus' interest in fine food and his determination to develop the Zodiac Room into a first-class restaurant for Neiman-Marcus customers. The recipes in this 303-page, pre-Helen Corbitt cookbook were tested by the Home Economics Department of the Texas State College for Women from the entries sent in by Neiman-Marcus customers from all over the United States with a number from international celebrities. A list of the contributors is included.

Helen Corbitt's Cookbook. Boston: Houghton Mifflin Company, Inc., 1957. Helen Corbitt's first published cookbook immediately became a classic and by March 1962 had gone into its fifteenth printing. She often introduces and comments on her recipes and, as if reluctant to say goodby to her readers, set a pattern used in her subsequent cookbooks by adding a section at the end which she labeled "This And That," a collection of cooking tips and recipes for which she had no other place in the book.

Potluck. Boston: Houghton Mifflin Company, Inc., 1962. This small, 181-page book was "designed to encourage an intelligent attitude toward leftovers and an experimental utilization of a whole raft of ideas." With her instinct for the tasty marriage of flavors, Helen's *Potluck* is a satisfying collection of delectable, rather easy to prepare recipes and menus.

Helen Corbitt Cooks for Looks. Boston: Houghton Mifflin Company, Inc., 1967. This 195-page handbook is a menu and recipe guide on how to live and be thinner on an 850 calorie-a-day month's diet which Helen developed at the Greenhouse spa in Arlington, a supply of tested recipes any dieter could enjoy while observing basic eating "dos and don'ts." In three concluding chapters she grants "Indulgences" to her non-dieting readers.

Helen Corbitt Cooks for Company. Boston: Houghton Mifflin Company, Inc., 1974. Helen Corbitt's third and largest cookbook of 434 pages was second in popularity only to her first. She responded to her friends and co-workers requests to "put down on paper the menus and recipes for the great many parties, large and small" which she planned. She graciously gives her friends credit for their good food ideas, and she divides the menus and recipes into three levels of expenditures.

Helen Corbitt's Greenhouse Cookbook. Boston: Houghton Mifflin Company, Inc., 1979. Helen Corbitt did not live to see this slender volume in publication, but her knowledge of good food prevails in this update of the 1967 "*Looks*" diet cookbook.

Helen Corbitt Collection. Elizabeth Ann Johnson (ed.). Boston: Houghton Mifflin Company, Inc., 1981. A large-sized compilation of the best of Corbitt's cookbooks, compiled by her long-time editor. A true cocktail-table book which few kitchens have room for.

Martha Mood
1908-1972

*"With a seeing eye,
an open mind
and a little courage"*

Martha Mood was to work continually in the arts in various media throughout her career, beginning with her art courses at the University of California at Berkeley in the 1920s and continuing until her death, but her most important medium as a distinguished artist was neither paint nor pencil nor charcoal nor clay nor the camera. She worked with distinction in all these skills, but in the late 1950s she began to concentrate in an ancient medium known as stitchery appliqué, "painting with fabric" or "drawing with yarn," which was to earn her well-deserved recognition. In 1962 she was able to write, with authority, an article for *House Beautiful* concerning the factual elements involved in developing and creating appliqué, but in print she could only partially convey to the reader the talent and training and imagination necessary to create such works of artistry.

Martha Wagele Mood was born on June 21, 1908, in Oakland across the bay from San Francisco. Both of her parents were children of German immigrants who had chosen to live in California. Her father, August Wagele, traveled to the United States with his parents from a village in the Black Forest and settled in Dry Creek Valley in Sonoma County, where he met Martha Glaser who had accompanied her well-to-do parents from Stuttgart, Germany. They were married in 1905 and settled in Oakland, where Gus went into the bakery business. Martha's mother often knitted, and the young girl at times visited an ill uncle who had taken up needlework. The mechanics of stitchery must have early caught the little girl's eye—the careful placing of the embroidery needle, the studied rise of the hand gently drawing the thread through the fabric, and the locating of forms within the designs before filling in the patterns of many-colored flowers or houses or clouds or sky.

When Martha was seven her family moved across the bay to San Rafael in Marin County. She and her older brother August, both talented, took piano lessons, but they also often played ball outside in the yard. Martha and her sister Helen enrolled in St. Raphael's Roman Catholic parochial school, but later at the Dominican College High School Martha was to experience a less kindly world than the one she had known with her family and in her early studies. Her high school classmates came from families more affluent and socially prominent than the immigrant Wageles, and Martha became something of an errand girl for the others. As demeaning as the situation was, the experience perhaps facilitated her later relationships with the wealthy patrons who came to buy her appliqué pieces for their homes, clubs, churches and office buildings. The experience also enhanced her capacities for expressing her own kindness and generosity to friends.

"I don't think she was even aware of how much she did for others," Jane Blaffer Owen, one of Martha's patrons recalled. "She gave me a sculpture, it was a contemporary Madonna and Child, not a pious madonna, just a healthy, proud country girl with her baby." Botanical artist-writer Jean Andrews also remembered Martha's generosity when, after telling Martha of her desire to teach stitchery to middle school art classes, she immediately rolled up a bundle of variously colored textiles for Andrews to use.

In addition to the generous nature she acquired from those high school years, Martha developed an intellectual inquisitiveness and an interest in research, the search for information "from books and from people." Through the years her personal library grew extensively with volumes concerning subjects that interested her. After she decided to use natural subjects in her appliqués—birds, animals and flora—she continually acquired illustrated books about them.

She was also a "spiritual person" and read widely in pursuit of information on world religions from the Quakers to Zen Buddhism and, late in life, on Christian Science and the teachings of the Episcopal church. When she began designing ban-

ners, altar cloths and robes for churches, the knowledge and
familiarity with the infinite variety of the symbols and colors of
those ancient art forms which she had gained from her years in
Catholic schools served her well. Martha learned from every
experience, refined her experiences by her reading, and enhanced her knowledge with her own innate artistic sensitivity.

After high school Martha took art courses at the University
of California at Berkeley, including a year's study at California
College of Arts and Crafts in Oakland. She wasted little time in
finding herself; early on she took classes in drawing, color,
design, balance, texture, art history and photography. Working
on her own under the dim "safe light" of the photography lab,
she explored the magic of developing film then left the acrid
smells of the lab to attend classes in studio painting where the
odors changed to the sometimes pungent scents of linseed oil
and turpentine and the flat distinctive scent of unprimed canvas. Following her classmates' preference for *avant-garde* clothing, she often wore a long, black cape. During discussions in
which only talent and interest in the arts mattered, she joined
her peers to analyze Picasso's Cubism or the Russian Abstrac-
tionists. And jobs after college.

After her graduation with honors as an arts major, Martha's
travels toward a career in the arts took a divergent road with
her marriage to John Homsy, an electrical engineering graduate
from a Syrian Catholic ranch family in the Fresno Valley. Whatever she was giving up seemed at the time worth losing for love.
For the most part Martha was able to renounce her out-of-the-
ordinary dress and the lifestyle and philosophy of the artist's
life, but she was unable to control the bravado with which she
spent too much of John's salary.

Martha's sprightly approach to money plagued most of her
life. As a child when she had asked her father why money was
so important, he had responded flatly, "Just wait until you don't
have any," but she never was to learn how to achieve a budgetary balance between income and expenditures. Checkbooks
and overdrafts remained a confusing and nebulous yet hard
reality, but Martha continued to read widely and visit museums
when she could. In college painting classes her work had shown
the influence of Matisse, and during these developing years she
found kinships with a wide variety of other artistic styles. She
was intelligent, imaginative, energetic and eminently practical

in her art, if not in her financial affairs. Texas architect O'Neil Ford was to comment two decades later that "Martha was art all day long."

She and John moved to San Pedro, California, where their two daughters were born—Ann in 1933 and Susan in 1935. Martha, with her sense of the playful, skillfully carved wood toys for the children, blocks decorated with artichokes and other vegetables, crib toys for them to play with, toy boxes to hold their treasures and, later, jigsaw puzzles with pieces large enough for little hands to slide easily into place. She also, however, professionally produced photographic illustrations for Dorothy Baruch's book *Parents and Children Go To School*.

With John's important business move to Honolulu, Martha established their new home amid the flowery landscape of the island and again seriously took up her photography, supplying book illustrations of fishermen, workers in the fields and hula dancers. During World War II the Homsys joined other local Americans living in Hawaii who provided hospitality for members of the United States armed forces temporarily in Honolulu pending other Pacific assignments.

On one of these occasions Martha met Beaumont Mood, who would become a pivotal part of her life. He was a photographer and she was pursuing her own career in photography, so the two had much to talk about. In quite a different setting, at a Quaker meeting she also became acquainted with Edgar Lehmann, another enlisted man, but she was soon to set aside her brief encounters with these two men. By this time Martha was finding that she and John Homsy shared few mutual interests; they divorced and she returned with her two young daughters to San Rafael where she found work in a photographic studio.

Beaumont "Beau" Mood, once again in Hawaii after being wounded in Saipan, discovered that Martha had been divorced and had returned to California. Discharged from the army several month later, he returned to his Fort Worth home but located Martha in San Rafael. Several weeks of telephone calls ending with a proposal of marriage convinced Martha that she could leave the security of her family and friends in California and share her talents as well as her life with him. She met Beau in Fort Worth and they were married. Ann, her elder daughter, lived with the Moods, but daughter Susan chose to live with her father.

Dallas had more openings in photography work than Fort Worth and the couple moved there. In Dallas Martha met three men with whom she would later be associated in San Antonio: she would work for architect O'Neil Ford; she would collaborate with his brother Lynn, an artist, woodcarver and craftsman; and she would share artistic knowledge with portrait painter Tom Stell, who described Dallas of that time as "a provincial kind of town . . . [but] a hot bed of enthusiasm and euphoria about the art going on in Dallas and Denton and Fort Worth—a kind of intellectual triangle up in North Texas, spawned by the federally funded Works Progress Administration and the National Youth Administration."

By the early 1950s Beau had a permanent job with Harper & Company, photographers on Main Street, and during the Christmas holidays Martha worked in a department store as a food demonstration saleswoman. Needing to rekindle her creative talents, she enrolled in a hobby shop ceramics class which gave her an opportunity to refine what she knew of the pro-cesses of creating clay art pieces. Experimenting with styles and techniques, she pursued the subtleties of color and glaze and learned the intricacies of firing her decorative clay tiles, figures, pots and vessels. The class was a good beginning, but she would have to wait before she could use her new-found expertise as a potter.

With an unexpected inheritance from a California relative, Martha financed Beau's venture into his own photography business. Everything went well until, in an automobile collision, a dashboard clock was flung into Martha's face and she was forced to begin long, painful months of delicate surgical operations in the slow process of rebuilding her face and forehead. The medical bills became so extensive that the couple sold their home and moved to an apartment complex to meet, even partially, the hospital and doctor bills which were to take them six years to pay. Martha had been "quite beautiful," but the accident permanently marred her features, although friends and associates whom she met after the accident were not aware of the remarkable change in her facial appearance. Instead they were to know a Martha Mood whose voice was "arresting, with its lyric, lilting tones, as if she had some exceptional news to tell you." She continued to live her life, as she described it, with a "seeing eye, an open mind and a little courage."

In 1952 the Moods, their fortunes at the lowest level since Martha's catastrophic injury, decided to establish a new life in San Antonio. With Ann away at The University of Texas at Austin, they loaded their car with photography equipment, books and some of Martha's ceramic art pieces, and left Dallas. With maturing talents she entered into the art-loving world of San Antonio, a gathering place for artists for the previous hundred years and a city which not only encouraged the creation of art but which also possessed private collectors and corporate buyers of art. The fabled Eleanor Onderdonk was serving as the guiding hand at the Witte Museum's arts and painting section, and Marion Koogler McNay had completed her museum-like mansion which offered to San Antonians a collection of paintings, prints and sculptures by modern American and French artists.

Martha and Beau found a house to rent on Augusta Street, auspiciously located just across from the Junior League tearoom "The Bright Shawl" whose clientele included many artists and patrons of the arts. Martha immediately converted the sunroom of the house into a studio for work in various art media—drawing, sketching, painting, photography and, ultimately, for her growing interest in stitchery appliqué—installing a large work table and hanging cages of birds from the ceiling amid an indoor jungle of potted plants. She soon found a job teaching art at Alamo Heights High School, and at the nearby San Antonio Art Institute on the McNay grounds she taught classes in ceramics. Even while continuing to create her own ceramic figures, she was also gaining a reputation as a stitchery artist.

The couple would live on Augusta for eight years before moving to the nineteen-hundred block of Broadway, still within easy commuting distance of the Witte Museum where she taught art classes for a time and worked with Harding Black, a foremost potter. She made puppets with Charles Long, who was both sculptor and photographer.

But before she was to begin her thirteen-year career in stitchery, she worked in the late 1950s with another medium. While Beau continued in photography, Martha was commissioned by O'Neil Ford to create ceramic lighting fixtures for the houses and buildings he was designing. Before long Beau left his business to facilitate the completion of the clay pieces which Martha designed. The couple's entry into the commercial world was solidified when Ford asked them to complete a contract, of mass-produced ceramic light fixtures for Dallas-based Texas Instruments, Inc., which had been started by a sculptor who did not finish the work. At the party celebrating the building's dedication in 1958, Martha's "beautiful clay pots and Lynn Ford's beautiful [wood] screens" were the featured architectural accents.

The Moods completed other ceramic work for Ford, supplying lighting fixtures for the Scribner Library of Skidmore College at Saratoga Springs, New York, in 1963. Propelled by the impetus of the contracts with Ford, they established their own business for designing and producing ceramic architectural lighting fixtures, to which they added fountains, murals and pottery figures. Martha did the designing and chose the colors; Beau handled the production, fine-tuning the "critical shaping of the [clay] molds, and supervising the final working with the clay, the firing and the glazing." Martha's chunky clay light fixtures, incorporating pierced openings with delicate crossed lines and flower-like patterns in bands of stunning red and blue and yellow glazes, seem almost to be an extension of her stitchery.

At first, Martha's interest in stitchery was in addition to her other art interests. Early in her appliqué-stitchery career she had often visited artist Margaret Pace's house-bound mother, taking along her bag of scraps and a book on appliqué. While demonstrating appliqué techniques and patterns to her elderly pupil, Martha sensed her own talent in this new artistic expression and, with consuming interest, she often took an unfinished piece to bed with her and worked on it into the night. During the day, the familiar sewing bag always accompanied her, for she could work on her stitchery almost anywhere.

Martha's transition to stitchery began as early as 1959, even while she was continuing to design for the Moods' ceramic business. One of her early experiments with appliqué techniques, for an abstract design she entered in a Witte Museum show, failed when the heavy glue she had applied to hold the textile pieces onto the backing caused the entire piece to sag and the individual, unhemmed pieces of cloth to unravel from the weight. Her practical solution was to sew the pieces firmly onto the background; at first she tried simple embroidery stitches which she already knew—crossstitch, running stitch, and daisy stitch—with little thought to the effect that more intricate stitchery could add to her designs.

As she worked, however, she began to incorporate more elaborate stitchery into the details of her "pictures," artistically selecting from a wider range of threads—cotton and wool for heavier textural effects, linen or pure silk, synthetic or metallic. When the threads were too thick or their texture too rough to draw through the fabric, or the fabrics too fragile, she learned to use the ancient "couch" or "Kloster" stitch to hold several long threads in place with other smaller stitches. Knowledge-able viewers of her appliqués are able to recognize a sampler of intricate stitches both functional and decorative.

Even more important than her variety of embroidery stitches, however, were Martha's selections from among the innumerable textures, colors and prints of the fabrics which became the individual figures in her work. She amassed a large collection of textiles to have on hand to select from; her consuming passion was for old fabrics, those with the patina of wear. Her longtime friend Dolores LaTorre recalled it was a "joke among Martha's friends that people had to hold onto their clothes when they visited her studio to keep her from taking the garment away from the wearer to incorporate into one of her pictures." For sewing her "cloth paintings," Martha estimated that she "used every kind of textured and plain material imaginable—velvet, corduroy and denim, a piece of army blanket, lace for a skunk's stripe, ostrich feathers, buttons for animals' eyes or a piece of somebody's long johns."

At an exhibition of her appliqués at the Witte in May 1967 she was awarded the prestigious San Antonio Art League's $500 Purchase Prize for her appliqué stitchery "San Antonio River." She would have a number of exhibits of her appliqués at the Witte, and one at Frost's elegant department store on Houston Street. With her commission to create a "San Antonio" appliqué for the 1968 Hemisfair World's Fair, Martha Mood became an internationally known stitchery artist.

The artist's long familiarity with landscape painting and with Cubism provided a basis for her artistic "half-closed eye" perspective. She patterned her arrangements of geometric triangles, cubes, squares, circles and arcs within a lively tension of interacting relationships. To incorporate all of the figures within the spatial limits of a stitchery picture, her "perspectives were foreshortened and figures stylized, so that although each element in the stitchery is immediately recognizable, the overall composition becomes quite abstract." None of her images of flowers, trees, leaves and foliage, ponds of water, or clouds is secondary in visual impact; she unabashedly employed clear visual guidelines such as bare, vertical branches to lead the viewer's eye into the whole picture, using curved branches to frame an object or animal which might otherwise be obscured.

Wherever Martha looked, the scenes she saw grew into pictures with trees, flowers, birds, clouds, sky, children playing. She often chose to recreate a Noah's ark of wild animals and birds in their native habitats, at times adding domesticated livestock, poultry, and dogs and cats. She cut out pillow ticking for zebras, spotted fabrics for giraffes, plaids for a tortoise shell, and puffy grey flannel for an elephant's baggy skin. Billowing puffs of printed materials became fantasy trees with branches and twigs outlined in simple embroidery stitches. Ponds of water in varying hues of blues hosted flamingos, ducks and open-mouthed hippopotamuses. One of Martha's appliqués, displayed at the San Antonio Country Club, depicts a shore bird scene of seagulls, running killdeer, herons, ducks, a white pelican, and a pair of flying terns. At one side of this picture she stitched a bare, curving tree that directs the viewer's eye to the cluster of birds at the center.

Among her most popular and original appliqués is the "First Families of Texas" series in which the artist recreated varying arrangements of Texas' wild animals. The first of the series, created in 1962 and now in the McNay Museum, is a vertical picture 67" x 32" of deer, skunks and an armadillo. She later expanded the idea into another popular series, "America's First Families," also using animals and birds.

The artist never left any area of her pictures without visual interest; flowers, shrubs, trailing snakes, coveys of quail, an owl high on a bare branch, a blue-grey rat, rabbits—each claims its colorful space within the unified overall pattern of solid and printed textiles of varying textures. An early appliqué, owned by St. Mary's Hall in San Antonio, depicted a mother opossum with a zipper pouch which the children could open to see her babies. Martha's "pageant of animals," with their eyes of colorful, shining, round buttons, gaze out at us with an almost quivering awareness, their vitality enhanced by the three-dimensional technique of their surroundings.

In her other creations the artist employed her drawing skills to illustrate the familiar jutting spires and rounded domes of San Antonio's old and well-known churches. Martha often selected narrative themes such as children at their games, horsemen's greeting one another in a plaza, or a bull fight. One patron requested a 105" x 53" vertical appliqué plat of his ranch, starting with the front gate and showing the main house, the outbuildings, the pastures, watering places and windmills.

Martha's appliqués in the McNay Museum include single-figure pictures such as "Sunbather," "Rooster," and a large "Black Cat in the Garden," a black polyester, satin and velvet cat lying amid green-patterned textiles. Figure appliqués were also popular with Martha's patrons; "In The Park" shows a mother and her two children clothed in warm pinks and apricots surrounded by colorful birds and flowers. In "Audience," a stunning group purchased by Margaret Batts Tobin and now on loan to the museum, the artist gathered a glittering array of operagoers in which the women are adorned with jeweled rings, earrings and necklaces and wear dresses of metallic textiles, laces and net. The museum also owns a Martha Mood ceramic bas-relief figure of a robed monk playing a cello.

O'Neil Ford remarked of her work, "When she started stitchery I realized that here was a unique artist," and Martha's highly individual art became internationally known. Art critic Mary Carroll Nelson wrote,

> Her Modernist aesthetic is revealed in her use of ambivalent space in shallow, overlapping planes; the sense of over all pattern and intense regard for textural variations that seemed rooted in Cubism. Yet Mood's humanism, faith, and buoyant love of the natural world of flora and fauna ally her versatile vision with artists as widely separated as Gaughin, Henri Rousseau, Roualt, Rivera, Shahn, and Grandma Moses.

Perhaps it was because Martha Mood often related her appliqués to architectural constructions that her works seem so much at home with the rough textures and earthtones of stone, brick or plaster walls of the private homes in which many of her tapestries hang. The Lyndon B. Johnsons were given a Martha Mood appliqué which complemented their ranch home setting; the large (37 1/2" wide x 53" long) piece recreates a cattle-working scene in which the artist used varied russet and ochre tones for the background and horses in contrast with the bluejean-clad cowboys and the bright red campfire.

She was also influenced by her travels. In the 1960s she visited anthropologists Dolores and Felipe LaTorre during their ethnological study of the Kickapoo Indians in Musquiz, Mexico, below Eagle Pass. Another exploration with her sewing bag was a nine-hundred-mile round trip with the John Rices from their La Mota ranch near Marfa and into the Big Bend along the Rio Grande. She also accepted the invitation of Jane Blaffer Owen to create a lighting fixture for a building and to teach classes in stitchery at New Harmony, Indiana, a community which Jane and her husband Kenneth Dale Owen were working to restore. During her stay in the early nineteenth-century settlement, she observed the orderliness of the garden beds defined by neat paths surrounding the brick and lumber buildings; here her artistic psyche related to the "exceptionally quiet" village set in the remote, woody terrain beside the wide Wabash River. Her ingratiating appliqué of a brown-robed St. Francis of Assisi amid a "choir of birds," which now graces the New Harmony Inn, reflects her response to the peaceful surroundings.

Enid Collins, another of the artist's friends, remarked that "Martha's life was full of difficulties," and that she "escaped into her work"; in some magic way she was able to overshadow her difficulties by losing herself in artistic creativity. Martha could not have created the enormous number of appliqués without the help of a loyal coterie of women friends who worked in the artist's studio. They often stitched on as many as half-a-dozen pieces at one time, following the embroidery axiom to "never pull out a stitch gone askew, embroider over it; if a short piece of thread, don't cut it off, use it up." Ann Drought, a member of the group, described their work as being done in an "aura of creativity, excitement and fun." The women often suggested themes which Martha then designed in a new appliqué, and sometimes they even named the finished tapestry.

After eighteen years, and apparently weary of patching up a marriage worn thin, Martha and Beau were divorced. In the 1966 San Antonio City Directory Martha's address is listed as Bandera Road, but her friends Jean Cauthorn and Martha Fuller offered her a place to live and work on their property at Helotes, a settlement just northwest of San Antonio. She lived there temporarily in a small stone house in such dire circumstances that Martha Fuller described the situation with the Mexican expression, *"Qué lástima!"* [What a shame!] The phrase stuck and was to become the name of Martha's new home when, encouraged both by her numerous friends and by her own ebullient spirit, Martha asked her daughter Susan Bragstad, now an architect from San Francisco, to help her design a new stone home and studio. Martha and Jean Cauthorn searched for and found architectural pieces from the recently cleared Hemisfair grounds to add to the building. Constructed on a functional plan, spaces were devised for both Martha's living needs and for her stitchery production—a long work table with enough room for the baskets of threads, shelves for the orderly storage of fabrics and, for purely aesthetic pleasure, places for Martha's ceramic pieces and dried flower and driftwood arrangements. One necessity was an adequate kitchen where she could cook and serve her ingenious meals.

At night Martha continued her solitary sewing, but she was not alone for long. By a remarkable coincidence Edgar Lehmann of Seattle, the young Quaker she had met in Hawaii, on a visit to his daughter in San Francisco, was taken to visit her friend Ann Homsy Woodward. Lehmann noticed and admired an appliqué on the wall and discovered the artist was Martha Homsy Mood and that she was no longer married. Lehmann telephoned her, and they arranged to meet after not having seen each other in over twenty-five years.

The couple married soon after they met again in Texas, and their move to the state of Washington entailed a sharp change in Martha's life and working routine. For a time they lived near Seattle in a rustic cabin with no conveniences, but she enjoyed the atmosphere of the remote surroundings. During the day, when her husband was in town at his business, she continued her stitchery, sending finished pieces to Helotes and receiving back pieces requiring her to add the finishing stitchery.

It was to be a too-brief interlude; when Martha became

seriously ill in 1970 she and Edgar returned to *Qué Lástima*. After months of continual visits from friends, the special help of Martha Fuller and Jean Cauthorn who brought Martha's dog to see her, and Edgar's devoted care, Martha died in her own home on June 15, 1972.

Of the over five-hundred appliqués created by Martha Mood, perhaps the most compelling exhibit is in the Ford-designed Margarite B. Parker Chapel beside the tall bell tower at Trinity University in San Antonio. Lynn Ford's exquisitely carved wooden doors and screens set off Martha's brightly colored appliqué banners hanging along the entry balcony railing of the church. She chose the "rich glass colors" of the south windows of the chapel for the traditional Christian symbols in her stitcheries, which are themselves like small jewels set within the subdued wood tones of the interior.

In this chapel visitors can view three separate aspects of Mood's work—the banners, two Portuguese-woven tapestries of scenes with Biblical quotations and, at the chapel office, four 54" x 48" tempera cartoons of the Biblical scenes she submitted for the Trinity University board to choose from for the two tapestries. Martha inscribed these last of her works with her usual signature "Martha Mood," but she added the letter "L" after "Mood" to recognize her marriage to Edgar Lehmann.

Poet-artist Amy Freeman Lee wrote of her friend Martha Mood, "She held every mineral, vegetable, insect, fish, reptile, bird, animal and man sacred and she treated them all with understanding, love and compassion."

REFERENCES

Dillon, David. "Arts and Crafts: A Legacy Of Design." *Texas Homes*, vol. 5 (October 1981).

Eaton, Jan, ed. *Mary Thomas's Dictionary Of Embroidery Stitches*. New York: Crescent Books, 1989.

George, Mary Carolyn Hollers. *O'Neil Ford. Architect*. Color photographs, W. Eugene George. College Station: Texas A&M University Press, 1992.

Haraszty, Eszter and Bruce David Colen. *Needlepainting, A Garden of Stitches*. New York: Liveright, 1974.

Henderson, Lester Kierstead and Shirley Koploy. *Martha Mood. The Sublime Heritage of Martha Mood*. 2 vols. Monterey, California: Kierstead Publications, 1980.

Huffstatler, Rebecca. Letter to Crystal Sasse Ragsdale, January 29, 1996.

James, Shirley. Letter to Crystal Sasse Ragsdale, February 20, 1996.

Lammers, Heather. Letter to Crystal Sasse Ragsdale, December 8, 1995.

Lance, Mary. *Lynn Ford, Texas Artist And Craftsman.* Photographs by Michael J. Smith. San Antonio: Trinity University Press, 1978.

Lehmann, Martha Mood. Biographical File. The Center for American History, University of Texas at Austin.

_____. Clippings File. Daughters of the Republic of Texas Library, The Alamo, San Antonio, Texas.

"Martha Mood Is Chosen League's Artist of the Year." *San Antonio Light* (May 14, 1967).

"Mood reproductions will be exhibited, sold." *San Antonio Express-News* (May 2, 1980). [Mood's appliqués copied in hand-woven tapestries]

Mood, Martha. "Make an Applique Tapestry." *House Beautiful*, vol. 104 (October 1962).

Nelson, Mary Carroll. "The Art of Stitchery; Martha Mood and Wilcke H. Smith." *American Artist*, vol. 49 (October 1985).

_____. "Martha Mood. The Sublime Heritage of Martha Mood." [book review] *American Artist*, 1 (October 1981).

"Old Texas Farmhouse restored for a family of five." *House & Garden* 140 (August 1971).

Passadore, Wanda. *The Needlework Book*. Italy: Alberto Peruzzo Editore, 1969.

Pitzer, Donald E. and Josephine M. Elliott. "New Harmony's First Utopians." *Indiana Magazine of History* LV (September 1979).

Rhodes, Glenda and Jack. Letter to Crystal Sasse Ragsdale, December 30, 1995.

"San Antonio River." [Martha Mood: appliqué/stitchery purchase] San Antonio Art League. Acquisitions list, 1925-1967, 16.

Sawyer, Eva Lynn. "Artist's Interesting Home Is a Studio Also." *San Antonio Light* (May 31, 1964).

Steinfeldt, Cecilia. *The Onderdonks: A Family Of Texas Painters*. San Antonio: San Antonio Art Museum Association by Trinity University Press, 1976.

Stewart, Rick. *Lone Star Regionalism, The Dallas Nine And Their Circle.* Austin: Texas Monthly Press, 1985.

Symbolism In The Margarite B. Parker Chapel and George Parker Chapel Garden [chapel folder]. San Antonio: Trinity University, n.d.

The New Harmony Inn [visitor folder]. New Harmony, Indiana, n.d.

INTERVIEWS

Jean Andrews and Crystal Sasse Ragsdale, Georgetown, Texas, October 10, 1995.

Heather Lammers and Crystal Sasse Ragsdale, San Antonio, Texas, January 9, 1996.

Dolores LaTorre and Crystal Sasse Ragsdale , Georgetown, Texas, October 10, 1995.

Glenda and Jack Rhodes and Crystal Sasse Ragsdale, 1995, 1996.

Tom Shelton and Crystal Sasse Ragsdale, San Antonio, Texas, January 9, 1996.

PHOTOGRAPHS

Mary W. McComb, San Antonio, Texas, "First Families of Texas" [one of the series], December 19, 1995.

Glenna P. Robbins, San Antonio, Texas, "First Families of Texas" [one of the series], November 15, 1995.

Dominique de Menil with Max Ernst's Retour de la Belle Jardinère.
Courtesy Menil Collection Library, Houston, Texas.

Dominique
de Menil
1908-1997

*"What is art
if it does not enchant?"*

"Dominique de Menil? Of course, she is from an old French family of art connoisseurs and was reared in an apartment in the Louvre."

"Her biographer will have to write volumes about her. . . ."

"I can see her in a thirteenth century-type tapestry designed Rockwell Kent style, in profile, wearing a classic 1930s hair-do."

"A tapestry is all very well to think about, but have you seen her real portrait Max Ernst painted before World War II?"

Only the first of these remarks is fantasy, but real or imaginary these snippets of conversations in French, German or English might have been heard at any de Menil-sponsored art exhibit opening in Houston, New York or Paris. Dominique and John de Menil's art collecting and their passion for art museums began when they were a young couple in Houston, and their reputation soon became international; when the de Menils issued an exhibit catalogue, the art world read it.

Dominique's family, the Schlumbergers, were French-German Protestants of Guebwiller in Alsace. Her father Conrad first came to Paris in the early 1890s for university study, taught physics, then worked to develop a process to measure electricity below the earth's surface. After his sobering experiences as a soldier during World War I, he became a firm pacifist and supported the politics of the French socialists. With his brother Marcel, who had studied civil engineering, and encouraged financially by their father Pierre Schlumberger, the brothers developed an electronic device to locate underground oil. By

1927 the process was becoming an essential part of testing equipment worldwide for the oil industry; in 1982 the net profits of the international Schlumberger company, in which the family members owned one-fourth interest, totaled well over a billion dollars.

Conrad Schlumberger had three daughters, all of whom provided the company with husbands invaluable to the company's success. Dominique was born in Paris on March 23, 1908, and grew up breathing the heady cultural and artistic air of Paris during the "peaceful" decades of the 1920s and 1930s following World War I. Although she at times underplays the influence of Paris, Dominique must have been touched by the beauty of the ancient city with its treasure-filled museums, grand palaces, imposing churches and public buildings, and its triumphal monuments and historic statues set in wide squares opening onto grand boulevards.

Despite the magnificence of Paris, Dominique recalled that

> as a child I hated living in a city, hated not to be able to walk on the grass in public gardens. From October to the end of June was like a long dreary day, waiting for the country and the excitement of meeting my cousins.

In the country she found other children and animals more to her liking as companions and maintained that she did not enjoy the company of adults, remembering,

> I found the conversation of grown-ups utterly boring and decided I would be a farmer. I tried my hand at it and succeeded to be put in charge of feeding and cleaning the cages of rabbits, of discovering the hidden nests of hens, and I even learned to milk a cow.

During vacations after World War I at the Schlumberger estate, Val-Richer on the Normandy coast, Dominique and her cousins saw portraits of heroes of the American Revolution and learned first-hand of the International Woman's Suffrage Alliance from their grandmother, Marguerite de Witt-Schlumberger, who was then head of the organization. Dominique's father encouraged her to study mathematics and physics at the Sorbonne, and she recalled,

> I learned a lot from my paternal grandfather Pierre
> Schlumberger. He was a born educator. I also learned
> some basics from a few good teachers in the *Lycée*
> (elementary school). I had a math teacher who made
> math exciting. I had also a wonderful teacher in
> French Literature. Texts from classic French authors
> (mostly Racine), became music to my ears.

In Paris Dominique worked in the Schlumberger family's
office as editor of *Proselec*, the confidential in-house magazine
of the *Societé de Prospection Electrique* later known as the Schlumberger Well Survey Corporation. Her heritage of generations of
Protestant forebears faced an abrupt change when she met
young banker Jean de Menil of an old, titled, French military
family. When they married on May 9, 1931, Dominique became
a Catholic. In her new faith with its varied religious experiences,
she discovered a spiritual richness as well as an appreciation
for beauty not fostered in her Puritan-Huguenot upbringing.

In 1939 Jean's financial expertise enabled him to join his two
brothers-in-law, one an engineer and the other a geophysicist,
in the Schlumberger company. In 1940 Dominique accompanied Jean to Romania where he "spent the whole summer in
discussions with the Romanian treasury officials" on international payments and currency exchange. When German troops
began taking control of the Romanian oil fields, he helped to
sabotage German railroads as part of the French Underground.
In 1941 he made his way to the Far East and from there to
Caracas, Venezuela. Dominique, who with great difficulty had
already fled to Spain with their two young daughters Christo-
phe and Adelaide and baby son Georges, sailed to meet Jean in
Caracas.

Soon afterward the family arrived in Houston, the oil capital of the world, to join the other Schlumberger company personnel in the United States. Houston was not unknown to the
family; in the 1920s the Schlumberger brothers Conrad and
Marcel had met in Texas with oil-company executives to publi-
cize their invention for locating sub-surface oil. Jean anglicized
his name to John, the couple moved to the River Oaks area, and
their two youngest children Francois and Philippa were born.

The de Menils found their place not with the showy "Wild-catters" but, rather, among the oil millionaire families of the city, the "Best Oil Money" who in the 1920s had begun "consolidating the real social, financial, and political power" in Houston. These families built their homes mostly in the River Oaks subdivision, following the modified styles of the Mediterranean, medieval, Georgian, American and Spanish colonial, and a few in the innovative modern contemporary and ranch styles. When the de Menils bought their San Felipe Road property adjacent to River Oaks, Dominique began to plan the family's new home, her first experience in what was to become a lifetime of working with architects. In 1948 they invited Connecticut architect Philip Johnson to Houston to discuss designs for the $75,000 house.

Dominique knew what she wanted—indoor spaces with room for potted plants and ample areas for the de Menils' five growing children. As he was to do later in his designs of the Rothko Chapel, Johnson did not take into account the Texas Gulf Coast's climate with its searing light, and his plans for the house failed to interact with either its Texas environment or with the de Menil family's lifestyle. Later structural and interior changes by other architects and designers made the house more to their liking. During the next decades the rooms would be adorned by the couple's growing art collection and would entertain internationally known artists and celebrities.

One of Dominique and John's earliest art encounters was having Dominique's portrait painted in Paris by the young Surrealist artist Max Ernst. The portrait did not please them, despite its delicate coloring and the symbolism of shells, and when the couple left Paris the painting remained behind where it luckily escaped the looting of their apartment by German occupation forces. The portrait was found unharmed after the war and became part of their large Ernst collection acquired as the couple grew to appreciate the artist's talent. After the war Dominique and John also renewed the acquaintance of a French Dominican priest, Father Marie-Alain Couturie, who became a guiding influence in their art collecting, encouraging and widening their appreciation of art of all cultures.

Not until four decades later, in 1987, would the de Menils' art collection have its own museum, a pleasant, unassuming, cypress-sheathed structure displaying the simplicity of the ranch style Dominique had first seen in Texas. The Menil Collection museum is set amid trees on its own ample grounds adjoining the Montrose section near downtown Houston. Before building the museum, however, Dominique would spend years learning about and experimenting with architecture while refining her appreciation of art. She approached the intricacies of art collecting with the realization that she did not have to own everything that appealed to her, that a certain art object "may not have been available, or the cost may have been prohibitive, or the work may have been enjoyable but not right for us," and she recalled, "sometimes I just decided not to buy." A painting or an art piece was accepted on trial while Dominique and John lived with it, seeing it in their home from day to day until they made their decision. If the art did not sustain a lasting appeal for them, it was returned to the dealer.

At times an art purchase or the development of an architectural plan was followed by periods of conflict. The first such conflict began with the couple's decision to purchase Barnett Newman's outdoor sculpture "Broken Obelisk." The acquisition began simply enough with a telephone call from Walter Hopps, an international art authority and director of the Corcoran Gallery of Art in Washington, D.C., who had tried unsuccessfully to persuade the museum board to purchase the sculpture. Dominique described the twenty-six-foot-tall, Cor-ten steel monument, an inverted obelisk with the tip's resting on a pyramid base and the top of the shaft cracked off, as a "virile and exalting monument" which "surges toward the sky like a symbol of man's aspiration and endeavor." In 1968, the year of Martin Luther King, Jr.'s assassination, the de Menils offered to finance part of its acquisition as a gift to the city if Houston would finance the remainder as a dedication to King's memory. When the city officials did not approve the proposal, the de Menils bought it themselves and ultimately placed it in a reflecting pool within sight of the Rothko Chapel located on Yupon Street at Sul Ross.

The Rothko Chapel itself had also brought its share of controversy, this time a private one between the de Menils and their architects. The chapel was planned to house Mark Rothko's 15-foot-tall color-field paintings in bands of deep shades of nearly monochromatic purples, browns, blacks and reds. Rothko completed the series of fourteen paintings in 1966, but the chapel's architectural designs became a source of irreconcilable visions. Philip Johnson saw the chapel as an 80-foot-tall, cone-shaped tower. During discussions with the de Menils he redrew the plans several times and the chapel height was lowered, but neither Johnson, Rothko nor Dominique was pleased with it. Johnson bowed out of the project, and Houston architects Howard Barnstone and Eugene Aubry completed the octagon-shaped chapel in 1971. The endless reworking of plans and model constructions led Aubry to comment later that Dominique "had a romance with the idea of architects but not with the reality" of the mechanics of building. When it later became evident that the rays from the Texas sun wiped out the dark colors of the "luminous abstractions," a *velarium* or sunshade was installed so that the subtle colors of the paintings became more discernible.

The de Menil's Rothko Chapel has become a universal sanctuary for all religious faiths, "a place of worship receptive to the essence and rites of ceremonies being performed." It is an icon in which international gatherings discuss, among several other colloquia, the various qualities of "Human Rights/Human Reality." Perhaps inspired by the chapel itself, in 1981 the de Menil family initiated the First Rothko Chapel Awards to "honor outstanding men and women who, often at great risk, have placed a commitment to truth and freedom at the center of their lives." In 1986, with the co-sponsorship of former President Jimmy Carter, the first Carter-Menil Human Rights prize, Second Rothko Chapel Award, and the first Oscar Romero Award were presented with Archbishop Desmond M. Tutu as keynote speaker.

Another confrontation resulted from Dominique's project in the late 1980s to restore and house two thirteenth-century frescoes from a tiny chapel in Lysi, Cyprus; her plans led to court hearings and depositions involving illicit trading of ancient artifacts, but Dominique and Walter Hopps, now the director of the Menil Collection museum, were able to retain the frescoes.

"My life has been such a surprise," Dominique once said. Not long after establishing their home in the booming city of Houston, Dominique and John had begun to take part in the art and intellectual activities of an unfamiliar American culture. They were "Radical Chic long before it was considered chic" in

Houston, as Isaac Arnold, Jr., chairman of Quintana Oil Company described the two young French *émigrés*, for they

> came as intellectuals to an intellectual void. Not only were they considered radical but really different. They had a foreign accent and political views that for Texas were extremely liberal.

Meetings which Dominique and John attended often brought disagreements and misunderstandings with their peers, whose backgrounds were for the most part Texas and the Old South. Houston had a large black population, and the de Menils soon spoke up against the inequalities in education and opportunities which existed between the white citizens who lived in other parts of Houston and the black citizens whose lives centered around Lyons Avenue in Houston's Fifth Ward. Perhaps influenced by the continuing antagonism between the two groups, in 1954 the couple set up the Menil Foundation, a "private, non-profit charity with the broad purpose of promoting understanding and culture, primarily through the arts." Years later John would leave his own art collection to the Foundation.

Dominique and John contributed to the American Civil Liberties Union and donated funds for black students' college careers. They also contributed to the refurbishing of the old Deluxe Theatre in the Fifth Ward and turned it into a museum for a number of their own African art objects. Their ideas on equality for Houston blacks seemed to crystallize when the de Menils discovered the electric personality of Mickey Leland, a young black activist from the Fifth Ward who had grown up in the Lyons Avenue world of black culture. He studied pharmacy at Texas Southern University, and then joined the protest movement against the traditional roles forced on blacks.

As the acquaintance grew into friendship between the de Menils and Leland, they urged him to run for Barbara Jordan's Texas Senate seat which she had vacated to seek a place in the United States Congress. Leland won the office and went on to replace Jordan again when she chose not to pursue her political career. He was elected to Congress in 1978 and continued to spend much time with the de Menils. After a trip to Africa which John de Menil had financed, Leland returned home with an expanded international vision for his ideas on the needs of blacks worldwide, but he was killed in a plane crash on another visit to Africa in 1989.

Although Houston, the state's largest city, was not a cultural wasteland—its Museum of Fine Arts, the first in Texas, had opened in 1924—Texas was still regarded by national and international standards as an arts backwater as late as the 1940s when John became a member of the museum's board. In 1950 he was elected chairman of the board of the recently organized Contemporary Arts Museum but soon found he faced opposing views from other board members who preferred to show works by local artists rather than by those more well-known.

Returning to the board of the Houston Museum of Fine Arts, John was influential in bringing James Johnson Sweeney, former director of the Guggenheim Museum in New York, as director of the museum in 1961. Sweeney, a scholarly critic who had written much on modern art in the 1930s and 1940s, was "an internationally known personality in a regional museum" and spent little time in Houston. He failed to please the board from the beginning and was fired when he questioned the authenticity and refused to accept a Fragonard painting as a gift to the museum from the influential Blaffer family. Another museum director from New York was hired who pleased the board but not the de Menils.

Dominique and John had given the Houston Museum of Fine Arts a number of monumental art pieces—a classic, third-century A.D. Roman bronze entitled "Portrait of a Ruler" in memory of Conrad Schlumberger, Calder's "International Mobile," and Jackson Pollock's "Painting No. 6"— and other Schlumberger family members also presented art gifts to the museum, but the couple withdrew their support from the museum and found another institution interested in their knowledge, their gifts and, perhaps most of all, their financial backing.

Their next choice was more to their humanistic approach to art and life, the scholarly setting of the small University of St. Thomas located on Branard and Montrose and directed by the Basilian Fathers of the French-founded, Canadian-based Congregation of Saint Basil. The de Menils' years of support of the institution began well enough with the couple's channeling enrichment funds, adding to the fine arts library, and presenting art pieces. In 1957 they called Philip Johnson back to Houston to develop a master plan for the campus for which Johnson took "an idea out of Thomas Jefferson's plan for the University of Virginia in Charlottesville." The "whole campus is really one building," is Johnson's description of the various structures with their unifying arcade.

John continued to follow the Schlumberger global business interests while serving on various art museum boards, but Dominique felt that for her there was more to museums than advising and funding and lending art for exhibits. She wanted to work actively with art. As a child she had "cut pictures from magazines" and arranged them on a wall, "but," she recalled, "nothing much was made of it." In Texas her latent talents in the arts flowered as she began creating exhibits of various pieces from their collection and writing essays, introductions and forewords to the exhibition catalogues.

At times Dominique may have had the feeling voiced by a museum-goer in a crowded exhibition, "Surely it would be nicer if it was your own private collection," but for Dominique a museum of her own was still in the future. When the talented museum director Jermayne MacAgy's contract was not renewed by the Houston Museum of Contemporary Arts in the late 1950s, the de Menils hired her as chairman of the art department at St. Thomas and paid her salary. She produced a number of spectacular shows for the school, but while working on an installation in 1964 she died suddenly. Dominique took over the college's art department and finished the shows Mac-Agy had scheduled. In the process she found her own career.

At St. Thomas she learned the expertise required for the rigorous behind-the-scenes running of a museum: the hiring of well-trained staff, the endless concerns in arranging for art exhibits, "the insurance, conservation examinations, guardianship, temperature and humidity reading of each gallery," the know-how of creating crates for and transporting art pieces, and the research for and publication of exhibit catalogues. Exhibitions of prints required the study of handmade papers and of dating them, knowledge of the inks used, the number of prints made, the location of the best specimens, and their ultimate framing. Even though Dominique became increasingly knowledgeable of all the mechanics of running a museum, she already knew the basic museum rule as espoused by Metropolitan Museum of Art director Thomas Hoving, "Collecting is what it's all about."

The de Menils' knowledge of art and their international enthusiasms and contacts were leading St. Thomas into cultural fields wider than the Basilian fathers saw as companionate with what they wanted for their Texas school. After arriving at an understanding with the St. Thomas directors, Dominique and John turned the school back to its owners, packed up their art library, and began to seek another place for their talents and money.

They did not, however, forget Houston's Fifth Ward and the blacks who lived there, and Dominique and John continued to be seriously concerned about the segregation of Houston's black citizens. The long history of the blacks in art also fascinated them, and in the usual de Menil style they set up funds to underwrite a study and hired a professional director and a staff of scholars in the 1960s to research the concept. The publication which resulted, *The Image of the Black in Western Art*, had been released in three of the proposed four-volume set by 1990.

Traveling among their homes in Houston, New York and Paris, Dominique and John enjoyed the crosscurrents of the international art world. They met artists, famous and aspiring, served on museum boards, viewed art for sale and on exhibition, and talked art with the various members of their Schlumberger family who were also well-known art collectors. In the early 1980s the French government honored the de Menils' collecting talents with a Paris exhibition of six hundred contemporary, Surreal and tribal objects including works the de Menil children had acquired. During the exhibition Dominique received the *Officier de l'Ordre des Arts et des Lettres* for her over thirty years of active support of French artists and especially of the Pompidou Center in Paris.

The art collected by the de Menils was eclectic—primitive objects, medieval pieces, Byzantine relics, the Surrealists, Minimalists and Cubists. John de Menil was especially interested in works by modern American painters. He had a "good eye" and at one time thoughtfully compared the vast, ten-thousand-piece de Menil art collection with the Schlumberger international oil interests by saying that "What is above the ground will some day be worth more than what is below ground."

In 1969 the couple offered financial support and other aids to the private, academically high-ranking Rice University in

Houston. With a tremendous creative output, Dominique and John developed the university's Institute for the Arts program, donated their art library, and built both the Media Center and the "temporary" art museum at University Boulevard and Stockton. With Dominique's experience in bringing together art, artists and collectors, the museum soon became an international exhibition center for the arts. In the Institute's *Newsletter*, 1970/1971, she wrote of the Institute's first year of accomplishments—the exhibition "Ten Centuries that Shaped the West," Greek and Roman art from Texas collections, and the show "The Black Experience" with Larry Rivers and six other artists. The Rice years were fulfilling ones for Dominique and John, but John did not live to realize the next step in their long devotion to the arts. He died on June 1, 1973, and it was for Dominique to continue their dreams.

In 1987 the de Menils' art collection was finally housed in its own structure, designed by Italian architect Renzo Piano who, with Richard Rogers in 1981, had designed an up-to-date research center from the rehabilitation of an outdated Schlumberger factory complex in the outskirts of south Paris and who, with his associates in 1977, had created the Beaubourg (the Pompidou Center) in Paris. Following Dominique's request, Piano and Richard Fitzgerald designed a museum which is "small on the outside, but as big as possible on the inside" to display and house the ten-thousand works of art it possesses.

Piano, from a sun-filled world and who likes indoor plantings, understands Texas' "light intensity and atmospheric conditions," and the skylight roof he developed for the Menil Collection's museum allows "natural light to enter and at the same time diffuse it gently throughout the interior spaces." Dominique and two other donors also commissioned Piano to create a mini-museum for artist Cy Twombly's works which opened in early 1995. In early 1997 the Byzantine Fresco Chapel Museum designed by Francois de Menil to house the restored pair of Cyprus frescoes was completed.

The chapel joins the other buildings on the de Menil-owned, twenty-three-acre site—the Rothko Chapel, the Barnett Newman sculpture and reflecting pool, the Cy Twombly Gallery, and the Menil Collection museum. On Branard across from the Menil Collection are the series of "Dominique Grey" and white 1920s bungalows, referred to by some as "Doville" in a spin-off of Dominique's nickname "Do," which form an "arts" compound of cottages housing the museum shop and some of the Menil Collection's offices. Other cottages are rented to writers, painters, musicians, filmmakers and photographers. Richmond Hall on Loretto provides space for "contemporary and experimental works of installation art and performance," and on the grounds facing Sul Ross and Branard, outdoor sculptures acquired by the de Menils form sharp images against Houston's skies.

Although Dominique and John de Menil did not transform Houston into a Paris-on-Buffalo-Bayou, they succeeded in putting Houston on the international art map and in bringing art collecting and the understanding of the enchanting art mystique to a sometimes reluctant Texas.

At Dominique's death on the last day of the year in 1997, her vibrant personality, her unstinting support of the arts, and her concern for the human condition brought an outpouring of appreciations from the artistic world over which she reigned. Architect Philip Johnson, her longtime associate—both friendly and acerbic—in numerous Houston building projects, said she was "an example of what a rich person can do for society," adding "She is selfless, very pure. She's my best friend and I'm in tears." Artist Robert Rauschenberg, whose landmark retrospective exhibition will open in the Menil Collection in February 1998, recalled that "She treated art as religiously as she lived." Philippe de Montebello, director of New York's Metropolitan Museum who has known Mrs. de Menil since the time he was director of the Museum of Fine Arts in Houston, recalled that her "collecting was literally a life's mission, and all for the public good."

REFERENCES

Auletta, Ken. *The Art of Corporate Success.* New York: G.P. Putman's Sons, 1984.

Barnstone, Howard. *The Architecture of John F. Staub.* Austin: The University of Texas Press, 1979.

Beauchamp, Tomi Ramona. "James Johnson Sweeney and the Museum of Fine Arts, Houston, 1961-1967." M.A. thesis, Department of Fine Arts, University of Texas at Austin, August 1983.

Browning, Dominique. "What I Admire I Must Possess." *Texas Monthly* (April 1983): 140-47, 192-209.

Colacello, Bob. "Remains of the DIA." Photographs, Jonathan Becker. *Vanity Fair* (September 1996): 173-74, 181-82, 186, 191, 198-200, 202, 204.

Cronin, Anne. "Museums: The Sluggers of the Cultural Lineup." *New York Times* (9 August 1995): B, 1-2.

de Menil, Dominique. "Rice Institute opening." *Newsletter*, Rice University Institute for the Arts (Winter 1970/71): 3.

_____. "The Rothko Chapel." *The Rothko Chapel* [Folder-Guide to the Rothko Chapel], Houston, 1991.

_____. Letter to Crystal Sasse Ragsdale, June 28, 1995.

Elliott, Keith. "At the Menil." *Texas Highways* (October 1988): 28-35.

Ennis, Michael. "Mrs. de Menil's Eye" [the Paris exhibition]. *Texas Monthly* (July 1984): 116-21, 172-74.

Ernst, Max. *Inside the Sight*. Houston: Rice University Institute for the Arts, 1973.

Freed, Eleanor. "Dominique de Menil: Rare Vision in the Arts." *The Texas Humanist* (September-October 1984): 42-46.

Gray, Lisa. "Good Bad Walter." *Houston Metropolitan* (October 1993): 42-45, 105-7.

Heagy, Philip. Letters to Crystal Sasse Ragsdale, June 16, July 13, September 7, 1995.

Hodge, Shelby. "Hostess passes hat with elegance." *Houston Chronicle* (7 October 1993): C-5.

Hoffman, Herbert. *Ten Centuries That Shaped the West*. Houston: Rice University Institute of the Arts, 1971.

Hofstadter, Dan. "Annals of the Antiquities Trade: The Angel on Her Shoulder." *New Yorker* (13 July 1992): 36-40, 42-65; (20 July 1992): 38-40, 44-49, 51-65.

Holmes, Ann. "Designs on the future." *Houston Chronicle* (7 October 1993): C-1, 5.

_____. "Humanitarian, patron of the arts de Menil, 89, dies." *Houston Chronicle* (1 January 1998): A-1, 20.

Hoving, Thomas. *Making the Mummies Dance*. New York: Simon & Schuster, 1993.

Johnson, Patricia C. "Why Twombly?" *Zest, Houston Chronicle* (5 February 1995): sec. 1, 8-10, 14-16.

"Larry Rivers and Six Artists Collaborate in *The Black Experience*." *Newsletter*, Rice University Institute for the Arts, (Winter 1970/71): 7.

Lewis, Hilary and John O'Connor. *Philip Johnson, The Architect in His Own Words*. New York: Rizzoli, 1994.

Magritte, René. *secret affinities*. Compiled from taped interviews by Dominique de Menil. Houston: Rice University Institute for the Arts, 1976.

McAuliffe, Mary. "The Erasure of the Canopy, Spatial Definition at the Menil Museum." *CRIT* 19 (Winter 1987): 32-37. Architectural student journal published in Washington, D.C.

McComb, David G. *Houston, A History*. Austin: University of Texas Press, 1981.

"Menil Exhibitions/Publications," [1955-1994]. Houston: Menil Collection, 1995.

Moorhead, Gerald. "Scenes From A Mall, Philip Johnson's University of St. Thomas Chapel." *CITE, The Architecture and Design Review of Houston* (Fall 1991): 8-9.

"Mumia Abu-Jamal Must have a New Trial." *New York Times* (9 August 1995): A-13. [full page ad with over a hundred signatures, including Dominique de Menil's.]

"Rites for de Menil, noted art patron, scheduled Tuesday." *Houston Post* (2 June 1973): A-18.

Russell, John. "Dominique de Menil, 89, Dies: Collector and Philanthropist." *New York Times* Obituaries (1 January 1998): B-8.

Schlumberger, Anne Gruner. *The Schlumberger Adventure*. New York: Arco Publishing, Inc., 1982.

Stiteler, Rowland and Don Robertson. "The Fifth Ward's Favorite Son." *Houston City Magazine* (June 1983): 47-50.

Tompkins, Calvin. "Profiles, A Touch For the Now." [Walter Hopps] *New Yorker* (29 July 1991): 33-38, 40, 42, 44-57.

_____. "The Piano Principle." *New Yorker* (22 & 29 August 1994): 52-53, 60-63.

Westbrook, Bruce. "Dominique de Menil, Her Legacy." *Houston Chronicle* (1 January 1998): D-1,7.

INTERVIEWS

Nancy Boothe and Crystal Sasse Ragsdale, Houston, telephone interview, 13 October 1995.

Phillip Heagy and Crystal Sasse Ragsdale, telephone interview, 18 September 1995.

Jeannine Henri and Crystal Sasse Ragsdale, Austin, telephone interview, 26 October 1995.

Rev. William J. Young, Congregation of St. Basil, Houston, and Crystal Sasse Ragsdale, telephone interview, 19 October 1995.

Mary Martin
1913-1990

Singing From the Heart

On November 9, 1938, theatre lovers in New York flocked to the Imperial Theatre for the opening of Cole Porter's new musical comedy *Leave It to Me*. The cast included such theatrical luminaries as Sophie Tucker, William Gaxton, and Victor Moore. The hit of the show, however, proved to be a young aspiring actress and singer from Weatherford, Texas, Mary Martin, who sang "My Heart Belongs to Daddy" sitting on a steamer trunk, clad in a fur coat and "undies" while doing a very mild striptease to the music. One of the Eskimos singing with Martin was a dancer, Gene Kelly, later to make his own mark on Broadway musicals.

Martin's wholesome manner and ingenue voice contrasted with Porter's racy lyrics to create a musical sensation that would launch her career on the Broadway stage. *The Daily Worker* noted that "Mary Martin is a debutante on the stage, where her name is surely destined for lights. . . ," while the *New York Telegram* told readers that Martin "has the freshness and vitality of youth, but she also has poise and the gift of devilish humor. . . ."

Mary Martin's "devilish humor" had been the hallmark of her growing up years in Weatherford and continued throughout her life. Coupled with her lyrical voice, it was to land her the part of a lifetime in 1954; as Peter Pan she brought Sir James M. Barrie's character to life for millions of fans young and old.

The curtain first went up on Mary Virginia Martin's life on

December 1, 1913, in Weatherford when her father raised the bedroom curtain to announce to the neighbors that his second daughter had been born. It was horse-trading day in the small Texas town and Preston Martin, a prosperous lawyer, often joked with his daughter that they had traded a horse for her. It was her mother Juanita Presley Martin, however, who instilled in Mary Virginia her love of music. Juanita taught violin at Weatherford Seminary and began teaching her young daughter to play the violin by age five. Although Mary could bow, she never became an accomplished violinist. What she did develop was a musical ear, and she later wrote of herself, "I sang from morning to night."

People in her hometown were soon aware that Mary Virginia had talent. Her lifelong friend Bessie Mae Sue Ella Yeager recalled that Martin, who often visited in her home and performed with Yeager's family, was extremely talented.

> Everyone in my family played an instrument, and we sang, families would get together and sing. But Mary was always so, so much more outstanding than anyone else. . . .

Mary and Bessie Mae presented recitals with Bessie Mae's playing the violin while Mary sang, danced, and once performed all five roles of a one-act play.

Elocution lessons were followed by voice lessons with the coloratura soprano Helen Fouts Cahoon, who was head of the music department at Texas Christian University. Cahoon convinced Martin not to pursue a classical career and not to push her voice, teaching her the invaluable lesson of controlling her breath. Martin credited Cahoon for saving her voice; years later she would resume voice lessons with her in New York.

Soon Mary Martin was performing regularly for groups and in school plays, learning her craft from the movies. When she was fourteen she met Benjamin Jackson Hagman, the grandson of Swedish immigrants, and began dating him during her senior year in high school. When she was sixteen her parents sent her to Ward-Belmont, a finishing school in Nashville, Tennessee. Although Martin enjoyed being with her friend Bessie Mae and continuing her music classes, she found school dull and missed her mother.

Juanita Martin, responding to pleas from her daughter, drove to Nashville with Ben Hagman and convinced the school to allow Mary to spend several days in town. In turn, Mary and Ben convinced her mother to allow them to marry secretly, and the two were married in Hopkinsville, Kentucky, on November 3, 1930. When the school discovered that Mary Martin was Mrs. Benjamin Hagman, she was allowed to leave school, and, delighted, she returned to Weatherford where the newlywed couple lived with Mary's parents. Larry Martin Hagman was born on September 21, 1931; thus, before she was eighteen, Martin was thrown into both marriage and family. As she wrote later in her autobiography, "I felt that Larry was my little brother, Ben my big brother." Her mother took over Larry's rearing and Mary became a dance teacher, practicing new routines with a dancer in Fort Worth. She also went to Hollywood to take advanced classes at the Fanchon and Marco School of the Theatre and to study with Nico Charisse, who taught modern dance for the school.

In Weatherford, the Mary Hagman School of Dance was such a success that Martin opened another school in Mineral Wells. Soon her dancers, the Martinettes, were performing everywhere and Mary, using the name "Mary Hagman, the Crazy Girl" was singing on the radio from the lobby of the Crazy Crystals Hotel. Further study in Hollywood resulted in her singing "So Red the Rose" at the Fox Theater in San Francisco and at the Paramount Theater in Hollywood. Returning to Weatherford, she opened still a third school in Cisco, and the Martinettes auditioned for Billy Rose's Casa Manana musicals to open in Fort Worth. When Rose hired her dancers but not her, Martin was hurt and bewildered. His words "Tend to the family, the diapers. Stay out of show business" hurt even more.

Stay out Martin could not, and she resolved to succeed in Hollywood even though she realized it would be at the cost of her family. She and Ben decided to divorce, but her father convinced her to wait a year before filing. Leaving her son Larry with her mother, she departed for Hollywood accompanied by her friend Mildred Woods and supported by a monthly check from her father.

From 1936 to 1938 Martin made rounds of auditions at movie studios, but Hollywood turned its back on the aspiring actress until she obtained singing jobs at the Cinegrille, a nightclub at the Hollywood Roosevelt Hotel, and at the Trocadero nightclub, where she originated a swing version of the classical "Il Bacio" which brought her acclaim and a year-long contract with Broadway producer Lawrence Schwab.

When June Knight dropped out of *Leave It To Me* to marry an oilman, Martin landed the job, and her photograph was featured on the cover of *Life* magazine. Martin began singing at a midnight show at the Rainbow Room in Rockefeller Center, but her New York triumphs were marred with sadness over the death of her father shortly after she had visited with him in the Weatherford hospital.

Hollywood finally took notice of Martin, and Paramount pictures signed her to a contract. Her first starring role was in the 1938 costume musical *The Great Victor Herbert* singing "Ah, Sweet Mystery of Life" and "A Kiss in the Dark." More films followed, including two with Bing Crosby. She reprised her hit "My Heart Belongs to Daddy" in *Night and Day*, a film about the life of Cole Porter starring Cary Grant.

The highlight of her Hollywood years was meeting story editor Richard Halliday at a dinner party. After a brief courtship, they decided during a romantic dinner that the most logical thing was to get married. They immediately drove to Las Vegas and stood in line at the registry office. When Richard signed his name "Halliday," Martin was surprised; she thought his name was "Holiday." Halliday presented her with a ring, designed with clasped hands which became the symbol of a love that lasted from their wedding day on May 5, 1940, to her husband's death in March 1973.

The birth of her daughter Mary Heller added impetus for the Hallidays' abandonment of Hollywood for the New York stage. Paramount, mired in the age of glamour girls, never used Martin's talents to their best advantage, and she took a leave from the studio. With Richard Halliday ready to assume the management of his wife's career, as well as the everyday aspects of their lives, including the decoration of their New York apartment and their farmhouse in Norwalk, Connecticut, Martin could devote her time and energy to performing.

Unfortunately, she turned down a lead role in the upcoming production of *Oklahoma* and chose instead to star in *Dancing in the Streets*, which never made it to Broadway. Then the producer Cheryl Crawford chose her to star in *One Touch of Venus* directed by Elia Kazan. Swathed in ethereal gowns by Mainbocher, dancing to music by Kurt Weill and choreography by Agnes De Mille, Martin was a Broadway success. The show ran for 567 performances followed by an extensive tour that ended in late 1945.

Still, Martin admitted that she "never felt like a star," and noted that Halliday

> surrounded me with the pampered, protected life that a star is supposed to have, but he expected me to behave like Mary Martin from Weatherford, Texas. Which is the only way I ever have felt, or ever will.

Bessie Mae Sue Ella Yeager also noted that Martin, throughout her lifetime, never evidenced any of the ego or mannerisms that so often marked a "star."

> .....she was very lucky, in that she never seemed to really lose a sense of who she was. I mean, in a very private sense, she was always Mary Martin from Weatherford, Texas.

Richard Halliday devoted his full time not only to managing Martin's career but in seeking out new plays for her. To keep their family together, their daughter Heller would go on the road with them, studying ballet and often appearing in her mother's shows. When Martin's mother died, her son Larry Hagman came to live with them. Unfortunately, Hagman had been the center of his grandmother's world; he had conflicts with Halliday, felt shut out of his mother's life, and chose to enroll in military school. As Martin later wrote, the "love and comprehension" they later found had to be postponed.

For her next project, Martin starred with Yul Brynner in *Lute Song*, a musical based on an ancient Chinese legend, that was a critical but not a commercial success. Rather than touring with the show, Martin chose to go to England to star in Noel Coward's *Pacific 1860*, a costume musical in which Martin felt she was miscast as Mme. Salvador. She refused to wear an ornate organdy bow on one of her costumes, and Coward labeled her "stubborn and impossible." Although the show ran for nine months in London, the star and the playwright refused to speak to one another.

Martin turned her back on the delicate, feminine roles for which she had become known to star in the national touring company of *Annie Get Your Gun* which had been a Broadway success with Ethel Merman. Martin determined that she would make the part her own and asked that opening night be held in Dallas. The play was a "smash," and Martin was especially proud of her daughter Heller's playing Annie Oakley's little sister. She basked in the Texas-style opening. Friends and relatives attended from Weatherford and all over Texas to watch her being inducted into the Texas Rangers and to see the mayor of Weatherford present her with a pearl-handled revolver—in a brown paper bag.

Annie toured until 1948, and Martin hated to see it close. The album of the show, produced with John Raitt singing the part of Frank Butler, remained one of her favorites. In her regret over the end of the *Annie* tour, Martin never dreamed that her biggest successes were yet to come.

"Apple-pie American" Nellie Forbush from Little Rock, Arkansas, seemed the part Mary Martin from Weatherford was destined to play, and director Josh Logan, who had directed Martin in *Annie*, knew it. Martin was eager to do the musical, based on two of James Michener's short stories in *Tales of the South Pacific*, but fearful of singing against Ezio Pinza's operatic voice. Although Pinza had several of the most successful songs in the show, Martin scored with "Cockeyed Optimist" and "Honey Bun" and brought down the house with her rendition of "I'm Going to Wash that Man Right Out of My Hair."

Clever staging by Logan and Martin had her washing her hair onstage, and the action caught the interest of women theatregoers as well as the press. Story after story focused on Martin's shampoo, her cropped hairstyle, and the glamorous turbans she wore offstage. Martin "charmed audiences with her clowning, and her acting and singing made each of her numbers a show-stopper. . . ." Critics enthusiastically praised Martin's performance; the *New York Sun* reviewer wrote:

> Martin . . . is completely captivating. She is festive
> and delightful in her lighthearted moments and is

entirely believable in her serious ones. She gives the performance of her career.

Martin won a special Tony award in 1948 for her work in the theatre. In 1951 the Hallidays made the decision to have Martin reprise her role as Nellie in London's West End, with Martin's son Larry playing a Seabee. Martin said of him, "He was a natural—like mother, like son." Although the London critics did not care too much for the play with its message of tolerance, the play ran for a year.

Martin's next play was also under the direction of Josh Logan, *Kind Sir*, a light comedy that later became a movie hit as *Indiscreet* starring Cary Grant and Ingrid Bergmen. It was not, however, a total success with either Martin or Hollywood idol Charles Boyer. Martin later noted that the only thing the critics praised were her costumes by Mainbocher, but the critic of the *Brooklyn Eagle* wrote:

> Mary Martin, doing it the hard way, with practically no help from the script, demonstrates that she is a legitimate actress of great charm and winning skill. . . .

The play was marred by Josh Logan's mental illness that kept him hospitalized off and on for a number of years. Martin realized that she missed the music, the songs, and the dance that musical theater offered. She had a chance to sing again on a television special sponsored by the Ford Motor Company in 1953; she and Ethel Merman's duet sitting on rehearsal stools proved to be the hit of the show, with Martin also contributing a comic sketch.

Then came the performance that Martin called "the most important thing, to me, that I have ever done in the theater. . . . I cannot remember a day when I didn't want to be Peter [Pan]." One of her closest Hollywood friends, the comedienne Jean Arthur, had played Peter on Broadway in 1950, and Martin had seen both a silent film version of the Barrie masterpiece in 1924 and Mary Morris in a London production. When Edwin Lester, director of the Los Angeles and San Francisco Civic Light Opera Company, suggested a musical version of the play, the Hallidays were enthusiastic. Cyril Ritchard as Captain Hook and choreography by Jerome Robbins assured that the musical would be a success, but rehearsals required endless hours learning to "fly" with wires, ropes, and pulleys under the direction of Peter Foy. She was determined to "fly all over the place," and Robbins choreographed a "flying ballet" with Peter and the children, Wendy, Michael, and John.

With Foy and his assistants' holding the control ropes, Martin did, indeed, "fly all over the place" and commented later ". . . I loved it so. The freedom of spirit—the thing Peter always felt—was suddenly there for me. . . ." It was there also for the children in her audiences, whether on the West Coast, on Broadway in 1954 where her daughter Heller played Liza, and during the television production. Children everywhere caught Martin's magic, especially during the musical production number "I've Got to Crow"; for years after, when Martin met children she had to join them in crowing. The critic of the *Christian Science Monitor* commented:

> In Miss Martin's sturdy, graceful, ebullient, unsentimental Peter Pan there is so firm a grasp on the spirit of youth that one recklessly follows Peter into Neverland.

In 1955 Martin played Sabrina, a part originally created for Tallulah Bankhead, in Thornton Wilder's *The Skin of Our Teeth* as part of the State's Department cultural exchange program. The play, which also starred Helen Hayes and George Abbot, was a family affair for the Hallidays; Heller played Gladys, the Antrobuses' daughter, and Larry played a small part in the production in Paris. Martin was not satisfied with her performance, but her Broadway performances received excellent reviews. The *New York World-Telegram* commented, "Mary Martin, as the excess (and provocative) baggage, Sabrina, has the time of her life, prancing about in red spangles. . . ."

During the production of *Skin of Our Teeth*, the Hallidays bought property in Brazil and began building a farmhouse that they named *Nossa Fazenda*, "our farm." The land was a working farm, and the Hallidays spent as much time as they could in Brazil. Halliday supervised crop planting and Martin opened her own boutique where she sold her needlework and other handicrafts. Over the years they spent many happy days there, where Halliday banned all telephones and Martin rested between shows.

While waiting for her next project, Martin went on tour with a dancer and a guitarist from 1958 to 1959 in "Music with Mary Martin/ Magic with Mary Martin," bringing her special brand of magic to audiences across the nation to "deafening applause," as reported in the *Houston Chronicle*. The deafening applause deepened when Martin opened in *The Sound of Music* in November 1959. The play, based on the autobiography of Baroness Maria von Trapp and with a cast focusing on children, was an instant success and the *New York Telegram* commented, "This is a role Miss Martin warms, lights up, and embraces. . . ."

With her husband's co-producing the musical with Leland Hayward, Martin worked with the original Maria, the Baroness von Trapp living in Vermont. The baroness taught her to play the guitar, and Martin taught the baroness how to yodel. After a time together, the baroness said to her, "Mary, you were born in Texas and I was born in Austria, but underneath we are the same Maria." She also worked with Sister Gregory to learn the ways of the convent, and the nun became a lifelong friend of the Hallidays. During the two years that *The Sound of Music* ran, Martin missed only one performance, another mark of her professionalism that endeared her to performers and producers alike.

After *The Sound of Music*, producer David Merrick offered her the part of Dolly Levi in *Hello Dolly!*, replacing Carol Channing for a tour that took her across the United States and to Canada, Japan, Korea, and Vietnam. While entertaining the service personnel, for security purposes her shows were never announced until an hour in advance, and Martin often played in aircraft hangers in heat up to 120 degrees, melting her makeup as she sang. She then opened the play in London's West End where, on her opening night, Londoners brought her back onstage for twenty-five curtain calls.

Martin said of her next musical play, *I Do! I Do!* that it was "like fate. It was meant to be in my life." Written and composed by fellow Texans Tom Jones and Harvey Schmidt and based on *The Fourposter* by Jan de Hartog, the play featured two people who told the story of their enduring marriage in music and song. Teamed with Robert Preston, Martin played in over five hundred performances, riding tricycles around the stage, performing an outrageous "Flaming Agnes" and a knee-slapping "When the Kids Get Married." She had fifteen costume changes, including five wigs, and was onstage through almost all the performance.

Martin and Preston were featured on the cover of *Life* magazine, and the *New York World-Journal Tribune* wrote of her performance, "Mary Martin will be the gift of youthfulness as long as she lives." Unfortunately, the play and a hysterectomy took a toll on her seemingly boundless energy, and *I Do! I Do!* was her last musical play. While on tour with the musical, she and her husband collaborated on a book about needlepoint, a lifelong passion for both of them. When the book was published, a bookstore near her New York apartment featured copies in their window with a handwritten sign, "Neighborhood girl makes good."

Retiring to Brazil, Martin and her husband welcomed many theatrical friends to their *fazenda*, and Martin returned home one day to find her husband on the front steps with a television crew and the TV host Ralph Edwards ready to present *This is Your Life, Mary Martin*. Her sister Jerry and her longtime friend Bessie Mae were part of the show, along with a cast of Brazilian children who sang "Do-Re-Mi" from *The Sound of Music*.

The death of her husband after thirty-three years of marriage devastated Martin, and she fled to her sister's home in Fort Worth. Then she spent a summer on Martha's Vineyard where her daughter Heller was married. She moved to Palm Springs to be near her friend Janet Gaynor, while often visiting with her son Larry Hagman and his family in Malibu.

With Hagman's becoming a movie and television star in productions like *I Dream of Jeannie*, Martin was amused to find she was known in Malibu as "Larry Hagman's mother." She also had time to delight in her grandchildren and lived to see a third Mary—Mary Devon DeMerrit, her granddaughter by Heller—and named another granddaughter, Heidi Hagman. One day Heidi told her grandmother that she had decided to be in theatre, perhaps in musical comedy. "If you're good, I'll let you be in my show," she announced.

Although Martin never starred in another musical, she did not cease performing. She took part in *A Celebration of Richard Rogers*, and in 1972 she was inducted into the Broadway Hall of Fame. She took time in 1976 to write her autobiography, *My*

Heart Belongs, and returned to her home town of Weatherford to unveil a statue to Peter Pan in her honor.

On her seventieth birthday, a benefit for the Boy Scouts of America was held in Los Angeles and Martin led the audience in "I Gotta Crow" from *Peter Pan.* She took part in the first Kennedy Center Honors, "A Celebration of the Performing Arts" in 1980. When England's Queen Mother celebrated her eightieth birthday in 1980, Martin and her son Larry Hagman sang two songs from *South Pacific.*

Even in her seventies, she found time to star in a television series called "Valentine," focusing on romance for senior citizens, which won a Peabody award. She also served as co-host on "Over Easy," a television show dedicated to seniors. Martin went to San Francisco to tape each of the shows, but in September 1981 she and her business manager Ben Washer, and Janet Gaynor and husband Paul Gregory, were driving to a restaurant after the taping, and their taxi was hit broadside by a driver's running a red light.

Washer died, and Gaynor died two years later of her injuries. Martin suffered a fractured pelvic bone but recovered and returned to San Francisco to mount the wires one last time to fly as Peter Pan to benefit the trauma center that had saved her life and which had been renamed to honor her. Her professional life became a series of one-night engagements, a short-lived appearance in a comedy, *Legends,* and a number of benefits.

In 1989 she planned a return to the musical stage as the narrator in *Grover's Corners,* a musical based on Thornton Wilder's *Our Town* by two of her favorite Texans, Tom Jones and Harvey Schmidt. The play was scheduled for production, but she became ill with what later proved to be cancer of the liver and colon. She nevertheless continued to travel, relishing seeing productions of *The Sound of Music* in New Zealand and Germany and celebrating the release of *Peter Pan* on video. Sales reached four million copies within three months.

In late 1990 she entered the hospital for further tests and found the cancer was spreading. She had made a request that her family not be present to see her die, and her son Larry came for a final visit with his mother on October 28. She returned home where Carol Channing came to sit at her bedside and tell her that she loved her; Channing later reported that Martin squeezed her hand, a memorable moment for her.

When Martin died on November 3, 1990, *Entertainment Tonight* featured her with a segment showing her as Peter Pan, flying into the heavens. Friends and colleagues gathered to honor the girl from Weatherford, Texas, at the Majestic Theatre on January 28, 1991. Florence Henderson recited "Mary's Creed," which ended with the hymnal words "I would look up—and laugh—and love—and lift," a fitting benediction for Mary Martin who, from the time she began to sing and act, had always performed from the heart.

REFERENCES

Balch, Jack. "A Theatre Portrait: Mary Martin." *The Theatre* (November 1959): 15.

Boardman, Gerald. *The American Musical Theatre: A Chronicle.* New York: Oxford University Press, 1978.

Browning, N.L. "Curtain Call for Mary Martin." *Saturday Evening Post* (November 1981).

Ewen, David. *Complete Book of the American Musical Theatre.* New York: Henry Holt & Company, 1959.

Gussow, Mel. "Mary Martin, First Lady of Musicals, Dies." *New York Times* (November 5, 1980).

Harmetz, Aljean. "Still the Cockeyed Optimist?" *New York Times* (September 8, 1977).

Hopper, Hedda. "The Mary Martin I Know." *Woman's Home Companion* (January 1956): 21-23.

Kazan, Elia. *Elia Kazan: A Life.* New York: Alfred K. Knopf, 1988.

Laufe, Abe. *Broadway's Greatest Musicals.* New York: Funk & Wagnalls, 1969.

Lerner, Alan Jay. *The Musical Theatre: A Celebration.* New York: McGraw-Hill, 1986.

Logan, Joshua. *Josh: My Up and Down, In and Out Life.* New York: Delacorte Press, 1976.

———. *Movie Stars, Real People & Me.* New York: Delacorte Press, 1978.

Mendelbaum, Ken. "Our Hearts Belong to Mary." *TheatreWeek* (November 19, 1990).

Martin, Mary. "Mary Martin." *Esquire* (March 1962).

———. *My Heart Belongs.* New York: William Morrow and Company, Inc., 1976.

"Mary Martin Sure to Captivate San Antonio." *San Antonio Express-News* (December 21, 1939).

Mast, Gerald. *Can't Help Singin': The American Musical on Stage and Screen.* Woodstock: The Overlook Press, 1987.

Mordden, Ethan. *Broadway Babies.* New York: Oxford University Press, 1983.

Reagan, Nancy. *My Turn.* New York: Random House, 1989.

Reminiscences of Bessie Mae Sue Ella Yeager. No. 72, SMU Oral History Project in the Performing Arts. New York Times Oral History Project. Sanford, N.C.: MCA, 1972.

Richards, David. "All about a Cockeyed Optimist." *New York Times* (November 11, 1990).

Rivadue, Barry. *Mary Martin: A Bio Bibliography.* New York: Greenwood Press, 1991.

Rodgers, Richard. *Musical Stages: An Autobiography.* New York: Random House, 1975.

Rosenfield, John. "Kind Sir Opening Festive." *Dallas Morning News* (September 28, 1953).

Shipman, David. *The Great Movie Stars.* New York: Bonanza Books, 1970.

Wright, Jeanne. "Mary Martin is Still Conjuring Up Magic." *USA Today* (March 22, 1989).

Courtesy Margo Jones Theatre Collection, Fine Arts Division, Dallas Public Library.

Margo Jones
1911-1955

"The Texas Tornado"

On October 17, 1948, staff writer Murray Schumach wrote in the *New York Times Magazine* that "a Texas tornado" had hit Broadway. The "tornado" was Texas-born Margo Jones, who had made her reputation in regional theatre as director of the Houston Community Players and as the innovative director of Dallas's Theatre '47 and Theatre '48.

In 1948 the "Texas tornado" was making her name on Broadway as director of Tennessee Williams's *Summer and Smoke*, the second production of Williams's with which she had been associated on Broadway. Long an admirer of Williams's genius, Jones told Schumach that Williams "hung the moon." Three years earlier as co-director of Williams's *The Glass Menagerie*, which won the New York Drama Critics Award in 1945, Jones had intervened when the producer decided that the play warranted a happy ending. "Tennessee, don't you change that ending. It's perfect," she told the playwright.

It was a long road to Broadway from the tiny East Texas town of Livingston, deep in the piney woods where Margaret Virginia Jones was born on December 12, 1911. The daughter of attorney Richard Harper Jones and Martha Pearl Collins Jones, Margaret Virginia had an affinity for music and played both the violin and piano at an early age. Playing duets with her sister Stella Nell was Margaret's first performing role, until both sisters and one of their three brothers contracted influenza in an epidemic that swept Texas in the 1920s. On New Year's Day of 1925, Stella Nell died of pneumonia, leaving Margaret as the only girl in the family.

Martha Pearl saw that her daughter had elocution lessons and coached her in "recitations." Watching her father in the courtroom inspired Margaret to want to become an attorney, "I used to sit in the courtroom and watch my father make speeches." But the theatre, not law, was to be her profession, although in the courtroom, she wrote later, "I was in the presence of drama, but it took me some time to realize that."

Growing up in a family of individualists, Margaret recited verses, danced, and performed for the family and in school programs. While in high school she participated in debate and declamation activities, doubled up on her school work so that she might graduate with Stella Nell's class, and determined to make a success of her life both for her own sake and for her sister's. Her individualistic streak led her to change her name, at one time considering changing it to Muriel, then signing notes to friends as "Margarette," and finally determining to call herself "Margo."

In 1927, a high-school graduate at the age of fifteen, Margo entered the College of Industrial Arts at Denton to major in speech and education. Although the college had no drama department, she had opportunities to perform in college productions; while other students were aiming for careers as actresses, Margo determined to be a director.

Her college years expanded her theatrical horizons beyond the amateur productions in which she took part. In the college library she read copies of *Theatre Arts* magazine, broadening her knowledge of theatrical movements, playwrights, and plays of both the past and of the present times. The theatrical period of the 1920s and 1930s was one of the richest in America, with Broadway presenting plays by Eugene O'Neill, Maxwell Anderson, Philip Barry, George S. Kaufman, and a host of other playwrights making American theatre history.

Her attendance at her first professional live stage production, by a touring company featuring Walter Hampden in *Cyrano de Bergerac*, opened "new vistas" for the aspiring director, and she attended touring company plays as well as productions of the Dallas Little Theatre. The little theatre or community theatre movement was sweeping American towns and cities, providing amateurs with directing and performing experience and enlivening a growing audience's theatre experience.

More importantly, many regional theatres were becoming showcases of new trends, new techniques, and new plays that could not find a home in traditional theatre.

Inspired by her readings in *Theatre Arts* and in drama theory and criticism, she began reading a play a day, a habit she continued throughout her professional life. She also received encouragement from two theatre "greats." When Dallas playwright John Williams Rogers spoke on campus, Margo took part in an open discussion and told him that she planned to be a director. Rogers sent her a copy of George Bernard Shaw's advice to directors, and Margo made it part of her developing theatre philosophy.

As a publicist for college productions, Margo also called on the *Dallas Morning News's* noted drama critic John Rosenfield, who recognized Margo's dedication and enthusiasm for theatre, helped her learn the angles of promotion, saw that she attended important films and plays, and became her mentor for life. In his prestigious columns, Rosenfield promoted Margo and the movement in Dallas for a regional theatre that would employ professional actors.

With her bachelor's work complete, Margo worked on her master's degree in educational psychology. Her thesis was an ambitious one titled "The Abnormal Ways Out of Emotional Conflict as Reflected in the Dramas of Henrick Ibsen." Focusing on three of Ibsen's strong women characters, Hedda Gabler, Ellida in *Lady of the Sea*, and Irene in *When We Dead Awaken*, Margo plumbed ways of turning ambition, coupled with emotional conflict, into mental health. As Helen Sheehy points out in her book-length study of Margo, it was not only an unusual topic for a college thesis, it was "a personal justification for Margo's own ambition."

Her ambition drove Margo until the end of her professional life. Receiving her master's degree in 1933, she didn't wait even one day to begin her life's work in professional theatre; after the morning's graduation ceremony she applied that afternoon for a job at the newly formed Southwestern School of the Drama where John Williams Rogers was teaching. She found "real inspiration" in all the classes given by theatre professionals, then she was off to attend summer school at the prestigious Pasadena Playhouse.

On the West Coast she was the only woman studying to be

a director under the guiding light of the playhouse director Gilmor Brown, who imbued his students with professionalism in the theatre. Margo received her first directing experience there and went on to direct *Hedda Gabler* and other plays at the Ojai Community Players. A whirlwind around-the-world trip, paid for by a fellow student who took Margo along to edit a book her husband had written on Hindu religion, gave Margo a chance to explore European and Oriental theatre, but to her, seeing New York "was the greatest thrill of all."

One memorable performance for her was the Group Theatre's production of Clifford Odets's *Waiting for Lefty*, in which the audience joined the actors at the end of the performance in the call, "Strike! Strike!" Home again in Texas, Margo determined to make her mark in theatre by participating in the WPA's Federal Theatre Project, sponsored by the Houston Recreation Project and designed to put unemployed actors and theatre technicians to work. Serving as assistant director for the project gave Margo experience working with actors, technicians, and designers. She both acted in and stage managed the production of *Pioneer Texas*, but when the Federal Theatre Project collapsed, Margo was out of a job.

Ever resourceful, she arranged to attend the Moscow Art Festival as a Texas centennial delegate, paying for the trip by covering the events for the *Houston Chronicle*. The trip expanded her knowledge of theatre and theatre people, and she waited in the lobby of a Moscow hotel to introduce herself to New York critic Brooks Atkinson, telling him, "Mr. Atkinson, my name is Margo Jones. You don't know me, but someday you will." Absorbing productions of the plays of Chekhov, Gogol, and Tolstoy, Margo was fascinated by Stanislavsky's Moscow Art Theatre and commented in her articles, "The theatre in Russia is the director." She also wrote that "The Russian theatre added to my belief that the theatre can mean and do much for the culture of the country."

Back in Texas, she took a job with the Houston Recreation Department training playground directors to put on children's plays. The pull of directing, however, remained strong, and she assembled a group of actors and artists to form the Houston Community Players. Her first production was *The Importance of Being Earnest*, for which cast members helped to defray the production costs.

The stylized production with set and costumes in black and white won a favorable review, and Margo staged her next production, *Judgment Day*, in a Houston courtroom. The novelty of the setting gained her newspaper publicity, and the production played to standing-room-only audiences. After her next two productions, *Hedda Gabler* and *Squaring the Circle*, Margo left for a West Coast vacation—and more theatre including Pasadena Playhouse productions and a performance of the Lunts in *Idiot's Delight*. She returned to Houston for a second season of the Players, growing in attendance and attracting fledgling actors such as Ray Walston and Larry Blyden, aspiring writers such as Rice student William Goyen and Cy Howard, and two future theatre directors who followed in Margo's footsteps, Nina Vance, founder of Houston's Alley Theatre, and Joanna Albus, founder of Houston's Playhouse Theatre.

From 1936 to 1942 Margo produced a wide range of plays planned to appeal to her Houston audiences. She produced her first original play, *Special Edition* by Houston newspaperman Harold Young, two original musicals, and one-act plays by Houston writers, mixing them with contemporary dramas and theatre classics. One of her most ambitious productions was *Sunrise in My Pocket*, a romantic, rambling play by Edwin Justus Mayer based on the life of Texas hero Davy Crockett. Although the play never received an anticipated Broadway production, Houston drama critic Hurbert Roussel wrote that Margo's direction of the play was "one of her best achievements."

The Houston years were productive ones for Margo, allowing her both to define her theatre philosophy and to determine to center her activities on a professional, residential theatre. She later wrote, "Being an idealist, I thought my place was in the little-theatre movements which sought exciting experimentation. The broad flexibility of this term attracted me tremendously."

With university professors' marching off to World War II, Margo had an opportunity to teach at the drama department of The University of Texas in Austin and to direct plays for the Austin Little Theatre and operas in conjunction with the music department. Often at odds with department administrators over her intuitive directing style and lack of academic discipline, Margo directed *The Eve of St. Mark*, a patriotic World War II drama by Maxwell Anderson.

While at the university, Margo gathered around her a group of aspiring theatre professionals who would "hitch their stars" to Margo's plans for a regional theatre. Louise Latham, a student in Margo's classes, performed as lead actress in *The Eve of St. Mark*, later appeared in ingenue roles for Margo's Dallas theatre, and went on to a successful career as a character actress in Hollywood. Margo also directed two plays of aspiring playwright Theodore Apstein, who also became a part of the Dallas theatre group and to whom Margo first read *The Purification*, a verse play by another aspiring playwright, Tennessee Williams.

Although she failed to persuade the drama department to produce Williams's plays, she spent a summer session at the Pasadena Playhouse and persuaded Gilmor Brown to allow her to direct *You Touched Me*, a play by Williams and Donald Windham. Margo, described by Williams as a "ball of fire," began heralding Williams as a bright new talent, and worked with him on revising the play. Williams, the first to call her "The Texas Tornado," was working as a Hollywood screenwriter at the time while writing another play, *The Glass Menagerie*.

Margo directed the premiere of *You Touched Me* at the Cleveland Playhouse and later at the Pasadena Playhouse, following it with a production of *The Purification*. While word of Williams's talent circulated through the movie colony, Margo worked to conceptualize her plans for a professional, resident theatre. Sharing her views with mentor John Rosenfield, she found him not only enthusiastic but determined that she should focus on Dallas as the site for her theatre.

Feeling that she needed to travel to research other theatres, with Rosenfield's help she applied for and received a Rockefeller grant and set off on her tour in the summer of 1944, talking with theatre professionals and studying regional theatres across the nation. During her travels she received the completed manuscript of *The Glass Menagerie* and was enthralled. She was torn between wanting to be associated with the production and needing to complete her grant and focus on her Dallas theatre.

She visited with Williams in St. Louis, and both he and his agent Audrey Wood recommended her to Eddie Dowling, who was to direct and star in the initial production of *Menagerie*. When Dowling offered her the position of co-director, Margo was quick to answer Broadway's call and take advantage of the opportunity to direct in the professional theatre. Taking a leave from her Rockefeller grant, she hired Joanna Albus as her production assistant and plunged into rehearsals.

"It's magic—sheer magic!" was the way Margo described the play, and the production made theatre history. Starring Laurette Taylor, Julie Hayden, Dowling, and Anthony Ross, with sets and lighting by Jo Mielziner, the production won critical acclaim. After a slow start, it played to packed houses and eventually made Williams's reputation as a major American playwright, won the Drama Critics Circle Award, was reprised on Broadway a number of times, and became one of the standbys of the regional theatre that so absorbed Margo's thinking.

A telephone call from John Rosenfield, intent on promoting a professional, regional theatre in Dallas with Margo Jones as director, sent Margo and Joanna Albus back to Texas. At a reception at the home of Eugene and Ruth McDermott, Margo "talked her dreams" of a regional theatre. The spirit of what was to become the Dallas Civic Theatre began with Margo, was spurred on by Rosenfield, and spread through Dallas's cultural community.

Persuading Mielziner and Williams to become members of the board of directors, Margo encouraged both to visit Dallas. Mielziner planned the remodeling of the Globe Theatre at Dallas's Fair Park, but the city condemned the building as a fire hazard. Undeterred, Margo drew around her the people she knew would provide the backbone of the theatre staff, Joanna Albus and June Moll, who resigned from The University of Texas drama staff to come to Dallas. Although Margo could not persuade Williams to become the theatre's resident playwright, she did encourage him to write about the planned theatre.

Waiting for a new theatre in Dallas, Margo went back to Broadway to direct *On Whitman Avenue*, which was not a critical success but which continued to run for over one hundred performances. Remaining in touch with fundraising plans for the Dallas theatre, she directed *Joan of Lorraine* starring Ingrid Bergman and written by Maxwell Anderson. With no stage experience, Bergman felt insecure with Margo's intuitive directing style, and Anderson fired Margo two weeks before the play's opening.

Visiting with Tennessee Williams in New Orleans, Margo found him busy on two new plays, *Streetcar Named Desire* and

Summer and Smoke. No doubt she shared with Williams the details of the new man in her life, her company business manager Manning Gurian. A professional business manager was vital to any theatre, and Margo later wrote that, "To have the respect of the town, the theatre must be run in as businesslike a fashion as a department store." Soon the two were sharing their private as well as their professional lives.

Fundraising efforts for the Dallas theatre had paid off, but still there was no building. Board members were frustrated, and Margo decided to begin a summer season of theatre-in-the-round in a renovated building in Fair Park. She had produced a summer season in Houston at the Rice Hotel and knew that Texas audiences would respond to good theatre performed in air-conditioned surroundings. Years of reading paid off when she traveled to New York to audition actors and select plays, and she selected *Farther Off from Heaven*, by the then-unknown playwright William Inge, for Theatre '47's season opener. Included in the five-play program were Margo's standby *Hedda Gabler* and the new play *Summer and Smoke* by Williams, who had waived his royalties for this premiere performance.

Working in repertory took its toll on the actors and production staff, but Margo was thrilled to learn that she had received the Pasadena Playhouse's Gilmor Brown Medal for "outstanding creative and artistic achievement." Opening night, sold out by the end of May, was a success, but ticket sales slumped until *Hedda Gabler* was on the boards. The world premier of *Summer and Smoke* opened with Williams and agent Audrey Wood's coming for a weekend performance. Broadway critic Brooks Atkinson found the play perfectly suited to theatre-in-the-round and told New York readers that "Something of consequence is rising here [Dallas] in addition to the thermometer." Margo was ecstatic when the summer season of Theatre '47 ended its run with a profit of $10,000 which could be applied to the fall's production expenses.

Margo visited with Tennessee Williams at Cape Cod, to finalize plans to take *Summer and Smoke* to Broadway, and met Marlon Brando who had come to try out for the part of Stanley Kowalski in *Streetcar*. When Joanna Albus left the Theatre '47 company to join the production staff of *Streetcar*, June Moll thought that her leaving was a blow to the theatre, that Albus had provided a needed balance to Margo. Moll recalls that

"Joanna Albus was the practical one, the one with her feet on the ground. Margo was the creative one."

Margo left for New York to hire production staff and audition actors for Theatre '47's fall season. Jack Warden was initially hired as production assistant but soon moved up to play such roles as Sir Toby Belch in *Twelfth Night* and Tony Lumpkin in *She Stoops to Conquer* before moving on to a successful movie career. Mary Finney joined the company, and a National Theatre Conference fellowship allowed Margo to add Louise Latham for the fall season.

Margo was dedicated to the repertory method of alternating actors in roles, explaining "We must remember that if we are to have great actors, we will have to create them, and I know of no better way than to give them an opportunity to play eight different roles during one season." She worked to balance her season between large-cast and small-cast plays, believing that "each play must be like a friend to the director; a play, like a person, has an individuality of its own, and this individuality must have a special appeal to the director."

Margo chose plays that would appeal to her Dallas audiences, still focusing on the works of new playwrights but alternating them with Ibsen, Shakespeare, and other classic playwrights plus a blend of contemporary ones. She continued to promote the works of Tennessee Williams during her first Dallas season and presented an evening of his one-acts including *This Property is Condemned*. The season was a success, and John Rosenfield announced that the *Dallas Morning New's* 1947 "Man of the Year" was a woman—Theatre '47's Margo Jones.

Margo and Manning Gurian, continuing to try to combine their personal and professional lives, determined to produce *Summer and Smoke* on Broadway, and by February 1948 they had raised the funds. Margo imported many of the Dallas cast for the Broadway performance, which included Ray Walston in his first notable Broadway performance. Opening on Broadway on October 6, 1948, *Summer and Smoke* played to mixed reviews, suffering from a proscenium stage production rather than the intimacy of the Dallas theatre-in-the-round. Nevertheless, Brooks Atkinson called the play "the most eventful drama on the stage today . . . a work of art."

Margo continued to promote regional theatre and served as the American National Theatre Academy's advocate for decentralizing the American theatre. She advised Nina Vance on her fledgling Alley Theatre in Houston, which used members of Margo's Houston Community Players as its founding company. Theatre '48 and '49 continued to prove that professional actors and skillfully directed productions could flourish far from Broadway.

Margo's belief in the power of Tennessee Williams's plays continued, and in 1949 she and Manning Gurian organized a traveling production of *Summer and Smoke* that played to excellent reviews and made a star of Katherine Balfour, who had played Alma in the Dallas production. While Gurian remained with the touring company, Margo returned to Dallas to get the first production of Theatre '49 on the boards. Jack Warden was leaving for a career in movies and television, and many members of the company were new, including a young drama student with a Texas background, Larry Hagman, son of Weatherford's Mary Martin.

Theatre '50 was a triumph for Margo. She directed *My Granny Van*, her first play with a distinctively Texas locale by a Texas writer, George Sessions Perry, and staged the world premiere of Irish playwright Sean O'Casey's *Cock-a-Doodle Dandy*. The hit of the season, however, was *Southern Exposure* by Owen Crump, a satire of the Old South that played well with Dallas audiences.

With the help of Theodore Apstein, Margo began writing her book *Theatre-in-the-Round*, detailing her philosophy of theatre and her belief that "with willingness and determination and hard work a professional theatre can be opened in every town in the U.S." She also spelled out her beliefs that the play and the playwright were linked, and that for a theatre to be both exciting and successful it would have to produce and develop new plays.

She went on tour to promote the book and found time to serve as inspiration to Zelda Fichandler, one of the founding partners of Washington, D.C.'s Arena Stage, and to introduce Nina Vance to agents. She rejoiced in the publication of old friend William Goyen's first novel, *House of Breath*, but was less than enthusiastic over Joanna Albus's plans to open a professional theatre-in-the-round in Houston. She no doubt desired to remain Texas's one-woman show.

Theatre '51 and '52 saw a new acting company with Ramsey

Burch's coming on to help with directing assignments and Jim Pringle's serving as technical director. Margo continued to alternate the classics her Dallas audiences adored with new plays by new playwrights, including *A Gift for Cathy* by Ronald Alexander who later scored a Broadway hit with *Time Out for Ginger.*

She and John Rosenfield sponsored The Round-Up, a theatre for Dallas's African-American community. Margo had William Saroyan write the play *The Lost Child's Fireflies* for the group and directed it herself. She also directed *Walls Rise Up*, a musical adapted from George Sessions Perry's novel, for which the integrated audience and the opening-night reception were a first for segregated Dallas.

Although Margo's professional career was flourishing, her personal life was in tatters. She had suffered a nervous breakdown in 1951 and been forced to take a rest. Her father's death from cancer and her breakup with Manning Gurian, who continued to center his life in New York and who later married the actress Julie Harris, took their toll on her. For a while she centered her romantic dreams on her longtime friend, novelist William Goyen, but eventually realized that for her life was, and always would be, the theatre.

Jim Pringle, who served as her technical director in the 1950s, recalls that Margo often said that the theatre was "her mother, her father, her lover, her husband, and her child. The theatre always came first; it was her entire life." He also felt that Margo's strength as a director was in her focus on the literary content of the play.

> Everytime we did a show, whether it was a classic or a new script, we were looking for something more than what came through in the script. . . .Her focus was always on the words and the playwright's intent. She was meticulous about interpretation and worked with the actors until she got the interpretation she wanted. . . .

She was approached by members of San Francisco's cultural community to open a residential professional theatre, and she began avid preparations for the project but failed to acquire the needed community support. Jim Pringle recalls that Margo's dream was to have a series of professional acting companies in Dallas, San Francisco, Detroit, Chicago, and St. Louis. Each company would develop a play and then perform in each of the other communities. The Dallas board, however, wanted her to focus her activities solely in Dallas.

Intent on keeping her in Dallas, on November 3, 1954, the Dallas theatre community honored her at a luncheon celebrating the tenth anniversary of her Dallas theatre. Messages were read from theatre professionals, including one by critic Brooks Atkinson who extoled her "dream come true."

With all the accolades, however, one of her strongest productions was still to come. She scheduled several comedies to precede Theatre '55's production of *Inherit the Wind*, by Jerome Lawrence and Robert Lee, which had been turned down by Broadway producers as too controversial. Margo believed the script, focusing on the Scopes trial of the 1920s and bringing fundamentalist religion into conflict with the issue of free speech, had all the makings of a surefire hit. "I think *Inherit* is one of the most exciting scripts I have ever encountered," she told the playwrights, and the production played to enthusiastic audiences and excellent reviews, breaking all production records of the Dallas theatre. John Rosenfield wrote that it was "one of the proudest . . . productions of our unusual theatre. . . ."

The Broadway production of the play, however, proved a disappointment for Margo. While producer Herman Shumlin used her to gain funding for the production, he refused to audition any of the Dallas cast members and legally challenged Margo's right to produce the play in repertory in Dallas while the production was running on Broadway. A Dallas judge refused to grant Shumlin an injunction, and *Inherit* continued to play to enthusiastic Dallas audiences.

To ease the tensions of her life, Margo took up painting, and at an opening-night party on July 11, 1955, she spilled oil paints on her apartment carpet. The managers brought in a professional cleaning service, and Margo sat on the carpet for hours reading scripts. Ill the next morning, she was admitted to the hospital with kidney failure produced by inhaling cleaning solvents. She was put on a dialysis machine but later lapsed into a coma. At the theatre on the evening of July 24, 1955, director Ramsey Burch assembled the cast for production notes and told them, "Margo died at eleven o'clock."

Her theatre company turned out for her funeral, and theatre

professionals including Tennessee Williams wired their expressions of shock and grief. Margo Jones went home to Livingston, deep in the East Texas piney woods, to be buried beside members of her family as praise for her theatre work poured in from around the country.

Across the years numerous theatre professionals paid homage to the woman who had often inspired them or encouraged their careers. One of the most heartwarming was Alley Theatre founder Nina Vance's accolade to her as the most influential person in her early theatrical career. In a taped interview with Orville Perkins, Vance noted:

> I idolized a great lady . . . she was a leader of great quality. . . .Whatever she was doing, I wanted to be part of it. . . .

Her legacy lived on, not only in the theatrical lives she had touched but also in the regional theatre she had helped create. Theatre '55 was renamed the Margo Jones Theatre and continued to operate until 1959 when soaring production costs spelled its finale. A cantata dedicated to her memory by Texas composers was presented by the Dallas Lyric Theatre, and the Eugene McDermotts established the Margo Jones Theatre at Southern Methodist University in her honor. Her alma mater, Texas Woman's University, also founded a Margo Jones Theatre, and playwrights Lawrence and Lee established the Margo Jones Award honoring theatre professionals who presented new works by playwrights in continuation of the tradition begun by Margo. Forty years after her death, Margo Jones's concept of a creative, regional, decentralized theatre is a reality across the United States.

Her greatest legacy, however, remains the tradition of theatre that she helped create in her native state. She had once written that she would like to take a cross-country trip in 1960 and be able to see good theatre everywhere. No doubt 1990s Texas would delight and amaze her, with professional theatre alive and well in Dallas, Houston, and Austin—the three cities where she worked and brought theatre-in-the-round to regional audiences. And no doubt she would have gloried in the fact that the years 1994 and 1995 saw two Texas playwrights, Robert Schenkkan, Jr. and Horton Foote, whom she had encouraged when he was an aspiring dramatist, receive the Pulitzer prize for drama. For "The Texas Tornado" it would have been a dream come true.

REFERENCES

Brown, John Mason. "Seeing Things—in the Round," *Saturday Review of Literature* (April 3, 1948).

Chinoy, Helen Krich and Linda Walsh Jenkins. *Women in American Theatre.* New York: Crown Publishers, 1981.

Clurman, Harold. *The Fervent Years.* New York: Knopf, 1945.

Flanagan, Hallie. *Arena.* New York: Duell, Sloan, and Pearce, 1940.

Freedley, George. "Central Staging," *Theatre Arts* (March, 1949.

Hicks, Ida Belle. "Margo Jones Finds Her Cherished Texas Background Key to a Career." *Fort Worth Star-Telegram* (December 1, 1946).

Holmes, Ann. "Dear Margo: And Now Look at that Dream." *Houston Post* (June 19, 1966): 18.

Jones, Margo. File, The Center for American History, University of Texas at Austin; Margo Jones Collection, Dallas Public Library, Dallas, Texas; File, Texas Room Houston Public Library, Houston, Texas.

_____. *Theatre-in-the-Round.* New York: Rinehart & Company, Inc., 1951.

Larsen, June Bennett. "Margo Jones: A Life in the Theatre." Doctoral dissertation, City University of New York, 1982.

"Lyric Theatre To Present Margo Jones Memorial Cantata At Concert Honoring Late Founder-Director of Theatre." *Dallas Morning News* (December 4, 1955).

"Margo Jones Theatre Closes." *Dallas Times-Herald* (December 6, 1959).

Neville, John. "New SMU Arena Theatre Will Honor Margo Jones." *Dallas Morning News* (January 11, 1969).

Rosenfield, John. "Great Woman Never Knew It." *Dallas Morning News* (July 31, 1955).

_____. "'Man of the Year' Is a Woman: Miss Margo Jones of Theatre '47." *Dallas Morning News* (January 1, 1948).

_____. "Margo Jones: Theatre Pioneer." *New York Times* (July 31, 1955).

Schumach, Murray. "A Texas Tornado Hits Broadway." *New York Times Magazine* (October 17, 1948): 52.

Stanley, Nina Jane. "Nina Vance: founder & artistic director of Houston's Alley; Theatre, 1947-1990." Doctoral dissertation, University of Indiana, 1990.

Stevens, David H., ed. "Theatre '50: A Dream Come True." *Ten Talents in the American Theatre.* Norman: University of Oklahoma Press, 1957.

Westheimer, David. "Margo Jones, theatre in Houston." *Houston Post* (May 9, 1988).

Williams, Dakin. *Tennessee Williams, An Intimate Biography.* New York: Arbor House, 1983.

Windham, Donald., ed. *Tennessee Williams' Letters to Donald Windham 1940-1965.* New York: Holt, Rinehart and Winston, 1977.

Zeigler, Joseph Wesley. "Margo Jones: Legacy and Legend." *Regional Theatre: The Revolutionary Stage.* New York: DaCapo, 1977.

INTERVIEWS

June Moll and Ann Fears Crawford, Austin, 25 May 1995.

Jim Pringle and Ann Fears Crawford, Salado, 26 May 1995.

Lila Cockrell
1922-

From Clubwoman
to Mayor

Texas politicians often revel in the saying, "Texas—where men are men and women·are mayors." The saying, now a part of the lexicon of Texas politics, characterizes the period from the 1970s to the 1990s when a number of Texas cities and towns boasted women as head of their municipal governments.

By 1990, eight percent of Texas cities had elected a woman as mayor. Corpus Christi has the distinction of having had one woman mayor succeed another in office, and El Paso claims the first Hispanic woman mayor in the state. Elective municipal offices, including the mayor's office, have proved strong training grounds for women, and a number of Texas women have used their municipal service to move up to other state elective offices.

In 1975 Texas elected the first woman to serve as mayor of a major metropolitan city in the United States. When Lila Cockrell, who had served in the WAVES in World War II, won the San Antonio mayoral race that year, one reporter commented that she was definitely "no Bella Abzug" and went on to note that "She is round-faced, sweet voiced and looks like she would be right at home in the kitchen or at a church social." The reporter, however, apparently overlooked the fact that Cockrell also had been "right at home" serving as president of the League of Women Voters in both Dallas and in San Antonio and had also been called "the ultimate woman club member." When the San Antonio Good Government League asked her to be part of their slate of city council candidates, her fellow women club members supported her candidacy.

Her election to the city council in 1963, only the third woman to be elected to a council seat in San Antonio's history, gave Cockrell an opportunity to voice her view concerning the duty of council members to serve the entire community. She believed that women would find a woman council member more accessible to their views and feelings. By 1969 she was serving as mayor *pro tem* of the city, but then she retired to private life for three years. In 1973 she was reelected to the city council, winning the largest number of votes of any of the candidates. The city of San Antonio had received numerous block grants, revenue sharing monies, and public works funding, and citizens were looking for new leadership in the mayor's office. Over and over again, Cockrell heard: "Lila, you would sure make a great mayor if only you were a man."

Despite being female, and with backing from the Good Government League, Cockrell ran for mayor in 1975. The race proved to be a hard-fought one. When Mayor Charles Becker bowed out, Cockrell's main opponent was John Monfrey, who charged the city could not afford Cockrell's spending programs. His public statement, "May the best man win," was a red-flag challenge to Cockrell.

Cockrell's agenda included an increased energy supply, providing for a long-range water supply for the city, more extensive public transportation, and revitalization of San Antonio's downtown area. Stressing the need for a stronger and more diversified economic base, Cockrell took her message to the voters but failed to win a majority in the primary election. In the runoff, however, she piled up votes on the city's north side to win the election with a total of 55,439 votes to Monfrey's 47,287.

The road to the mayor's office had been a long one for Lila Cockrell, but one on which she had taken every advantage along the way. Born on January 19, 1922, in Fort Worth, Texas, she was the daughter of Velma and Robert Bruce Banks. When her father died, her mother took her to her family home in Forest Hills, Long Island, but then the family moved back to Fort Worth when Velma Banks married Judge Ovid Winfield Jones. Lila attended Paschall High School in Fort Worth and Ward-Belmont Junior College, then she went on to earn her B.A.

degree in Speech with honors from Southern Methodist University.

One month after graduating from SMU she married Sid Cockrell, a reserve office in the U.S. Navy. Sid was called to active duty after the bombing of Pearl Harbor, and the couple lived together at Fort Sill, Oklahoma, and later at Fort Jackson, South Carolina, until Sid was shipped overseas. Wanting to contribute to the war effort, Lila was commissioned an ensign in the WAVES and attended officer training school at Smith College in Northampton, Massachusetts. There the trainees marched up and down the hills, learning to call cadence, to follow commands, and to identify ships and aircraft. It was all totally new and they had to learn in a "big hurry," for their training period lasted only ninety days.

She was stationed in the Bureau of Ships in Washington until her husband retired from service. Her pregnancy with her daughter Carol was the end of her service career. Serving in the WAVES during World War II was an experience she never could have obtained at any other time, and she was glad to have trained and served and to have taken advantage of the opportunity open to her. She remains justly proud of her award of recognition as the commanding officer of the company judged "best commanded and performed" in the bureau. In her later years, she commented, "I traded in an ensign commission for motherhood—first class, I hope."

Since her high-school years sitting around the family dinner table, Lila had been exposed to political discussions. Her parents and grandparents, active members of the Republican party, were very interested in both government and politics. During high school she was very active in debate and later believed that participating on the debate team was instrumental in helping her research issues, prepare arguments, and develop rebuttals to an opponent's comments. Her high school years also gave her a glimpse of male bias; when all-male members of an oratory group called the Senate refused to allow women to join, she organized the Little Congress with an all-female membership.

Living with her family in Dallas, she was consumed with her duties as wife and mother. Her interest in civic issues remained strong, however, and about four months after her second daughter Cathy was born, Lila was leading a discussion group for the League of Women Voters in her living room, Cathy nestled in a basket by her side. At one time her discussion group included twenty-five young mothers with twenty-five children. Each mother contributed a quarter toward hiring a babysitter for the group.

She served as a board member and as president of the League of Women Voters, and she became active in the United Nations Association. When her husband was appointed executive director of the Bexar County Medical Society and moved the family to San Antonio, Lila thought that she should stay at home and concentrate on her family. Within two years, however, she was serving as president of the San Antonio League of Women Voters and as president of the Horace Mann PTA.

As president of the league from 1959 to 1963, she represented the group before city council, and the Good Government League had an opportunity to see her in action. When they were considering candidates for council, they felt it was time for a woman on the ticket and that Lila Cockrell was just the woman for the job. Her daughters, then in junior and senior-high school were not so sure. "Nobody else's mother had ever run for public office, and they were unsure about how having a mother on city council would affect their lives," Lila recalls. As both girls became older, they also became strong supporters of their mother's political career.

The GGL made the job easier by raising money for their slate of candidates, strong progressives who they thought represented a common-sense approach to government. While there was a great deal of interest in her from both the media and the voters because she was both a woman and a newcomer, Lila was very conscious of her role as the first woman candidate. "If I didn't do a good job," she recalled, "there was always the possibility that the door would slam for other women."

Many people teased her, and newspaper articles commented that the council would have to mind their "p's and q's" if a lady were to serve. But serve she was determined to do. Women were just beginning to get their feet wet in the political arena, and running for council gave her an opportunity to be both role model and mentor. She remembers that when she went to pay her filing fee for her initial race, she wore a hat and gloves. She twice ran for council as Mrs. S.E. Cockrell, Jr., and it was not until her third race that she became "Lila."

Her red, white, and blue campaign hat soon became a conversation piece at ladies' luncheons where she went to solicit votes. When she was elected, she credited her strong showing to women voters and to the push for women in elected office. Her victory was one of the last for the Good Government League, which dissolved in 1976. In each of her subsequent races, she ran as an independent, drawing votes from both Democrats and Republicans.

Stressing increased tourism to the city and a downtown revitalization program, Cockrell went about bringing together her divisive council members to back her programs. Major problems faced the city of San Antonio, including the adoption of a city master plan and efforts to provide protection for the environmentally sensitive Edwards Aquifer, the underground source of the city's water supply.

At the end of her first term, Cockrell was given high marks for promoting San Antonio and won the "master publicist" award from the San Antonio Advertising Federation, but many of her programs remained uncompleted. Cockrell also extended her influence as a woman mayor by serving as the president of the Texas Municipal League and as president of the National League of Cities. In 1977 she became the first woman elected to the board of the U.S. Conference of Mayors.

When Cockrell announced for a second term, John Monfrey challenged her again, announcing that "Taxpayers Can't Afford Lila." Council member Dr. José San Martín also challenged the mayor, but once again Cockrell and Monfrey faced each other in a runoff. Her campaign was designed to project an image of her as an "experienced leader with vision" and one who was "tough, courageous, but compassionate." Her strategy paid off and she won the election, defeating Monfrey in the runoff with 62,447 votes to Monfrey's 43,039. She accepted the challenges of attracting new industries to the Alamo City and of solving the problem of dealing with threatened strikes by city employees. She also learned how to play tough in the political arena. "There are times when you just have to be tough," she recalls, "I try to be tough and ladylike at the same time."

Her second term was a difficult one, with the organization of the city council changing from nine members elected citywide to a council of eleven members, ten of whom were elected from single-member districts. Each new council member came into the political arena with an agenda designed to benefit his or her specific district, and the mayor found that she "had to be tough." She recalls that her toughest job was "turning district concerns into a cohesive plan designed to benefit the city as a whole."

In 1979, aware that council member Henry Cisneros might well make a bid for the mayor's office if she decided not to run, Cockrell announced early that she would seek a third term. She built her campaign around the business partnership she had formed in the city, stressing the fact that construction was up and unemployment down. Citizens liked her leadership style and her ability to pull the Alamo City out of its economic decline. During her campaign, veteran San Antonio political reporter James McCrory described her.

> Behind the brown eyes and her oversized owlish glasses is a mind that is full of facts and figures ready to be recalled when needed—a woman deadly in debate, as befits a person who was a notable debater during her school years. . . .

In this third of her mayoral races, she was opposed by former council member Charles Becker, who criticized her out-of-town trips. Cockrell invited Mayor Tom Moody of Columbus, Ohio, to speak on her behalf during the campaign and to explain how such trips were important to the Alamo City. Speaking at the Henry B. Gonzalez Convention Center, Moody enthused, "I came to thank you for giving Lila to the world." Cockrell won the election handily, gaining 50,363 votes to Becker's 29,045.

Although Anglo domination of city hall was being challenged by a number of Hispanic groups, including COPS, Communities Organized for Public Service, Cockrell continued her role as mediator, striving to bring council members together for the good of the city. In 1980, however, with her husband Sid's recovering from a heart attack and retiring as consultant to the Bexar County Medical Society, Cockrell decided not to seek a fourth term and left the path open for Henry Cisneros to become the first Hispanic mayor of San Antonio in the twentieth century.

After her retirement from office, the media credited her

with winning her major battles, including overseeing the downtown revitalization of San Antonio, increased tourism for the Alamo City, and the settlement made with Coastal States Gas Corporation over a suit concerning natural gas pricing. Her third term as mayor had also brought another electoral change for San Antonio, with the city's moving to single-member districts and the mayor elected by the populace at large.

During the interim in her political career, Cockrell served as executive director of United San Antonio, helping to get increased jobs for the city and to increase its economic growth. With the death of her husband Sid in 1986, however, Cockrell began looking for new challenges and a return to political life, and by September 1988 she was testing the waters for another term in the mayor's office. Strong contenders were incumbent mayor Henry Cisneros and city council member Nelson Wolff. Although both Wolff and Cockrell were seen as likely to continue the agenda set by Cisneros, when Cockrell announced her candidacy the council members signed on to support her, citing her leadership abilities. With no formidable opposition, Cockrell gained 59.6 percent of the vote, outdistancing six other candidates.

Crime in the Alamo City was one of its most serious problems, and providing police protection throughout the greater San Antonio community was one of Cockrell's top priorities during her fourth term. She inaugurated the "Mayor's Forum," a televised talk show, and worked with the president of Mexico to make San Antonio the "business gateway" to Mexico. She invited Mexico's president Salinas to visit San Antonio and was thrilled when Salinas first mentioned the concept of NAFTA, the trade pact that now embraces the U.S., Mexico, and Canada, to a group she led to Mexico City in 1990. "We came back home knowing that we had been privileged to sit in on a little piece of history," she recalls, pointing proudly to the fact that San Antonio leaders took a very strong role in promoting the NAFTA agreement.

Her tenure in office was nevertheless a difficult one, with the Alamo City's facing a $31 million budget deficit plus difficult decision-making over the choice of a new city manager. When Cockrell supported a weak mayor-strong city manager form of government for San Antonio, her critics began to look to other leadership for the mayor's office. In her final campaign, running against strong challenges by Nelson Wolff and council member Maria Barriozobal, Cockrell ran third on the ballot and Wolff won the mayor's office.

Cockrell might well have settled down to a life as a doting grandmother; but as much as she relishes her role as grandmother to Carol's daughter Annalee and Cathy's merged family of three children, life still holds challenges for her. "I've always enjoyed my life, whether in or out of public office," she recalls, and remains flattered when people ask if she would return to elective office. After thirty years in public office, however, she knew the time was right to move on to other challenges and allow younger women to pick up the mantle of elected public office.

She is proud to recall her role as the leader of Texas's most historic city during difficult years of transition. She had a vision for San Antonio, that "it would be recognized as an international center, not merely a Texas town that was growing up rapidly," and she counts among her major accomplishments putting that vision into reality. During her first term as mayor, she initiated activities designed to establish rapport with Texas's sister republic of Mexico. She told the U.S. State Department that she wanted San Antonio to be a welcoming city, and she invited Mexico's President Echaverria to visit San Antonio in 1976 to open a Mexican trade fair.

After a stint as executive director of the United Services Automobile Association, she continues to enjoy an active business life as president of her travel agency, Travel by Design, and as chair of the World Affairs Council bringing speakers on foreign policy issues to San Antonio. She also chaired the 1992 Camino Real Conference, an economic development conference bringing together four southwestern states and Mexico. Sports has always been an interest of hers and her husband's, and she served as a member of the Alamo Sports Foundation and on the first board of the Alamo Bowl, serving as chair of hospitality and doing what she does best—meeting and giving a warm welcome to people who come to San Antonio.

Congressman Henry B. Gonzalez appointed his city's former mayor as chair of a commission to study severely distressed public housing. The commission toured public housing developments, identifying major problems and making constructive suggestions for improvements. When Cockrell gave a copy of the commission's report to Henry Cisneros, she was not yet aware that he was to become Secretary of Housing and Urban Development in the Clinton administration.

Her abiding passion for the arts led her to be founding chair of Arts San Antonio and she remains on the board. She also serves as an honorary board member of the San Antonio Museum Association, as a trustee of the Southwest Research Institute, and on the advisory board for the Texas A&M Engineering Extension Service.

Lila Cockrell looks back to the years as city council member and mayor as years of opportunity for her as well as for other women seeking opportunities in the business and political arenas. She always felt that it was important to have a woman's point of view in politics and that her abilities in interpersonal relations were a great help to both the council and the city. She served as mayor of San Antonio during years of change which were often years of conflict. Throughout these years she always tried to act like a lady, the image she projected from her first to her fourth campaigns. She recalls, however, "When you're mayor, you have to be made of steel."

REFERENCES

Casey, Rick. "Lila exits at height of power." *San Antonio Express* (April 5, 1981).

———. "Lila starts slowly in mayor marathon." *San Antonio Express* (September 30, 1988).

Cobler, Sharon. "Running 'big household' mayor's lifestyle." *Dallas Morning News* (October 10, 1975).

Coggins, Cheryl. "Mayor watched by bodyguards." *San Antonio Express* (October 9, 1977).

Davidson, Vickie. "Cool, calm Lila blazed her own trail to success." *San Antonio Express-News* (April 30, 1977).

Diehl, Kemper. "Cockrell building campaign with slow, methodical care." *San Antonio Light* (November 13, 1988).

Don Politico. "S.A.'s Two Politicians of the Decade." *San Antonio Light* (January 6, 1980).

Eames, Steven M. "Woman Mayor Calming Politics in San Antonio." *Houston Chronicle* (October 10, 1975).

Edwards, Thomas. "Mayor backs crime-fighting tactics." *San Antonio Express-News* (June 4, 1989).

"Ex-WAVE Lila Wary of Female Draft." *San Antonio Light* (January 27, 1980.)

Krelsberg, Luisa. "Women Mayors: They Run Homes and Cities Too." *Family Weekly* (January 29, 1978): 4-5.

Lauder, Patricia and Beverly Bentley. "Cockrell began her political interest early." *San Antonio Express* (November 18, 1980).

Langley, Roger. "Lila calls for city strategy." *San Antonio Express* (February 1, 1976).

"Lila nominated for league post." *San Antonio Express* (December 6, 1977).

Lippman, Laura. "Mayor's race scenarios a blend of past, future." *San Antonio Light* (September 30, 1988).

Martinez, Gebe. "The cards are on her side." *San Antonio Light* (February 5, 1989).

"Mayor Lila Cockrell." *The Broadcaster* (October, 1979).

"Mayor Lila Decides to Lead." *San Antonio Light* (May 23, 1976).

McCrory, James. "Cockrell sails past Monfrey." *San Antonio Express-News* (April 17, 1977).

_____. "Lila defeats Monfrey: Independents win six seats." *San Antonio Express-News* (April 16, 1975).

_____. "Lila keeps mayor's job." *San Antonio Express-News* (April 8, 1979).

_____. "Lila: No political patronage." *San Antonio Express-News* (January 27, 1977).

_____. "Mayor has best win record." *San Antonio Express* (April 5, 1979).

_____. "Runoff: Lila vs. Monfrey." *San Antonio Express-News* (April 3, 1977.)

_____. "Seven runoffs in city races." *San Antonio Express-News* (April 2, 1975).

McKinney, Wilson. "Every hour counts in the life of Mayor Lila." *San Antonio Express-News* (June 15, 1975).

Scalise, Celeste. "Analysis of Campaign Techniques in the Cockrell Campaign." Research paper.

Smith, Cathy. "Lila Cockrell: Reliable, diplomatic, thorough . . . and a lady." *San Antonio Express* (May 7, 1989).

Willis, James R., Jr. "An Overview of the Career of Lila Cockrell." Research paper, senior seminar "Women in Politics." Department of Political Science, University of Texas at San Antonio, Spring 1978.

Wiser, Deborah. "Lila: It could be disastrous." *San Antonio Express* (April 3, 1976).

_____. "Lila Won't Run Again." *San Antonio Light* (December 9, 1980).

_____. "Mayor to Run Again." *San Antonio Light* (December 14, 1978).

Wood Jim. "After 100 days, Cockrell still forging ahead." *San Antonio Express-News* (September 10, 1989).

_____. "Lila making preparations to run again." *San Antonio Express-News* (December 3, 1977).

_____. "Politician of the Year." *San Antonio Express-News* (December 23, 1979).

"Woman Gets SA Mayor Race." *Dallas Morning News* (April 2, 1975).

"Woman Mayor Thrilled." *Dallas Morning News* (April 17, 1975).

INTERVIEWS

Lila Cockrell and Ann Fears Crawford, San Antonio, 29 December 1993.

Celeste Scalise and Ann Fears Crawford, San Antonio, 28 December 1993.

Courtesy Evin Thayer Studies, Inc.

Kathy Whitmire
1946-

Running the City

When certified public accountant Kathy Whitmire was elected controller of the city of Houston in 1978, she became the first woman ever elected to a major political office in Houston. What Whitmire had promised the citizens of the Bayou City was what they received—a businesslike approach to government and eventually a mayor who guided the city for five successful terms through one of the worst recessions in its history.

A native Houstonian, Kathryn Jean Niederhofer was born on August 15, 1946, and grew up poor in northeast Houston with a Germanic, abusive father, Karl Niederhofer, who thought being a secretary was a "good enough job for a girl." Politics was always important to her family, but her father thought that politics was no life for a woman. Her mother Ida concurred, believing that a life in politics was too bruising; she never wanted anyone saying anything negative about "her little girl."

Her mother's explosive temperament and her father's abusiveness led to continual clashes within the home. When Kathy was four years old and her brother Tom was six, they spent much of their time on their grandparents' farm in Walker County. When the two children were not helping with farm chores, their mother had them pouring over the pages of the encyclopedia, determined that her children would have a good education.

Whitmire credits her mother for the fact that both she and her brother were straight-A students.

> She deserves 1,000 percent of the credit. . . .She was
> the one who was making learning exciting for us
> when we were preschoolers. She was going to make
> sure her kids had every opportunity they could. . . .

Ida saw that her children had music and square-dance lessons, and by the time young Kathy was in junior-high school she could play both the piano and French horn and twirl a baton. Ida often talked of her own unhappiness to her daughter, and as early as when she was in the fifth grade Kathy began encouraging her mother to get a divorce. It took another twenty years, and only after daughter Kathy had acquired a lawyer, filed the papers, and bought a duplex for her mother, but Kathy's parents were divorced by 1976.

Whitmire remembers sitting in class in high school studying about presidential elections and dreaming that one day she would like to be married to a political candidate. Her dreams never encompassed the idea that she would run for public office, but the ambitious teenager did set herself goals. Besides excelling in her academic subjects, she was involved in R.O.T.C., the drill team, the choir and band. She was graduated as a Jesse Jones scholar from San Jacinto High School in 1964, then she entered the University of Houston to study accounting and was graduated with honors in business administration in 1968. She earned her master's degree in accountancy in 1970. The university's College of Business Administration awarded her its Distinguished Alumna Award in 1979, and in 1982 the university's alumni organization presented her with its Distinguished Alumnus Award.

Her marriage to fellow student Jim Whitmire in 1967, after only a five-month courtship, began a partnership in business and politics that continued until her husband's death in 1976. Jim's death was a tremendous blow to her; her husband, who called her "Kid" and who was extremely affectionate, had been her biggest supporter. The two were always together after their first meeting in college, and she served as his campaign manager in both of his unsuccessful campaigns for city council in 1973 and 1975. When her husband developed complications from diabetes, Whitmire remained always by his side, helping with his dialysis treatments. After he died, she began the sad task of closing their office and finishing a course he had been teaching at Texas Southern University.

Determined to continue her husband's political ambitions, and inspired by the meeting of the National Women's Political Caucus in Houston, Whitmire entered the race for the city controller's office in the wake of feminist protests against the firing of Harris County Treasurer Nikki Van Hightower. Whitmire signed up volunteers from among the one thousand protesters who had stormed city hall to protest the firings. Gaining the controller's office, however, was only the first hurdle Whitmire had to overcome.

Her blonde petiteness gave many people the idea that Whitmire was a person who could be walked over, but Whitmire took the same businesslike approach to her appearance as she did to running the city. Adopting a rather severe, "dress-for-success" fashion style, including pinstripe suits and floppy bow ties, Whitmire soon exerted a strong stance as city controller, often challenging Mayor Jim McConn over budgetary matters.

Openly criticizing the mayor for not showing copies of proposed city budgets to council members prior to the meetings held for their adoption, she also challenged the mayor for first establishing a hiring freeze and then issuing exceptions without informing the controller's office. She continued her opposition to the mayor into her second term, and by 1981 it was no secret that Whitmire would enter the mayor's race running on a strong plank calling for ethics in government.

Challenging Houstonians to make their city a great one that "serves its people," and asking them to work toward "combining our resources and uniting our spirits," Whitmire inaugurated a series of task forces combining public officials, private citizens, educators, and labor leaders. Her priorities included community development through upgrading deteriorating neighborhoods and cutting administrative costs.

She came under attack for not revealing the names of members of her advisory boards and commissions whom she had appointed before she took office, but Governor Mark White responded to the charges by saying that she did not have to reveal the names because her advisers served on task forces which were not supported by public funds and which functioned outside city government.

With little support from the city's establishment, Whitmire

challenged McConn for the mayor's office, positioning herself both as a liberal on social issues and as a fiscal conservative. She defeated McConn, pushing him to fourth place on the ballot, but faced a runoff with Harris County sheriff Jack Heard who promised Houstonians to restore law and order. With her broad-based support Whitmire beat Heard, gaining 62 percent of the total vote. She won 90 percent of the African-American vote, 60 percent of the Hispanic vote, and split the Anglo vote with her opponent.

She also gained the support of the Houston Gay Political Caucus. Few Houstonians paid attention when an anonymous letter was circulated that she endorsed teaching homosexuality as an alternative lifestyle, but her support would elicit controversy in future campaigns. She was inaugurated Houston's forty-eighth mayor and first woman mayor at 9:30 in the morning on January 2, 1982, with a city council meeting at 11:00 a.m. For the inaugural ball held at the Albert Thomas Convention Hall that evening, Whitmire specified there be no dress code.

Once in office, Mayor Whitmire found herself under fire for not supporting a gay activist to teach a course for police department cadets. City councilman Ben Reyes joined the critics of the mayor's appointment policies when he accused Whitmire of slighting Hispanics when she made top-level administrative appointments. Feminists also took the mayor to task for supporting Anthony Hall over Nikki Van Hightower for an at-large position on city council. Hall won the election and joined the mayor's team, working for her agenda throughout her terms in office.

At the end of her first term, Whitmire was challenged by former supporter Bill White and seven other political unknowns. Standing on her record, Whitmire swept to victory, winning 64 percent of the vote and avoiding a costly runoff, the first Houston mayor in fourteen years to be elected without a runoff. She credited her victory to her businesslike approach to government, to her task-force approach to running the city, to a decrease in Houston's crime rate, and to her appointment as chief of police of Lee Brown, an African American who had served as Atlanta's police commissioner when serial killer Wayne Williams had been arrested and convicted. Brown, intrigued with the idea of being the first African American appointed to the post by an Anglo mayor, accepted the position.

"Someone had to break the ice, and Kathy had enough nerve to do it," he told a reporter for *Texas* magazine in 1996.

Houston's crime and violence were regular features on the nightly news, and Brown set about improving the department's image and sending minority officers as police teams into Houston's diverse neighborhoods. While gaining high marks among law enforcement officials for his innovative, neighborhood approach to law enforcement, Brown was never popular with the men and women he sent out onto the streets, and he eventually left Houston to serve as police chief of New York City and later as drug czar for President Bill Clinton.

Whitmire is quick to focus on the fact that the city's drug problem and the effect that it had on the crime rate was the biggest problem she faced during her terms as mayor. During the first half of her tenure in office, the crime rate continued to drop until crack cocaine arrived on the scene and reversed the trend.

The police unions posed yet another problem for her. She believed strongly in reforming the way the city managed the uniformed personnel, but the police and firefighters were controlled by laws passed by the state legislature. It was against state law to give a police officer a promotion based solely on performance, and she found it was illegal even to give merit raises. The only measure of police effectiveness was a numerical score on an objective test. The state laws of Texas mandated law enforcement personnel, but to Whitmire these restrictions seemed illogical, were out of line with all the principals of effective city management, and provided little incentive for the police to do a good job.

Fighting the police and firefighters unions was the toughest battle she ever fought, and she fought it tenaciously. She spent most of her political capital on her reform efforts, but this was the effort where she accomplished the least. It earned her the ire of the unions, who opposed both her and Brown during her subsequent campaigns.

Despite conflicts in her administration, in a contest to choose Houston's best boss Whitmire placed second to Houston television personality Ron Stone. The qualities that employees liked in Whitmire were her understanding, her abilities as a goal setter, her sensitivity, her organization, her firmness, and her progressive thinking. She had worked hard to improve her image. When fashion guru Mr. Blackwell listed her as one of the year's worst-dressed women in 1983, and *People* magazine noted her resemblance to actor Dustin Hoffman in drag for the movie *Tootsie*, Whitmire abandoned her owlish glasses for contacts, cut and streaked her hair, and began looking more stylish and glamorous at social and political events.

After two terms in office, Whitmire had chalked up an impressive record as Houston's mayor. She believed in appointing strong leaders and letting them do their jobs. Efficiency had always been her watchword, and major construction projects including the George R. Brown Convention Center were completed in record time and within budgets. City services improved, notably in public works and garbage collection. Under Brown's administration, public safety had improved and Houston had the lowest crime rate among the six largest cities in the United States.

Gay rights became an issue in her 1985 campaign for a third term when former Houston mayor Louie Welch attempted to regain the office. At Anthony Hall's urging, Whitmire supported a gay rights referendum which was approved by the city council. Council member John Goodner, with the support of many of the city's clergy, mounted a petition drive to call for a plebiscite to attempt to defeat the referendum.

With support from Welch and his forces, Goodner's drive for a plebiscite was successful and the referendum went down to defeat. Whitmire's credibility suffered, and rumors circulated that she and Hall were involved romantically. Because of her support of the referendum, other rumors circulated that she was gay. The rumors persisted even after her campaign staff leaked the names of the numbers of males whom she was currently dating.

Welch's political campaign focused on restoring Houston's boomtown status and attracting business and residents to the Bayou City. Campaigning on economic development and jobs, on leadership, and on crime, Welch scored political points with his fight against gays. He blundered, however, when he suggested, on a television microphone he did not know was open, that an effective cure for the AIDS epidemic was "to shoot the queers." Houston's gay community printed T-shirts bearing the slogan, "Please Louie, don't shoot," and the former mayor immediately dropped eleven points in the polls.

While 25 percent of the voters thought the AIDS epidemic was a major issue, the majority of Houston voters thought that leadership and the economy were more important. Whitmire defeated Welch with 59 percent of the vote; African Americans again voted overwhelmingly for Whitmire.

In her bid for a fourth term in 1987, Whitmire ran against six political unknowns with largely underfunded campaigns. Voters overlooked the city's still sagging economy and returned the mayor to office with 73 percent of the vote. Her nearest challenger, businessman Bill Anderson, received only 12 percent.

Running for her fifth term in office in 1989, however, Whitmire faced the formidable challenge of former mayor Fred Hofheinz. Aware of Hofheinz's strength, Whitmire hit the campaign trail, citing the fact that she had accomplished many of the programs that Hofheinz had failed to achieve, including improving the police force, passing a regional mobility plan, and improving water pollution. She pointed to her clean up of Buffalo Bayou, accomplished under court order, as one of the high points of her administration.

Whitmire also made the war on drugs a major issue, pointing to her support of the Houston Crackdown on Drugs and her efforts as head of the U.S. Conference of Mayors in gaining federal funding for the city's drug abuse programs. Whitmire once again stood on her record of bringing the city through its economic crisis and in setting its course toward new economic growth.

Calling for an amendment to the city charter to limit the mayor to four consecutive terms, Hofheinz urged voters to turn Whitmire out of office, saying that "the only way to clean up city hall is to defeat her." Whitmore entered the race trailing Hofheinz by ten percentage points in the polls, but Hofheinz's mudslinging negative campaign worked against him. Whitmire outcampaigned the former mayor to win the office with an overwhelming vote of 65 percent, holding her support among Houston's African Americans and splitting the Anglo vote with her opponent.

By 1990 Whitmire was looking forward to an unprecedented sixth term as Houston's mayor. Controversial issues, however, concerning her ousting of Metropolitan Transit Authority Chairman Bob Lanier whom she had appointed to the post, and her continued support of a controversial rail issue, hindered Whitmire's reelection bid. A number of city politicians called for a referendum to allow the voters to vote on the rail issue, but Whitmire continued to support the proposed MTA system that would have cost citizens one billion dollars.

Bob Lanier decided to challenge Whitmire for the mayor's office. Whitmore, knowing that he would use the MTA system as a political issue in the upcoming campaign, continued to lobby to block a rail referendum at the state level. She earned the ire of State Representative Sylvester Turner and Senator Don Henderson, both of whom supported a referendum and presented separate bills to that effect before the state legislature. Turner made the decision to file against her in a race marked by bitter campaigning on all sides.

She hired a California political consulting firm to focus her image, but Whitmire's opponents portrayed her not as the reformer she had been when first elected, but as a "go-along, get-along" leader who looked the other way when sweetheart deals were being made at City Hall. One longtime political observer noted that Whitmire had become one of those political figures who "forgot who brung 'em," neglecting people who had supported her when she first ran for office. She never fully realized that compromise has always been the keyword in politics, and she never responded to the give-and-take of politics. Texas writer Molly Ivins summed up the good and the bad aspects of her political style.

> . . . she is the compleat technocrat, the perfect yuppie politician, a manager to the bone. But there is courage, determination and discipline there as well. . . .

Her longtime feud with the police union and the firefighters added fuel to the race when, with Houston in the grip of a crime wave, the police wreaked havoc on her political campaign by branding her an impediment to public safety. Soon polls showed that the voters found the once highly dedicated mayor both distant and out of touch with the city she had guided successfully since 1981.

Many voters found Whitmire too much of technician at a time when the city, still suffering from the economic downfall of the oil industry, was more in a need of a cheerleader at the head of its government. There was little doubt that the voters no longer viewed the mayor as the reform candidate but as a symbol of retrenchment and the status quo. Many of her long-time supporters deserted the mayor, and Turner siphoned off many of her liberal supporters. Whitmire won only 20 percent of the vote and failed to gain a place in the runoff. Lanier went on to capture the mayor's office in the runoff election against Turner, and Whitmire commented that, "Losing is no fun. I've run for office eight times, and I've only lost once. I think that's a pretty good batting average." Term limits was an important issue to many Houston voters, and Whitmire credits her loss to a desire for change and the "term limits mood."

When speaking to groups of women who plan to run for elective office, Whitmore stresses the fact that to be a winner, you have to want to win an election more than anything else in the world. She counsels that if they're not ready to put winning at the top of their list and give it all their energy and all their time, they shouldn't even file. "That's what it takes to win elective office."

She considers her most important contribution while in the mayor's office as "pulling the city together and getting it going in a new direction" when the economy hit rock bottom. During her first bid for the mayor's office, she had run on issues that had little to do with economic development; after the recession hit, the top priority became turning the Houston economy around.

> Let's face it. We lost 230,000 jobs in Houston during the 1980s, and we hit bottom in 1987. We've shown moderate growth ever since. These economic accomplishments have to be those that stand out.

Using her coalition and team approach to solving problems while she was mayor, the city had put together a public sector/private sector working group called the Greater Houston Partnership to promote the city. Even after Whitmire left office, the group continued to work to upgrade Houston's image and to promote economic progress throughout the city.

Like many mayors, Whitmire points with the pride to the brick-and-mortar accomplishments of her terms as mayor. The George Brown Convention Center, which has made it possible

for the Bayou City to host larger conventions, and the Performing Arts Center, which links Houston's downtown theatres,
music hall, and restaurants in a revitalized civic area, are major
renovations adding to Houston's economic progress. Whitmire
also cites the improvements along Buffalo Bayou as major
accomplishments.

The former mayor continued her political involvement as
director of the Rice University Institute for Policy Analysis and
through teaching courses in political science and business at the
Houston university. She also served as a political commentator
for Houston television stations, focusing particularly on campaigns and campaign strategy, and many journalists and political watchers speculated that she would reenter the field of
elective politics.

She continued to be involved with the "cause" oriented
groups, many of these carrying over from her days as mayor
and several dealing with the reform of law enforcement. During
her last term as mayor, the Police Foundation asked her to join
their board of directors, and she also served as treasurer of
Scenic America, a national coalition with the goal of improving
the visual environment. Boston University contacted her to
chair a national policy panel to develop proposals to finance
drug treatment programs, and the policy panel for Join Together published a report on how communities could finance
substance abuse services.

Women's issues remain her "gut-level" interest, and she
also remains active with the American Institute of Certified
Public Accountants. Although Whitmire ceased practicing accounting actively when she entered the public arena, the majority of incoming CPA's are now women, and the group has
created an executive committee on women and family issues.

When a new opportunity in the business world beckoned,
Whitmire accepted the presidency of Junior Achievement, Inc.,
although it required a move to Colorado and away from Houston where she had spent all of her personal and professional
life. Heading the fastest-growing, nonprofit education organization in the world was more than Whitmire could resist, and
she left Houston in August 1994. When Harvard beckoned,
however, she left Junior Achievement to teach a course in
women and politics and to become a fellow at the Institute of
Politics at Harvard University's Kennedy School of Govern-

ment. In July 1996 she joined the faculty of the University of Maryland to establish a policy institute.

Although she had left her mayor's office, she remained vocal about her opposition to Mayor Bob Lanier's administration, feeling that he had undone many of the reforms of her administrations through neglect. She remains a firm advocate of public transportation, and feels it is a priority necessity for Houston. "We dream of great cities, and what they are all about is people," she recalls.

> What's special about Houston is the people. But to make a city great, public transportation is essential. Although we made major improvements in our public transportation system, we never got to the point that I wanted us to.

In March 1996, when Whitmire was nominated to become president of the American Public Transit Association, a lobbying group composed of municipal transportation entities, rumors circulated throughout Houston that Mayor Lanier opposed her nomination. Lanier denied any intervention in the process, but other transit officials noted her association with the head of the nominating committee, Alan F. Kiepper, chief of Houston Metro. When the vote of the association was taken, Whitmire fell short of the required two-thirds majority. Although the nominating committee had endorsed her overwhelmingly, she lost in the overall voting when eight major transit agencies, including Houston Metro, threatened to resign from the group if she were chosen. One executive charged "partisan politics," noting that the "nay" votes came from Republican transit agencies who did not want a Democrat in office.

Whitmire told the media that she thought the chairman of the nominating committee would have liked her to withdraw when controversy loomed, but the woman who had been involved in controversy ever since she first ran for the Houston controller's office stated, "I've never been known as a quitter." The next week she was back at Harvard teaching her course in "Women in Government."

Even though her teaching career and speaking duties have taken her from the Texas scene, Whitmire's Texas roots remain important to her. She does not rule out a return to the Lone Star State—or another run for elective office. Statewide office continues to beckon, and she won't rule out seeking the state comptroller's office. Her legacy as Houston's five-term woman mayor remains a strong one, and in summing up that legacy, one political analyst commented: "She brought the city into the 21st century in public administration."

REFERENCES

Barret, Karen. "A New Breed of Woman Mayor: The Realpolitik of Kathy Whitmire." *Ms.* magazine (August 1982): 24-30.

Bernstein, Alan. "Leading and following in the unique Whitmire style." *Houston Chronicle* (February 17, 1991): D-2.

Boatright, Joyce. "Whitmire on politics versus the glass ceiling." *Houston Woman* (January 1989): 8-28.

Bonavita, Fred. "Whitmire lead down as race nears the vote." *Austin American Statesman* (October 24, 1989): A-2.

Brewton, Pete. "Whitmire ready to fight for civil service changes." *Houston Chronicle* (June 24, 1982): B-1.

Budd, Millie. "Kathy Whitmire: Introducing Madame Mayor." *Houston Business Journal* (January 4, 1982): Section 2.

Canetti, Barbara. "Closet Politics: What the gay rights referendum meant." *Houston City* magazine (March 1985): 22-92.

_____. "Welch vs. Whitmire: Politics or Personalities." *Houston City* magazine (October 1985) 52-118.

Carreau, Mark and Tom Kennedy. "Whitmire Readying Her List." *Houston Post* (July 18,1982): A-1.

Chadwick, Susan. "The Kathy Ratings." *Texas Monthly* (October 1985): 158-254.

_____. "Whitmire vs. Whitmire." *Houston City* magazine (October 1983): 51-53.

Curtis, Tom. "A Woman's Place . . . is in City Hall." *Houston City* magazine (November 1978): 6.

Elkind, Peter. "Mayor, Council Locked in Bitter Struggle." *Texas Monthly* (February 1985): 118-69.

Ely, Jane. "He ran so poorly, she ran so well." *Houston Chronicle* (November 11, 1989): A-3.

_____. "Whitmire will run for mayor." *Houston Post* (March 16, 1981): A-1.

Feldstein, Dan. "Whitmire loses bid to be named president of transit association." *Houston Chronicle* (March 11, 1996): A-1.

Flynn, George. "City controller—controversial or calm?" *Houston Post* (March 26, 1978): D-3.

Fraser, Babette. "Whither Whitmire?" *Houston City* magazine (November 1978): 47-124.

Fulenwider, Barbara. "Whitmire talks about women and politics." *Matrix* (April 1981): 1.

"Getting Down to Business." *Texas Monthly* (January 1982): 69-71.

Gilbert, Julie. "She's not just playing politics." *Houston Post* (December 3, 1985): C-1.

Gilchrist, Gail. "Kathy's Closet." *Houston Post* (November 11, 1989): D-1, D-5.

Grandolfo, Jane. "Citizen Whitmire." *Houston Metropolitan* (February 1993): 31-87.

Hart, Joe. "Mayor Whitmire in eye of political storm." *Houston Business Journal* (March 18, 1985): 15-17.

"Houston at the crossroads." *The Economist* (October 26, 1985): 30-31.

"Houston mayor rides out storms in bid for second term." *Austin American Statesman* (November 6, 1983): H-2.

"Houston: Wind of no change?" *The Economist* (October 8, 1983): 22.

Ivins, Molly. "Women in the News: Kathy Whitmire." *Working Woman* (March 1987): 120-24.

Kennedy, Tom. "First 100 days." *Houston Post* (April 14, 1982): A-1.

_____. "Police, Fire Fighters Plan Drive to Defeat Civil Service Changes." *Houston Post* (June 8, 1982): A-14.

_____. "10 items on a very private mayor." *Houston Post* (January 2, 1984): C-26.

Kirtzman, Andrew. "Whitmire wins a 5th term." *Houston Post* (November 8, 1989): A-1.

McNeely, Dave and Dinah Wisenberg. "Her Honor." *Ultra* (April 1982): 62-64.

Nocera, Joseph. "Fantasy Island." *Texas Monthly* (November 1983): 167-261.

Palomo, Juan R. "Whitmire, Others Testify on Civil Service Law Reform." *Houston Post* (May 27, 1982): A-26.

Pugh, Clifford. "Lee Brown." *Texas* magazine. Houston: *Houston Chronicle* (April 28, 1996): 6-18.

Recer, Paul. "Kathy Whitmire resumes reshaping of Houston." *Dallas Morning News* (January 8, 1984): A-1.

Reinert, Al. "The Three Kingdoms of Kathy Whitmire." *Texas Monthly* (November 1991): 159-82.

Roberts, Wade. "In Houston, it's 'Her Honor': How She Did It." *Texas Observer* (December 4, 1981): 1-12.

Simmon, Jim. "Voters stay with Whitmire." *Houston Post* (November 9, 1983): A-1.

_____. "Whitmire coasts back into office." *Houston Post* (November 6, 1985): A-1.

Snyder, Mike. "Whitmire vows a more responsive City Hall." *Houston Chronicle* (January 3, 1982): A-1.

Swartz, Mimi, Ann Powell, and Eloise Tusa. "Houston's 20 Most Powerful Women." *Houston City* magazine (September 1982): 31-37.

Taylor, Gary. "Lalor vs. Whitmire." *Houston Digest* (March 12, 1984).

Trounson, Rebecca. "Intense, enigmatic describe Whitmire." *Houston Chronicle* (October 8, 1989): A-1, 18.

Watson, Burke. "Anti-Whitmire campaign heats up." *Houston Chronicle* (April 26, 1985): B-1.

Whitmire, Kathy. Biographical File. The Center for American History, University of Texas at Austin.

_____. Clipping file. Texas Room, Houston Public Library, Houston, Texas.

_____. "Inaugural Address (January 2, 1982)."

_____. "The State of the City." Address delivered to the Houston Chamber of Commerce (January 21, 1982.)

"Whitmire loses office after 10-year tenure." *Daily Texan* (November 8, 1992): 2.

"Whitmire will seek unprecedented sixth term." *Austin American Statesman* (August 16, 1991): A-2.

Wittenberg, Pete. "Whitmire to head national group." *Houston Post* (July 27, 1994): A-1.

INTERVIEW

Kathy Whitmire and Ann Fears Crawford, Houston, December 15, 1993.

Cyndi
Taylor Krier
1950-

From Statehouse
to Courthouse

To some veteran Texas politicians, Judge Cyndi Taylor Krier's career in Texas politics headed the wrong way. She has moved in a nontraditional route from working at the national level in Washington, D.C., to the state level as a Texas senator, then to the local level as a Bexar County judge. To Krier, however, her career changes make sense. She sincerely believes that the government closest to the people governs best, and she wants to be involved where government can and will make a difference.

The woman who has always been "determined to make a difference," was born on July 12, 1950, in Beeville, Texas, the daughter of Robert Stevens Taylor and his wife, Mary McGuffin Taylor. When Cyndi was eight years old, her parents divorced and her mother moved to DeNero, Texas, to give her daughter the care and support of a grandmother. Cyndi grew up in a home that housed three Texas women, and she recalls the strength of both her mother and her grandmother, Emma McGuffin. Her grandfather had been the first postmaster in DeNero, and when he died his wife took over as postmistress. Her mother made the twenty-four-mile drive every weekday to work with the postal service in Beeville, but when Emma McGuffin died, Mary Taylor moved with her daughter back to Beeville.

Mary Taylor was a very strong single parent, and Krier feels that "everything I am is because of my mother." She stressed the values of reading and education to her daughter, and she also talked about issues that were important. As a federal employee, Taylor was barred from participating in politics, but she spent a good deal of time talking about political issues around the dinner table. A woman relative of her father's had also succeeded her husband in office, as a county commissioner in Bee County. "It never occurred to me," Krier states, "that women could not serve in elective office."

An honor student at George West High School, Cyndi was involved in many extracurricular activities, played basketball, and learned how to excel and how to make the most of team-work—valuable skills that have paid off for her in her political life. Her English teacher sponsored the Young Republican Club and took the group to San Antonio to hear Barry Goldwater speak, and Cyndi had her first taste of Republican politics. Although her father's family had been Democrats, she knew she was destined to be a conservative.

At Trinity University in San Antonio she worked on Richard Nixon's campaigns, and when she transferred to The University of Texas at Austin to major in journalism, she continued her campaign work for Republican candidates. As a reporter for the *Daily Texan*, the student newspaper, her first assignment was to interview Student Body President Joe Krier concerning the university's cutting down trees along Austin's Waller Creek, a move that raised the ire of environmentalists. During the interview it was raining, the bulldozers were moving, and Taylor's notes washed right off the page. As a member of the university's house of delegates representing Jester Dormitory, Taylor told Joe Krier she didn't want him to appoint her to committees just because she was a woman, so he didn't. She admits that the man who was to become her husband was not as liberated as he is today.

Graduating from UT in 1971 with a bachelor's degree in journalism and one of the highest grade-point averages in the department's history, she went to work for the Republican Party of Texas. She edited a statewide newsletter and spent longer than she could stand answering the telephone with "Go party of Texas." Then she enrolled in law school.

While working for the Republican Party, she had met Beryl Milburn, vice chair of the party at that time and one of the state's most active and prominent Republicans, who was appointed in 1973 to serve as vice-chair of the Texas Constitutional Revision

Commission. Although still in law school, Taylor served as Milburn's assistant, gaining valuable political experience and learning the ways of state government. In 1974, between her second and third years in law school, she applied for and was accepted as a White House intern at the height of the Watergate scandal. All the interns were kept busy answering the many inquiries that poured into the White House concerning President Nixon and Watergate.

During the summer Taylor was assigned to work with Anne Armstrong, then special counselor to the president in charge of youth, women, Hispanics, and the National Park Service. Taylor would arrive at the office very early to prepare the week's political analysis, which Armstrong would then report on in Cabinet meetings. The week that Nixon resigned, Armstrong's office submitted a report, *Hispanics Under the Nixon Administration*, that Taylor had helped prepare. The document had a one-week lifespan, for soon there was no Nixon administration.

On August 8, Vice President Gerald Ford met with the interns before he met with President Nixon. Knowing that the president's resignation was imminent, the vice president was very reassuring to the interns. His message to them was that, no matter what happened as the result of Watergate, they should stay involved and not turn away from politics.

After the president's resignation, Taylor stood in the East Room while Nixon said goodbye to his staff. "It was a real testing experience as to whether or not I would stay in politics," but Ford's words served as a reminder of how important political involvement was. She resolved to stay. "Anne Armstrong will always be my political ideal," she recalls, and she counts both Beryl Milburn and Armstrong as strong political mentors in her life. Writing speeches for Anne Armstrong provided her with experience for her own speechmaking in the Texas Senate and as Bexar County judge.

Taylor came home to Texas to finish law school then, after graduating in 1975, returned to Washington hoping to get a job in the political arena. Her longtime friend Douglas Harlan, a power politician in the Texas Republican party, suggested that she call on Senator John Tower's office as a courtesy, and she landed a job as Tower's administrative assistant. Her primary duties included dealing with Texas voters and jobs, plus walking Texans through senate confirmation hearings. She also worked on legislation, principally with the Federal Election Commission and judiciary matters.

She worked for Tower's office throughout 1975 and 1976 then returned to Texas to work for President Ford's campaign in Texas. Back in Washington to work for the Republican National Committee dealing with rules and committees for the group's national convention, her greatest thrill was being able to sit in the presidential box while President Ford delivered his acceptance speech.

Senator Tower asked her to come to Houston to supervise his 1978 election campaign, moving her to San Antonio once his state office was established. Tower's win over Democrat Bob Krueger was a close one, and Taylor was involved in the recount that sent Tower back to the U.S. Senate. While working with the campaign, Taylor lived with newspaper columnist Jan Jarboe, who was dating Joe Krier's best friend, and Taylor and Krier began dating. It was an unlikely political melding, for while Taylor was working on Tower's campaign, Krier and Sam Millsap were running Democrat John Hill's bid for governor of Texas. The couple, however, found they shared an interest in politics and good government. "We're both interested in making our city, our state, and our country better places in which to live."

On April 1, 1979, she went to work for the law firm of Lang, Lado, Green, Coghlan & Fischer, specializing in civil cases. Her commitment to Republican politics remained strong, and she actively recruited women into the political process. She continues to work for women in office, feeling that it is important for women to participate in politics in both parties.

She continued to see Joe Krier, and their marriage in 1982 drew comments from friends about their Republican-Democrat coalition. Cyndi always compared their political marriage as being much like a Dallas Cowboys' fan's watching a football game with a Washington Redskins' fan.

Cyndi Krier continued her involvement in Republican party politics, serving as vice-chair of the Bexar County party from 1979 to 1981 and as attorney for Representative Alan Schoolcraft after his contested election. Lt.Governor Bill Hobby named her to a bipartisan commission to propose legislative reforms for the Texas Election Code, and in 1981 Governor Bill Clements appointed her to the Governor's Task Force for

Women and Minorities. She served on the candidate recruit-
ment committee of the Bexar County Republican party and
admits that she knew that someday she would run for political
office.

That day came in 1984 when she began to look at a race for
the Texas 26th Senatorial District, where incumbent Senator Bob
Vale seemed vulnerable. President Ronald Reagan had carried
the district in 1980, and Republican governor Bill Clements had
received half the votes of the district in 1982. Senator Tower was
looking for Hispanics to run for office, and the district seemed
a likely one. The Bexar County Republicans found their Hispanic candidate in automobile dealer Ernesto Ancira but, before
the filing deadline, party members discovered that Ancira did
not live in the district. Cyndi Taylor Krier resolved to run, but
the party insisted that they wanted a Hispanic. "So did my law
firm," Krier told them, "but they found a woman would do just
as well." Eventually, so did the Bexar County Republicans. She
contacted June Deason, an experienced Republican campaign
manager, and told her, "I'll do this only if you run my campaign."

The day before the filing deadline, she met with the head
of her law firm then, at an early morning meeting on deadline
day, the members of the firm gave her their approval. By seven
o'clock that evening she had filed. She admits that she never
had time to ponder all the negatives or where the money was
coming from. She, Deason, and her husband sat down, set a
budget, and went to work.

Krier knew that her campaign, with its clear-cut, liberal-
conservative split within the district, would have to draw
Democratic support as well as Republican voters. Direct mail
publications went out to Republicans, and she enlisted the
personal support of Texas Republicans in Congress and Governor Bill Clements. Her first fundraising effort, put together by
women, was aimed at "godmothers" and favorite aunts, appealing across the board to both Democratic and Republican
women. She netted twenty thousand dollars.

To women in San Antonio, she was the woman candidate
who could beat Vale and bring a woman's voice to the Texas
Senate. While speaking to a group of Mexican American Business and Professional Women, one woman told her, "I am a
Hispanic. I am a woman, and I am proud of being both. There

are already Hispanics in the Texas Senate. That part of me is represented. But there are no women."

Knowing that her opponent's record in the senate was a lackluster one, she adopted as her theme "A Senator We Can Be Proud Of" and played on the fact that *Texas Monthly* had named Vale one of the "Ten Worst Legislators" at the end of the 1973 session, describing him as "the kind of politician who confirms your most cynical fears about politics." She pointed out that the State Bar had reprimanded him for abuse of legislative continuences, and that her opponent "displayed disrespect for the law" by failing to respond to three outstanding warrants against him in Comal County.

She strove to make her campaign a broadbased one and never took victory for granted as she campaigned door-to-door across the highly diverse district. She also began running television commercials in September, before her opponent, and credits the commercials with securing her name identification and giving her campaign credibility.

Senator Vale was unconvinced that an untried woman politician could defeat a twenty-year incumbent. Ten days before the election both candidates were invited to speak before the Metropolitan Congregational Alliance, but Vale failed to appear, sending word that he had an important meeting to attend. One of her campaign workers, walking door-to-door, discovered Vale weeding his garden, and Krier let the members of the alliance know that Vale was pulling weeds while she was talking with them.

Her door-to-door campaign and her focus on ethics paid off; she won the election on November 6, 1984, with a total election vote of 95,069 to Vale's 60,068, an impressive victory for a woman candidate who had never before filed for elective office in Bexar County. She found herself newsworthy as the first woman and the first Republican to represent San Antonio in the Texas Senate, and as the sole woman senator during her initial session.

During her campaign, Krier had cited the fact that over eighty percent of Vale's campaign contributions had come from special interests, including a $15,000 donation from South Texas millionaire Clinton Manges. After her election, when political action committees for organizations that had failed to back her contributed $16,200 to help her retire her campaign debt, Krier astounded Texas politicians by returning the funds, stating, "it is critical to me that I go to Austin without any question of whether I am indebted to anybody but the people of Bexar County."

During the 1985 legislative session, Krier was appointed by Lt.Governor Hobby to serve on the finance, education, and jurisprudence committees. She was to achieve a 97 percent voting record and pass twenty-eight bills, but her initial effort, her proposed bill designed to create municipal courts of record in San Antonio, seemed for a while to be a disaster. She knew her bill was important because of the city's twenty-thousand-case backload in which many of the cases would be automatically appealed and dismissed. Her colleague Frank Tejeda had agreed to sponsor the bill in the Texas House of Representatives, and Krier had lobbied her bill, obtaining what she thought would be an overwhelming majority.

Then her male colleagues decided to play a joke and began asking outrageous questions and offering opposition. When they voted against the bill she was confused and perplexed, and some senators told her, "Well, I told you I would vote for your bill, but I lied." When she found out the practical joke was an initiation rite for freshman senators, she jokingly rescinded her invitation for senators to visit San Antonio for Fiesta. Finally, Lt.Governor Bill Hobby overrode the veto and cleared the way for the bill's passage.

Despite being the only woman senator during the session, and only the sixth woman to serve in the upper house in the history of Texas, when she forgot her identification card she was denied entrance to the House of Representatives to hear Governor Mark White deliver his State of the State address and had to listen to it upstairs from the gallery. When the Speaker sent a staff member to apologize, Krier's reaction was simply, "I think he said the same thing to the folks in the gallery as he said to the folks on the floor." Senator Chet Edwards presented her with a huge identification card so that the guards would recognize her for what she was—Texas's lone woman senator. "I'll wear it around my neck," Krier joked for reporters.

The only woman senator also led what the media labeled as the senate "brahaha" after Krier was informed of the senate dress code requiring senators to wear sneakers only with socks and to abandon bras only if the lack of a bra did not prove a distraction. Krier defended the right of senators to wear sneakers and to eschew bras, asking if male senators were required to wear any particular type of underwear.

Krier passed twenty-eight bills during her first session, all of which became law. "If someone had told me going into the session that I was going to pass twenty-eight bills, I would have taken it [her record] and run," she recalls. One of the most significant bills she passed, and one of which she is justifiably proud, was the bill establishing Sea World, bringing the nation's fifth-largest theme park to San Antonio, a city whose main business remains tourism.

She worked with Representative Senfronia Thompson to pass legislation declaring February 15, 1975, as Susan B. Anthony Day in Texas, and she also passed a resolution honoring her former mentor John Tower for his service to the United States Senate. Another pivotal issue for her was eliminating legislative continuances in which legislators who were lawyers often postponed active court cases until after the legislative session. Her proposal, however, met with stiff opposition and died in committee.

Krier worked ardently for revision of state laws dealing with child abuse and family violence. The Bexar County Task Force dealing with these issues helped spur her efforts, and she passed bills designed to educate teachers and law enforcement personnel in recognizing signs of neglect and abuse.

Another bill allowed judges to restrict access to a child who had been abused. The bill was the result of a San Antonio case involving Melissa Robinson, who was taken from school by her father in violation of a protective order. The mother called the police, but they could not find the order as it had not been properly filed. By the time the order was found, the girl's father had killed Melissa and committed suicide. Krier's interest was a heartfelt one. She knew the bill could not bring back Melissa, but it was designed to help save other children, giving police the right to make an arrest where there is a history of child abuse or family violence and when the life of a child is threatened.

In 1988, with campaign contributions from business interests joining those of her original supporters, and with Democrats such as Lt.Governor Bill Hobby and U.S. Representative Albert Bustamante endorsing her, she easily defeated her Democratic challenger, "Nef" Garcia. During the 71st legislative session, family abuse became a very personal issue. Texas was one of fifteen states that exempted spouses from being tried for sexual abuse, and Krier was determined to change the status to allow prosecution for spousal abuse. She had become dedicated to the issue of abuse against women when her mother, Mary Taylor, was attacked and raped by a sixteen-year-old who was a chronic inhaler of spray paint. Although the boy later hanged himself in jail, Krier continued to work against the weakening of laws against stores selling spray paint to juveniles.

At the end of the session, *Texas Monthly* named her "The Most Valuable Player" in the legislature, and she received a humanitarian award from Centro del Barrio. A San Antonio radio station also named her one of the "Top Ten Most Influential People in Bexar County."

Commuting between San Antonio and Austin might well have proved a problem for the "power couple" of Cyndi and Joe Krier, but Mary Taylor cooked and packaged frozen dinners for the two so that they were not reduced to eating junk food on their weekends together. Becoming disenchanted with the direction that the Democratic party was taking in the late 1980s, Joe Krier switched his allegiance to the Republican party; their life together, however, became even more hectic when Joe accepted the presidency of the Greater San Antonio Chamber of Commerce just in time to begin promoting the proposed Alamodome. When asked if their jobs conflicted or overlapped, Cyndi Krier commented, "I stay out of his business, and he stays out of mine."

With the legislature's facing a special session in 1991, Krier was approached by Republican operatives to run for the state comptroller's office, but she told them she wanted to continue to serve in the senate, focusing on worker's compensation issues for the upcoming session. She left the door open for a possible run, however, despite the fact that a number of Republicans tried to force her to take a firm stand against abortion. Standing firm on waiting for a Supreme Court decision, she told the media:

> I . . . have the hardest time talking to those against abortion, and against birth-control. I am not a single-issue voter, and I am not about to become a single-issue politician.

During the 1991 session, however, she had served as a "whistle blower," filibustering against the state's not following the Constitution. The only woman to ever have filibustered during a legislative session, she wore her sneakers and stood at her desk for nine hours, standing firm on the fact that state spending should not increase more than the population and inflation within the state. Although her bill failed, her efforts led to the state's following the law in 1992. Krier, however, had always prided herself on being a team player and felt that her filibuster put her at odds with some fellow senators.

During her two terms in the Texas Senate, Krier worked well with Lt.Governor Bill Hobby, but when Hobby retired she early on crossed swords with incoming Lt.Governor Bob Bullock. She had actively campaigned for Bullock's opponent, Republican Rob Mosbacher, Jr., and she felt that she and Bullock had not been "the best of teammates." She felt the relationship was not good for her, not good for him, and not good for the state of Texas.

She did not want to spend her life fighting people and wanted to be more constructive and productive. When Republicans began to encourage her to run for a district judgeship in Bexar County, she sat down and, an inveterate listmaker, listed all the reasons she should run and then all the reasons she shouldn't. She made the decision to run in 1992 for an open seat created when District Judge John Longoria retired to run for the state legislature. A firm believer in term limits, she felt she could leave the senate since conservatives and other Republicans had been elected to advance the conservative agenda. In addition, the commute between San Antonio and Austin had begun to wear on her, and she felt that she was ready to do "hands on" work at the local level.

With her husband Joe holding the family Bible and with her mother at her side, Krier took the oath of office as county judge on December 8, 1992. She had soundly beaten Democrat Tommy Adkisson with 58 percent of the vote, and she told supporters, "This is a good day for me to look back and offer thanks and look ahead and ask for help," restating her campaign pledge to "open the courthouse to everyone" by opening appointments to everyone and calling for competitive bidding. Once again Krier had made history, becoming both the first woman judge in Bexar County history and the first Republican judge in the modern period.

When she became Bexar County judge, her supporters gave her a broom as a symbol that the courthouse needed cleaning up, but her administrative style often conflicted with longtime county politicos. Some called her a "prima donna" and others called her "pedantic," but even her most vocal critics admitted that, as the county's top administrative official, she was both "hard-driven" and "well-intentioned." Criminal justice had been a priority for her in the senate, and it remains one for her as a judge. With more prisoners convicted of violating state laws remaining in county jails, she continues to work for the state to assume its responsibility toward inmates.

Being a woman judge, she feels, is important. She stands firmly by the idea that the heart of representative government remains having people in elective office that are representative of the population. To her, having women in state legislatures, on commissions court, as judges, and in Congress does not mean they are going to vote differently, but they are going to prioritize issues differently and often they will present issues differently.

Krier often reflects on her own political career and feels that now in the 1990s it is much easier for a woman to run for political office and win. She feels that women must remain active, vital leaders in political parties everywhere. She was happily surprised, during a trip to observe elections in Russia in 1993, at the number of women there who were running and making strong showings.

Child abuse, family violence, and child support remain priority issues with her, a carryover from her service in the Texas Senate. Although she and her husband have never had children, she is active in the San Antonio Children's Shelter and looks for ways in which she, as county judge, can be an advocate for children. Issues dealing with juvenile justice remain a priority, and she feels that she has a couple of thousand children in Bexar County, even if she has none at home.

And children may well figure in her future career plans. The woman who moved from the Washington political scene to the Texas Senate to Bexar County judge can envision a life for herself after politics. Surprisingly, she feels that perhaps she might like to be a kindergarten teacher. "I keep going from the big picture down to the little one," she observes, "looking for ways to change lives one by one."

REFERENCES

"County judge determined to overhaul Bexar court." *Victoria Advocate* (July 5, 1993): 2.

Davidson, Bruce. "Krier: Compromise on continuances necessary." *San Antonio Express-News* (February 17, 1985): A-6.

_____. "Long road to acceptance has been bumpy for Krier." *San Antonio Express-News* (July 4, 1993): A-4.

Donahue, Terry. "Krier barred from House floor." *San Antonio Express-News* (January 16, 1985): A-9.

Eskenazi, Stuart. "Krier being viewed as the top GOP candidate for Bexar County judge." *San Antonio Light* (December 17, 1990): B-2.

Jarboe, Jan. "Krier's victory offers lesson." *San Antonio Express-News* (November 8, 1984): B-7.

Kase, Kathryn. "Krier bill Ok'd after fake nays." *San Antonio Light* (March 15, 1989): B-4.

_____. "Krier not afraid to play 'hardball,' defy labels." *San Antonio Light* (April 28, 1985): B-6.

Kid, Bill. "Krier in historic filibuster." *San Antonio Light* (July 24, 1991): B-4.

Knaggs, John. "Krier a coming presence in GOP politics." *Austin American-Statesman* (May 13, 1995): C-3.

McCrory, James. "Krier urges Bexar help send more women to Texas Senate. *San Antonio Express-News* (November 3, 1992): B-2.

McNeely, Dane. "Republican will stand out as only woman in Texas Senate." *Austin American-Statesman* (December 25, 1994): C-2.

Padilla, Gloria. "Krier makes history for Bexar." *San Antonio Express-News* (December 9, 1992): B-1.

_____. "Krier's mom, mate watch swearing in." *San Antonio Express-News* (January 11, 1989): B-1.

"Politician of the Year: Cyndi Taylor Krier." *San Antonio Express-News* (December 30, 1994): L-1.

Robison, Clay. "San Antonio, like state, is GOP territory." *Houston Chronicle* (June 23, 1996): C-2.

Salazar, Rosanna. "Krier, Zaffirini will help give Senate the female touch." *San Antonio Light* (January 11, 1987): B-3.

"Senate 'brahaha' coverage irks freshman Krier." *San Antonio Light* (January 10, 1985): B-4.

Sheridan, Martha. "Cyndi Krier: Learning her legislative ABCs." *San Antonio Express-News* (April 26, 1987): L-11.

Silverman, Dwight. "Power couple." *Houston Chronicle* (December 10, 1989): C-3.

Swibold, Denise. "Sen. Krier enters race for Bexar County judge." *San Antonio Light* (January 3, 1992): B-5.

Tangum, Rick. "A state senator dedicated to the Legislature." *San Antonio Light* (June 21, 1987): C-4.

INTERVIEWS

Cyndi Taylor Krier and Ann Fears Crawford, Austin, June 17, 1985.

Cyndi Taylor Krier and Ann Fears Crawford, San Antonio, Bexar County Courthouse, December 28, 1993.

Eddie Bernice Johnson

1935-

Making Ideas Work

In November 1992, Eddie Bernice Johnson of Dallas won election to the United States Congress, the first African-American woman from the Dallas area and the first Texas woman since Barbara Jordan to go to Congress. The newly created 30th Congressional District had turned out in force for the Texas politician and granted Johnson 74 percent of the vote. Since her win only one other Texas woman, African-American Sheila Jackson Lee of Houston, has joined her colleague in the U.S. House of Representatives.

Eddie Bernice Johnson's victory was only one of a number of firsts for a woman who had proved her mettle on the Texas political scene and who was considered one of the major players in Democratic politics in the state. Born on December 3, 1935, she was one of three daughters and four children born to Edward and Lillie Mae Johnson in Waco, Texas. During her childhood, her mother read to the children from English novels and the family attended plays at Baylor University, although they could only attend on "black day."

Deeply involved in community affairs, her parents were staunch Democrats and stressed political involvement to their children. When African Americans gained the right to vote in Texas elections in 1944, her parents worked to register their neighbors and see that they went to the polls. Her mother was always active in community affairs; Johnson remembers her as a "little crusader" and feels she has followed in her mother's footsteps.

Although her father was often away from home with his trucking business, Eddie Bernice considered him her "best friend" and often slipped out of bed to greet him when he arrived home at night. She revered him as her hero but shocked him when, as a college student, she announced she thought she would become a Republican. Another shock followed when she converted to the Catholic religion; she remained a Catholic until she married a Baptist. She also remained a Republican until John F. Kennedy was elected president.

Her parents instilled in her the idea that neither race nor color should be a barrier to her achievement, and after graduation from high school she entered St. Mary's College at Notre Dame University to earn a nursing degree. For the first time she was plunged into an all-Anglo world. As the only nursing student from Texas, she soon earned the nickname "Tex." She was later to earn a Bachelor of Science in Nursing from Texas Christian University and in 1976 was to be named to TCU's board of trustees.

After graduation from St. Mary's in 1955, she obtained a position as a psychiatric nurse at the Veteran's Administration in Dallas with the promise of a room in the nurses' dormitory. When she arrived in Dallas, however, the administration was surprised to discover she was an African American; suddenly no room was available in the all-Anglo dormitory and she was banished to a rooming house near Dallas's Fair Park.

She often volunteered for special assignments but was turned down for many. The overt racism was most apparent when her superiors deemed it necessary to explain she really *was* qualified for her job. Racism and the way she was treated almost defeated her, and she considered taking a job out of the South. When her chief nurse heard she had acquired a scholarship to New York University, she counseled Johnson to remain in Dallas, telling her she needed to persevere not only for herself but "for her people." Persevere she did, and within eighteen months Johnson was promoted to head nurse.

While working at the Veterans Administration she met Lacy Kirk Johnson on a blind date, and the two married. They had one son, Dawrence Kirk, and Johnson was kept busy with her job, her marriage, and her son until an incident brought racism home to her and launched her political career. Shopping at a downtown department store for a hat to wear to a friend's wedding, she was appalled to find that African-American women were not allowed to try on hats or shoes in Dallas. Perplexed because African Americans in Waco were allowed to try on clothes in all the city's department stores, she immediately put down the hat she had chosen, refused to buy it, and went out and organized a group of fifty African-American women to boycott the department store and other stores that would not allow women to try on clothes before buying them. Group action made a difference, and soon the stores were allowing African Americans to try on clothes before purchasing them.

The boycott helped Johnson realize that political action was the only way to change the system, and soon she was campaigning for African-American candidates, pushing her son in his stroller while distributing campaign literature in shopping centers for a host of candidates. Although African Americans won few races, she feels that the effort was worthwhile because black citizens in Dallas became aware of the strength of their African-American community.

A divorce from her husband proved devastating to her and her son, but her political consciousness increased. When the Reverend Zan Holmes, serving in the Texas House of Representatives, suggested that she run for the House from District 33-0, her first reaction was a negative one. She felt that she had just been through a difficult divorce, she had a son to rear, and she would have to give up her job with the Veterans Administration where she was secure as a nurse.

Holmes, the leader of the Dallas black community who once described Johnson as that "rare combination of blackness, brains, beauty, and boldness," continued to encourage her to run for the state legislature, and the time seemed right. Stanley Marcus of the prestigious Dallas department store offered her a job as executive assistant to the store's personnel director with the understanding that she would run for public office. District 33-0 seemed tailor-made for her, but she still had qualms about making the personal sacrifices that political life involved. Her strongest advocate was her son, who kept saying to her "Why don't you do it?" and took cooking and homemaking classes in school to help out at home while she was campaigning.

Even after she had filed her candidacy papers she had second thoughts, "What have I done?", but there was little time to ponder for the race was on and she was rated as the underdog with a campaign budget of only $5,000. Working day and night from her dining room, often making calls herself, she pointed to her civic involvement and her work at the Veterans Hospital. She cited her work as an organizer of the Cedar Crest Civic Club and with the League of Woman Voters, Business and Professional Woman's Club, and Women for Change. In 1963 she had served as president of the National Council of Negro Women.

Although her opponent, Berlaind Brasher, was a lawyer supported by the establishment and had a significant campaign war chest, Johnson had the support of many community leaders and the veterans she had worked with. She also had an inspiring mentor, Federal Judge Sarah T. Hughes, who had won a seat in the Texas House of Representatives in 1931 and had been appointed a federal judge in 1961. Johnson launched a door-to-door campaign with her fourteen-year-old son by her side, taking the issues to the people. "I just had to win," she recalled, and win she did by a landslide. She said of her success at the polls: "I didn't base my campaign on being a woman or a black. I am interested solely in the people and in reflecting the needs of the constituency."

Before taking her seat in the Texas House of Representatives, she won still another victory when she was elected in June 1972 as vice-chair of the Texas State Democratic Convention, the first African-American woman to serve in the position. In December, one month before the opening of the legislative session, she and the other African-American members going to the House met at her home and formed the Black Legislative Caucus.

When the session opened in January 1973, Eddie Bernice Johnson became the first black woman from the Dallas area to serve in the legislature, and soon she became the first woman to chair a House Committee and one not traditionally considered a woman's area—Labor. As a former psychiatric nurse, mental health with a focus on upgraded facilities was a priority; she also focused on prison reform, better health care, and health insurance for the elderly.

In March 1973 Johnson and two other state legislators filed a class-action complaint with the Equal Employment Opportunity Commission charging that State Comptroller Robert Calvert's office restricted opportunities for women. An investigation by the EEOC revealed that discrimination did exist. Calvert stormed back, calling Johnson a "nigger woman" in the media and declaring she had been "giving him hell" and "doesn't know what she's talking about." With Dallas Representative Paul Ragsdale, Johnson called a press conference demanding that Calvert adopt fair hiring practices or resign—or she would call for his impeachment.

Governor Dolph Briscoe hedged on the issue, saying he "deplored" racial statements but telling the press he didn't know if Calvert had actually made the statement. Lt.Governor Hobby, however, warned heads of state agencies to adopt fair hiring practices or their budgets would not be honored. The Calvert incident provided impetus for Bob Bullock's hard look at the comptroller's office as a possible elective position in the Texas political world.

Johnson served for three sessions in the legislature; her major success in the 1977 session was gaining passage of a neighborhood preservation loan fund bill to make loans to modernize inner-city housing. After her third session, word began circulating that Johnson was being considered for a position with the Carter administration. She received the appointment in August as director of the Dallas regional office of the Department of Health, Education, and Welfare, overseeing programs in Texas and four other states.

Johnson saw her job as once again working for the people, sorting out problems and improving the delivery of services to them. Many of her constituents in her legislative district, however, resented the fact that she had taken the position and charged her with deserting her responsibility to them and leaving them without leadership. Nevertheless, her position with HEW extended her management and negotiating skills and was, according to her, a "never-ending task." She remains justly proud of the job she did as an HEW administrator, commenting:

> I have worked hard and I think I have done an acceptable job. . . .I would hope that some young person, one day, would see me as role model.

After the defeat of President Jimmy Carter, Johnson began looking for another political opportunity, and word began to circulate that she intended to run for the U.S. Congress in 1982 from the new 24th District. When her father developed cancer, however, she postponed campaigning for any seat. She nursed him during his terminal illness and then cared for her mother during her final illness. She founded Eddie Bernice Johnson and Associates, a business and consulting firm located in the Dallas-Fort Worth International Airport and dedicated to helping businesses expand or relocate in the Dallas-Fort Worth area. She also served as a consultant to Sammons Corporation and became a founding member of the Board of Directors of Sunbelt National Bank.

Then, in 1986 when veteran state Senator Oscar Mauzy retired, the seat in the 23rd District also seemed tailor-made for her, although it was a much larger district extending from Tarrant County to Oak Cliff. Once again Johnson used her door-to-door campaign tactics to win the seat, defeating state Representative Jesse Oliver in a close runoff victory in the Democratic primary and then going on to defeat Republican Darrell Castillo, a financial analyst and political newcomer, with 78 percent of the vote. "I feel complimented by the voters," Johnson stated, and noted that she wanted to remain accessible to the voters although her senatorial district was five times larger than her house district. Her priorities as state senator remained people-oriented and focused on supporting education, reducing insurance costs, and increasing economic development and fair-housing, particularly within inner-city Dallas. She served on senate committees dealing with Finance, Health and Human Services, and Education, and proved to be a leader on issues pertaining to minorities and women.

In 1991 Johnson chaired the Senate Subcommittee on Congressional Redistricting and was instrumental in carving out a new district, the 30th Congressional District in Dallas composed of 60 percent African-American or Hispanic voters and 40 percent Anglos. Her political experience and expertise discouraged many potential candidates from filing against her, and the *Dallas Morning News* commented that she "sat down at the table with some of the most skilled political gamblers in the nation—the Texas congressional delegation—and came away victorious." Johnson denied that she had created the district essentially for herself, although she had announced her decision to run during a hearing of the subcommittee. She said her candidacy was not the issue but "whether or not there is a district in Dallas County where black voters can vote for a candidate of their choice."

In commenting to Emily's List, a group that promotes women in the political arena, Johnson noted that her congressional agenda would be much like her agenda in the Texas Senate.

> . . . .I will continue to adhere to my principles and beliefs. And I will remain steadfast in what I believe is the right position to promote fairness and equality for everyone.

Johnson scored a remarkable victory with 107,830 votes to Republican Lucy Cain's 37,853 votes. She stressed the fact that she would be continuing to work in Congress on the issues that she considered important as the nation approached the twenty-first century: pay equity for women, preschool education, parental leave, reproductive choice, and subsidized housing with tax incentives for investors. With forty million Americans uninsured, striving for better health care remained a top priority. "We must do something today to make our tomorrows possible," she said.

As a freshman member of Congress trying to be an effective spokesperson for her constituents and to attend the myriad committee meetings, Johnson found her work often both "disjointed" and "frustrating." Her priorities remained those of her Dallas constituents: the economy and more jobs. She also continued her work to eliminate discrimination against women and minorities. Writing a column for the *Dallas Morning News*, the congresswoman spoke out on congressional issues important to her community. In one column she pointed out that "getting young people ready for work should never be the sole responsibility of the school systems," and she noted the importance of federal School to Work programs.

Among bills she sponsored in Congress relating to health matters were a number relating to women's health. Among these were amendments to the Public Health Service Act increasing the number of health professionals, providing for research, and education regarding menopause. She sponsored amendments to the Social Security Act extending Medicare to military retirees and their spouses, providing information about family planning, and requiring state Medicaid plans to provide coverage for mammography and for coverage of an annual mammography for women sixty-five years or older. She co-sponsored measures to establish offices of women's health within government agencies.

She also sponsored the Advancement of Women in Science and Engineering Work Force Act and co-sponsored bills to improve the interstate enforcement of child support, to establish comprehensive early childhood education programs, and to provide federal assistance to early childhood education programs. Of importance to African Americans were the bills she co-sponsored calling for the redesign of the one-dollar coin commemorating Dr. Martin Luther King, Jr., establishing the National African-American Museum in the Smithsonian Institution, and designating the route from Selma to Montgomery as a National Historic Trail.

When six Republican voters in Dallas and Houston charged "gerrymandering" of districts in those two cities, claiming that the districts were drawn to give minorities more political influence, the Supreme Court took the redistricting plan by the state under consideration. After its ruling that "districts were constitutionally suspect if race was the primary factor in drawing them," Johnson, whose congressional district was one of the ones under scrutiny, commented, "If race was the predominant factor, we would have a lot more black seats in Texas." In June 1996 the Supreme Court ruled that three congressional districts in Texas, including Johnson's 30th Congressional District, had been "racially gerrymandered." Texas Attorney General Dan Morales stated that "We now accept the ruling as the law of the land and will abide by it."

In the subsequent race, Johnson faced an unusually large number of opponents. One former staffer, Lisa Hemby, ran against her but without any party identification. Hemby's candidacy brought her headlines with former Dallas Cowboy Roger Staubach and two former Dallas mayors' supporting her, and with her claims that Johnson treated her staff poorly. Nevertheless, Johnson won the race without a runoff over Republican Representative John Hendry, garnering 55 percent of the vote. Hendry commented of Johnson's candidacy, "She was just real powerful."

Hemby's charges during the 1996 race caught the media's attention because there *had* been a significant turnover in Congresswoman Johnson's staff during her first two years in Congress. In July 1996 her top aide John Cones resigned his staff position, charging that Johnson used "official resources for personal and campaign efforts" and claiming that she required staffers to drive her, pick up dry cleaning, and prepare campaign expense reports. Johnson responded that Cones was a misfit whom she was planning to ask to resign. She further stated that she had always checked with the House Ethics Committee concerning campaign affairs. She *had* been fined $44,000 for violations of campaign-finance laws in April 1996, but she herself had discovered the problems and reported them to the Federal Elections Commission.

Looking back over a career filled with "firsts" and outstanding achievements, Eddie Bernice Johnson continues to serve as a role model for other women who want to achieve success in the political world. She has much practical advice to give to young women in Texas.

I say work hard and hang in there. This is our world too. . . .Get involved in civic groups, educational groups. Be active in the appropriate groups for whatever you choose to accomplish. Spend time making your ideas work.

For Congresswoman Eddie Bernice Johnson, "making ideas work" has been a lifelong goal for which she continues to strive.

REFERENCES

Aguirre, Richard R. "Johnson, Price headed for political showdown." *Dallas Times-Herald* (August 5, 1990): A-1.

Attlesey, Sam. "Remap official to seek seat in new district." *Dallas Morning News* (May 16, 1991): D-12.

Barta, Carolyn. "Candidate Won on Issues." *Dallas Morning News* (July 5, 1972): A-1.

_____. "Higher Office Pondered." *Dallas Morning News* (November 28, 1973): B-1.

_____. "Johnson Pushes Bias Fight." *Dallas Morning News* (September 20, 1973): B-1.

Bennett, Elizabeth. "New face on state political scene." *Houston Post* (June 16, 1972): D-1.

_____. "Legislator sets example." *Dallas Times-Herald* (January 14, 1975): D-1.

Calhoun, Ron. "Rep. Johnson gets HEW post." *Dallas Times-Herald* (August 11, 1977): A-3.

Camia, Catalina. "Eddie Bernice Johnson settles complaint by former employee." *Dallas Morning News* (September 8, 1995): A-6.

_____. "Lawmaker's top aide quits, alleges improper use of staff." *Dallas Morning News* (July 20, 1996): A-6.

_____. "Rep. Eddie Bernice Johnson fined $44,000. *Dallas Morning News* (April 23, 1996): A-16.

Castlebury, Vivian. "Bernice Johnson: Do your homework." *Dallas Times-Herald* (January 2, 1975): D-1.

Coggins, Phil. "Taking the Fifth." *D* magazine (November 1993): 41-44.

Daniel, Carol. "Eddie Bernice Johnson: Family Helped Her Succeed." *Waco Tribune-Herald* (February 14, 1979): A-1.

Fish, Dottie. "Six Women Will Be in New Legislature." *Dallas Morning News* (November 19, 1972): D-5.

Griffith, Dotty. "Johnson Sees Challenge as HEW regional head." *Dallas Morning News* (September 6, 1977): D-4.

Henderson, Lana. "Eddie Johnson." *Dallas Times-Herald* (June 6, 1979): C-5.

Hecht, Peter. "Johnson adds to legacy of firsts." *Dallas Times-Herald* (January 13, 1987): E-4.

Johnson, Eddie Bernice. Biographical File. The Center for American History, University of Texas at Austin, Texas.

_____. Biographical File. Texas and Local History Room, Dallas Public Library, Dallas, Texas.

_____. Biographical File. Texas Legislative Library, Texas State Capitol, Austin, Texas.

_____. "Preparing students for jobs." *Dallas Morning News* (January 28, 1996): E-8.

Kilday, Anne Marie. "Johnson making transition from Texas to DC." *Dallas Morning News* (April 25, 1993): A-14.

Lenz, Mary. "Female legislators ready for office." *Dallas Morning News* (December 3, 1972): D-3.

Keever, Jack. "Sole Brothers." *Texas Monthly* (January 1975): 20-29.

Morehead, Richard. "Democrats Drop Orr for Johnson." *Dallas Morning News* (June 14, 1972): B-1.

Northcutt, Kaye. "The Calvert flap." *Texas Observer* (October 5, 1973): 4.

O'Connor, Colleen. "Eddie Bernice Johnson." *Dallas Morning News* (February 1, 1987): E-1.

Sanders, Bob Ray. "Divided We Fall." *D* magazine (February 1986): 92-162.

Seymour, Kelly B. "Johnson to run again for Senate." *Dallas Times-Herald* (November 4, 1989): B-3.

Wade-Adams, Norma. "Johnson leads in redrawn District 30." *Dallas Morning News* (November 6, 1996): A-33.

_____. "Johnson's surprising win defies runoff predictions." *Dallas Morning News* (December 7, 1996): A-22.

Weddington, Sarah, et.al. *Texas Women in Politics.* Austin: Foundation for Women's Resources, 1977.

Wiessler, Judy. "Justices quash racial districts." *Houston Chronicle* (June 14, 1996): A-1.

Williams, Ruth. "'Rules are not made to inhibit, but to better serve'." *Downtown News* (May 1, 1978): 1.

Winegarten, Ruthe. *Black Texas Women: 150 Years of Trial and Triumph.* Austin: University of Texas Press, 1995.

Zimmerman, Ann. "U.S. Reprehensible." *Dallas Observer* (October 31-November 6, 1996): 26-37.

INTERVIEWS

Mike Green and Ann Fears Crawford, telephone interview, Washington, D.C., November 20, 1996.

Jack Keever and Ann Fears Crawford, Austin, Texas, August 5, 1993.

Molly Ivins

1944-

"Having It All"

Although she sounds like she was born in the creek bottoms of East Texas, Molly Ivins was born in Monterey, California, on August 30, 1944, one of three children of James E. and Margo Milne Ivins. Her father was serving in the Coast Guard on the West Coast when she was born, but when Molly was three he moved his family to Houston where he joined Tenneco as general counsel, moving up the corporate ladder and settling his family in prestigious, conservative River Oaks by the time Molly was seven years old.

Taller and smarter than most students at Sidney B. Lanier Junior High School and St. John's School, Molly plunged into reading and tried to play basketball with little success. She even tried smoking to stunt her growth, which would eventually propel her to an awesome six feet. Molly was often at cross purposes with her teachers and even more so with her father who, having a hearing problem, often screamed for effect. The two often engaged in shouting arguments around the dining table over issues such as civil rights. She received encouragement, however, from teachers at St. John's and explored issues of liberalism by reading her best friend's parents' copies of the *Texas Observer*, the state's liberal and literary journal.

There was a time in her teenage years when Molly wanted to write the great American novel, until she realized that a very great number of people had the same ambition and that "some of us were not going to make it. I decided that I'd better think of something else." Then she decided it would be romantic and adventurous to be a foreign correspondent.

> I knew I wanted to be a journalist, and I thought that
> I would be a foreign correspondent, get to wear a
> trenchcoat, be paid fabulous sums of money, go
> around the world, and have adventures in any num-
> ber of exotic places.

She followed her mother Margo and grandmother, Fauchon
Hathaway, to Smith College, winning the Sophia Smith award,
the college's most prestigious leadership honor, and spending
a year at the Institute of Political Science in Paris studying
history, philosophy, and languages. Home for summers in
Houston and pursuing her ambition to be a journalist, she
worked for the *Houston Chronicle*, serving in what is known as
the "snake pit" for women reporters—food and fashion. She
even served as the editor for the bride's report.

Ivins soon realized that, to get ahead in the world of journalism, she would need a graduate degree, so she completed a
master's degree at Columbia University and began applying for
newspaper jobs. The *Minneapolis Tribune* had a reputation as one
of the best daily newspapers in the United States, and in 1967
Ivins landed a job as the paper's first police reporter. "Actually,
my size worked for me," she recalls. "You can't send a sweet,
dainty, little thing out to cover crime."

Crime however, was almost nonexistent in Minneapolis, but
Ivins paid her dues, learning the ways of the daily newspaper
world and earning a reputation as a solid writer, good at her job.
She soon was writing a column on "Movements for Social
Change," covering Native Americans, militant African Americans, radical students, and feminists. She also learned to deal
with editors, who were never intimidated by her size.

> They never pussyfooted around. It was always, 'Iv-
> ins, get your ass out there.' I have literally towered
> over every editor I have ever known.

By 1970 she was yearning for sturdier journalistic fare and
for the opportunity to speak out for the liberal issues that
dominated the era. She found her niche as co-editor of the *Texas
Observer*, the liberal monthly published in Austin and the voice
of liberalism in Texas and throughout the South. The job paid

only $125 a week but Ivins loved it. She felt at the time that it was the best job in American journalism, and money was never an issue:

> I loved working on the *Observer*, and I didn't mind one bit that it didn't pay much. What did I care? I was young. I was healthy. I didn't have a family. I met fabulous people.

To Ivins, the six years she spent on the *Observer* were her maturing years in the world of journalism. "Some people think of their college years as the happy, golden time," she recalls. "Writing for the *Observer* was my golden time, a time of joy, laughter—and learning." She worked alongside such dedicated journalists as Larry Goodwyn and Willie Morris and considers the *Observer* to be the best graduate school of American journalism in the country.

> You study under the moral suasion of Ronnie Dugger, who walks on a higher moral plane than most mortals on this earth. You have that fabulous journalistic tradition to live up to, and you get to make your own mistakes. That is, of course, the greatest privilege of all.

While co-editing the *Observer* with Kaye Northcutt, Ivins came to journalistic grips with the Texas legislature, commenting on the foibles of "The Lege" for the journal, as well as on all things Texan in an occasional column for the *New York Times*, the *Nation*, and the *Atlantic*. Once when calling the members of "The Lege" to task, she admonished the state's voters: "All right, goddammit, you elected them," also noting that "In lobbyist-legislator circles, available women are referred to as 'sweat hogs'."

Being a Texas woman herself, and writing during the time when feminists were speaking out against chauvinism, she explored the sexist culture of Texas in print and in speeches to women's groups. She found that Texas women deal with a degree of sexism that is missing in most of the country.

> Sexism is reinforced by the peculiar culture of Texas. First, there's the Southern woman on the pedestal,

coming into East Texas from the Old South. You get
the machismo of the Spanish tradition. You get the
machismo of the culture in which football is the
ultimate religious experience. And, of course, we are
only allowed to stand on the sidelines with pom
poms and cheer while the guys play the game. . . .

Also impacting Texas women is the myth of the
frontier and the Old West as presented by all those
John Wayne movies, in which he steps up to some
distressed, ditzy lady who has gotten herself
stranded in the middle of a strange place and says:
'Don't worry, little lady, I'll take care of you. . . .'

Time and time again she points out to women the reality of
frontier Texas, that women "were tough as hell and equal to any
man," but she notes that all the strains of Texas culture have
created a "particular kind of sexism that we have had to deal
with all our lives."

She dealt with feminist causes with the acerbic humor that
she brought to bear on the denizens of the Texas House of
Representatives, but she never avoided taking on tough issues
such as gun control and noted in 1973 that 1,164 Texans had been
murdered with firearms in 1971 and that the "National Rifle
Association is still terrorizing politicians." Gun control did not
become a reality in Texas until the 1990s.

In 1974 Ivins and eleven other American journalists went to
the Soviet Union on a cultural exchange program sponsored by
the U.S. State Department and the American Council of Young
Political Leaders. She found that "gloomy weather makes
gloomy people," and that Moscow was "on a par with Abilene,
Amarillo, and Lubbock." She found Leningrad lively, however,
and wrote that the trip had given her a far stronger "opinion on
the durability of detente between the USSR and the U.S.A." She
never lost her ability to get angry over just causes but, unlike
most editors of the *Observer*, she used her wit to put her points
across. She once said that "most *Observer* editors lose their
humor . . . but the longer I stay, the funnier I get."

The stay, however, was coming to an end. Turned down by
The University of Texas for a part-time job on the journalism
faculty, on June 15, 1976, Ivins left the *Observer* to join the *New
York Times* and was assigned as chief of their Rocky Mountain

bureau. She worked there until 1980, cruising the area in her Chevrolet Blazer and writing mostly environmental stories. She knew that working for a fabulous newspaper like the *Times* was considered the height of journalistic success, but working in New York was dreadful. "However," she says, "if you're a thousand miles away from New York in a gorgeous stretch of country, you can have a wonderful time."

She often found herself writing a type of story that she abhorred; she calls them "vulture stories" where the journalist knocks on the door of a family during a tragedy. During the Iran hostage crisis, there were a few families in her area being hounded by the press. "They were so tired of talking to me," she recalls. "I simply left them alone."

She was not above shocking the *Times* editors with her salty language and downhome wit. On one occasion when she covered a ritual chicken slaughter, she labeled it a "gangpluck" knowing full well that the editors would cut the expression from her story. She still considers the staff of the *Times* "the finest group of practicing journalists in America."

The journalist, who has never planned her career and who says that on her tombstone should be written: "She never made a shrewd career move," reveled in the opportunity to return to Texas in the 1980s. The *Dallas Times-Herald*, then a counterpoint to the conservative *Dallas Morning News*, called and asked her to join their staff, promising, "You can write what you want to, and you can say whatever you want to." Working on the *Times-Herald* gave her the opportunity to do what she does best and likes best to do—"raising; hell and makin' people mad!" And Dallas was a fabulous place to do just that. Once again she found that she was the person called by journalists from New York to Washington when they wanted "the real skinny" on Texas politics.

Her salty style, however, often conflicted with the upward-mobility mentality of the Dallas establishment. Ivins never minded taking on banks, corporations, and Republicans in print, going so far as to label Ross Perot a "chihuahua" and characterizing the feisty politician as "all hawk and no spit." Soon the *Times-Herald* editors were receiving complaints and being asked to curb her tart tongue and acid pen. Ivins found she was the target of right-wing paranoia and began receiving an extraordinary amount of hate mail, but once again she was dispatched to cover "The Lege," finding that the "good ole boys" hadn't changed overly much and that the Texas legislature was still what she once characterized as "the land of no vision."

For some time she had been mulling over the idea of gathering her columns together into a book. When the *Times-Herald* folded, she had several months of unemployment and began selecting the columns and contacting publishers. Then in 1990 she went to work for the *Fort Worth Star-Telegram*, the paper she once called "the best unread paper in Texas," telling them she didn't need much money but did need the same freedom to write what she wanted that she had with the *Times-Herald*. She got it and, as she says, "It doesn't get any better than that in journalism."

Her columns for the *Star-Telegram* were among some of her best, often extoling her views on the Lone Star State and all its peculiarities.

> I dearly love the state of Texas, but I consider that a harmless perversion on my part, and discuss it only with consenting adults. If Texas were a sane place, it wouldn't be nearly as much fun. . . .

Never standing back from an issue, she took on the Republican budgetcutters with the warning:

> The Republican budget remains a recipe for the most astonishing transfer of wealth from the Have Nots to Haves ever contemplated in an apparently sane country. . . .

Among her best articles were the ones that captured Texas's greats and not-so-greats. Her column on Barbara Jordan, written after the Texas politician received the Presidential Medal of Freedom, provided a glimpse into the political background of the Texas politician:

> Barbara Jordan single-handedly forced the whole Establishment to draw the first black congressional district Texas ever had. Jordan used the system to beat the system. . . .

Her syndicated column also gave her an opportunity to take on national politicians, noting that Pat Buchanan was "a racist, sexist, xenophobic, homophobic anti-Semite" but "a fairly likable human being," and chronicling the often-absurd remarks of President George Bush. She once commented on the former president that, "Calling George Bush shallow is like calling a dwarf short," and she ranked both Bush and former President Ronald Reagan as "merely amiable doofuses." Her columns continued to call politicians to task for meddling with abortion rights, ignoring equity for mental health in medical insurance programs, and even for their lack of good manners in public debates

Soon, however, she was cast in the unlikely role of best-selling "arthur" when her first book, *Molly Ivins Can't Say That, Can She?*, spent over twelve months on the best-seller list. The book's title came from billboards that the *Times-Herald* spread across Dallas when the business community, protesting her columns, withdrew their ads for two weeks. She found herself plunged into the world of press interviews, autographing appearances, and speaking engagements.

Her sharp tongue and rapier wit had made her a celebrity known everywhere as the state's resident political humorist but with a decided punch. Success, however, proved challenging and often bewildering. She found herself going to a psychiatrist to determine if she had a strong case of "fear of success"; for some time she had felt that her success might be because of her size or because she was just lucky. It took some time for her to discover that her success was attributable to the fact that she is merely "damned good."

She also points to the fact that growing up in the 1950s she, like other Texas women, were never groomed for success. As she recalls, "your choice of role models was a Kilgore Rangerette or Ma Ferguson." She nevertheless has a decided fondness for Texas women and found mentors within the field of journalism, recalling especially Edith Asbury at the *New York Times* and Vivian Castlebury of the *Dallas Times-Herald*. She also found role models within the field of Texas politics; she has known Ann Richards since before she entered politics, and the former governor still serves as a role model to Ivins. Just as she finds humor in the Byzantine world of Texas politics, Ivins can laugh at the cultural foibles of Texas women. "You know, when we haven't seen each other for a long time, our greeting is: "'Ooooooh, honey. I'm glad to see you.' We sound just like we're calling hogs!"

The success of her first book gained Ivins increased media coverage and the opportunity to speak to groups across the nation. She had always accepted speaking engagements since her stint as an *Observer* editor in the 1970s, once traveling to Texas A&M University, at the request of a student group, to challenge the school's ban on political speeches. When the administration threatened to cancel the organization's charter, the students moved the speech to the Methodist student center. Ivins recalls that she did her best to "incite a riot," but only about seven people showed up, listening silently to what she had to say.

But with her book's success, Texans and people across the nation were listening intently, and even the most conservative of women's groups continue to applaud her salty language and pungent comments on Texas politics and the world in general. She never tempers her language to suit a particular group, and the applause she receives, mingled with uproarious laughter, whether from university students or a group of the state's librarians, is often loud and long. She continues to be committed to delivering one *pro bono* speech each month on the First Amendment, a promise she made to one of her strongest mentors and best friends, the late John Henry Faulk, who was blacklisted from radio and television in the 1950s. One of her most poignant columns celebrated the life of Faulk, whose name now graces the former Austin Public Library. Ivins wrote of him that he denounced "fascists and racists and a splendid assortment of know-nothings and pinheads who sinned against the Bill of Rights."

Her second book, *Nothin' But Good Times Ahead*, brought her even more fame and longer lines at bookstores to obtain her autograph. She is working on a third volume to be published in Spring 1998, and continues to write three columns a week for the *Fort Worth Star-Telegram*. Her columns are now syndicated in over two hundred newspapers nationwide. She also writes articles for small progressive magazines which don't pay much but allow her to use her wit and determination to communicate to the nation's liberals, and she contributes an occasional article to magazines, including her feature on House Speaker Newt Gingrich which appeared in *Playboy* in 1996. Ivins labeled the Speaker "the single silliest public official east of the Texas legislature" and claimed that the point man for the Republican "Contract with America" "has no ideas, no principles, no integrity, and by and large he's a damn fool."

In February 1996, "60 Minutes" announced that Ivins would be one of a corps of columnists, along with Stanley Crouch and P.J. O'Rourke, who would be commenting on news stories each Sunday, engaging in a back-and-forth repartee on timely topics. Designed to put a "little spark in the program," the debate seemed staged and Ivins appeared somewhat wooden in the program's format. When the idea for the program was first announced, Ivins had commented: "I'm keeping my day job. . . . The chance of my becoming a TV star at my age is pretty remote."

Soon the "spark" had burned out and the segment was abandoned, but Ivins continues to appear on the McNeil-Lehrer report and other TV programs, commenting in her usual ribald style on Texas and politics in general. She has also taped pilots for a number of television shows, but she has consciously tried to slow down, looking for projects that allow her to remain in Austin for longer periods of time and to spend time with friends. She relishes her sanctuary in South Austin and frolicking with her dog Athena, a real clown who makes Ivins laugh all the time.

She recalls that when she was a teenager, she thought that when she was twenty-one, she would know exactly what it was she wanted to do. Then when she was thirty, she hoped she would, and when she was fifty, she felt sure she would know. But the journalist is now happy with what she's doing although she wishes she were doing a bit less. She's also learning to live with and accept Molly Ivins as Molly Ivins.

> As I grow older, I get more comfortable with myself. More comfortable with the fact that I'm not perfect, and that there are some things I will never be able to do. Every year is a year's more experience and knowledge.

The years sit well on her. Her columns in the 1990s reflect a wide range of subjects and a journalistic maturity but have never lost the spark of feistiness mingled with dedication and zeal that marked the columns she wrote for the *Texas Observer* in the 1970s. Only the issues have changed. Longtime friends don't expect her to slow her pace one bit and fully expect that the journalist who once said that the secret of life was "having it all," will still be "raisin' hell and makin' people mad" well into the twenty-first century.

REFERENCES

Benatar, Giselle. "Good Golly, Miss Molly!" *Entertainment Weekly* (September 27, 1991): 12-13.

Carter, Bill. "Columnist Ivins to join '60 Minutes' format." *Austin American-Statesman* (February 14, 1976): C-3.

Denison, D.C. "The Interview: Molly Ivins." *Boston Globe* magazine (January 12, 1992): 24.

Green, Michelle and Anne Mauer. "The Mouth of Texas." *People* (December, 1991): 99-102.

Hays, Susan. "Ivins earns 'No-bull' prize for literature." *Daily Texan* (October 23, 1991): 4.

_____. "Molly Ivins did say that." *Daily Texan* (April 4, 1991): 15-17.

Herndon, John. "Molly Ivins sez anything she wants to." *Austin American-Statesman* (October 10, 1991): B-1,4.

Holder, Dennis. "Molly Ivins Can Say That (And Will)." *D* magazine (May, 1985): 174-253.

Holloway, Diane. "Ivins 'keeping my day job' despite '60 Minutes' role." *Austin American-Statesman* (February 16, 1996): B-1.

Ivins, Molly. "Barbara Jordan's freedom medal shows our progress." *Austin American-Statesman* (August 2, 1994): C-3.

_____. "Buchanan's manifold flaws." *Fort Worth Star-Telegram* (February 25, 1996): C-3.

_____. "Gramm never mastered 'works well with others.' *Austin American-Statesman* (February 18, 1996): C-3.

_____. "Kids more important than tax cuts." *Fort Worth Star-Telegram* (November 26, 1995): C-4.

_____. "Lib in Longhorn Country." *New York Times* (October 18, 1971): D-34.

_____. *Molly Ivins Can't Say That, Can She?* New York: Random House, 1991.

_____. "The 1973 gun control editorial." *Texas Observer* (March 2, 1973): 23.

_____. *Nothin' but Good Times Ahead*. New York: Random House, 1993.

_____. "No villains; just asses." *Texas Observer* (June 18, 1971): 21.

_____. "The Observer goes to the Soviet Union." *Texas Observer* (November 1, 1974): 23.

_____. "Political Asylum." *Ms* magazine (June, 1988): 26.

_____. "Practicing Nuance Down at Luby's." *The Nation* (November 8, 1986): 481.

_____. "Ramifications in the Hilterland." *The Progressive* (December, 1987): 37.

_____. "Political Writing: A State of Lazy Journalism." *Texas Humanist* (November/December, 1994): 26-28.

_____. Typescript of Newt Gingrich article for *Playboy* magazine. Supplied to Ann Fears Crawford by the office of Molly Ivins, June 1996.

_____. "When others buckled, John Henry Faulk stood strong." *Dallas Times-Herald* (April 11, 1990): C-15.

Knapp, Deborah. "Observer Coeditor Says Sexual Bias Continues." *Daily Texan* (April 22, 1976): 4.

"Molly Ivins On the Road." *New Yorker* (October 31, 1994): 22.

Morris, Anne. "Bawdy Politic." *Austin American-Statesman* (September 27, 1993): C-1.

"Observer in Exile." *Daily Texan* (June 10, 1076): 5.

Porterfield, Billy. "When a colleague gets famous, you try the best you can to help." *Austin American-Statesman* (August 25, 1994): B-1.

Roberts, Raequel. "Taking Texas to Task." *Houston Post* (October 24, 1991): C-1,2.

Swartz, Mimi. "The Price of Being Molly." *Texas Monthly* (November, 1992): 138-66.

Wehmeyer, Peggy. "Observer Editor Blasts Texas Politics." *Daily Texan* (February 6, 1976): 1.

INTERVIEWS

Molly Ivins and Ann Fears Crawford, Austin, Texas, May 22, 1996.

Courtesy Texas Senate Media Services.

Judith Pappas Zaffirini
1946-

*The Senator
from South Texas*

In November 1987, Judith Pappas Zaffirini from Laredo won election to the Texas Senate, the first Hispanic woman to serve as a Texas senator and the first woman to chair the influential Texas Senate Hispanic Caucus. It had been a difficult goal that she had pursued diligently, just as she has pursued all the goals she has set for herself throughout her life.

Judith Pappas was a member of a multicultural family that had always been devoted to Democratic politics. Born in Laredo on February 16, 1946, the third daughter of George Santiago Pappas and Nieves Mogas Vidaurri Pappas, Judith could point with pride to her paternal grandfather, Santiago Pappas, a Greek immigrant who had served on the Laredo City Council and married a Hispanic woman. Her husband's father had come from Italy and had also married a Hispanic woman. The two grandfathers studied English and Spanish together and stood up for one another when each was married.

Judith entered St. Peter's Elementary School early, because she cried to go when her sisters left in the morning, but by the second grade she found school too boring and begged to quit. Her mother allowed her to stay home for one day but put her to work washing dishes and cleaning house. Judith learned the value of education and was back in school the next day.

From the time she was a child, she was involved in politics. With her sisters, she has given the job of calling citizens on the telephone to ask if they needed rides to the polls or if they needed a baby sitter so that they could have free time to vote.

As a high-school student she continued her political participation, handing out bumper stickers for Democratic candidates and collecting funds for city-council candidates. When she entered The University of Texas to study communications, she often held as many as three part-time jobs but nevertheless found time to work for Democratic candidates. In Austin she worked for Gus Garcia in his campaigns for city council and supported both Irma Rangel and Ernestine Glossbrenner, South Texas women, in their successful races for the Texas House of Representatives.

In 1965 she married her childhood sweetheart, Carlos Zaffirini, and the couple continued at The University of Texas where Carlos worked toward his law degree and Judith earned two degrees in communications, a BS in 1967 and an MA in 1970. In 1967 Carlos became chief of staff for Senator Wayne Connally of Floresville, and Judith wrote press releases and speeches for the senator while she was still in school.

During the 1967 legislative session, she and Carlos both worked on bringing a four-year college to Laredo, coordinating efforts between the mayor, community leaders, and the Texas Coordinating Board for Higher Education. The Coordinating Board rejected their request even though a prominent Laredoan, Dr. Joaquin Cigarroa, was a member of the board, but the cause would occupy both Zaffirinis for the next several years. Their state senator was Wayne Connally, the brother of Governor John Connally whose main agenda was higher education for Texans and who was interested in Laredo's acquiring a four-year university. The supporters for the college did manage to acquire funding for a Center for Higher Education which offered junior and senior-level courses on the campus of Laredo Junior College, so in part they won their battle.

Judith and Carlos returned to Laredo in 1970 and she began teaching speech and journalism at Laredo Junior College, also serving as the college's director of public relations. In the late 1970s she began the grueling commute to Austin each week to work on her doctorate in communications. After lunch on Sunday she left for Austin, studied on Sunday night, attended classes until ten on Monday night, then rose at four in the morning to drive back to Laredo where she taught classes at Laredo Junior College until nine on Tuesday evening. It was a happy day when she was granted her Ph.D. in 1978.

Both she and her husband remained politically active in Democratic state and local politics and were still concerned that Laredo should have a four-year university. She had other concerns such as the needs of the mentally ill and the mentally retarded, for whom she was involved not only as a volunteer but as a volunteer lobbyist before the state legislature. "I certainly learned the difference between the Senate and House of Representatives," she recalls. "From my lobbying experience, I realized that a senator was much more powerful than a house member, and I began to realize that the senator from our district was working much more closely with San Antonio than with Laredo."

She also realized that her senator, John Traeger of Seguin, was a member of the lieutenant governor's team and more actively involved with statewide issues than with the needs of the constituents closer to home. "He didn't go to Crystal City or to Roma," she remembers. "Many times, when we were trying to lobby a local issue, we couldn't get in to see him. We had to work with his aide." She and other local leaders worked toward electing a senator who would focus on local issues, a senator who would visit with people in small towns and who knew the people in the district.

Meanwhile, Zaffirini was establishing herself as a prominent Democrat from her area. In August 1980, as a member of the Texas State Democratic Executive Committee and the Hispanic American Democrats, she attended her first Democratic National Convention, serving on the platform committee and as a whip for President Jimmy Carter. She caught the eye of an NBC correspondent who interviewed her on national television, and President Carter's Hispanic advisors lauded her as "one of the most articulate Chicano political organizers in the country." In the same year, Texas Press Women named her their Woman of Achievement. In 1981 the Texas Mexican American Women's Political Caucus also named her its Woman of the Year.

In 1982 Zaffirini was one of several people in the district who considered a race for the Texas senate. She began to feel ill, however, and feared that she might have cancer. She went to a physician in San Antonio, who suggested she give up caffeine and change her bra style. The pain persisted, and a glimpse of herself in her dressing-room mirror caused her to exclaim "this is not my body." She realized that she might be pregnant. She and Carlos had been married for sixteen years and had never had a child. She had suffered four miscarriages but kept them secret from all except her sister and her husband. Now she was thirty-six years old, but her physician dashed her hopes when he told her she was not pregnant.

She thought that she was, but she was hesitant to purchase a pregnancy test and sent her husband in to buy one, whispering to him, "Don't tell them it's for me." Carlos had to laugh, "Who do you want me to tell them it's for?" Playing it safe, Carlos brought two of the tests, and they received two positive results.

Finally the doctor confirmed her pregnancy. She called her sister and asked, "What is the last thing you expect me to tell you about myself?" Her sister replied: "Ronald Reagan appointed you to something." When she told her sister she was pregnant, Celita began crying and then called her mother, who also began crying. "All over town people were crying because they were so happy for me," she recalls with genuine pleasure.

To Judith, "faith and family came first," so she put aside any thought of running for the senate; the most important thing was to have a healthy child. Then the doctor told her there were problems—that the baby was in danger of being born retarded or with brain damage. With her firm pro-life, anti-abortion values, and knowing that after four miscarriages this might well be her last chance to have a child, she made the decision to have her baby, no matter what the costs. She went on a health and reading campaign, gaining over forty pounds by eating over one hundred grams of protein a day, including four glasses of milk and liver twice a week. She also absorbed over one hundred books on nutrition, pregnancy, birthing, and child rearing, and resolved to have her baby without the aid of drugs.

On March 23, 1982, after eighteen hours of labor, Carlos, Jr. was born, the answer to her prayers, her own "little miracle" as she calls her son. He was a healthy child from the first, and she breast fed him to insure his immunity from childhood diseases. For nine months she and the baby were never separated. If she was at the office, so was Carlos, Jr.; if she was at home, he was at her side.

In 1985 she again considered a race for the senate, secretly thinking that perhaps she would once again become pregnant.

The Democratic network of which she was very much a part was looking for a senatorial candidate who would give them access to the system and who would be responsive to their needs. They were not particularly looking for a Hispanic or a woman, but after considering six possible candidates, the network decided that Zaffirini had the best qualifications and the best chance of winning in the twenty-county district that spread from Webb County to Bexar County and from Laredo to San Antonio. Her networking throughout the community paid off, and she proved to be an effective fundraiser.

One of the items on her campaign agenda was retaining the Center for Higher Education in Laredo. The Select Committee on Higher Education considered downgrading the Center or closing it, but with Zaffirini actively working for its support, Laredoans formed the Webb County Committee on Higher Education, collected more than twenty thousand signatures in support of the Center, and once again won the battle.

In her campaign she drew four Democratic opponents, including a strong contender for the senate seat, State Representative Billy Hall also from Laredo. Despite a grueling schedule throughout the campaign, Zaffirini never lost sight of her family responsibilities. To her, being a good wife and mother was just as important as being a good senator. During the campaign she spent only two nights away from her family, and two nights away during the runoff. She caught up on her sleep in the car, using a friend, family member, or campaign aide to drive her to speaking engagements.

Her first campaign also saw her focusing on organizational skills, planning each week's activities and organizing her closet so that clothing was matched and ready to wear in an instant. Organization was a necessity, for her campaign was a high-energy, grass-roots one with Zaffirini's taking her message to many of the small towns that had never even seen their state senator.

Her organizational skills extended to preparing huge scrapbooks covering issues and reactions from voters, a practice she has continued for bills and issues facing the Texas Legislature. She announced her personal pledge to go door-to-door in every county in the district and to work for jobs and economic development. Never far from her campaign focus was her commitment to families, declaring that she would work to see that "the father has employment, the children have education, and the entire family has proper health care."

Her tremendous energy on the campaign trail paid off. The *Laredo Morning Times,* in the forefront of the newspapers endorsing her candidacy, noted that she "is energetic, educated, has knowledge of the issues, tremendous organizational abilities, charisma, and the ability to deal with the majority of voters of South Texas." In a runoff she faced Hall, who tapped the state's political action committees for funding for his campaign.

One of the primary issues in the runoff became the "open-container law" designed to prevent Texans from driving while drinking intoxicating beverages. As chairman of the House Liquor Regulations Committee, Hall killed the law by assigning it to an unfriendly committee, and the liquor lobby poured funds into his campaign. Zaffirini spoke out in favor of tough DWI and drug laws and in favor of closed-container legislation. In its endorsement of her candidacy, the *San Antonio Express-News* noted that she was "free of the old-style" politics, and the *San Antonio Light,* adding its endorsement, stated that she had the "ability to represent the diverse interests of this sprawling district." She went on to win sixteen of the counties in her district, but lost her own Webb County.

In the general election she faced Republican Bennie Bock, who called on Zaffirini and her campaign staff to take drug tests, which they did with all, including the candidate, testing free of drugs. During the hard-fought runoff, an elderly Hispanic man, horrified that a woman was running for the Texas Senate, admonished her: "Everybody knows that women are supposed to stay home and clean house." She laughed and replied, "Yes sir, that's exactly what I'm going to do. I did the dusting off in May, swept up in June, and I'm going to mop up in November."

Zaffirini won the general election with 52 percent of the vote, even winning a recount demanded by Bock, and joined Senator Cyndi Taylor Krier and Senator Eddie Bernice Johnson in the senate chamber. Lt. Governor Bill Hobby assigned her to committees on Health and Human Services, Intergovernmental Relations, and Natural Resources, and to the subcommittee on water. In addition, he named her as ex-officio member of a new committee to examine Texas programs on alcohol and drug abuse.

With State Representative Henry Cueller she worked for a bill that established Laredo State University as a four-year school, deleted a law that would have allowed the Coordinating Board to close the school, and gained a School of International Trade for the university. She also successfully sponsored bills that made parental kidnapping a felony and rape of a spouse illegal. Her work in passing a bill prohibiting abortions of viable fetuses, except when the mother's physical or mental health was at risk, the first anti-abortion law passed in Texas since 1857, won her an award from the Texas Coalition for Life.

She continued her fight against alcohol and substance abuse by sponsoring bills for counseling treatment for minors on drugs, bills for drug-abuse education programs, and bills that strengthened laws for DWI by minors. Mindful of her campaign promises, she worked hard for the creation of enterprise zones, for economic development, and for water rights in rural areas. She also co-sponsored a bill that called for the Texas Education Agency to reduce the dropout rate of students to no more than five percent.

Despite an intense work schedule, Zaffirini returned to Laredo each weekend to spend time with her family. She was well known for her baking, often rewarding fellow legislators, capitol reporters, and staff with the cookies and cakes that had won her a plaque from her son's kindergarten class as "the best cooker in the whole world." At the end of her initial session she earned another accolade from Laredo's mayor of which she's justifiably proud: "Our senator is the best senator we've ever had." She was also inducted into the National Hispanic Hall of Fame and received the LULAC Medal of Honor.

"It's as important to me to be a good wife and mother as to be a good senator," she says. No matter what is on the legislative agenda, Christmas Eve always remains special with more than one hundred family members' gathering to sample her home-made specialties, including *encilantradas*, *puerco adobado*, sour cream cheesecake, and praline pecans. Her party table holds twenty-one main dishes and her dessert table boasts fifteen items—all made by her. She keeps notes on her recipes like she keeps files on senate bills.

In November 1990 she won a second term with 68 percent of the vote, carrying all twenty counties in her district. Looking forward to the upcoming legislative session, she joined twelve other senators in opposing measures that would declare Texas an "English Only" state and end the state's printing of documents in Spanish. During the 72nd legislative session, she was reappointed to committees dealing with natural resources and health and human services and also acquired a seat on the Senate Education Committee. She won accolades for her "momma" agenda, continuing to push for health, education, and child-related issues. She passed a bill that established an office for prevention of developmental disabilities and that established three task forces to study issues related to disabilities. Her fight for fairer worker's compensation measures for the state earned the Heroine Award from the Texas Chamber of Commerce.

During the 72nd legislative session meeting in 1991, she continued her focus on women and children by passing legislation that required convicted sex offenders to register with police in any town or city where they intended to live for more than seven days. She also passed bills designed to toughen birth certificate registration and to mandate education classes for midwives. At the end of the 1991 regular session, Zaffirini won a distinct award—a perfect attendance and voting record for her four years in the senate. During the three regular sessions and eight called sessions, she had cast 9,108 votes and had passed 107 bills, a remarkable achievement and one of which Zaffirini is justifiably proud. "Maintaining this record required meeting the challenge of taking a stand on all issues, no matter how controversial," she told the media.

In September 1991, Lt. Governor Bob Bullock appointed Zaffirini to serve on the important Legislative Education Board dedicated to maintaining legislative oversight over educational policy. He then appointed her to the Senate Finance Committee to replace Senator Frank Tejeda, who was running for U.S. Congress. In making the appointment, Bullock noted her "superior service" and called her "a hard worker and a dedicated lawmaker." Because of legislative redistricting, Zaffirini was required to run for a third term in 1992, but she ran without opposition.

With her district's encompassing the UT-medical center in San Antonio and The University of Texas at San Antonio, as well as extending to El Paso in West Texas, Zaffirini's concentration on health and education issues became increasingly important in the senate. Many political watchers expected her to aim at higher office, possibly choosing to follow Bob Bullock in the lieutenant governor's office.

Before the 1993 legislative session opened, Zaffirini was elected to head the Texas Senate Hispanic Caucus, designed to focus on issues having an impact upon Hispanics across the state. Lt. Governor Bullock appointed her to chair the Senate Health and Human Services Committee, the first woman ever to serve as chair of a major senate committee.

The senator and the lieutenant governor made major headlines across the state in January when Bullock introduced her at a Texas Chamber of Commerce breakfast by commenting that the senator would get her bills passed during the session if she would "cut off her skirt about six inches and put on some high heels." Feminist groups and the media assailed the lieutenant governor for sexist remarks that might well have been construed as sexual harassment in the workplace. Some suggested that Bullock was in need of sensitivity training. Zaffirini, however, with her good sense and good humor, refused to be offended and said she always took Bullock's remarks "with a grain of salt—lots." She told the media that "I know hatred when I see it. I know bigotry. I know chauvinism. This was not any of those." Bullock defended his remarks, saying that Zaffirini was a senator for whom he felt "a great deal of respect and affection," adding that he always made fun of Zaffirini's skirts and that she called him "an old mothbag."

Critics persisted, insisting that Zaffirini should have taken umbrage at Bullock's remark as the sexist slur that others considered it. Zaffirini commented that she took more notice of Bullock's actions, and that he had recently appointed her to the chair of the Health and Human Services Committee. Editorial writers for the *Fort Worth Star-Telegram* commented on Bullock's humor but noted that the remark was just one of the many that "shape the way society thinks about women." Republicans called on Bullock to apologize and tried to make the issue a partisan one. Governor Ann Richards, citing the lieutenant governor's positive record on hiring women, commented that Bullock "has been giving me fashion advice for years and I have been giving him advice on what to say to the press. I ignore him and he ignores me."

When Bullock was named "Mr. South Texas" in February

1993, Zaffirini commented that he richly deserved the honor, citing his "ability to solve controversies, his success in meeting needs with limited resources, and his determination to improve our quality of life." When the Gulf Coast Council of the Boy Scouts of America named Zaffirini their Distinguished Citizen of 1993, Bullock commented, "I have been blessed with a lot of good things in my life, and at the top of that list is my special friendship with Senator Zaffirini."

Zaffirini once more made headlines in March 1993 when Bullock presented her with a special gavel for casting her 10,000th consecutive vote, still maintaining her 100 percent voting record. Senator Carl Parker ungallantly commented, "If I had a husband that would support me, I could do that too." The media immediately chastised Parker for his "smart-alecky and irrelevant remark," but Zaffirini refused to comment on what she construed to be a "chauvinistic statement."

At the close of the 73rd legislative session, Zaffirini had passed fifty-four bills focusing on revoking licenses of drunk drivers, a statewide plan for immunization of children, a plan by which race or ethnicity could not be used in placing children for adoption, and supporting a volunteer advocacy program for abused or neglected children. Other bills focused on children's issues, rights of mental patients, higher education in South Texas, an academy for Foreign Language and Culture, and reducing the risks of transporting low-level radioactive waste.

High on her agenda remained higher education in South Texas, and she sponsored a bill that expanded Laredo State University to a four-year institution and changed its name to Texas A&M International University. Other bills she sponsored ensured that $65.4 million went to education in South Texas and that state funding in the amount of $23.6 million went to health and human services.

Speculation continued to mount that Zaffirini would run for higher office, but she told the press, "I'm not even tempted. . . . I'm not a career politician. I ran because there were needs to be addressed." She herself speculated that she might cut her time in the senate to fourteen years.

Among her proudest achievements is her leadership of the Health and Human Services Committee. Before the session even started, she held hearings for the senators who had prefiled bills, instructing her staff to hold hearings when the senators wanted them even if it meant a hearing at eight in the morning or at ten at night. "I pledge to the senators who have bills set for hearing that we will maintain a quorum," she says. "We start every hearing on time, and we stay as long as we need to to complete the hearing."

She has a test for health care that she learned from former Surgeon General Antonia Novella. "Health care should be accessible, accountable, affable, adequate, affordable, and available." She is also concerned that health care meet the needs of all Texans. "Health care is a critical problem in our state, because our state is so big. What might work in Dallas or Houston might very well not work in smaller communities."

Overcoming Republican challenger Fernando Cantu in November 1994, Zaffirini prepared for another four years that she felt "would be the best." However, in March 1995 the senator was again involved in controversy when she proposed that Texas A&M International University be transferred to The University of Texas system, citing the fact that the university could take advantage of UT programs in Latin American studies and medicine. State Representative Henry Cuellar supported the move, but critics of the move charged that Zaffirini had proposed the move in order to become president of the institution.

The president of Texas A&M opposed the measure, but the Senate Finance Committee approved the move. Opposition continued to mount; students held a statewide rally to keep the school part of the A&M system. Lobbyists worked the legislature for both sides while she and Cuellar held public forums in Laredo. The bill was assigned to the House Committee on Higher Education, under the chairmanship of Representative Irma Rangel of Kingsville, a graduate of Texas A&M. Insisting that the votes were not there to send the bill to the floor of the House, she allowed the bill to die in committee. The university remained part of the Texas A&M system.

In 1996 Zaffirini faced opposition from Republican CPA James Whitworth in a race which brought into question Zaffirini's views on abortion. She remained strongly pro-life even though the Democratic platform supports a woman's right to abortion. Whitworth charged her with soliciting the support of the religious right, but Zaffirini won the election with 67 percent of the vote, claiming that "The reason I get reelected is good, old-fashioned hard work."

By December 1996, the senator had prefiled a number of bills to be considered in the legislative session beginning in January 1997. A bill high in priority for her would restrict children's access to tobacco; other bills dealt with indigent health care programs, child care, parenting, abuse of the elderly, abuse and neglect of children, and child services in nursing facilities.

When the 1997 legislative session opened on January 14, the state lay in the grip of an ice storm. Determined to maintain her perfect attendance record and not to miss the opening day of the session, Zaffirini hooked a ride to Austin with a highway patrol officer and was there when senators unanimously elected her president *pro tempore* of the senate, the fifth woman in Texas history to receive the honor. Noting her penchant for early morning meetings, Republican senator Bill Ratliff told the members that his only fear was that Lt. Governor Bob Bullock might fall ill and that Zaffirini would convene the Senate at 5:00 a.m.

Senators, both Democrat and Republican, praised Zaffirini for her perfect attendance at committee meetings and at floor votes, the only senator to hold such a record. On Saturday April 19, both Governor George Bush and Lt. Governor Bob Bullock left the state so that she could hold office as Governor-For-a-Day. Many prophesied that she might well be Texas governor in the not so distant future.

With her positive attitude, her organizational skills, and her strong work ethic, Senator Judith Zaffirini looks forward to remaining in the Texas Senate until the twenty-first century. She is one of Texas's political women who has made her political philosophy work for her. As she says about her opponents, "You've got to outwork, outsmart, and outspend them."

REFERENCES

"A Woman of Substance." *Hispanic Magazine* (March 1993): 10.

"Bob Bullock." *Fort Worth Star-Telegram* (January 23, 1993): B-4.

"Boy Scouts of America Gulf Coast Council Distinguished Citizen Award." *Laredo Morning News* (August 17, 1993): C-3,8.

Cash, Wanda. "Zaffirini shows who wears pants in Senate." *Galveston Daily News* (April 8, 1993): B-2.

Critchell, Peter L. "Zaffirini at home at first convention." *San Antonio Express-News* (August 15, 1980): A-1.

Davidson, Bruce. "Forget usual party politics in this Texas Senate race." *San Antonio Express-News* (April 21, 1996): A-2.

_____. "Zaffirini championing state 'momma agenda'." *San Antonio Express-News* (June 25, 1989): B-2.

_____. "Zaffirini's foe needs Demo vote." *San Antonio Express-News* (May 16, 1996): B-5.

Diehl, Kemper. "Laredo native puts energy into race for 21st District." *San Antonio Express-News* (December 15, 1985): M-2.

_____. "Zaffirini content as a senator, has no plans for higher office." *San Antonio Express News* (August 22, 1993): L-3.

Driver, Don. "Zaffirini, Wentworth win reelection." *San Antonio Express-News* (November 9, 1994): M-4.

Fisher, Mary M. "She sandwiches legislative duties, family." *North San Antonio Times* (August 20, 1987): 6.

French, Pat. "Zaffirini to run for Senate." *Laredo Times* (December 19, 1985): 1.

Fuentes, Diana R. "Panel approves UT link for campus in Laredo." *San Antonio Express-News* (March 10, 1995): A-2.

_____. "Poll gives backing to school transfer." *San Antonio Express-News* (March 20, 1995): A-2.

_____. "Zaffirini becomes the first Hispanic female in Senate." *Laredo Morning Times* (January 14, 1987): A-1.

_____. "Zaffirini takes great strides to cover sprawling district." *San Antonio Express-News* (January 24, 1993): A-3.

Herrera, Mike. "Zaffirini landslide." *Laredo Morning Times* (December 22, 1995): E-5.

_____. "Zaffirini: the choice." *Laredo Times* (April 6, 1986): D-3.

Herrick, Thaddeus. "A&M foe lives to fight another day." *Houston Chronicle* (January 4, 1995): C-4.

Hight, Bruce. "Senate clears ban on drinking, driving." *Austin American-Statesman* (March 16, 1987): D-5.

Hutton, Jim. "Zaffirini touts knowledge, cash for campaigns." *San Antonio Express-News* (July 27, 1994): B-3.

Jarboe, Jan. "Fitness may win race for Senate." *San Antonio Express-News* (March 4, 1986): A-11.

Keever, Jack. "Sen. Zaffirini a whirlwind with priorities." *Houston Chronicle* (August 6, 1989): C-4.

Kidd, Bill. "Bullock appoints Zaffirini to Senate finance panel." *San Antonio Light* (September 14, 1991): D-7.

Lenz, Mary. "Richards brushes off Bullock skirt remark." *Houston Post* (January 23, 1993): B-1.

Loddeke, Leslie. "Bullock's remark no surprise, but Zaffirini's reaction to it is." *Houston Post* (January 28, 1993): B-3.

McNeely, Dave. "Bullock's skirt joke wasn't wise." *Austin American-Statesman* (January 24, 1993): C-3.

Ramsey, Ross. "Bullock's 'chauvinist' remark." *Houston Chronicle* (January 22, 1993): D-4.

Labbe, J.R. "Just a joke? Then why aren't more women laughing?" *Fort Worth Star-Telegram* (January 27, 1993): E-6.

Lamensdorf, Marilyn. "Officials oppose local plan." *Laredo Morning Times* (January 11, 1989): A-1.

_____. "Texas senators oppose 'English Only' bill." *Laredo Morning Times* (December 1, 1988): A-1.

Ray, Steve. "S. Texas lawmakers gain legislative clout." *Corpus Christi Caller-Times* (June 13, 1993): D-1.

Santos, Richard G. "Bexar County rediscovers state Sen. Judith Zaffirini." *San Antonio Express-News* (September 21, 1991): D-4.

Scharrer, Gary. "Zaffirini sets record for attendance." *El Paso Times* (March 11, 1993): A-1.

Scott, Stephanie. "Campus plan now in trouble." *San Antonio Express-News* (April 20, 1995): B-2.

Sills, Edward. "Zaffirini's power increases with Senate appointments." *San Antonio Light* (January 14, 1993): B-3B.

Smithson, Shelley. "A&M Laredo transfer in trouble." Bryan College Station *Eagle* (April 20, 1995): A-1.

"Thumbs up." *Dallas Morning News* (March 12, 1993): B-5.

Walt, Kathy and Polly Ross Hughes. "Lawmakers all smiles on opening day." *Houston Chronicle* (January 15, 1997): A-1.

Wright, Andrea. "Judith Zaffirini knows her way around the Senate and the kitchen." *Corpus Christi Caller-Times* (January 30, 1991): D-5.

Zaffirini, Judith. "Health, human services budget $23.6 billion." *Laredo Morning Times* (July 4, 1993): B-2.

_____. "Laredo State U. funding." *Laredo Morning Times* (March 14, 1993): B-2.

_____. "Senator sponsors, passes 54 bills during session." *Laredo Morning Times* (June 13, 1993): B-2.

_____. "State watching out for its resources." *Laredo Morning Times* (August 8, 1993): B-2.

_____. "Zaffirini summarizes legislative program." *Laredo Morning Times* (January 20, 1993): B-2.

"Zaffirini heads Hispanic Caucus." *San Antonio Express-News* (December 24, 1992): D-6.

INTERVIEW

Senator Judith Zaffirini and Ann Fears Crawford, Texas Health Science Center, San Antonio, March 16, 1994.

Kay Bailey Hutchison

1943-

From Newsroom to Senate Chamber

On June 5, 1993, Texas State Treasurer Kay Bailey Hutchison won a landslide victory over Democrat Bob Krueger to become the first Texas woman to win a seat in the United States Senate. The election marked yet another historic milestone; when Hutchison joined Republican Phil Gramm in the senate, it was also the first time since the period of Reconstruction that both U.S. Senators from Texas had been members of the Republican party.

After campaigning across the state with Gramm and Hollywood actor Charlton Heston, Hutchison had swept all areas of the state with 67.3 percent of the vote to Krueger's 32.7 percent. Her Republican victory cut deeply into traditional Democratic strongholds in both East and South Texas and won the votes of many Democratic women. The media had focused heavily on the campaign, and *Glamour* magazine had labeled her the Republican party's "dream candidate."

Party leaders looked to Hutchison to provide a conservative balance to the five Democratic woman senators. After conferring with Senate Minority Leader Bob Dole, Hutchison took her place among senate Republican stalwarts, but her victory was marred by charges brought by Travis County District Attorney Ronnie Earle concerning her activities as state treasurer.

Allegations concerning her actions against state employees in the treasurer's office arose early in the campaign when Sharon Amman, daughter of former Texas governor John Connally who was backing Republican Jack Fields, charged

Hutchison with striking her with a binder. Other employees charged that Hutchison berated and pinched them. Days before the election, Krueger's campaign managers had charged that Hutchison, following her successful 1990 campaign for state treasurer, had given a job to former San Saba County Judge Tom Bowden in exchange for his endorsement of her in the race. Both Hutchison and Bowden denied the charges.

Then, on June 8 three days after Hutchison's landslide victory over Krueger, a Travis County grand jury subpoenaed records and fourteen treasury employees because of allegations of official misconduct that might well have resulted in both misdemeanor and felony charges. An anonymous caller informed Texas media sources of the grand jury action well in advance of the subpoenas, and Republican sources were quick to cry "foul," charging that the grand jury investigation was politically motivated. Hutchison's press secretary called it a "political witch hunt." Despite the allegations of improper conduct, Hutchison was sworn in as the first U.S. woman senator from Texas on June 15, 1993.

Her becoming a U.S. Senator was only one of many "firsts" in Kay Bailey Hutchison's political career. A native Texan whose great great grandfather, Charles Taylor, signed the Texas Declaration of Independence, Kay Bailey was born in LaPorte, Texas, on June 22, 1943, the daughter of Allan Bailey, a real-estate developer, and his wife, Kathryn Sharp Bailey.

In elementary school, Kay read numbers of historical biographies and resolved to become a lawyer. She was a prom queen and cheerleader at LaMarque High School, and after graduation in 1993 she enrolled at The University of Texas in a special three-year undergraduate program that led to law school. Actively involved in college life, she was a nominee for UT sweetheart, a Bluebonnet Belle nominee, the sorority editor for the UT yearbook, and a member of the Student Government Coordinating Board. She also served as varsity cheerleader for the 1963 Longhorn football team.

The idea of a woman cheerleader in law school was so unique that the UT Law Forum ran an article on Bailey, written by a fellow law student named Ronnie Earle who was later to meet Hutchison in a courtroom. Earle wrote of her, "Anyone talking with Miss Bailey soon gets the impression that she considers Law School more important than the win-loss record of the Longhorns."

She was graduated from The University of Texas with a Bachelor of Law degree in 1967 and was briefly married to a medical student. The marriage, however, ended in divorce. She worked for a Galveston law firm for a year but found breaking in with a law firm difficult; heads of firms tended to ask questions about what might happen if she got married and had a baby.

Bailey next took a job as a political reporter with Houston's KPRC-TV, covering the courthouse and the political beat. An interview with Anne Armstrong, then serving as co-chair of the Republican National Committee, led to a job in 1981 as Armstrong's press secretary in Washington. Although Bailey worked for Armstrong for only seven months, she counts Armstrong among her mentors and one who inspired her to run for elective office.

By 1971 redistricting had opened up additional seats in the Texas legislature, creating opportunities for minorities, women, and Republicans to gain access to legislative seats. Taking advantage of the opportunity, Bailey returned to Texas and filed for a seat as a Republican. Her opponents took advantage of her frequent support of Democrats as well as Republicans. One challenged her on the fact that she was not married, while another claimed that she had not belonged to the Young Republicans while attending The University of Texas. Bailey acknowledged her support from both Republicans and Democrats and campaigned on the need to build a two-party state in Texas. Running in the wake of the Sharpstown scandal, she stated that "voters were fed up with 'one-partyism' in Texas" and noted that the failures of conservative Democrats meant gains for both liberals and Republicans.

Early in the 1972 campaign, she charged that Texas was not acting responsibly in its budgeting and called for a move to hold down taxes—a campaign issue that she would carry over into her race for the U.S. Senate. Although liberals captured an additional fourteen seats in the elections, Bailey won 67 percent of the vote from the conservative neighborhoods of West University Place, Afton Oaks, and part of Bellaire, and joined six other Republicans in the legislature.

While serving in the Texas legislature, Bailey co-sponsored bills to reorganize the Texas Highway Department and a bill to create a mass transit system for the city of Houston. She also helped pass a bill to improve the treatment of rape victims in Texas, legislation that prevented rape victims from becoming the persons on trial. She also served as vice-chair of the Intergovernmental Affairs Committee and as a member of the House Ways and Means Committee. A highlight of her legislative career was taking part in the 1974 constitutional convention that attempted to revise the Texas Constitution.

Of importance to her later senate race was her careful avoidance of being labeled a feminist while in the Texas legislature, stating:

> I consider that I am a representative of women . . . and that I will always make sure that areas where there is discrimination, I will be involved in trying to correct that. But I don't know what the definition of a feminist is . . . I'm not focused just on those issues.

In 1976 Bailey considered entering the congressional race when Houston Democrat Bob Casey was nominated for a seat on the Maritime Commission, and many political onlookers expected her to run for Congress. Later she would regret that she did not enter the race, but she noted that hard-line Republicans opposed her moderate stance. Conservative Ron Paul won the Republican nomination but was defeated by Democrat Bob Gammage; Hutchison remains convinced that she could have beaten Gammage.

Her legislative focus on mass transpiration paid off when, after two terms as a state legislator, Bailey was appointed to the National Transportation Safety Board by President Gerald Ford, who then named her vice-chair. Both Texas senators, Republican John Tower and Democrat Lloyd Bentsen, supported her nomination. Even though aviation-oriented groups opposed her, citing her lack of technical expertise in transportation safety, her nomination sailed through the Senate Commerce Committee.

Her assumption of office placed Bailey in the national spotlight for the first time; *Redbook* magazine in 1976 named her as one of the most prominent Texas women, and *Glamour* chose her as one of ten outstanding working women in America. The Congress of Houston Teachers named her Texas's Outstanding Young Woman of the Year and Most Outstanding Texas Legislator for 1976.

During her tenure as a state legislator, however, Bailey met Ray Hutchison, then serving as a state representative from Dallas, and Bailey resigned her position on the National Transportation Safety Board to return to Texas to be married on March 16, 1978. She campaigned actively for her husband when he challenged Bill Clements for the governor's office. Although her husband lost the election, Hutchison continued to win accolades in Houston and was named both Woman of the Year, by Houston Baptist University, and Outstanding Young Lawyer in Houston by the Houston Bar Association. Determined to expand her recognition within the business community, she accepted a position as vice president and general counsel for the Republic of Texas Corporation, the holding company that owned Republic National Bank. She also served as co-founder of Fidelity National Bank in Dallas.

The pull of politics, however, remained strong, and in 1981 Hutchison decided to run for Congress. Republican Steve Bartlett, who had served as an at-large member of the Dallas City Council, had already filed to run in the Fifth Congressional District, so the Hutchisons moved into the Third District. Despite the move, redistricting pitted the two Republicans against one another, and the campaign became a bitter one.

Hutchison led in the Republican primary, carrying 42.02 percent of the vote to Bartlett's 22.43 percent. The two candidates' positions on issues were quite similar, and consequently the runoff became a campaign based on personality. When a smear letter aimed at Hutchison circulated three days before the runoff, Ray Hutchison pointed the finger at Bartlett's supporters, but Bartlett defeated Hutchison in the runoff and went on to defeat Democrat Jim Nees.

After the congressional loss, Hutchison once again turned her talents to the business world, investing in a design showroom and buying McCraw Candies, located in Farmersville. Working to improve both sales and profits, she immersed herself in the company but continued to look for a statewide race. Many of her supporters thought she might run for the attorney general's office, but in 1990 she chose to enter the race for state treasurer, the post Ann Richards was vacating to run for governor.

With Democrat Nikki Van Hightower, the former treasurer

of Harris County, challenging Hutchison. the race was another "first" in Texas, marking the first time in the state's history that two women had run for the same major statewide office. Hutchison based her campaign on her banking and financial experience although, as the *Austin American-Statesman* pointed out in its endorsement of Van Hightower, Hutchison had "no known public finance experience."

Hutchison stated that her goals were "to streamline the operations of the [treasurer's] office and to centralize the supervision of state bond issues," while Van Hightower stressed "maximizing the state's investment revenue and updating the system of cash management technology." Hutchison set as one of her priorities reclaiming the state's AAA bond rating, a move that she felt would save the state $25 million a year in funds that could be used to "build prisons, drug treatment centers, and schools."

The race was a hard-fought one. Van Hightower charged Hutchison with conflict of interest, citing Ray Hutchison's position as a bond attorney, while Hutchison countered by challenging Van Hightower's record as executive director of the Houston Women's Center. With Republican Clayton Williams' losing momentum in his race for the governor's office, Hutchison feared that her race was in jeopardy. Even with former president Gerald Ford campaigning across Texas for Hutchison, she was unable to claim victory until well after midnight of election night. She won the race with 49.9 percent of the vote to Van Hightower's 46.7 percent.

As soon as Hutchison took the oath as state treasurer, political observers began speculating that she might challenge Ann Richards for the governor's office in 1994. Speculators relished the thought of Hutchison, often characterized as a woman of "demure reasonableness" who once appeared at a Republican district convention looking "like Little Bo-Peep" according to one observer, challenging the acerbic and assertive Democrat Richards. Hutchison projected an image of a sweet, young girl, defending her looks by stating that "People don't like to yell at little girls," but a 1980 article in *Texas Business* had more accurately depicted her as "A kitten on the surface; a lioness underneath." She traveled the state for five years, even going so far as to purchase Wrangler western wear for tours of the rodeo circuit in order to stay in touch with Texans. Few observers doubted that she was headed for a higher office.

The opportunity came in 1993 when Hutchison chose to challenge Richards's appointed candidate Bob Krueger and two other Republican challengers, Jack Fields and Joe Barton, both members of the U.S. House of Representatives, in a race for the U.S. Senate. Hutchison was correct in predicting that the woman's vote would be an important factor in the race. With almost one-half million more women than men registered to vote in Texas, both Krueger and Hutchison made strong appeals for the woman's vote. Krueger maximized his strong pro-choice stance while pointing out that Hutchison's Republican challenger, Joe Barton, had told the *Dallas News* that, "On the issue that is most important, [Hutchison] is with the Right to Life Community."

Krueger won the endorsement of the Texas Women's Political Caucus and the National Abortion Rights Action League. Hutchison, declaring that she would vote to confirm an anti-abortion Supreme Court Justice, won the endorsement of Phyllis Schlafly's Eagle Forum. Hutchison's campaign received a boost when conservative media personality Rush Limbaugh, who had met Hutchison at the Republican National Convention, made favorable comments concerning her on three segments of his national television show.

When the votes were cast on May 1, Hutchison led in the balloting with 28.99 percent of the vote and faced a runoff against Krueger, who had received 28.66 percent of the vote. Hutchison's political consultant Karl Rove found no surprises in his candidate's leading, stating that pollsters had "failed to gauge the breadth or depth" of his candidate's support and noting that Hutchison had effectively put together a coalition of "urban conservatives, suburban voters, and younger working women."

As soon as the votes were counted, the hotly contested runoff began. Both candidates barnstormed the state, Krueger charging Hutchison with vacillating in her support of abortion rights, and Hutchison labeling Krueger a "political insider," telling voters that "we have a choice between continuing the old bygone era . . . and a new generation of leadership for America." Because the candidates' stands on economic and foreign policy issues were remarkably similar, the runoff dissolved into a contest of personalities, media, charges, and countercharges.

Both candidates were fiscal conservatives and stood as moderates with their respective political parties. In addition, both candidates made a strong appeal to women, but Hutchison counted on Democratic women to support her.

Social issues became the battleground upon which the two candidates differed and debated. Krueger took a pro-choice stance; Hutchison's departure from the anti-abortion stand she had taken in her 1982 Congressional race led Krueger to label her "multiple choice on abortion." Running in 1992, she now favored parental consent but opposed making abortion services available as part of a national health plan. Hutchison's attempt to walk a tightrope on the abortion rights issue angered both pro-choice and anti-abortion rights advocates.

The candidates also differed on the issue of gay rights; Krueger stated that the rights of gays to serve in the military should be left up the Joint Chiefs of Staff. Declaring that the presence of gays in the military would undermine morale and discipline, Hutchison opposed allowing gays to serve in the military.

A series of debates provided Hutchison with an opportunity to project herself to the media. In person and on television, Hutchison came across as clear and concise while Krueger appeared dull and stuffy, often seeming to be preaching to the voters. Hutchison's television commercials showed her as a calm, assured woman moving graciously through crowds of people; Krueger came across as distant and remote.

Political consultant Karl Rove, who helped plan Hutchison's campaign, noted that throughout the campaign she "managed to keep her positive message going . . . and that combined with her enormous credibility made the campaign work." He also cited her credibility, which had appeal to both Republicans and Democrats.

> She had an appealing positive personality and was not a Washington insider, which was important, and she had a certain balance. She is a very outstanding speaker and a charismatic personality. That combination was extremely powerful and worked for the campaign.

Her high-profile win against Governor Richards's appointed candidate brought her even more attention when she took her seat in the U.S. Senate in June 1993. Her unofficial appearance on the House floor to save two federal projects important to Texas caused the House Republican whip, Newt Gingrich, to comment on the rarity of a new senator's appearing on the House floor, "I don't know if she could have gotten away with it if she weren't a freshman and weren't so charming." Gingrich went on to note her effectiveness and that members "just melted" when she urged them to support the space station and the supercollider, projects important to the Lone Star State. The space station narrowly survived a House vote, but the supercollider was defeated in a vote intended to cut federal spending.

The media continued to focus on the ongoing grand jury investigation of her campaign, but Hutchison announced that she intended to be a "full-time senator for Texas" and noted that the investigation was clearly politically motivated. Her first appearance on a Washington talk show ended abruptly when host John McLaughlin insisted on pursuing the grand jury investigation into her service in the Treasury Department. A profile in the *Washington Post* focused so heavily on Hutchison's cheerleading days at UT that women protested the newspaper's belittling her ideas.

Her image as a sweetly demure, smartly dressed, conservative woman had always drawn the media's attention. Texas journalist Molly Ivins labeled her the "Breck Girl," and as late as July 1995, *D* magazine featured her on its cover clad only in a stars-and-stripes bikini. The cover story labeled her "Legislator of Love," and an illustration featured her as a busty cheerleader with "GOP" adorning her red sweater.

Scrutiny came from the political sector as well, particularly when Hutchison broke from time to time with Texas's other Republican senator Phil Gramm on important votes. Congressional expert Norman Ornstein noted that "she is a moderate on social issues and a fiscal conservative, she might be a harbinger of things to come," while Al From, president of a the Democratic Leadership Council, stated, "One thing she has done is protect herself from the hard religious right and made inroads to traditionally Democratic votes."

In the Senate Hutchison aligned with fiscal conservatives, but she often voted with Democrats on social issues. She voted against the family emergency leave issue but voted for one version of the Brady gun-control bill, typically a woman's issue. She has proved tough on crime, adding an amendment to a crime bill preventing criminals from applying for federal financial aid for students.

The defining issue, however, and one that many women's groups find pre-eminent, is abortion. She supports a woman's right to abortion and voted to make obstructing access to clinics a federal offense; however, she voted to deny women the right to federal funds for abortions.

In a poll conducted by the *Houston Chronicle* and the *Dallas Morning News* in September 1993, 40 percent of Texans approved of the job she was doing in the senate, while 56 percent of Texans surveyed thought that the charges filed against her by Travis County district attorney Ronnie Earle had been politically motivated.

In a move that made headlines across the state for months, the Travis County grand jury indicted Hutchison and two of her former aides on charges of official misconduct and tampering with evidence and government records. Through her attorneys, Hutchison stated that the charges were a plot by Democrats to influence her reelection chances and complained that the Travis County grand jury was stacked with Democrats. In January 1994, Hutchison's attorneys requested a change of venue, and the trial was moved to Fort Worth. Hutchison, the first U.S. senator from Texas to be charged with a crime while in office, and only the tenth senator to be charged in the history of the United States, agreed to testify in her own behalf and jurors were chosen.

In a surprise move on February 11, Travis County District Attorney Ronnie Earle asked Judge John Onion to dismiss the case. Onion refused and had the jury sworn in. The judge then asked Earle to present his case but Earle refused, claiming that the judge would suppress key evidence against the senator. Defense attorneys, claiming that the documents and computer records from the Treasury Department had been illegally seized without a search warrant, asked the judge to direct the jurors to find Hutchison not guilty.

Judge Onion issued the order, and Hutchison was declared not guilty. She told the press, "The only crime I committed was doing a great job as state treasurer and winning an election by a landslide." To the media Earle defended his not presenting the case by saying that if he had proceeded, with the judge's not allowing all the state's evidence to be presented, the state would have lost the case. He felt that such a loss would have "set a dangerous standard for other officeholders." The district attorney admitted both that "justice has been denied" and that, before the evidence was presented to him, he had believed that Hutchison was "Rebecca of Sunnybrook Farm."

Molly Ivins called on Hutchison to answer questions about her guilt or innocence, and the media also bemoaned the fact that a jury did not have the opportunity to judge whether she was guilty or innocent of the charges brought against her, wondering if the aftermath of the dismissal might well harm her when she ran for her seat in 1994. The outcome of the case also led to questions about reform of the system and the rules that govern elected officials in Texas.

In 1994 Hutchison sought a full six-year term, opposed by Democrat Richard Fisher who put over $3,000,000 into the race to unseat her. Hutchison announced that she would continue to work for new laws relating to illegal immigration, fighting crime, and welfare, tax code, and health-care reform. In endorsing her, the *Houston Post* pointed to her "thoughtful and balanced approach" and that she had "sought to represent all the people."

The race degenerated into name calling, with Fisher's labeling her the state's "temporary interim junior senator" and a public official who was "arrogant with power." Hutchison labeled him a "pinball" driven by the polls. She also challenged him to a series of debates, calling for Texans to focus on values and to make a strong stand on changing government. She pointed out that she had reduced her office budget by 24 percent and had hired an ethnically diverse office staff. She also noted her strong stand on term limits. When the votes were counted on November 8, 1994, Hutchison had won a significant victory, capturing 60 percent of the vote to Fisher's 39 percent.

Preparing for the upcoming session of the 105th Congress scheduled for 1997, Hutchison gave up her seat on the Armed Services Committee to serve on the Appropriations Committee, charged with funding government programs. Hutchison took a place vacated by Gramm when the senior Texas senator moved to the Finance Committee. With her stated focus on balancing the budget, without depriving Texans of programs important to their welfare, she told the media:

> As we continue to move toward an era of balanced federal budgets, which I strongly support, it will be crucial for Texas to have a seat at the table . . . I want to ensure that . . . our state is confident that the money it sends to Washington is returned to Texas in a fair share. . . .

She urged a revised welfare plan and circulated a letter signed by twenty-eight senators stating that freezing welfare funds would hurt growing states such as Texas. She worked hard to prevent the closing of Kelly Air Force Base in San Antonio, but she broke with Republicans to oppose the extension of benefits to Admiral Frank Kelso, involved in the navy's Tailhook scandal. She also enlisted the aid of other women in Congress to strengthen federal protections against stalking. She and Senator Phil Gramm opposed the section of the immigration reform plan that would deny public schooling to children of illegal immigrants, but she urged the government to block the entrance of illegal immigrants into the state.

In October 1995 her alma mater, The University of Texas, named her a distinguished alumnae along with another Texas Republican woman, Beryl Buckley Milburn. However, with the Republican state convention scheduled to meet in San Antonio in June 1996, anti-abortion activists moved to prevent Hutchison's attendance as a member of the delegation to the national convention. The support of presidential candidate Bob Dole, Texas Governor George W. Bush, and her fellow senator Phil Gramm, against the efforts of Texans United for Life, assured that Hutchison was part of the delegation headed for San Diego. At the convention she proved to be a media attention-getter, and her speech with its jocular barbs at President Clinton was broadcast during prime time. Her role at the convention assured that she would be a major player in Republican national politics.

As one of nine women in the United States Senate, Hutchison will play an important role in lawmaking as the nation moves toward the year 2000, and she plans to collaborate with Democratic Senator Barbara Mikulski and other senators on issues important to women. The year 2000 may also prove to be an important one for the senator from Texas. Many Republicans in the Lone Star State are saying that Kay Bailey Hutchison may well be one of the names submitted for vice president on the Republican party ticket for the first presidential election in the 21st Century.

REFERENCES

Attlesey, Sam. "Senator seen in poll as victim of politics." *Dallas Morning News* (September 30, 1993): A-1.

Bailey, Brad. "Kay Bailey Hutchison: Legislator of Love." *D* magazine (July 1995): 28-30.

Bernstein, Alan. "Most in poll cite politics in Hutchison indictment." *Houston Chronicle* (September 30, 1993): A1.

Burka, Paul. "The Trials of Senator Sweet." *Texas Monthly* (November 1993): 134-38.

Cullen, James. "Looking for Kay." *Texas Observer* vol. 85, no. 11 (June 4, 1993): 8.

Cullum, Lee. "Hard work pays off." *Dallas Morning News* (June 8, 1993): B-1.

Davidson, John. "The Woman Who Would be President." *Elle* (November 1994): 120-26.

Dart, Bob. "Washington takes notice of Hutchison," *Austin American-Statesman* (June 27, 1993): B-2.

Edmonds, Patricia. "Hutchison." *USA Today* (September 30, 1993): 8.

Elliot, David. "Texas' first woman senator says voters sent a message." *Austin American-Statesman* (June 6, 1993): A-1.

_____ and Dave McNeely. "GOP women follow lead of Hutchison." *Austin American-Statesman* (June 20, 1993): B-1.

Eskanazi, Stuart. "Despite charges, GOP may place all bets on Hutchison for Senate race." *Austin American-Statesman* (October 5, 1993): B-1.

_____. "Hutchison Indicted." *Austin American-Statesman* (September 28, 1993): 1-A.

"For Hutchison." *Houston Post* (October 23, 1994): C-2.

Garcia, James E. "Close of ethics trial opens questions of public expectation." *Austin American Statesman* (February 13, 1994): A-12.

Gonzalez, John. "Ex-aide accuses Hutchison of lying." *Austin American-Statesman* (October 23, 1993): A-1.

Hutchison, Kay Bailey. Biographical File. The Center for American History, University of Texas at Austin, Texas.

_____. Biographical File. Texas Room, Dallas Public Library, Dallas Texas.

_____. Biographical File. Texas Room, Houston Public Library, Houston, Texas.

_____. Legislative File. Legislative Library, Texas State Capitol, Austin, Texas.

_____. "Innovation can be economic boon to Texas," *Austin American-Statesman* (July 30, 1992): B-2.

_____. "Why I ought to be senator." *Houston Post* (October 16, 1994): C-1.

"Hutchison on Clinton's side this time." *Houston Chronicle* (September 29, 1996): A-16.

"Hutchison's defense tactics deplorable." *Austin American-Statesman* (October 21, 1996): A-22.

Ide, Arthur Frederick. *From Stardom to Scandal*. Las Colinas: Monument Press, 1994.

Ivins, Molly. "Hutchison still owes answers." *Houston Post* (February 16, 1994): C-2.

_____. "The next casualty." *Texas Observer* (September 2, 1994): 12.

Jamieson, Kathleen Hall. *Beyond the Double Bind: Women and Leadership*. New York: Oxford University Press, 1995.

Jennings, Diane. "Kay Bailey Hutchison: Taking the lead for the Texas GOP." *Dallas Morning News* (March 3, 1991): D-1.

"Judge quashes four out of five charges against Hutchison." *San Antonio Express-News* (December 29, 1993): A-1.

Kay, Michele. "Hutchison carving hard-to-define niche." *Austin American-Statesman* (December 5, 1993): B-1.

Kilday, Anne Marie. "Hutchison takes Senate oath." *Dallas Morning News* (June 15, 1993): A-4.

Knaggs, John. "Outcome of Hutchison case weighs on GOP in 1994." *Austin American-Statesman* (January 8, 1994): B-2.

_____. "Publicity may outweigh verdict in Hutchison trial." *Austin American-Statesman* (October 9, 1993): A-23.

McDonald, Greg. "Texas senators see their power growing." *Houston Chronicle* (December 5, 1996): A-4.

McNeely, Dave. "Officials must walk fine line between jobs, campaigns." *Austin American-Statesman* (September 30, 1993): B-2.

Moline, Carrie. "A kitten on the surface; a lioness underneath." *Texas Business* (September 1980): 26-28.

Murchison, William. "The Dupe of Earle." *Texas Republic* (March-April 1994): 30-33.

"Nine Women to form a powerful new force in the 105th Congress." *Houston Chronicle* (December 8, 1996): A-6.

Palomo, Juan R. "Jury denied chance to certify senator innocent?" *Houston*

Post (October 21, 1993): A-25.

Ratcliffe, R.G. "Grand jury indicts Hutchison." *Houston Chronicle* (September 28, 1993): A-1.

_____. "Hutchison case may change rules." *Houston Chronicle* (February 14, 1994): A-10.

Robertson, Nan. "The Washington Shuffle." *Modern Maturity* (September-October 1996): 33-38.

Roth, Bennett. "Hutchison backs rewriting GOP platform on abortion." *Houston Chronicle* (December 20, 1995): A-4.

Rothschild, Scott. "Documents implicate Hutchison." *Austin American-Statesman* (February 14, 1994): B-1.

Selby, Gardner. "Hutchison lawyers seek 'equal' jury. *Houston Post* (October 21, 1993): A-19.

_____. "New fight over Hutchison records." *Houston Post* (February 16, 1994: A-1.

_____. "On the road with the candidates." *Houston Post* (September 25, 1994): A33-35.

White, Jerry. "Bomb threat delays Hutchison trial." *Austin American-Statesman* (February 8, 1994): B-4.

_____. "Earle balks; Hutchison walks." *Austin American-Statesman* (February 12, 1994): A-1.

_____. "Earle defends decision to drop Hutchison case." *Austin American-Statesman* (February 18, 1994): A-1.

_____. "4 Hutchison charges rejected." *Austin American-Statesman* (December 29, 1993): A-1.

_____. "Hutchison and Earle share a past and a present." *Austin American-Statesman* (September 12, 1993): A-1.

_____. "Hutchison, Earle differ on meaning of acquittal." *Austin American-Statesman* (February 13, 1994): A-1.

_____. "Hutchison indictment in jeopardy." *Austin American-Statesman* (October 19, 1993): A-1.

_____. "Hutchison to be tried in Fort Worth." *Austin American-Statesman* (January 12, 1994): A-1.

_____. "Hutchison to testify in her defense." *Austin American-Statesman* (January 8, 1994): A-1.

_____. "Hutchison trial goes beyond courtroom." *Austin American-Statesman* (February 8, 1994): A-1.

_____. "Senator's team presents case to public." *Austin American-Statesman* (February 17, 1994): A-1.

Yeager, James. "Lone star girl." *Texas Observer* (July 16, 1993): 8-9.

INTERVIEWS

R.G. Ratcliff and Ann Fears Crawford, telephone interview, Houston, December 6, 1996.

Karl Rove and Ann Fears Crawford, Austin, September 22, 1995.

INDEX